The Cell Phone Reader

Steve Jones
General Editor

Vol. 34

PETER LANG
New York • Washington, D.C./Baltimore • Bern
Frankfurt am Main • Berlin • Brussels • Vienna • Oxford

The Cell Phone Reader

Essays in Social Transformation

EDITED BY
Anandam Kavoori and Noah Arceneaux

PETER LANG
New York • Washington, D.C./Baltimore • Bern
Frankfurt am Main • Berlin • Brussels • Vienna • Oxford

Library of Congress Cataloging-in-Publication Data

The cell phone reader: essays in social transformation /
edited by Anandam Kavoori and Noah Arceneaux.
p. cm. — (Digital formations; v. 34)
Includes bibliographical references.
1. Cellular telephones—Social aspects.
2. Wireless communication systems—Social aspects.
3. Technology—Social aspects. I. Kavoori, Anandam P.
II. Arceneaux, Noah. III. Series.
HE9713.C44   303.48'33—dc22   2005025658
ISBN 0-8204-7919-5
ISSN 1526-3169

Bibliographic information published by **Die Deutsche Bibliothek**.
Die Deutsche Bibliothek lists this publication in the "Deutsche
Nationalbibliografie"; detailed bibliographic data is available
on the Internet at http://dnb.ddb.de/.

Cover design by Joni Holst

The paper in this book meets the guidelines for permanence and durability
of the Committee on Production Guidelines for Book Longevity
of the Council of Library Resources.

Table of Contents

The Cell Phone Reader

Introduction

Anandam Kavoori and Noah Arceneaux

The cell phone presents itself at the periphery of contemporary discourse about media and culture. TV cops use it as they rush to crime scenes, teenagers use it to connect with their peers, terrorists are traced through calls made on their cell phones, extramarital affairs draw sustenance from them, and war correspondents cradle them on bumpy tank rides. Such images, however, do not do justice to the central role that this technology has begun to play in contemporary society.

Cell phones lack the hype of the Internet, but they have achieved the status of a mass medium. They have begun to shape how we communicate, their use has created new forms of media-centered relations, and in the marketplace they have begun to influence patterns of media ownership and acquisition. In the developing world, the cell phone is often the *first* phone for many individuals, opening new possibilities for communication in areas that never installed the cumbersome, expensive infrastructure required by land lines. In the world of television news, cell phones made an impact with the first video of the London Metro bombings coming from cell phones—giving birth to a new term, *cellevision*. In the cell phone's intersection with other media technologies—text messaging, the World Wide Web, and digital photography and video—the device has changed how we look at an omnipresent cultural technology: the "telephone."

In this anthology, we take aim at identifying the key cultural dynamics that underlie this rapidly changing and mobile (no pun intended) sociological landscape. Written by established experts and new scholars, the chapters employ diverse research methods and different perspectives, ranging from utopian to dystopian, though they all share a focus on the intersection of culture and technology. Many of the contributors use the term *cell phone* for this device, one uses *mobile phone*, while another spells it as a single word, *cellphone*. We made a deliberate decision not to standardize this terminology, as this discrepancy highlights the way language itself changes to accommodate new technological innovations. (Indeed, as more capabilities and features are integrated into portable phones, the initial communication function may fade into the background and the word phone itself may no longer even be applied to these devices.)

Taken together, the chapters in *The Cell Phone Reader* set out to achieve three important goals:

1) To provide a broad, systematic, theoretical accounting of what the cell phone as a

cultural technology entails. The chapters connect cell phones with existing paradigmatic frames in media and sociological theory, showing how this technology relates to, and changes, those frames.

2) To provide a sustained analysis of the how issues central to the project of cultural studies generally and identity politics specifically are impacted by cell phones. The focus is not just on media use but on how systemic changes in culture are impacted by the use of such technologies and, equally, how identity politics frames the composition and use of such technologies.

3) To provide a cross-disciplinary and global accounting of the shape, structure, and form of the cultural order that is emerging in the wake of cell phones. This is done through an accounting of global trends and through chapters drawing on different cultural and ethnographic contexts that allow for a rethinking of the nature of the cell phone as a cultural technology, simultaneously technological and political, personal and sociological.

■ ■ ■

The book is organized into three sections, "Theorizing Cell Phones," "Identity Politics and/of/in the Cell Phone," and "International Perspectives." The chapters can be used independently or as parts of lesson blocks focused on the subjects of each of these sections.

Section 1 frames the later works with chapters that orient the topic of cell phones within a larger history of the study of technology and culture and within separate but interlinked bodies of sociological literature.

The chapter by Paul Levinson, one of the pioneers in the study of the cell phone, provides an introductory word on the subject. He locates the cell phone as a form of human technology that is analogous to the human brain, and situates the device within the long technological and experiential history of media technologies, such as writing and printing, the telegraph, photography, sound cinema, and television. He examines how such technologies have had structured relationships to the sensate world in limited ways and how the cell phone has transformed that relationship. The cell phone, he suggests, "does more than mix the digital and the physical. . . . [I]t not only integrates speech into the forest, the beach, the automobile, the city streets, but also has begun to subsume, to blend into the mix, all the media that the Web has already brought into its precincts."

The chapter by Adriana de Souza e Silva examines how hybrid spaces merge the physical and the virtual in a social environment created by users connected via mobile technology devices. She suggests that portable interfaces transform our experience of space, contributing to hybrid spaces. The chapter problematizes the cell phone within a range of such technologies, including PDAs, Palmtops, and laptops as types of "nomadic technologies." Specifically, the chapter details key concepts of materiality, wearability, immersion, and presence and relates these issues to the sociological implications of mobility and the inhabitation of these hybrid spaces. Special attention is paid to issues of body physiology and the idea of being always connected, in contact with digital spaces.

Janey Gordon's chapter provides an overview of the current use of the cell phone and suggests that it has become not only a part of our popular culture, but also a tool of the public sphere. On occasions the ability of the individual to have access to a mobile phone may have a significant influence not only on personal choices and actions but also on national and international events.

She discusses how during 2001, in January in Manila and on September 11 in New York City, the cell phone played a part in world events. In the Philippines, cell phone technology—specifically text-messaging—played a critical role in a major political upheaval in the country. On September 11 in the United States, this same technology gathered significant press attention, as it linked doomed airline passengers and panic-stricken office workers of the World Trade Center with friends and family members. These two events are presented as case studies illustrating how changes in our personal behavior and the organization of our societies have already been influenced by the extraordinary expansion of personal communication.

The well-known scholar Rich Ling provides an innovative framework for examining cell phones. Using the notion of the "nomos"—which stands for the active nature of family life (in contrast to Durkhiem's notion of "anomie" or normlessness)—and drawing from research on couples in Norway, he examines how the cell phone functions normatively and ritualistically to structure conversation, routines, and the practice of family life. Ling suggests that the cell phone as a cultural technology functions to support the broader goals of nomos and of social integration. The larger focus of Ling's study is communication and coordination within families, and this chapter illustrates how deeply the device has been embedded into the mundane routines of daily life.

In the realm of news-gathering practices, cell phones have already proven their value on a number of occasions, and the chapter from Wendy Robinson and David Robison focuses on the 2004 tsunami disaster as a case study of this phenomenon. Inspired by Foucault's theory of the panoptic, the authors ruminate on the idea that the spread of mobile media technology in South Asia may also entail a "creeping westernization"; cell phones are accompanied not only by technological infrastructure but by ideological baggage as well.

The second section of the book begins with Collette Snowden's chapter on SMS as a cultural tool and the constitutive nature of this media technology, which is embedded in niche identity politics. This theme is then discursively elaborated by the other chapters in this section, which focus on teen horror film culture (Allison Whitney), religion (Heidi Campbell), people with disabilities (Gerard Goggin and Christopher Newell), and African Americans (Davin Heckman).

The chapter by Snowden examines the application of SMS, or text messaging, and illustrates that the popularity of this form of communication was not expected by the telecommunications industry. The many different uses of SMS have dramatically altered our perception of what a phone can be and how it can be used. This chapter discusses how SMS became a global phenomenon generating a multibillion-dollar income stream for telecommunications companies, changing fundamental aspects of language and communication.

Although the similarities between the "unexpected" rise of SMS and developments in earlier forms of media are not her primary focus, Snowden does note that the phenomenon of radio "broadcasting" was also unforeseen by the industries that dominated early wireless technology. As a further example of the parallel between old and new technologies, the first acknowledged text message was a Christmas greeting, while the first musical broadcast was of holiday music, transmitted on Christmas Eve 1906 by inventor Reginald Fessenden.

Whitney examines the relation between cell phones and the American horror film, arguing that much of the impact of new communications systems may be understood through their representation in popular culture. Beginning with an examination of the telephone in theater and silent cinema, Whitney traces this thread up to the present day and argues that the horror film is the genre most invested in the anxieties aroused by changes in the social order. As such, it is an ideal arena for exploring the social disruptions brought by the cell phone, such as the conflation of public and private space and the blurring of identities.

The chapter explicates these generic shifts through an analysis of Wes Craven's highly successful *Scream* trilogy (1996, 1997, and 2000), a series of horror films in which the killers' reign of terror and the heroines' counterstrategies are largely contingent on cell phones and their infrastructure. The films' popular and commercial success is due largely to their careful mapping of social dynamics onto the technical specificities of the cell phone and the habits of its users. The chapter concludes with a discussion of the film *Cellular* (2004), in which this technology plays a pivotal role.

Campbell's chapter considers the religious use and perceptions of mobile technology by investigating how religious groups utilize text messaging in order to create social-religious networks. Building from these observations, Campbell then discusses the innovation of the "kosher phone" by the ultra-Orthodox community in Israel. It would be difficult to find a more concrete, clearly defined example of how a community's cultural (and in this case religious) values can literally shape the form and function of a new technology.

Goggin and Newell's chapter draws upon critical disability studies and cultural studies to offer an account of disability and cell phones. The chapter considers the use of cell phones by people with disabilities, discussing in turn first-, second-, and third-generation mobile networks and handsets, noting inaccessibility and barriers that have affected both cell phone design and their usage.

Goggin and Newell investigate how the cell phone has intersected with crucial aspects of identity, community, and politics in the lives of people with disabilities. The rise of text messaging in Deaf culture is explored, a change that is displacing prior networked technologies such as the TDD (telecommunications device for the Deaf). In a discussion of the innovation of a cell phone/camera for Blind users, Goggin and Newell also reveal some truly innovative technological developments, such as a device that translates "colors" into "sounds."

Heckman's chapter discusses the media effects of wireless technologies in the African-American community. Beginning with a general discussion of the uses of cell phones and pagers by black artists in rap songs and videos, and contrasting this opulent image with the economic realities of inner-city communities, this chapter identifies a cultural ambivalence to these new technologies. An analysis of three films featuring black male protagonists who are threatened by technology (the mainstream blockbuster *Enemy of the State* [1998], the less successful *Bait* [2000], and the independently produced *I Got the Hook Up* [1998]) provides additional insights into technological anxieties, which persist across class lines but reflect class concerns. This chapter concludes with a discussion of interpolation, credit practices, surveillance, and technological dependence, commenting on the disciplinary aspects of what is commonly considered a "liberating" new technology.

The concluding section of the book examines a range of cultural contexts of cell phone use—drawing on both local cultural issues and diverse theoretical frameworks. The cell phone has many names across the world: "kanny" in Finland, "portable" in French, "movil" in Spain, "moto" in Thailand, "sho-ji" in Japan, "makhmul" in Arabic, and the ubiquitous "mobile." The chapters in this section explore some of the cultural specificities and discursive and historical aspects of local and global cell phone use.

Bahíyyih Maroon explores the cultural implications of the rise of cell phone use in Morocco. As in many African nations, the government of Morocco holds the primary license to fixed telephone lines within the country. The general conditions of housing, along with the price of a single line, means that utilizing a phone in one's home usually entails very little privacy. These conditions have contributed to an astounding growth pattern of cell phone use within the North African nation. Drawing upon first-hand ethnographic accounts, Maroon illustrates that the advent of cell phones, which are subject to competitive pricing and market economy principles—unlike the monopolized fixed line—has radically shifted the dynamics of communication. She argues not that the exponential rise of cell phone use is merely the emergence of a new habit or way of conversing, but rather that the cell phone in the Muslim African context is an instrument that allows users to bypass previous models of public behavior and establish alternative modalities of social exchange. In a potent example of this dynamic, Maroon documents one family in which the father disables the household land line when he departs, thus exerting not only symbolic but *literal* control over the communication abilities of his wife and children. In such an environment, a cell phone is bound to have a dramatic, and immediate, impact upon the lives of its users.

Paul Leonardi, Marianne E. Leonardi, and Elizabeth Hudson explore the use and social construction of the cell phone from three distinct cultural contexts—the United States, Latin America, and the Ukraine—to begin to understand the similarities and differences in the way the cell phone is translated from a material into a cultural artifact. Whereas most studies of the cell phone suggest that use is linked to shared perceptions of utility, the authors' findings reveal that when culture is considered as an integral variable in the social construction of the cell phone, contradictions surface between the processes of perception and use. The findings of focus group studies showed that the presence of contradictions between perception and use persisted across the three cultures included in this study, while the social organization of the contradictions differed across cultures.

The concluding chapter, by Anandam Kavoori and Kalyani Chadha, examines discourses around the cell phone in the developing world, with a focus on India. Focused on a textual analysis of cell phone advertising and a visual record of advertising in India's urban landscape, it suggests that there is a need to rethink the discourse of digital celebration and euphoria that has accompanied the cell phone in the developing world, especially India. They argue that the themes emergent in the advertising of cell phone firms provide for a vision of the future of technological development that reifies issues of linguistic hegemony, technological solutions, a consumerist (rather than a citizenry) culture, and reiteration of the traditional discourses of masculinity, gender, and class. It suggests that we think of the cell phone as a cultural technology, intimately connected with issues of global capitalism and cultural hegemony.

■ ■ ■

Each section of the reader thus has a thematic unity, and the overall book is held together by the thrust of the theoretical work that is being done by each chapter as it relates to the links between culture and technology as seen in the case of the cell phone. Needless to add, the import and impact of this reader must in the end begin with you, the *reader*.

Acknowledgements

Figure 1 (p. 27): NTT DoCoMo Wristomo
Copyright 2003, NTT DoCoMo, Inc. All Rights Reserved

Figure 2 (p.37): Motorola Dyna-Tac 8000X
Copyright 1994-2005, Motorola, Inc. All Rights Reserved

Section One

Theorizing Cell Phones

The Little Big Blender: How the Cellphone Integrates the Digital and the Physical, Everywhere

*Paul Levinson**

All human technology begins with the human brain—not only because the brain invents technology and directs its use, but because the biological brain is a template, a model, for all technological media.

The single most salient feature of the brain and the way it operates is that it is a little big blender. It's little in the sense that it only weighs about a kilogram or so; it's big and it's a blender because with this kilogram of material, we see, hear, smell, taste, touch, dream, project, recall. In other words, all of the things we communicate about are processed in this portable command center we have here in our heads. It is therefore entirely natural that as we invent communication technologies, we invent devices that, like the brain, integrate a lot of processes. The cellphone is currently the leading example of such a device, and is also the best example in history.

One-Dimensional History

As natural as this progression to more integrated media is, however, it is extremely difficult from a technological standpoint. It took a very long time. If you look at the history of media and communications, you see that most of the early and middle and even recent media do not integrate and blend very much, and instead emphasize and extend a single process. Writing, for example, extends just our vision.

As Marshall McLuhan pointed out in 1962 in his *Gutenberg Galaxy*, the process of both writing and reading is antisocial and antisensory, in that what's happening is you're taking the whole world of thoughts and sounds and sights and steamrolling them into a series of squiggles on a wall or on a page, a very one-dimensional approach to the world from the point of view of communication. Indeed, as writing developed and continued along those lines, the invention of mass printing made the written word even less sensory

*Author's note: An earlier version of this chapter was delivered as a lecture on April 23, 2005, at the New York Society for General Semantics Colloquium, American Museum of Natural History, New York City.

than it was when it was handwritten, when there was a variety of writing styles. You can look at a handwritten piece of work even today and get some sense of the person who wrote it. Not so with print on a page, where it's all standardized. Although print helped written words reach many, many more people—and in that sense was a more socialized kind of writing than what the hand conveyed—it was nonetheless a very unidimensional, antiseptic kind of socialization.

Going ahead a few hundred additional years. If you think about what the telegram does, it's the height of that stretch and removal from the sensory world. In fact, the telegram is three levels of abstraction removed from reality: Morse Code is an abstraction of written language, which in turn is an abstraction of spoken language, which in turn is an abstraction of the real world. So the price that we paid as human beings for this miracle of instant communication—communication at the speed of light, which is what we get with the telegraph—was a complete loss of the sensory basis of communication.

Retrieval of the Sensate World

However, that loss was remedied about fifty years later, when the telephone brought us back to just one level of abstraction beyond physical reality—with speech. In one fell swoop, the telephone not only got rid of the Morse Code of the telegraph but also of the written word. Furthermore, the telephone brought into play emotional nuance, tone of voice. And so 1876 marks a crucial point in the development of media, communication, and language.

Meanwhile, photography—on the scene about fifty years earlier than the telephone and about the same time as the telegraph—had made a remarkable change in the way we communicate about the visual world, because now for the first time we did not have to rely on written descriptions or on painters' subjective impressions of the world. Instead, we could look at a photograph and see the world pretty much as it was. Paul Delaroche in 1839, upon seeing photographs for the first time, explained—in French, but I'll give you the English translation—"From today on, painting is dead." Of course he was wrong, because painting went on to do things that photography could not. A Cézanne or a Monet painting shows you something that is beyond photography: it presents an impression of the world, not a recording of the world, which is an important difference.

But although photography and the telephone in the nineteenth century restored literal sensation to technological communication, the two were still by and large singular in the way they presented and communicated information. The telephone, notwithstanding its advance back to reality, still conveyed only one dimension of that reality—the human voice. And the same with photography: it presented only the visual. Motion pictures added motion into the mix, but it was still at first purely visual. Radio allowed sound to be communicated instantaneously to mass audiences, and this was a remarkable development, but this was still sound only.

The Emergence of Composite Media

It wasn't until the advent of "talkies" that sound—more precisely spoken words—expanded the sensory tableau of media. *The Jazz Singer* in the late 1920s was the first film in which we began to see some integration in media, and this integration of course was the combination of sight and sound and the capacity in now-talking motion pictures that allowed us, the viewers, to see and hear what the story on screen was all about.

This led to another turning point, which was instigated by television in the 1950s. Television is the first medium that truly began to integrate more than just two things. First of all, it did integrate—as motion pictures with sound had already done—pictures and words, but it also integrated something else that was extremely important. It integrated prior media, by in some cases showing motion pictures, and also co-opting radio's content. As a matter of fact, some of the biggest stars of radio in the late 1940s, such as Jack Benny, left radio and went into television. Some of the most successful shows on television, such as *Gunsmoke*, were derived directly from radio. Sometimes that had unfortunate consequences for the stars. The original star of *Gunsmoke* on radio was William Conrad, who later went on to play the overweight detective Cannon in the eponymous television show. This was in the 1970s, in what I call the "defective detective" era on television. All of the detectives had some kind of problem—Ironside was in a wheelchair, Longstreet was blind, Barnaby Jones was about ninety years old, and Cannon was overweight. The main suspense in *Cannon* was Will Cannon get the bad guy or will he drop dead of a heart attack?

But William Conrad as Cannon had a great voice, and back in the 1940s he was Sheriff Matt Dillon, with the same basso profundo delivery. Conrad sounded great, but he didn't look the part, and that's how James Arness came to play Sheriff Dillon on the CBS television version of *Gunsmoke*. So this transition from radio to television had unforeseen consequences.

But the important point for the purposes of this essay is that in television you can see the prior integration of media such as radio and motion pictures. McLuhan again was aware of this as early as the 1960s, when he realized that one of the things that new media do is they take as their content prior media. Motion pictures did that with novels and theater, and each in its own way became a contributor to the content of motion pictures.

The Dawn of the Digital Age

By the 1980s there was a new communication device that was attracting a lot of attention: the personal computer. And when it hooked up to the Internet, the personal computer became one of the most integrated and integrating media in human history. Media for the first time began to do what the human brain does. Back in the mid-1990s, I realized that the Internet could be aptly described as the "medium of media," because on the Internet you could read a newspaper, browse through a book, leaf through a magazine even though it had no paper pages, and exchange mail. You could have a live conversation via instant messenger. You could watch television shows, or listen to radio programs. You could even have a telephone conversation. In other words, you could do through the Web in one way or another just about everything these individual media had been doing in some cases for thousands of years when people were speaking or writing.

But one thing that the personal computer and the Web did not do—and by and large still do not—is integrate the digital realm, the realm of cyberspace, the place we inhabit when we go onto the Web, with the physical world all around us. That place out there, the one we reach when we log on, with this place here, the room in which I am now sitting as I write this. Or the place that you and I might be in if we were talking in person. Or the place in which the people are walking outside of this room, outside this building on the Fordham University campus, on Fordham Road, or in the New York Botanical Gardens or the Bronx Zoo. What I mean, in other words, is just the plain old physical world, this real world that in one way or another had been victimized by every medium that was ever invented. Not only because of the way that writing flattened out communications, as mentioned above, but because even up to and including the Internet and the personal computer, to use these media the ticket you had to purchase was far more profound than the cost or purchase price of the personal computer. The entry fee was turning your back on the physical world.

I saw this very clearly when my family and I would go up to Cape Cod in the mid-1980s and I would bring along my computer to do some work online. Here we were on Cape Cod, in this cottage by the beach; it was beautiful out there, but any time I wanted to do anything on the computer, I couldn't be on that beach. I had to be seated at a desk looking not at the ocean but at a computer screen—and that was about the best circumstance vis-à-vis the real world in which a computer could be used. Most of the time, during the rest of the year, the circumstance was being stuck in an office nowhere near a beach. It just was as Jacques Ellul, a mostly incorrect critic of technology (even a broken clock is right twice a day) had noted in his book *The Technological Society*. What is it like to live in a technological world? Look at the human being stuck in a cubicle with no fresh air, Ellul observed. That person is no different from a fly on flypaper. When we were using our personal computers, we were the flies and the screen was the paper.

Cellphonic Freedom

Which brings us to the cellphone—because, first and foremost, what the cellphone did and does increasingly is, for one of the first times in human history, allow us to communicate, to have all of the benefits of communication, without being stuck in place behind a desk indoors. You can use the cellphone walking on a beach, walking down the street, driving a car (perhaps not the safest thing in the world, but still it can be done). There are certain cellphonic predecessors that we can now clearly see as leading up to this important breakthrough. I describe them in some detail in my book *Cellphone: The Story of the World's Most Mobile Medium and How It Has Transformed Everything* (2004). Among them is the Kodak camera, which for the first time in history—this would be in 1888—allowed people to go around and take photographs with a relatively small camera rather than having to go to a photographer's studio. Skipping ahead about seventy years, in the 1950s we encounter the transistor radio, which allowed people to listen to the radio while walking down the street. But none of those did more than just one thing: taking pictures in the case of the Kodak camera, listening to music and words in the case of the transistor radio. And what the cellphone initially allowed us to do was just one thing: have conversations with people, any place we might be, any place they might be.

By the way, I am not claiming that that's purely good and problem-free. All technologies are two-edged swords. The price we pay for being able to call someone any place any time we might want is that anyone can call *us* any time he or she desires. And we might not want to talk to that person or anyone else at that particular time. So the cellphone has ushered in what I think of as the golden age of the little white lie. There have always been little white lies, but now explaining why it is that you have not answered your cellphone has become an art form.

Children and teenagers are especially adept at this; they're really smarter than adults when it comes to new media. Parents were initially suspicious of cellphones, but then they realized, *Hmm . . . if I give my kid a cellphone, this is a way we can stay in touch.* Kids thought the cellphone was great—for a completely different reason. "Thanks, give me a cellphone." *I can call my friends.* But when parents called and said, "Where are you? What's going on?" the kids responded, "Oh, I'm sorry, Mom. I was in a 'pocket' where my cellphone wasn't working." Or they could try a flat-out lie. "What do you mean? It didn't ring." Or, "I'm sorry. It must have accidentally shut off." Blatant lies, but understandable—all in the service of protecting the right of people, in this case kids, not to be called.

So this cellphonic reach is a two-edged sword, for both parents and children, and indeed for everyone who has a cellphone. But by and large it is a step forward. When we evaluate whether a new medium is good or bad, we need to add up the positives and the negatives. I think the positives do outweigh the negatives regarding the cellphone. In fact, I don't know any parents or children who have given up their cellphones.

Blending More Than Talking

But the cellphone does more than mix the digital and the physical, more than allow conversation with someone any place in the world from anywhere you happen to be. It not only integrates speech into the forest, the beach, the automobile, the city streets, but has begun to subsume, to blend into the mix, all the media that the Web has already brought into its precincts, and indeed many media that have flourished for decades or more before the Web. Let's look at some of the highlights.

Instant messaging online has become texting on the cellphone. This is an especially fascinating and subversive development. If you were texting someone right now, as you were reading this, there would nothing socially inappropriate or sleight-of-hand in that action. After all, your own private time is yours to use as you wish. But if you were in an auditorium listening to me deliver this essay as a lecture—or if you were at a conference table at a departmental meeting where I was talking about the cellphone—and you were texting with someone outside of the room, you would be not be fully attending the lecture or the meeting. Your physical body would be there, but your mind would be elsewhere. You in effect would be partially pretending to be at the lecture or the meeting. You would be defrauding the other people at the lecture or meeting of your complete presence.

Now, this is certainly not the only possible use of texting. And many lectures and meetings may not deserve our complete attention—indeed, I fully admit to texting during meetings and lectures myself. After all, being the chair of communication and media studies at a major world-class university obliges me to attend a lot of boring meetings. So if I'm sitting there at a meeting with deans and important people, I can look like I'm paying attention, while I'm actually having a text conversation. (Don't worry, anyone, if you're reading this—I would never text and pretend to be participating in a meeting with *you*. The meetings you convene and/or attend are always of keen interest to me.) But then I teach a class called Intro to Communication and Media Studies that has 120 students. I'm one hundred percent sure that during my lectures there are students who use their cellphones to have text conversations. So those texting students are able to create the impression that they're there, which they are physically but not mentally or pedagogically.

How can this "absent-minded" texting student be handled? Well, there are obvious, heavy-handed remedies. For example, there are professors who say, "I'm not going to allow any cellphones in my classroom." But how can this be implemented? Frisk every student who comes into the classroom? Cellphones are getting smaller and smaller. And while we're on the subject of cellphones in classrooms, what do you do when you're giving an open-book exam, which is the type of exam I usually give? It's one thing for students to look at their notes, look at their text; it's quite another for them to text someone who had the class last year. But how can a professor tell the difference between a student who is looking at a text and texting? In a class of 120, that's nearly impossible.

So there's not much that can be done about students texting in classrooms. And there's nothing at all to be done about people like me who text during faculty convocations.

The Pits and the Heights

Some unintended consequences of the extended cellphone and its unspoken uses are far more sinister than texting. Cellphones increasingly work as cameras, allowing the person in possession of such a cellphone to snap pictures of everyone from Grandma to Fido, and then send them anywhere in the world, instantly, via the Web. But if you log on to the Web today and do a search for something called "upskirts," you'll find more than 2 million websites that display these snapshots. What are they? Well, usually some guy—this kind of cellphonic photographer is usually a guy—is hidden somewhere, crouching low and out of sight, and happily taking shots of women who are walking by. In department stores, where many of such photos are taken, it is especially easy to hide behind some clothing, point your camera upward, and capture what's underneath any unsuspecting skirt that walks by. But that's just the beginning. For not only is the privacy of these women invaded, but a split second after the photograph is taken, it can appear on the Web and will be available to everyone around the world—in many cases, free of charge. In Japan, laws have already been enacted against this. Closer to home, in White Plains, New York, there has been talk about outlawing the use of cellphones in bathrooms—apparently cellphonic photographers have been taking unauthorized photos in the john as well.

That's the worst of the cellphone. On the bright side, all kinds of new services have been cropping up in the cellphonic mix machine. Not only is the cellphone a camera, a device that can take video clips, and in some cases audio-visual clips. We've seen the cellphone develop into a receiver of television programs. MTV will soon have a cellphonic channel. As a matter of fact, two kinds of special new programs that are basically the same will soon be available for use exclusively on cellphones. One company calls them "V-casts." That's Verizon. And the other—I think much more imaginatively and usefully—calls the programs "Mobisodes": mobile episodes. These are little stories, no more than two to three minutes in length. I like them for two reasons: One, as a short story writer, I'm pleased to see small literary stories return to the popular culture. (There was a time, about a century ago, when the short story was a staple of many magazines.) And second, the short form in cellphonic television marks an important reversal. Until now, on television, something that was a minute or two in length was usually a commercial. The entertainment, the reason for watching television, was always much longer and something that was punctuated by commercials. Now entertainment that is the length of these commercials is the show on cellphones.

Other highlights: *Playboy* may soon be available on cellphones. Hey, there's nothing wrong with nudity for consenting adults—it goes at least as far back as ancient Egypt— and the phone screen is too small to be seen by very many unwelcome eyes. And radio is available on cellphones right now. This is historically highly appropriate—the transistor radio in the 1950s was the first easily portable electronic medium. It's almost as if a week doesn't go by without some new application of the cellphone. So this little device that we can carry in our hands and our pockets is itself getting smaller and smaller, is becoming more and more like the human brain and allowing us not only to talk to anyone any time we might want while allowing them to talk to us, but also to tap into the cornucopia of all human information and receive it any time we might like.

It's always fun when you say something years ago and then are proven right. In my 1979 doctoral dissertation *Human Replay: A Theory of the Evolution of Media*, I argued that, contrary to critics of technology, media were actually getting more human, more consonant with human perception. I said we were going to someday see a situation in which anyone, in any place, could hook into the totality of all human communication and receive whatever they pleased from that. I did not imagine that this would come in the form of a cellphone, but that's exactly what has happened. The someday of my prediction in the 1970s is right now, brought to us by the little big blender of the cellphone at the beginning of the twenty-first century.

Gauging the Nuances of Utopia

But we need to be aware that getting what we want—or, in this case, what I predicted we would invent and employ, in response to our need for human communication in our media—is not undilutedly beneficial. In addition to the more obvious abuses discussed above, we need to be aware of the ways in which this new ubiquity of communication, the accessibility of the cornucopia of information, may put unwanted pressures on us, and change things that we might not want to change. To give you a recent historical example that predates the cellphone by a decade or two: Once upon a time, the phone caller was anonymous. And then caller ID was introduced. Now, caller ID is by and large beneficial because it puts out of business the obscene caller. But it also puts out of business me when I was fourteen or fifteen years old and I was calling this girl up because I was madly in love with her. I called her and she wasn't home so I was able to hang up and call back later, maybe a day or two later, and be as cool as if I were calling her for the first time. In contrast to today, when caller ID would enable her to say, "Oh, Paul Levinson tried to call me yesterday." We might say that the anonymity of the caller was, in my fourteen-year-old self's case, an unintended benefit of the phone—which caller ID in pursuit of other important benefits has now taken away.

The cellphone, as we have seen, continues to create problems as it solves or reduces others. Being on call, being available twenty-four hours a day, seven days a week, having to explain why we don't want to talk, is probably the single biggest universal problem created by the cellphone. We come from a tradition of information scarcity, of commu-nication being difficult, but now the tables have completely turned. I'm not too worried about this, because I think we'll develop a series of customs and expectations, a social sinew that prepares us and allows us not to talk when we don't want to. In other words, for the cellphone to continue to serve us, we'll need to develop a society in which it's okay not to talk at a particular time.

I suspect kids will be leaders in developing such customs. I know that my daughter, who is eighteen, seems to get this already. I'm amazed that her phone rings and she says, "I'm not going to bother to answer that. It's Laurie." My daughter doesn't seem at all upset by that. I'll ask her, "Isn't Laurie going to get angry?" And my daughter says, "No,

I just didn't want to talk to her." That's part of a new social acceptance of noncommunication.

For more serious problems caused by the cellphone, we may need new laws—as in the case of upskirts. Laws against use of handheld cellphones by automobile drivers also make sense. But, in general, I think laws are not a very good way of dealing with social problems. Various laws have been proposed for other difficulties that the cellphone creates. For example, in New York, the city council enacted a law that Mayor Bloomberg did not sign. The gist was to make it illegal for a cellphone to ring in the theater. It is indeed distracting to hear a cellphone ring when you're enjoying a play or a movie, but no more so than a person snoring loudly right behind you, and there are no laws against that. (I have a policy with my students: it's okay if you fall asleep as long as you don't snore so loudly as to drown out my fascinating lecture.) Informal custom seems a far better way of regulating such social annoyances.

Remedial Media

When we examine the evolution of media, we also find a third way of reducing or eliminating discomforts and problems caused by new media: neither laws nor customs, but improvements in the technologies themselves. I call such technological adjustments "remedial media" (see my *The Soft Edge: A Natural History and Future of the Information Revolution*, 1997).

The window opens up a great historical example (see Wachtel 1977/1978, for its analysis of the window as a medium of communication). Once upon a time, people lived in dwellings in which holes in the wall were the only way to see outside. Windows were an excellent improvement—or remedial medium—because they let people see out, without cold air and rain coming in. But the window also created a problem: it not only let dwellers look out, but let strangers on the outside look in. The window, in other words, created the Peeping Tom. Laws and customs, of course, were directed against this invasion of privacy. But technology offered a far better remedy: the curtain, the Venetian blind, the window shade.

Modern technologies of remedial "window shade" media abound. Television was criticized by Lewis Mumford (see, for example, 1970) for confining to us to an omnipresent, with no past or future, no means of retrieval. Within a few years, the VCR provided a fine remedy for that problem. Today, TiVo and similar technologies continue to make anything on television as retrievable as the pages of a book.

The telephone has been the recipient of numerous remedial media in the past fifty years. Telephone answering machines, call waiting, and caller ID all solved problems of missed calls and the like. But, as with any technology, the remedies themselves occasionally created problems. Consider call waiting: If I'm talking to you, and I put you on hold because another call comes in, and I come back to tell you, "Sorry, I've got to take the other call," what does that make you and your call: chopped liver?

Indeed, the cellphone can be seen as an archetypical remedial medium that both solves and creates problems. The biggest problem with the land line telephone was that you had to be in a specific place—a home, an office, a public booth—to make (and in the case of home and office, to receive) a call. Solved with the cellphone! But the little big blender also engenders numerous problems, serious and trivial, as we have seen. No need to despair, however. Remedial media can and will be applied to the remedial medium of the cellphone.

The common denominator in all of these developments is human rationality. Contrary to Jacques Ellul (see, for example, 1964), who sees us as totally, inextricably dominated by technology, it turns out that we call the important shots in media evolution. Human assessment and invention, not mindless obeisance to technology, decides where we go with any and all media.

The little big blender of the cellphone is thus by and large in very good hands: our own.

References

Ellul, J. (1964). *The technological society*, trans. J. Wilkinson. New York: Vintage.

Levinson, P. (1979). *Human replay: A theory of the evolution of media.* Ph.D. diss., New York University.

Levinson, P. (1997). *The soft edge: A natural history and future of the information revolution.* London and New York: Routledge.

Levinson, P. (2004). *Cellphone: The story of the world's most mobile medium and how it has transformed everything.* New York: Palgrave/Macmillan.

McLuhan, M. (1962). *The Gutenberg galaxy.* New York: Mentor.

Mumford, Lewis (1970). *The pentagon of power.* New York: Harcourt, Brace, Jovanovich.

Wachtel, E. (1977/1978). "The influence of the window on western art and vision." The Structurist 17/18: 4–10

Interfaces of Hybrid Spaces

Adriana de Souza e Silva

> *People are going to stop carrying around things like laptops....*
> *More and more devices are going to fit in your pocket. People*
> *will discover that their mobile can handle video, work like a*
> *Palm Pilot and be a phone. It's much more powerful than what*
> *they have at home. . . . And what will we call these non-phones?*
> *"We're calling them communicators."* — *Jan Uddenfeldt*

Introduction

Since their inception, cell phones have been regarded as mobile telephones. This is not surprising, since the cellular technology had been created to allow many people to share the same radio frequency in adjacent cells in order to transmit voicelike telephone. In the last twenty years, however, since the first cell phone was commercially released, the devices have acquired other functions, such as text messaging, video and image transmission, Internet connection, location awareness, and gaming.

Therefore, instead of being studied as wireless voice devices, cell phones are analyzed as portable microcomputers, embedded in public spaces. Changing the concept of the cell phone also implies looking at it in different ways: as a wearable, ubiquitous, and social device. Moreover, it implies the redefinition of existing correlated concepts, such as the Internet, as well as our very notion of presence and space.

Hybrid spaces merge the physical and the digital in a social environment created by the mobility of users connected via mobile technology devices. Cell phones are digital interfaces that make us "inhabit" these hybrid spaces. Mobile and portable interfaces are embedded in physical space, promoting the blurring of borders between physical and digital spaces. The emergence of mobile technology devices has contributed to the possibility of being always connected to digital spaces. It has become possible to literally "carry" the Internet wherever we go, feeling as though we are everywhere at the same time. And because they move around with us, mobile devices also make us aware of the physicality of digital spaces. Furthermore, cell phones and other mobile devices, such as Palmtops and PDAs (personal digital assistants), are responsible for the feeling of being always connected, in contact with digital spaces.

Understanding and investigating some characteristics of mobile interfaces, such as ubiquity, wearability, and transparency, it is critical to conceptualize mobile devices, as well as to foresee how they will mediate our social interactions in the future. For more important than the technological developments is to realize how mobile devices become embedded in contemporary's society and culture, and how different cultures create distinct uses for the same interface. Mobile phones can be regarded as entertainment and collective communication interfaces, therefore being used also in pleasurable parts of life: for promoting sociability, art making, and game play. After the introduction of image and video, as well as GPS (global positioning system) capabilities, mobile phones began to foment new types of sociability and develop new perceptions of physical spaces.

Moving away from a technological determinism by which new technology changes society, this study analyzes ways by which the mobile is socially appropriated, therefore being transformed into a wearable computer, as well as a fashion item. On the other hand, mobile devices also reshape our subjectivity, our sociability, and the spaces we inhabit: urban spaces, digital spaces, and imaginary spaces.

Ubiquitous Computing:
An Earlier View on Embedding the Digital in the Physical

Already more than ten years ago, Mark Weiser (1996), from the Computer Science Lab at Xerox PARC (Palo Alto Research Center), predicted that we would be moving toward a third era in the history of computers. The first era he called mainframes, characterized by one computer being shared by lots of people. At this time, computers were run mostly by experts. The second phase, which spanned the last decade, was called the personal computing era, when person and machine stared uneasily at each other across the desktop. Each personal computer was meant to belong to one person. Next comes ubiquitous computing, or the age of calm technology, when technology recedes into the background of our lives, and the computer-human relationship is characterized by many computers for one individual person. Thus, ubiquitous computing happens when computers are embedded in our daily lives and no longer part of a distant reality. In this sense, "ubiquitous computing is roughly the opposite of virtual reality. While virtual reality puts people inside a computer-generated world, ubiquitous computing forces computers to live out here in the world with people" (Weiser 1996).

Weiser was a visionary, for as early as 1987 he and his group at the Electronics and Imaging Laboratory at Xerox PARC started thinking about spreading out computers ubiquitously in the environment. The idea was to make computers embedded into the physical world, albeit not perceivable. He believed that the future of interface design was leading us to an era of invisible interfaces. "A less-traveled path I call the 'invisible'; its highest ideal is to make a computer so embedded, so fitting, so natural, that we use it without even thinking about it" (Weiser 1996). But isn't that the primary goal of computer technologies? Since the invention of the personal computer, it has been constructed with layers of interfaces (monitor, hard drive, floppy drive, operational system) that tried to approximate the user and to make the machine itself transparent to the user. These interfaces were means of rerepresenting the digital for humans, in a language that would be understandable to us. The more imperceptible the interface, the more the user felt she could communicate with the machine.

However, the goal of personal computers' interfaces was to make the relationship between one user and one computer so natural that the user could be immersed in the digital environment without even realizing its detachment from the physical space. This approach to computer interfaces was responsible for the myth of the immateriality of digital spaces, which was also a consequence of the transition from a culture of calculations to a culture of simulations (Turkle 1995, p. 41). The graphic user interface (GUI) simultaneously hid the code behind the screen, allowing an intuitive relationship to the personal computer, and also simulated the physical world, nearly saying, "You no longer need the physical desk because all your actions can now take place on the virtual desktop." The shift from personal computers to calm technology inverts this relationship. Arguing that "the world is not a desktop," Weiser (1994) tried to figure out what the metaphor for the computer of the future would be.

The main problem he identified regarding PCs was their obvious visibility. They required too much of our full attention. A good technology, according to him, functions like a tool. A tool, when properly used, disappears as a function of its use, moving to the background of our attention. Weiser supported the claim that calm technology would move back and forth between the center and the periphery of our attention. For example, "the ink that communicates the central words of a text also, through choice of font and layout, peripherally clues us into the genre of the text" (Weiser and Brown 1996). Conversely, bad typography or poorly constructed sentences tire the user without apparent reason. When talking about transparency and functionality, Weiser probably had in mind functionalistic rules that guided the design of objects, buildings, and pages during most of the twentieth century. According to functionalistic movements, the form of an object should follow its function, thus making the object disappear according to its use. The same, in this case, was valid for typography: good typography should "disappear" to give the meaning of the text visibility.

Nonetheless, a calm technology would move to the foreground of our attention when, for example, the user needed to control the device. This movement backward and forward, from the periphery to the center of our attention, created, according to Weiser and Brown (1996), a natural relationship to technology. When things are in the periphery, we are still aware of them, but they do not require full attention. Also, Weiser and Brown stresses that not all technologies should be calm. Telephones, for instance, are not calm technologies, because they require our full attention when ringing. However, as will be discussed later, they are indeed ubiquitous.

During the 1990s, Weiser's group at Xerox developed some prototypes they envisioned would be the ubiquitous computers of the future. These prototypes included boards, pads, and tabs. The LiveBoard allowed, among other functions, remote drawing collaboration, and was sold to schools until 1998. The ParcPad maintained constant network connectivity and was used for radio, protocol, and mobile networking. Finally, the ParcTab could be used with one hand and included a location-sensitive, agent-based infrared network. These devices foresaw much of the critical functionalities in today's cell phones, like mobile networks and location-based services.

Weiser also foresaw consequences for the use of ubiquitous computing: surveillance and control. Once one creates computers that are invisible and extensive, it becomes hard to know who is controlling what and who is observing what. N. Katherine Hayles

(1996, p. 6) observes that in the beginning of the 1990s "employees at the PARC are provided with interactive badges that communicate with sensors in the ceilings, which in turn signal confirmation about the employees' locations to a computer network."

Yet in the 1990s researchers and artists at PARC were not so much concerned with surveillance, but with bringing the digital world inside the physical environment. A critical question at that time was how to represent the digital information in the background of physical space. Natalie Jeremijenko, an artist in residency at PARC, created the Dangling String (1995), an eight-foot piece of plastic spaghetti that hung from a small electric motor mounted in the ceiling. The string monitored network activity, becoming "nervous" and emitting sounds if traffic was heavy, and "quiet" if traffic was slow. The Dangling String hung in an unused corner of the research center's hallway and did not interfere with employees' movements around the office space. On the other hand, it was an important tool to hear and visualize network activity without the need to be connected to a desktop computer.

Transforming bits into a palpable experience is also the aim of Hiroshi Ishii and the Tangible Media Group at the MIT Media Lab. Ishii (1999, p. 232) declares that he has been inspired by Weiser's vision of ubiquitous computing. However, he points out that his group's goal is not only to make computers ubiquitous per se, but also to transform physical objects into interfaces to interact with digital environments. Ishii differentiates tangible bits from the traditional GUI, virtual reality, and augmented reality, although he admits to also being influenced by augmented reality research. Nevertheless, while augmented reality generally superimposes graphical data on physical space, Ishii's group creates graspable physical objects that function as interfaces. The interfaces created by his group belong to at least one of the following categories: (1) interactive surfaces between physical and virtual spaces; (2) graspable physical objects that couple bits and atoms; and (3) ambient media, represented by background interfaces such as sound, light, and airflow. These ambient media, from which Jeremijenko's Dangling String is an example, aim to transform the entire physical environment into an interface. By creating sensible environments, Ishii brings computation from the digital desktop to the physical world. He also points out another trend from this computational locus shift: the move into our skins/bodies.

Wearable Computers: Carrying the Digital Space

While ubiquitous computing and tangible bits are related to spreading out computer technologies around the physical space, thus transforming the physical environment into an interface, wearable computing focuses on adapting this technology to the body, allowing computers to move with us. The concept of wearable computers includes fashion and clothing, besides being related to identity and personality. Wearable computers have many common points with the ubiquitous interfaces. First, they are meant to be transparent, since the user should not be "annoyed" by the presence of the computer. Second, they bring digital space into physical reality, allowing the user to be constantly connected. Third, they change our perception of physical space by merging digital data inside it. Finally, wearable computers can also be regarded as tools.

Hayles (1999, p. 34) points out different meanings acquired by tools throughout the centuries. In the nineteenth century, mainly due to the Industrial Revolution, using a specific tool could shape the body, as the woodcutter becomes strong due to the use of an axe. Later, in the twentieth century, the human being was transformed from a tool user to a toolmaker. Yet in the twenty-first century the emergence of the posthuman changes again the meaning of the word *tool*, from something detached from the body to a prosthesis (part of the body).

Hayles (1999, p. 84) tells that in the 1970s Gregory Bateson asked his graduate students if a blind man's cane could be considered part of the man. "Most of his students thought that human boundaries are naturally defined by epidermal surfaces. . . . However, cybernetic systems are constituted by flows of information. In this viewpoint, cane and man join in a single system, for the cane funnels to the man essential information about his environment." Being an important mediation between the man and the world, the cane becomes a transparent tool, and therefore part of the man. The cane's value is then defined by the information extracted from the world and transmitted into the man's mind. In the twenty-first century, these tools are getting smaller, connecting the subject with digital data.

Furthermore, tools are also used to extend one's mind into the physical environment; according to Daniel Dennett (1996, p. 146), words and writing are extensions of our memory. Thus, while the blind man's cane can be regarded as a tool that allows the flowing of information from the environment into the man's mind, words can do the opposite, offloading information from our minds into the world. Although words are culturally the most important tools, computers can also be regarded as "tools for thought." Furthermore, computers are not only extensions of thought, but also extensions of the physical world into our minds (they work as part of our bodies, as well as extensions of contiguous spaces).

Significant inventions in the area of wearable computers (Rhodes 2005) started to take place in the 1970s. Steve Mann (1996), who designed a backpack-mounted computer in 1981, points out three main characteristics for wearable (or existential) computers. First, they are part of the self, and not a separate object carried by the user. Second, the apparatuses should be controlled by the wearer. Finally, they should be constant; that is, they should never be turned off. When not used, they go into sleep modes, but they are always ready to turn themselves on whenever required. The second and third characteristics are aligned with Weiser's description of *ubiquitous* computers, devices that should always travel back and forth across human attention, automatically and/or via user control. The first characteristic, though, excludes mobile technology devices from the category of wearable computers. I will argue that this concept is suitable to change to include mobile phones.

Mann (1996) points out that existential computers can be used for all facets of living, and not just as places to work, as desktop computers have been frequently regarded. Therefore, wearable computers belong to the ludic side of life.[1] When a computer can be carried around, it becomes an intrinsic part of our lives, for there's no longer the need to go to a computer—it is always with us.

It's interesting to think that wearable computers have developed simultaneously to the GUI in desktop computers. Although in the very beginning the graphic interface has been skeptically viewed by programmers, soon it became synonymous with computers and considered a more natural way of getting in contact with the digital domain. The power of the graphical interface to pull the user into the virtual environment overshadowed the material interfaces used to manipulate it, focusing on the information space. On the other hand, wearable computers should be carried by the user, making the physical interfaces much more visible. Throughout almost two decades wearable computers have been awkwardly viewed, since the physical apparatuses used to interact with the user were not at all "transparent." The first wearable computers were heavy and clumsy, requiring too much of an effort from the user. The production of smaller and comfortable interfaces has been accomplished mainly since the late 1990s.

Wearable computers and small interfaces contribute to creating more natural relationships with technology, including them in our everyday life without the need to really perceive them. Therefore, they also become a part of our bodies. The miniaturization of interfaces might not be crucial, but it is surely a critical factor to the emergence of mobile communication devices.

Mobile Technology Devices: Combining Mobility and Communication

Ubiquity

Cell phones and other mobile communication devices share some characteristics with ubiquitous and wearable computers, but differ from them in other respects. Mobile technologies are supposed to be small in order to be carried. Similar to wearable computers, they should be wireless in order to allow the user to move freely through the physical environment. However, cell phones do not fit into Weiser's description of transparent technologies, because they require the full attention of the user. This feature is inherited from the telephone, whose ringing always demands an interruption of any previous conversation or action in order to answer the call. As Marshall McLuhan (1994, p. 268) observes, we feel compelled to answer a ringing public phone even when we know that the call cannot concern us. According to Sadie Plant (2002), who developed a report on the social use of cell phones for Motorola, public use of mobile phones creates an additional tension, because only the person to whom the call is made is in a position to respond. This situation irritates many people, because they feel disconcerted by this new electronic soundtrack invading public spaces. Moreover, many people state that "just the knowledge that a call might intervene tends to divert attention from those present at the time," placing the cell phone always in the center of attention of a group (Plant 2002, p. 30).

Plant (2002, p. 31) creates three categories for the public reception of calls on cell phones. The first one she calls flight, which is characterized by the user immediately moving out of the group to talk in privacy. The second, suspension, is related to recipients who stay in the same place but stop whatever they are doing for the duration of the call. Finally, persistence describes users who try to stay engaged with the nearby context, as much as possible paying attention to what they were doing prior to the incoming call. All three situations are characterized by at least a minimum disconnection from the nearby context and the fear of close peers of being "abandoned" by the person who has answered the phone. However, this paradigm shifts. Cell phones do take people out of the nearby context, but also bring distant people to the actual context. This movement in and out of physical space promotes new types of sociability and communication patterns. Moreover, in places like Japan, Finland, and Sweden, cell phones largely changed their roles from personal communication devices to social communication interfaces, engaging nearby friends in the conversation with distant peers, thus promoting a larger "multiuser" experience.

Overhearing private talks in public spaces is indeed disturbing for many people. Consequently, cell phones have been placed on some public places' "blacklists." There are restrictions on the use of mobiles on British, Japanese, Swiss, and American trains. "Restaurants in cities as diverse as Cairo and Chicago have introduced 'no-mobile' policies or 'mobile-free' zones in an attempt to maintain the senses of privacy and personal space which are considered crucial to their atmosphere" (Plant 2002, p. 36). It's interesting to note, though, that signs of "silent rooms" in trains or other public spaces are only viewed where the technology has become ubiquitous. On the other hand, ubiquity also promotes familiarity with the technology. Artist and curator Sara Diamond (personal communication, April 17, 2003) observed that in London's subway and buses, dealing with cell phones is quite ordinary. London citizens are traditionally introspective people, but it seems that the cell phone changed their way of dealing with public/private matters, for they talk openly about all (personal) topics in public places. In the U.K., a research study conducted by Telecom Italia attested that as much as 1.1 percent of the population admits they try to listen to other people's conversations on cell phones (Fortunati 2002a, p. 52). However, the same research states that 21.1 percent of U.K. citizens are annoyed by public use of cell phones, the highest percentage in western Europe.[2] Likewise, most Germans disapprove the use of cell phones in public spaces; 50.1 percent think, "What a show!" when seeing somebody using their mobile phone in public (Fortunati 2002a). This reaction is connected to the old belief that mobile phones should be used only for emergency calls. As a result, many think people should refrain from using their phones in public, unless extremely necessary. Plant (2002, p. 34) tells us that "in 1988 a German business man died in a fight provoked by what was perceived to be ill-mannered use of his mobile."

Certainly ubiquity per se is not connected to mobility, but mobile devices can be ubiquitous, as long as they can be viewed and used anywhere. Technologically speaking, ubiquity can be defined as the ability to communicate anytime, anywhere via computer devices spread out in the environment. Ideally, this connectivity is maintained regardless of the location or movement of the mobile entity. This location independence should be available over an area that could be physically too large for any single wired medium, such as an ethernet cable. Obviously, wirelessness enables greater ubiquity than is possible with wired media, especially when one is in motion. Moreover, many wireless hosts spread out over the environment allow the user to move freely around physical space while being always connected.

Broadening the meaning of the word ubiquitous beyond technological aspects, it means something "present, or seeming to be present, everywhere at the same time" (Agnes 2000, p. 1550). In this sense, cell phones are becoming ubiquitous technologies. Recent statistics show that in many parts of the world, including the United States, cell phones surpass the number of telephone land lines (Teleco World 2005). However, while this inversion happened in the United States only in 2004, in Latin American countries, like Brazil, there were more cell phones than land lines as early as 2003. In December 2004, the country had 65.61 million cell phone users versus 40 million fixed lines ("Anatel confirma" 2003). Interestingly, in December 2003 there were 46 million mobile phone subscribers in the country, indicating a growth of almost 50 percent from 2003 to 2004, while the number of fixed land lines has remained almost the same since 2001 ("Estatísticas gerais do Brasil" 2005).

Mobile phones are not only replacing land lines faster in places where access to land lines is difficult to establish, and expensive, but they are also substituting for fixed Internet use. In countries like Brazil, where the rate of Internet users was stable at 8 percent of the population between 2001 and 2003 (ICT 2005), cell phone ownership rate grew 10 percent (from 16 percent to 26 percent) in the same period. In 2005 the cell phone penetration rate represents one third of the country's population. It is also possible to foresee that the more cell phones are equipped with mobile Internet capabilities, like remote data access, location-based services, and multiuser communication, the more this tendency will continue. In many countries where the development of fixed Internet and telephone land lines is not so widespread, cell phones are generally the first computer and the first telephone of many citizens.

The main difference, thus, between mobile technology devices and previous wearable and ubiquitous computing devices is the ability to communicate among people. Mobile technologies, especially cell phones, not only allow connection with digital data, but they also contribute to forming new types of communities. In some parts of the world, like Japan and Finland, cell phones are no longer only two-way communication devices, which is the main characteristic of the traditional telephone. Eija-Liisa Kasesniemi and Pirjo Rautiainen (2002, p. 182) observe that in Finland, where the use of SMS is frequent, "the recipient of the message is generally unaware of the number of people involved in composing the message and the time spent in formulating it," because the message is usually sent under the sender's name only. They observe teenagers' behavior in buses and trains in that country while using their cell phones. Most of the time, the teenagers have the device in their hands at all times. When receiving a call, frequently the conversation is shared among the group. Also, when writing SMS, they ask friends about the content and show received messages to the group.

As long as cell phones are ubiquitous, they can also be regarded as tools, since they turn out to be so natural that one does not even perceive they are being used. As Joshua Meyrowitz (1985, p. 109) comments about the use of the traditional telephone, "speaking to someone on the telephone . . . is so natural that we almost forget about the intervening medium." In this sense, telephones are also transparent. Is the cell phone becoming a transparent interface like the telephone? Here we must distinguish between two meanings of transparency. One is the transparency proposed by Weiser (1996), which is applied to a device that doesn't frequently require our attention and that can be in the background of our lives. Another meaning is related to tools that do not show up because they are functional, and their use is already embedded in our everyday lives. For example, when one talks on the phone the focus stays on the person on the other end of the line, not on the phone itself. Likewise, when one writes, the focus is on the words employed, and not on the pen itself—unless it is an uncomfortable pen, and then it does not exert its functional task. Both meanings of transparency are connected, since calm technology should be functional and tools should recede to the background when not in use.

Wearability

Mobile phones can also be regarded as wearable devices, even though, unlike wearable computers, mobile technology devices are not meant to be worn. However, among all mobile communication technologies, cell phones are the closest to the body. They are generally placed in pockets, belts, or purses, becoming an indispensable accessory for everyday life. Yet Italian researcher Leopoldina Fortunati (2002a, p. 46) inquires whether mobile phones are really portable technologies. "If we look at the phenomenology of its use, its position on the surface of the body is both precarious and uncomfortable." She argues that the difficulty in finding an appropriate place for the cell phone on the body limits its wearability because "the tendency is to free it from its new place at the earliest opportunity and put it somewhere else" (Fortunati 2002a, p. 47). For example, it is common to leave cell phones on tables in restaurants, bars, or trains. The impact of this "placeless" cell phone could be computed by the London's Lost Property Office, which reported that mobiles have replaced umbrellas as one of the most common returned items between April 2000 and March 2001 (TfL 2001).

Studies on the design of cell phones are conducted with the goal of trying to make them more "wearable" or to adapt clothes to carry them. Fortunati (2002a, p. 47) also mentions that Nokia "has teamed up with a European fashion house to create clothes specifically designed to incorporate mobile communication technologies." The IBM pervasive wireless industry[3] explores ways to make technology wearable and ubiquitous. One of its earlier prototypes included a wearable "jewelry" cell phone. It consisted of a pair of earrings, a necklace, a watch, and a ring that at first glance look like ordinary jewelry. Reporter Tom Spring (2000) explained how it worked: "When you get a call, a tiny light starts blinking on your ring. The phone number of the person calling is displayed on the watch. You answer the phone by pressing a button on your watch. Next, you hear the call through your earring, which has a tiny speaker embedded in it. You then speak to the necklace, which has a tiny microphone inside and acts as a mouth-piece."

Current research on fashion and technology is being conducted to make new devices more embedded in the body and personalized, enabling information access anywhere, anytime.[4] In 2003 NTT DoCoMo, the main mobile communication company in Japan, announced the development of a new wearable cell phone: a wrist phone. Besides being a portable phone, the Wristomo assumes a standard handset shape when opened. Like most good watches, it is waterproof. Furthermore, it sends and receives e-mails, and is provided with location-based service that informs the user about restaurants, weather, and transportation, depending on the user's location. The Wristomo is not based on I-mode 3-G standard,[5] but, according to journalist Anthony Newman (2003), "it is an important step in making PDAs and phones—and their connectivity —'ubiquitous' like watches." As technological innovations never come alone, almost simultaneously Samsung announced the first GPRS[6] watch phone in Europe. Samsung's phone is based on GSM,[7] the European standard for mobile communication (Samsung 2003). Measuring 37.8 by 64 by 17.7 millimeters, the phone was scheduled to go on sale across Europe at the end of 2003 as the world's smallest GPRS phone in the Guinness list of world records. Both the Wristomo and Samsung's watch phone represent attempts to make mobile communication more wearable and available, without being uncomfortable. "With your phone strapped to your wrist, you never have to worry about leaving it behind," comments Newman (2003). It is still early to predict whether cell phones are going to migrate from handsets to

Fig. 1
NTT DoCoMo Wristomo

"wristsets," but definitely they are becoming fashion items, personalized and smaller. Cell phones are already wearable devices in Japan. The Japanese keitai[8] is certainly not only a phone; it is also a personal item and part of the identity of many young teenagers. Plant (2002, p. 44) comments that "in many parts of Pacific Asia, girls wear their mobiles as functional jewelry: in Bangkok they are carried in fur-edged plastic pouches worn as necklaces."

Sara Diamond (personal communication, April 17, 2003) argues that despite cell phone manufacturers' concern with the device's design, frequently an emphasis on aesthetics leaves functionality on a second plane. For example, internal antennas decrease reception quality, and smaller handsets have less durable batteries. However, wearability is critical to transforming cell phones into ubiquitous interfaces, with all the characteristics a ubiquitous device might have: transparency, popularity, omnipresence, and pervasiveness. As Fortunati (2002a, p. 48) argues, "if the Walkman 'dresses' the ear, and microchips remain inserted in the body for long periods, the mobile involves not only the ear, but also the mouth and voice." When it is not being used, the mobile phone generally stays close to the body most of the day.

The popularity of cell phones over other mobile technology devices, like laptops and PDAs, is due to their portability—and their price, naturally. As Plant (2002, p. 26) notes, they are especially popular in Japan because people are used to living in confined spaces, "which makes them reluctant to own or carry something as large and heavy as a laptop, but delighted to pocket a small, light, multifunctional keitai." Even in other places in the world, as long as cell phones acquire other functions that are not limited to the traditional telephone, they tend to substitute for other mobile devices because they are easier to carry and more affordable.

Immersion

Although cell phones might be easily forgotten, while in use they can be really demanding. It is common to hear comments about people who spend more time talking on the phone than interacting with others in their vicinity. Therefore, mobile phones are frequently considered nonsociable media. Howard Rheingold (2002, p. xxii) observes that in trains and buses passengers prefer to talk to somebody who is physically absent than with other people who are in the same vehicle. Yet that is not a big deal, for, since the emergence of the train as a transportation technology, communication inside the wagon has been awkward, leading to the habit of reading during the trip (Schivelbusch 1986, p. 75). Partly because the typical train trip is short in duration, conversations with people who are no more than strangers—and who will probably never be seen again—is generally not initiated. With the further development of advanced transportation technologies, like the automobile and the airplane, this situation did not change. However, cell phones have created different communication patterns—for example, the enfolding of contexts.

According to Hayles (personal communication, November 19, 2002), "the context is becoming enfolded, so that there is no longer a homogeneous context for a given spatial area, but rather pockets of different contexts in it." For example, someone talking on a cell phone is part of the context of people who share the same spatial area, but she is also part of a distant context, because she is talking to someone who is spatially remote from her area. Hence there is a context that is created by the spatial proximity of people and inside it another context that is created by the cell phone. This might have been a feature of other media as well, such as the TV or land line telephones. The difference promoted by mobile technologies, however, is precisely the possibility of moving through space. The first popular experience of enfolding contexts while moving through space was perceived with the Walkman in the early 1980s (Hosokawa, 1987), but these folded contexts were not connected to two-way communication. The Walkman mixed the present context of the urban environment with a soundtrack that did not belong to it, but was particular to the person who wore the device.

Interestingly, many issues raised by the widespread use of the Walkman as a wearable technology are applied to cell phones today. For example, Hosokawa (1987, p. 7) inquires whether or not using the Walkman implies a loss of contact with reality. While walking through space, the Walkman listener is in a world whose sounds do not correspond to the environment she sees. The ability to choose the soundtrack to the world also isolates the listener from contact to other people in the vicinity, and the physical environment becomes a background to the listener's thoughts. According to Hosokawa (1987, p. 21), "The practical meaning of the Walkman is found in the distance that it creates between the reality and the real, the city and the urban, and mainly between the other and the self. The Walkman destroys the context of the city, and promptly places any incoherent situation in its context."

Due to its ability to isolate users from interpersonal interaction in public space, the Walkman technology provoked a lot of public debate (Licoppe and Heurtin 2002, p. 99). Although cell phones are communication devices, many times they have also been regarded as responsible for taking people out of the physical environment and isolating users. Differences from the Walkman, however, are many. First, mobile phones are generally used to interact with other people. Second, mobile phone interactions are unexpected, while the Walkman has a constant behavior while on. Furthermore, interaction with the cell phone is not only limited to incoming calls, but can also include nearby peers. Conversely, cell phone screens, displaying all sorts of games, personal assistance, and the Internet, turn the mobile phone into a highly immersive device.

Machiko Kusahara (personal communication, January 16, 2003), professor at the Waseda University in Japan, tells a story about a man waiting for a train in the Tokyo subway. He was so immersed in his cell phone screen that he unconsciously crossed the security line of the subway toward the rails, and did not realize when the train came. By a fraction of seconds he was not hit by it. This story raises some issues. First, how does the cell phone screen compete so successfully with the urban background? Technically speaking, suggests Erkki Huhtamo (personal communication, December 15, 2002), professor of media archaeology at UCLA, immersion is defined as an exclusion from the surroundings, in a situation where the user does not see the borders that separate the digital and the physical environment. The cell phone, in turn, has a clear frame that is defined by the tiny screen. Therefore, there is no way of applying the traditional immersion concept to the cell phone. However, "what is the feature in the cell phone that may exclude the surroundings so powerfully?" questions Huhtamo. According to critical theorist Norman Klein (personal communication, November 8, 2002), "there's no longer need of the screen, because the real world around us has become the screen." Klein believes that when people talk on the phone while walking, they just move through the space, but they are not actually there. Moreover, this absent presence transforms physical space into a nonplace, because people do not interact with anyone in their vicinity. Therefore they become walking avatars. An avatar is one's representation in a space in which one is not. This perspective, Klein says, "generates a culture of tremendous paranoia and isolation.

The more we promote an invasion of privacy in public spaces, the more we make ourselves isolated from the world around us."

Within this context, there are two opposing ways of looking at cell phones. One, following Klein, considers them as technologies that promote isolation. The other regards mobile phones as technologies that enhance communication. According to Klein, mobile technology devices detach us from the physical world around us, projecting our presence in virtual spaces. Conversely, in physical spaces we are represented by many disembodied, distributed presences, like answering machines. For Klein, we increasingly live in virtual spaces.

Given this fact, the second question is, does immersion depend on the screen itself? The man with the cell phone in Tokyo could have been reading a newspaper or a book, and the level of "disconnection from the present context" would be the same. Similarly, while playing a game, even if the screen is small like in a Game Boy, the level of disconnection with the surroundings might be really strong. Therefore immersion does not depend only on our vision, but also on touch, smell, and sounds. Most of all, immersion depends on imagination. Like the Walkman user who "reinvents" the city soundscape by replacing its original soundtrack with the sound that comes from the device, the cell phone user also reinvents urban spaces, no longer disconnecting from them, but connecting in a different way.

In any case, what we learn about mobile communication technologies is that they simultaneously change our communication patterns and also transform our relationship to space. Therefore, there is no point in discussing whether cell phones take us out of physical space or promote sociability among nearby users, because the space in which communication happens is no longer physical or virtual; it is hybrid. A hybrid space encompasses both instances in one, enfolding contexts and connecting people who are distant and close.

Presence

Mobile technologies also change our sense of presence. Presence has always been an important concept in digital environments, to the extent that the creation of an avatar has been required to represent one's body in the digital world. The avatar is the interface of an absent physical body. Kenneth Gergen (2002) explains how technologies such as the Walkman, books, computer screens, and telephones have the power to exclude us from the environment in which we physically are. For him, these are technologies that promote an absent presence, for when talking on a cell phone, for example, "one is physically absorbed by a technologically mediated world of elsewhere" (p. 227). This statement is partially true, especially regarding fixed telephones, but it is also important to consider two additional things. First, the fact that one is absently present in this context might mean that she is presently absent in another context. Fortunati (2002b, p. 519) believes that the "ambiguous dimension of presence/absence in space also means the restructuring of the sense of belonging to a place." Therefore, the feeling of belonging to one's communicative network is no longer dependent on a specific place or physical presence, but on space and message exchange. Interestingly, researcher Mizuko Ito (in Rheingold 2002, p. 6) observes that Tokyo thumb tribes consider themselves "present" at a gathering if they are in touch via SMS: "As long as peers participated in the shared communication of the group, they seemed to be considered by others to be present." This distributed presence allows users to participate physically in one social event, while being "in communication" with people at another social event, creating a double social network, and the ability to be "present" in both places.

Second, we must consider a very peculiar characteristic of mobile phones, especially in Scandinavian countries and Japan: communication that takes place in the contiguous physical environment. Mobile phone screens differ from movie theaters' screens, for example, in that they are embedded in the environment. A completely separate environment, similar to a black box, must be created in order to watch a movie on a theater screen, to disconnect it from the physical world around us. A similar situation has been produced by the TV, which generally occupies a specific place inside one's house. The goal of these screens is to disconnect the spectator from the nearby context. While watching TV or seeing a movie, generally no conversation occurs. Conversely, cell phone screens are embedded in the physical world, they are mobile, and they travel around attached to the user. Although they can also promote immersion, frequently it has been noticed that the "shared use" of cell phone screens promotes communication and interaction among people who inhabit the same physical environment. Alexandra Weilenmann and Catrine Larsson (2002, p. 95) developed a study on local use and sharing of mobile phones in Sweden and concluded, among other things, that "the remote communication, i.e., the phone calls they [teenagers] receive or make, as well as the SMS messages they receive or send, are accounted for in the ongoing local interaction. Teenagers thus share the communication they take part in with their co-present friends."

Sociability: Creating Multiuser Environments

In the aforementioned mobile interaction, not only the communication as an abstract entity, but often the phone as a physical medium is shared. Therefore, cell phones become no longer "private" objects, although they can be very personal. Via several examples, Weilenmann and Larsson (2002) show that cell phones in Sweden are often shared to enable a whole group to talk to a remote person. "Instead of one person talking and 'shielding' her/himself from the group while doing it, everyone present involves themselves, and are allowed to involve themselves in the ongoing conversation" (p. 98). Thus the mobile becomes a collaborative resource for teenagers, rather than a private phone. Mainly allowed by the widespread use of SMS in Scandinavian countries, the social communication promoted by cell phones is much more than merely a group communication.

While cell phones still cannot be regarded as "wearable" devices, they are definitely viewed as extensions of the body, mainly the extensions of one's hands. Plant (2002, p. 23) shows that except for in the United States and in Latin American countries, where the word for the cell phone comes from the technology that enables them, in almost all other parts of the world the words for the device are connected to mobility, hands, and portability. For example, in French it is called *le portable*. Finns name it *kännykkä* or *känny*, which refers to an extension of the hand. In Germany a cell phone is a *handy*. In Spanish, *le movil*. Plant (2002, p. 23) goes further, explaining that "In Arabic it is sometimes called *el mobile*, but often a telephone *sayaar*, or *makhmul* (both of which refer to carrying). . . . In Thailand it is a *moto*. In Japan it is *keitai denwa*, a carried telephone, or simply *keitai*, or even just *ke-tai*. In China it is *sho ji*, or 'hand-machine.'"The shift from cellular phone to mobile or handy shows a transformation from a technological to a personal device. It represents the moment when the technology is no longer just a tool, but rather part of ourselves, and part of our identity.

On the Consequences of a Mobile Interface

Mobility and Imagination: Enfolding Contexts

Huhtamo (personal communication, December 15, 2002) argues that understanding cell phones requires that we look at early stages of mobile technology, which includes the history of portable sound. More than a technological history, it is a history of imagination, and of imaginary devices that were never really implemented. Early mobile sound devices included car radios in the 1940s, bicycle radios, radio bracelets, as well as hybrid devices that combined radio and photographic apparatuses in the beginning of the last century. Reasons why the radio-camera did not succeed are unclear, but it might be due to the inability to send the pictures after they had been taken. While the combination with the camera did not succeed, portable radio devices have been a great success. Until recently, however, portable communication has been successful only in imaginary realms. Huhtamo also suggests that imaginary visions develop more slowly than the technology itself, which means that even though new technologies arise, present fantasies might come from earlier times. Conversely, fantasies from earlier times produced never-implemented technologies. The wrist phone used by the cartoon character Dick Tracy included features like video streaming that are only now being implemented in cell phones. Other technologies, like the videophone, remained successful only in fiction, as in reality they did not work. Barry Brown, Nicola Green, and Richard Harper (2002, p. 9) tell us that in the 1970s AT&T spent over $500 million to develop the videophone. However, by 1973, there were only one hundred public videophone subscribers. Therefore, according to Huhtamo, there is no synchronous mode between the history of the imagination about technology and the history of technological development.

Cell phones transform (urban circulation) spaces into (social) places both by enhancing communication among people who are close in physical space and by extending communication to hybrid spaces. Both cases involve communication with people who are not sharing the same contiguous physical space, and both cases change our perception of space by enfolding distant contexts into the present context. The enfolding of spaces promoted by cell phones nourishes people's imagination about distant contexts and worlds. There are always two contexts involved in a cell phone (or telephone) conversation. According to Plant (2002, p. 47), "to overhear a conversation is to listen in to one of these worlds. To overhear just one of its sides is to be neither fully admitted nor completely excluded from its worlds." A young teacher in Chicago admits that, because she could not hear both sides of a conversation, she frequently found herself drawn into speculations about the missing sides of the dialogues in an attempt to fill the gaps (Plant 2002, p. 47). Mobile phone conversations overheard in public spaces are like narratives about other spaces in the minds of nearby people. As strangers generally know nothing or very little about the person who is talking on the other side of the phone, they can imagine whatever they want about the spoken topics. This situation is different when considering shared cell phone use among teenagers. In these circumstances, the distant context is a present part of the nearby context.

One can argue that fixed telephone calls also enfold distant contexts into the present context, nurturing imagination. However, land line phones (except for pay phones) are not generally used in public spaces, restricting the number of people who might overhear a conversation and fixing the context in which the conversation happens. A home phone, for instance, is used by family members whose contexts are not completely unknown to each other. Conversely, the mobile phone user is usually in motion, so calls are received in quite different contexts. The mobile enfolding of contexts is also connected to a technology that is necessarily embedded in the environment and part of other contexts. For example, "in Tokyo, people are expert navigators of busy city streets, railway platforms, and subways while keeping an eye on their keitai. In Beijing, the new skill is more likely to involve riding a bicycle while making and taking mobile calls" (Plant 2002, p. 50). The mobile phone creates a culture "in-between."

The most common question at the beginning of a cell phone call—"Where are you?"—is not only a practical question, but also an attempt to contextualize the conversation, to try to imagine where the other person might be. This was not at all an issue with fixed telephones, because the context was always already given. Furthermore, fixed phone lines are connected to places, and not to people. Similarly, IP addresses on the Internet are connected to servers, not to people. One person can use many different hosts, but a brief look at the IP numbers reveals where a message has been sent from. Mobile phones, in contrast, have no fixed location. Cell phones decontextualize the conversation, and demand its recontextualization. As a result, while fixed telephones and the Internet connect people in a virtual space, cell phones bring this virtual conversation place into physical space, creating a hybrid environment. In a mobile network, the users are the moving network nodes.

Mobility and Space: Public, Private, and (Non)Surveillance

The physical place in which the cell phone is located has always been an unknown geographical location for those on the other end of the line. In addition, the fact that the cell phone has become a personal item frequently represents for teenagers freedom from parents' surveillance. It is true that many parents give cell phones to their children in order to monitor their activities, or to make them "available" at all times. Nevertheless, one can always lie about one's physical location, and choose whether or not to answer a call depending on the number displayed on the screen.

The existence of one common fixed telephone line in a house enabled members of the family to answer calls intended for other members and therefore possibly "monitor" who was calling whom. It was possible to have an idea about who was on the other end of the line—and sometimes overhear conversations, if the phone were in a common place of the house. "Mobile phones do not allow this type of mutual surveillance anymore. For many teenagers this is the technology of freedom, while for many parents it is the technology of losing control" (Kim 2002, p. 73).

Consequently, the traditional perception of public and private spaces has changed. Much has been asked about whether cell phones privatize public spaces or publicize private spaces. This is the same case of whether the cell phone is responsible for taking one in or out of physical space: the borders have been blurred and it is hard to define what is private and what is public. The very concepts of private and public have been transformed. Is a cell phone conversation on public transportation publicizing one's private space? Or is the phone user privatizing the public space of the bus? What is the difference between a conversation on a cell phone and a conversation with the person seated beside you? Is it different because the other person on the cell phone is not physically present?

Gergen (2002, p. 230) splits communication interfaces into two categories: monological technologies and dialogic technologies. The first, which includes TV, radio, and film—that is, broadcast media—brings public into private. (The TV in a house functions as a window opened to the world.) They insert outside voices into daily life circumstances, but there are few means by which one can respond to them. Conversely, dialogic technologies include telephones and cell phones. These interfaces, according to Gergen, privatize spaces in the sense that the incoming outside voices are generally available to only one person at a time. Gergen suggests that the emergence of advanced communication technologies like the telegraph in the past century promoted an erosion of face-to-face communication. Interestingly, "when the telephone entered cultural life early in the twentieth century, it primarily served as an extension of face-to-face relations" (p. 236). The Internet can function both as a monological technology (when used to access information) and as a dialogic medium (when used for two-way and multicast communication). Nevertheless, the Internet has rarely been regarded as an extension of face-to-face communication. Due to the possibilities of reinventing the self and assuming "multiple identities," it is more like hiding oneself under the barrier of the interface than extending "real" communication.

Cell phones also play an important role in creating a private space for teenagers in Japan. As Japanese people are used to living in very small places and sharing one phone line with the entire family, the ownership of a cell phone creates a private space for communication. As Rheingold (2002, p. 4) observes, "in Japan, adding wired telephone lines to home is expensive, but it is less expensive for teens to have their own personal mobile numbers." Also, because much of the communication is accomplished via text, other members of the family are not able to overhear the conversation. This fact might partially explain why cell phones in Japan are so popular among teenagers and why the same is not true in the United States. In the United States, families tend to live in bigger houses. Also, land lines are very cheap and frequently one family house has more than one fixed line, allowing each member of the family to have his or her own private line. Privacy in the United States does not depend on the new mobile interface. Ito (in Rheingold 2002, p. 23) notes that "Americans move between private nucleated homes, private transportation, and often private offices and cubicles as well, with quick forays in the car to shop occasionally (not daily grocery shopping as in Japan), and use of public space and restaurants has the sense of an optional excursion rather than a necessity."

Accessing the Internet via mobile devices will, therefore, change what we understand by the Internet. With the addition of location-awareness technology, the Web will be increasingly connected to places and progressively distant from the old notion of a nonplace. Moreover, the idea of "entering the Internet" is most likely to disappear, since 3G mobile phones are always connected.

Although cell phones can be used differently in diverse parts of the world, they promote this blurring of borders between public and private spaces, enfolding the private within the public, bringing the public to the private, and creating private/public mobile islands. Especially among teenagers, mobile phones are not only instruments to build their privacy, but also enforcements of their social public identities. Plant (2002, p. 45) argues that youngsters without cell phones "can feel—and really be—excluded from the social networks to which their friends belong."

Mobility and Microcoordination

Another important consequence of the widespread use of cell phones is the ability of microcoordination. Microcoordination is the result of a series of short phone calls in order to establish appointments and update the other party of real-time events. In the past, one was only available for communication while in the office, or at home, or close to any land line phone. Nowadays, with the possibility of being always available, scheduling and rescheduling appointments becomes easy. Chantal de Gournay (2002, p. 194) points out three characteristics of the mobile interface: reachability, immediacy, and mobility: "Immediacy is an advantage common to both the mobile and the corded telephone. Reachability is an advantage of the mobile phone but it depends on the cooperation of its owner, because, if he or she is unavailable, the result is the same as with a corded phone. Mobility is unquestionably the distinguishing characteristic." Microcordination depends on the three characteristics working together. In Korea, Shin Dong Kim (2002, p. 70) writes, there has been a change in the way people schedule appointments. If before appointments were generally scheduled weeks in advance, so people could organize their schedules, after the cell phone the coordination time became much more dynamic. Kawamura (in Rheingold 2002, p. 5) suggests, "Kids have become loose about time and place. If you have a phone, you can be late." Microcoordination affects not only users' perception of time, but also the perception of public spaces. First, the use of cell phones for microcoordination spreads out and diversifies meeting places. Second, it is used to coordinate instant gatherings and "flash mobs" in specific sites of the city. Third, it can be used to develop imaginary spaces over the city space, as in the case of pervasive gaming.

The power of cell phones in the macrocoordination of political actions, as in the case of President Estrada in Manila, has been noted (see Janey Gordon's chapter this volume). However, another phenomenon related to microcoordination occurring in the United States has been called "flash mobs." It consists of dozens or even hundreds of people with cell phones who gather suddenly, perform some specific but innocuous act, and then promptly scatter. Journalist Rob Walker (2003) tells us that in August 2003, "a mob formed at Toys 'R' Us in Times Square, stared at an animatronics Tyrannosaurus rex, then fell to the floor with screams and a waving of hands before quickly dispersing." These weird actions took place in San Francisco, Minneapolis, London, and Berlin and received attention partially because they were weird, and partially because they were organized via cell phones, pagers, and Web sites.

On the Developments of the Mobile Interface

From Emergency Calls to Social Networks

Michael Benedikt (2000, p. 34) points out that until the 1940s the telephone, which is now taken for granted as a conversational device, had been envisioned merely as a different type of telegraph. Hence people used telephones only for important messages, and would hang up as soon as the essential message was relayed. Similarly, cell phones have also been viewed as "urgency" devices. We have frequently heard that cell phones are useful for emergencies or urgent messages, and that is why they should be carried around all the time. With cell phone development, however, we realize that mobile phones not only are evolving in the same direction as land line telephones, being used for long conversations, but are also used as a mix of pager (SMS), digital camera (camera phone), video camera, personal organizer (PDA), microcomputers with mobile Internet (WAP, wireless application protocol), and game device.

As occurs with every new interface, it takes a while until users can figure out the meaning of the new device. New meanings from new technologies are generally socially and culturally created. In the early years of cell phone development, for example, many people considered it a cordless traditional phone, thus keeping their mobiles at home, like a replacement or additional fixed phone. Fortunati (2002a, p. 47) writes that European research (at Telecom Italia in 1996) "found that one owner out of five never used their mobile phone outside the four walls of the house." This fact is easily understandable from a historical perspective about former uses of past new interfaces and communication media. For example, Janet Murray (1997, p. 66) comments that early film was viewed as a mix of photography and theater, and it was called photoplay (*photo* plus *play*). This concept consistently influenced earlier film aesthetics, in which the camera was generally statically placed at the movie scene, like an observer who was watching a play in a theater. Much later, shooting alternatives with cuts and closeups were developed, more fully exploring what the camera could do.

The same is true for the cell phone. Even if not considered a "replacement for the cordless phone," cell phones have been attributed specific functions in order to acquire meaning as a new interface. Considering mobile phones as "emergency" devices is one example. Talking in public on a cell phone was not considered polite, but its use was justified when the calls were extremely important and urgent.

The use of the mobile phone also differs depending on users' ages. Recent research (Ling and Yttri 2002, p. 147) shows that the oldest users still focus on issues of safety and security. Middle-aged users focus on the coordination potentials of the system, like microcoordination and appointment calls. Finally, the youngest users have the most distinct profile, using the cell phone as an expressive medium for social purposes. Therefore, younger users actually discover new meanings for the interface and explore new usage possibilities. According to Tom Standage (2001, ¶ 9),

> Because it used the same wires, the telephone was originally seen as merely a speaking telegraph, but it turned out to be something entirely new. The same mistake is already being repeated with the internet. Many people expect the mobile internet to be the same as the wired version, only mobile, but they are wrong. . . . Instead, the mobile internet, although it is based on the same technology as the fixed-line internet, will be something different and will be used in new and unexpected ways.

From Telephone to Remote Control, and Game Device

The first public call from a cell phone was completed more than thirty years ago. In 1973 Martin Cooper, a Motorola researcher, called a public phone from a cell phone in New York (Fontoura 2003). However, the first model of cellular phone authorized for public use was only released ten years later, in 1983. It was Motorola's DynaTAC 8000X. At that time, consumers paid as much as four thousand dollars for the device. Looking briefly at the old model, it seems silly that today people discuss portability concerning the tiny existing cell phones. The first cell phone could be mobile, but it was definitely not easily carried. The device weighed around 1 kilogram, and was 25 by 3 by 7 centimeters. The battery lasted twenty minutes when the phone was in use. Nevertheless, it was a great improvement over car phones, the only type of mobile communication technology existing since the 1940s.

If cell phones have been on the market for twenty years already, why didn't they become popular until the late 1990s? The history of cell phones is considered a history of (non)development (Brown et al. 2002, p. 7). Technology to produce mobile phones has existed since the 1940s. However, it took thirty years to make the first phone call, and ten more years to commercialize the mobile devices. Then, fifteen years passed until mobile phones were culturally assimilated. Since 1997/1998, cell phone ownership increased exponentially all over the world. This development is partially related to the commercial growth of SMS since 1999. Also the I-mode standard in Japan in 1998, followed by the emergence of the first camera phones, contributed to the success of the mobile. Indeed, the triumph of the cell phone is based on the fact that it is no longer just a phone. In countries in which mobile phones have the highest penetration rates (in East Asia and Scandinavia), people do not use cell phones only for talking; mobile phones are mostly used to send messages and e-mails, to access information on the Internet, and for entertainment purposes.

Fig. 2 Motorola
Dyna-Tac 8000X

Location Awareness/GPS

Location awareness is a simple and effective feature of some mobile phones. There are two different ways by which the cell phone can be aware of its position. One is accomplished by cellular positioning, which indicates the device location through the triangulation of radio waves detected by the cell phone. Another much more accurate way uses GPS systems embedded in the phone to determine its position in relation to the transmission tower. The system, connected to a constellation of satellites, gives the device's position with a small error margin. A cell phone enabled with GPS or cellular positioning is necessary for the development of location-based services, such as information about the weather, restaurants, or facilities that are in the vicinity of the mobile phone user. Other possible uses are mobile yellow pages, find-a-friend, personal mapping services, and location-based games.[9]

NTT DoCoMo (2003) announced the first GPS mobile phone in Japan in March 2003. The phone "enables users to determine their location at the mere touch of a button, and download maps and information about the area. GPS accuracy is within 10–50 meters." By means of the new system, which is part of the I-mode standard, users can access information about public transportation and restaurants, as well as routing to help find specific locations. Furthermore, users can also find each other.

Camera Phones

Another important feature acquired by cell phones is the ability to take pictures and create videos. Ilpo Koskinen, Esko Kurvinen, and Turo-Kimmo Lehtonen (2002) conducted research in Finland about the social effects of using camera phones among youngsters. Among other things, they point out (2002, p. 21) a shift in the reason for taking pictures. Originally, a photograph replaced memory. One would take a picture in order to remember a place or a person. Today, with digital mobile images, taking a picture is a means of commenting on the present and creating sociability. "In a digital world, an image can be responded to with another image" (p. 33). Koskinen gives several examples in which cell phone users take pictures from their everyday life and send them to friends, with or without text. These pictures can sometimes come in a series, creating a visual narrative. Accordingly, friends generally answer with another image: a different one, or the same image manipulated (pp. 32–65).

Formerly, cell phones were seen as introducing a feeling of "control" over one's life, enabling users to organize spatial and temporal relationships to people. I have dealt with a couple of examples in which researchers emphasize micro- and macrocoordination among cell phone users, scheduling and coordinating meetings. However, Koskinen et al. (2002, p. 77) argue that "when e-mails begin to contain images, this feeling of control is secondary. The significance of mobile phone use lies rather in its potential for creating sociability."

> Generally these images are not sent while working or doing "serious" things: The impetus to establish contact with others is often quite simply that one has a bit of time and is able to free oneself from the flow of busy routines. In this sense, sending mobile visual messages is similar to the recreational use of a mobile phone while, for instance, waiting for a bus or a train or being on the way and "nothing happening." (p. 78)

Naturally the ability to send and receive pictures is a characteristic of cell phones with Internet connection.

Internet (WAP and I-mode)

Most devices in the Western world access the Internet with WAP (Wireless Application Protocol). Using WAP, content can be delivered over the Internet to most current wireless networks, including the new networks with GPRS and 3G. Nevertheless, WAP has been viewed skeptically by most mobile phone users, due to the fact that it is hard to use, does not have much content, and is expensive. A study conducted in the U.K. in January 2000 recruited twelve users to test WAP usability. Among other tasks, users were asked to locate the address details of the Imperial College in London using the business directory service on the Orange Portal site. Ten out of the twelve users used the Internet regularly, ten owned a mobile phone, three had shopped online before, and eleven were aged thirty or younger. Despite their expertise, "only two were able to complete the task, and it took them over 25 minutes of searching to find what they looked for" (Helyar 2002, p. 198). WAP technology in Europe was originally based on GSM network, and users were charged according to the "air time" used. The large amount of time spent finding simple information meant that WAP was a very expensive service. An alternative came with GPRS network, which charged users according to the amount of data they downloaded. Even so, the cost is still expensive and the service has not become simpler to use.

In addition, the quality of graphics and information users can access via WAP is generally frustrating. Koskinen et al. (2002, p. 113) comment that "WAP was marketed as a 'mobile Internet,' which made users and business analysts expect a visual quality and service level compatible with that of the World Wide Web." However, WAP is a completely textual interface and could be more easily compared to SMS. The amount of content is also very low. Unless a Web site is written in WML (website META language), a WAP phone cannot access it. Therefore, the number of WAP sites is not very large (especially compared to the number of I-mode sites in Japan). According to the Mobile Data Association (Marriot 2003), the main reason to use WAP sites is to download mobile games and ring tones.

I-mode in Japan became more popular mainly for two reasons. First, the quality of the Web sites and graphics displayed on its screen make it worthwhile to browse. Second, it is based on cHTML (compact HTML), which is very similar to HTML. Therefore, it is easy for nonexpert users to upload content and exchange information, just like on the Internet. Using I-mode is much easier than dealing with WAP: "Before accessing a site, WAP users must agree to pay extra charges and even type in URLs to browse through sites other than the service provider's portal. I-mode phones have a one-button browsing method, eliminating the need to type in web addresses" (Batista 2000, ¶ 20).

The PC-based Internet had a similar development. In the beginning, the Internet was merely textual. Although many multiuser environments still function in a textual interface, the introduction of images and graphics online revolutionized and popularized Internet use, mainly because it became much easier to navigate the information space. With cell phones, we perceive the change from a small black-and-white screen to larger colored displays. In a not-so-distant future, it might be that even larger mobile screens are not enough to display large amounts of information. Mobile technology developers are still careful when talking about the technology that will come after the third generation, or 4G. Björn Krylander, chief executive of UbiNetics, a U.K.-based telecom technology company, suggested in a interview with the *Financial Times* (Baxter et al. 2003, p. 2) that some form of glasses or retina projection device might be the solution to displaying the outcome of a mobile Internet connection that will range from 100 megabytes (MB) to 1 gigabyte (GB) per second in 4G networks.[10] As a result, the visual component will acquire more importance in mobile networks and embedded technology.

However, this kind of change tends to be slow. Krynlander (Baxter et al. 2003) also points out that the more pervasive a technology is, the longer it will take to be replaced by a newer one, because people become used to it. Therefore, each mobile generation tends to have a longer life than its predecessor. "While 2G (GSM) has had a 10–12 year heyday, 3G will last 15–18 years, taking the arrival of 4G to 2019" (p. 2).

Conclusion

In combination with image transmission and Internet access, improvements in the display and projection capabilities might significantly change the perception of what a mobile phone is. Moreover, it is not possible to transfer information across media without changing the meaning of the information. For example, a movie viewed on a cell phone screen is not the same movie watched on a large screen. Therefore, the mobile Internet will carry other meanings and uses than the actual World Wide Web, mainly because it is mobile, and it is developed to be used in transit. While we cannot see the future, the study of current characteristics of mobile interfaces helps us to project future developments.

We saw that much of what has been discussed and developed in the 1980s and '90s about ubiquitous and wearable computers are now characteristics of mobile devices. Moreover, the merging of GPS devices and cell phones creates smart-phones with location awareness, which are potentially useful for location-based services, but also for playing location-based mobile games and for creating communities of peers according to their location, such as the Japanese ImaHima[11] and LoveGetty (Iwatani 1998). These new uses for mobile technologies merge digital and physical spaces, creating hybrid spaces, which are social spaces formed by the constant mobility of users who carry portable devices continuously connected to the Internet and to other users. More important, we should be aware that the way we use specific interfaces never depends solely on the technological inovations but rather on the social use we make of them.

Acknowledgments

Research for this paper was supported by CAPES (Commission for Enhancement of Graduate Researchers, Brazil), a doctoral fellowship from CNPq (National Research Council, Brazil), and the Department of Design—Media Arts (UCLA).

This paper is part of my Ph.D. dissertation entitled *From Multiuser Environments as (Virtual) Spaces to (Hybrid) Spaces as Multiuser Environments: Nomadic Technology Devices and Hybrid Communication Places*, defended in the School of Communication at the Federal University of Rio de Janeiro, Brazil, February, 2004.

Notes

1 *Ludic* means anything that is related to play, games, and entertainment. It describes a pleasurable activity performed just for the sake of pleasure.

2 Based on this fact, Crispin Jones, associated with IDEO, developed the piece *Social Mobiles* in order to criticize people who are annoyed by cell phones. Retrieved April 7, 2005, from www.ideo.com/case_studies/Social_Mobiles/index.html.

3 Retrieved April 15, 2005, from www-1.ibm.com/industries/wireless.

4 The Fashion and Technology show on Siggraph 2003 (San Diego) explored these issues, including an electric shock jacket from the Wearable Computing Group at MIT, and special garments to accommodate cell phones.

5 Third-generation cellular system. "Third Generation Cellular Systems include the possibility to offer data services without the need of establishing a connection (permanent connection) and speeds up to two Mbps. The main systems are WCDMA and CDMA2000 1xEV. The ITU refers to 3G as IMT-2000." Retrieved April 7, 2005, from www.teleco.com.br/glossario.asp?termo=3G.

6 GPRS, general packet radio service, is a "system that can be implemented as a layer over GSM systems. GPRS allows data services without the need of establishing a connection. It is considered an intermediary step (2,5G) to the third generation of cellular systems (3G)." Retrieved April 7, 2005, from www.teleco.com.br/glossario.asp?termo=GPRS.

7 GSM, global system for mobile communication, "originally known as Group Special Mobile, is a second generation digital cellular system developed in Europe and used in the majority of the world. Initially developed to the range of 900 MHz, GSM had afterwards a version adopted to 1800 and 1900 MHz." Retrieved April 7, 2005, from www.teleco.com.br/glossario.asp?termo=GSM.

8 *Keitai* or *Ke-tai* is the word for cell phone in Japan, which roughly means "an extension of one's hand."

9 A comprehensive list of location-based mobile games can be found at Paul Baron's Web site. Retrieved April 22, 2005, from www.in-duce.net/archives/locationbased_mobile_phone_games.php.

10 As a comparison, the faster modem connection today goes up to 56 kilobytes (KB) per second; 100 megabytes (MB) represents 100,000 kilobytes.

11 "ImaHima is the Japanese expression for 'are you free now?' It is a mobile, location-integrated, community and instant messaging service allowing users to share their current personal status (location, activity, mood) publicly and privately with their buddies and send picture and instant messages to them" (ImaHima, Inc., 1999-2004). Retrieved April 22, 2005, from www.imahima.com/www/en/ps/service_imahima.html.

References

Agnes, M. (Ed.). (2000). *Webster's new world college dictionary*, 4th ed. Cleveland, OH: IDG Books Worldwide.

"Anatel confirma: No de celulares ultrapassa o de fixos." (2003). *Teleco: Informação para o aprendizado contínuo em telecomunicações*. September. Retrieved April 7, 2005, from www.teleco.com.br/comentario/com01.asp.

Batista, E. (2000). "WAP or I-mode: Which is better?" *Wired News*, August 30.

Baxter, A., C. Brown-Humes, R. Budden, I. Cheng, J. Moules, M. Nakamoto, et al. (2003). "Talking 'bout a generation: Beyond 3G to 4G [FTIT Review, Special Report]." *Financial Times*, October 29, pp. 1–2.

Benedikt, M. (2000). "Cyberspace: First steps." In D. Bell and B. M. Kennedy (Eds.), *The cybercultures reader* (pp. 29–44). New York: Routledge.

Brown, B., N. Green, and R. Harper. (Eds.). (2002). *Wireless world: Social and interactional aspects of the mobile age*. London: Springer-Verlag.

De Gournay, C. (2002). "Pretense of intimacy in France." In E. Katz and M. Aakhus (Eds.), *Perpetual contact: Mobile communication, private talk, public performance* (pp. 193–205). Cambridge, UK: Cambridge University Press.

Dennet, D. (1996). *Kinds of minds: Toward an understanding of consciousness*. New York: Basic Books.

Estatísticas Gerais do Brasil. (2005). *Teleco: Informação para o aprendizado contínuo em telecomunicações*. March 4. Retrieved April 5, 2005, from www.teleco.com.br/estatis.asp.

Fontoura, A. (2003). "Primeira ligação de celular completa 30 anos." *JB Online*. April 3. Retrieved April 5, 2005, from jbonline.terra.com.br/jb/online/internet/destaque/2003/04/onlintdes20030403002.html.

Fortunati, L. (2002a). "Italy: Stereotypes, true and false." In J. E. Katz and M. Aakhus (Eds.), *Perpetual contact: Mobile communication, private talk, public performance* (pp. 42–62). Cambridge, UK: Cambridge University Press.

Fortunati, L. (2002b). "The mobile phone: Towards new categories and social relations." *Information, Communication, and Society* 5(4): 513–28.

Gergen, K. (2002). "The challenge of absent presence." In J. E. Katz and M. Aakhus (Eds.), *Perpetual contact: Mobile communication, private talk, public performance* (pp. 227–41). Cambridge: Cambridge University Press.

Hayles, N. K. (1996). "Embodied virtuality; or, How to put bodies back into the picture." In M. A. Moser (Ed.), *Immersed in technology: Art and virtual environments* (pp. 1–28). Cambridge, MA: MIT Press.

Hayles, N. K. (1999). *How we became posthuman: Virtual bodies in cybernetics, literature, and informatics.* Chicago: University of Chicago Press.

Helyar, V. (2002). "Usability of Portable Devices: The case of WAP." In B. Brown, N. Green, and R. Harper (Eds.), *Wireless world: Social and interactional aspects of the mobile age* (pp. 195–206). London: Springer-Verlag.

Hosokawa, S. (1987). *Der Walkman-Effekt.* Berlin: Merve Verlag.

ICT—Free Statistics Homepage. (2005). *International Telecommunication Union.* March 16. Retrieved April 7, 2005, from www.itu.int/ITU-D/ict/statistics/.

Ishii, H. (1999). "Tangible bits: Coupling physicality and virtuality through tangible user interfaces." In Y. Ohta and H. Tamura (Eds.), *Mixed reality: Merging real and virtual worlds* (p. 229–46). Tokyo: Ohmsha/Secaucus.

Iwatani, Y. (1998). "Love: Japanese style." *Wired News,* June 11.

Kasesniemi, E., and P. Rautiainen. (2002). "Mobile culture of children and teenagers in Finland." In J. E. Katz and M. Aakhus (Eds.), *Perpetual contact: Mobile communication, private talk, public performance* (pp. 170–92). Cambridge, UK: Cambridge University Press.

Kim, S. D. (2002). "Korea: Personal meanings." In J. E. Katz and M. Aakhus (Eds.), *Perpetual contact: Mobile communication, private talk, public performance* (pp. 63–79). Cambridge, UK: Cambridge University Press.

Koskinen, I., E. Kurvinen, and T.K. Lehtonen. (2002). *Professional mobile image.* Edita, Finland: IT Press.

Licoppe, C., and J. P. Heurtin. (2002). "France: Preserving the image." In J. E. Katz and M. Aakhus (Eds.), *Perpetual contact: Mobile communication, private talk, public performance* (pp. 94–109). Cambridge, UK: Cambridge University Press.

Ling, R., and B. Yttri. (2002). "Hyper-coordination via mobile phones in Norway." In J. E. Katz and M. Aakhus (Eds.), *Perpetual contact: Mobile communication, private talk, public performance* (pp. 139–69). Cambridge, UK: Cambridge University Press.

Mann, S. (1996). "'Smart Clothing': Wearable multimedia computing and 'Personal Imaging' to restore the technological balance between people and their environments." September 30. Retrieved April 6, 2005, from http://wearcam.org/acm-mm96/acm-mm96.html.

Marriott, K. (2003). "29 million WAP page impressions per day during July 2003." *Mobile Data Association.* September 1. Retrieved April 6, 2005, from www.text.it/wap/default.asp?intPageId=558.

McLuhan, M. (1994). *Understanding media: The extensions of man.* Cambridge, MA: MIT Press.

Meyrowitz, J. (1985). *No sense of place: The impact of electronic media on social behavior.* Oxford: Oxford University Press.

Murray, J. H. (1997). *Hamlet on the holodec: The future of narrative in cyberspace.* New York: Free Press.

Newman, A. (2003). "View: The future of mobile phones?" *InfoSync World,* April 10. Retrieved April 6, 2005, from www.infosyncworld.com/system/print.php?id=3411.

NTT DoCoMo. (2003). "NTT DoCoMo to introduce first GPS handset." NTT DoCoMo press release, March 27. Retrieved April 5, 2005, from www.nttdocomo.com/presscenter/pressreleases/press/pressrelease.html?param[no]=215.

Plant, S. (2002). *On the mobile: The effects of mobile telephones on social and individual life.* New York City: Motorola, Inc.

Rheingold, H. (2002). *Smart mobs: The next social revolution.* Cambridge, MA: Perseus.

Rhodes, B. (2005). "A brief history of wearable computing." *MIT Wearable Computing Project.* Retrieved April 7, 2005, from www.media.mit.edu/wearables/lizzy/timeline.html.

Samsung. (2003). "SAMSUNG Electronics showcases the world's first GPRS wrist watch phone on sale in Europe Q4 2003." Samsung press release, March 13. Retrieved April 15, 2005, from www.samsung.com/PressCenter/PressRelease/PressRelease.asp?seq=20030313_0000004250.

Schivelbusch, W. (1986). *The railway journey: The industrialization of time and space in the 19th century.* Los Angeles: University of California Press.

Spring, T. (2000). "IBM gets fashionable with wearable cell phone." *PC World,* November 3. Retrieved April 7, 2005, from www.pcworld.com/news/article/0,aid,33322,00.asp.

Standage, T. (2001). "The Internet, untethered." *The Economist,* October 11.

Teleco World. (2005). *Teleco: Informação para o aprendizado contínuo em telecomunicações,* April 14. Retrieved April 20, 2005, from www.teleco.com.br/pais/us.asp.

"TfL Los Property Office: Interesting statistics." (2001). *Transport for London.* Retrieved April 7, 2005, from www.tfl.gov.uk/tfl/ph_lpo_stats.shtml.

Turkle, S. (1995). *Life on the screen: Identity in the age of the Internet.* New York: Simon and Schuster.

Walker, R. (2003). We're all connected? *New York Times,* August 24. Late Edition—Final, section 6, p. 11, column 2.

Weilemann, A., and C. Larrson. (2002). "Local use and sharing of mobile phones." In B. Brown, N. Green, and R. Harper (Eds.), *Wireless world: Social and interactional aspects of the mobile age* (pp. 92–107). London: Springer-Verlag.

Weiser, M. (1994). "The world is not a desktop." *ACM Interactions* 1(1): 7–8.

Weiser, M. (1996). "Ubiquitous computing," March 17. Retrieved April 7, 2005, from www.ubiq.com/hypertext/weiser/UbiHome.html.

Weiser, Mark and Brown, John Seely. (December 21, 1995). "Designing calm technology," Xerox Parc. Retrieved October 13, 2005 from http://www.ubiq.com/hypertext/weiser/calmtech/calmtech.htm.

The Cell Phone:
An Artifact of Popular Culture
and a Tool of the Public Sphere

*Janey Gordon**

This chapter provides a context-setting framework for the cultural impact of cell phones. It gives an overview of the current use of the cell phone and suggests that the cell phone has become not only a part of our popular culture, but also a tool of the public sphere. On occasions the ability of the individual to have access to a cell phone may have a significant influence not only on personal choices and actions but also on national and international events.

Twice during 2001, in January in Manila and on September 11 in the United States, the cell phone played a part in world events, which must alert academics to its far-reaching effects in communication and culture. In the Philippines, cell phone technology—specifically text messaging—played a critical role in a major political upheaval in the country. On September 11, 2001, this same technology gathered significant press attention, as it linked the ill-fated hijacked airplane passengers with friends and family members. These two events are presented as case studies illustrating how changes in our personal behavior and the organization of our societies have already been influenced by the extraordinary expansion of personal communication. "[C]ontrol over media production is diverging and new, sometimes less traditional, content providers are entering the media industries. However, research on media convergence has mostly addressed stationary settings. But with the growing phenomenon of mobile information technology, it is becoming increasingly important to consider mobility as a dimension of media convergence and mobile media as a new research field" (Nilsson, Nuldén, and Olsson 2001, p. 34).

Introduction

The cell phone has unique functions and characteristics in its cultural uses that it does not share with fixed line telephony. The areas of sociology, linguistics, and politics all may be significantly changed by the ability of the individual to have routine access to such a relatively cheap mobile communications device.

*Author's note: This chapter is based on an earlier article published in *Convergence* 8, no. 3 (Fall 2002).

In the mid-1990s, use of the Internet greatly increased, due to simpler software and cheaper connections and access. At the time it was hailed as a library, a communications system, a demonstration of democracy. However, as information is increasingly made available to Internet users, those without access, whether because they lack the inclination or the knowledge or the wealth, risk being disempowered. A further restriction for many Internet users is the lack of accessibility once they are away from a fixed terminal; a problem that does not affect cell phones.

In 2004 cell phone usage overtook fixed line usage, 1.5 billion cell phones to 1.2 billion fixed lines ("Mobile phone sales" 2004). The current take-up of the cell phone has exceeded the industry's expectations, and the consumer has been active in defining usage; for example, in the use of the SMS text message. Increasingly it is the norm to be immediately contactable. Those without cell phones are regarded as eccentric. This is particularly true among younger users: cell phone usage among the fifteen- to thirty-five-year-old group may be regarded as being at market saturation, over 90 percent in some cases (Ofcom 2004a).

Along with the extraordinary ability to communicate in situations in which people were previously regarded as unreachable, the cell phone also may chart its user's location and movements. In addition, the provider offers the "service" of listing all contacts to and from that handset. Consequently, matters of privacy and civil liberties have arisen that need urgent examination and definition.

However, it is the cell phone's development as an artifact of popular culture and its role within the public sphere that have emerged as being of unforeseen importance.

The rapid take-up of the cell phone is indicative of the value that is put upon it and the pleasure that many take in its use and functions. A secondary market has developed in the imaginative personalizing of the handset, with the sale of such items as ring tones, fascias, wallpaper, and lanyards.

But users have also found unpredicted ways of using their handsets. It may be argued that a new and enhanced public sphere might be developed by the use of mobile technology. There have been instances of the phone being used to circumvent oppressive or intimidating situations. In the Philippines the text message was used to provide a quick way of passing on information and rallying support among the population to expedite the overthrow of President Estrada (Gordon 2002), and in the United States the cell phone was used by the victims of the September 11 terrorist attacks to make a final contact with their families.

Andreas Nilsson, Urban Nuldén, and Daniel Olsson (2001) examined the way in which cell phones were being used in three popular public events. They showed that the cell phone's mobility led it to be used by spectators to follow the event closely using SMS text messages from the organizers and utilizing the Internet via WAP phones. In one event the audience was asked to phone home to confirm their personal safety and at this point the system became overwhelmed and ceased to function, causing frustration among the users. Nilsson et al. extrapolated that these modes of use were indicative within a wider context. Their observations are not disputed, but it is suggested that the cell phone's roles can be more far reaching than simple personal communications.

Current Features and Their Usage

In 2003 it was estimated by the cell phone industry that by 2006 there would be a global usage of 25 percent, but in 2005 this is already the case. The reality has overtaken the industry's own hype. There are now 1.52 billion cell phone users globally ("Cellular stats, 2004" 2004; Internet World Stats 2005). The developed countries clearly inflate this figure, but the market in handset ownership in the developed countries has slowed and is maturing. For example, in the U.K. in January 2005, the mobile phone providers reported 58.4 million active subscribers, out of a population of just under 60 million, although it was noted that some subscribers have more than one cell phone (Ofcom 2005, p. 39). Around 79 percent of all U.K. adults subscribe to or use cell phones. The penetration of handset ownership is over 90 percent among some sectors of the population, particularly young adults (Ofcom 2004b, p. 35). The greatest area of growth in the market is in the developing countries of Africa, where usage more than doubled during 2004, although this is still only 6 percent of the population ("Cellular stats, 2004" 2004), and also in China, where 25 percent of the population now use cell phones ("Mobile subscriber growth" 2004).

One particular aspect of the cell phone market that has been consumer led is the short message service or text message. The text message was originally given away as an additional service but now accounts for a high amount of the cell phone traffic. In the U.K., users now send around 70 million texts a day, more than one a day per head of population (MDA 2004; "UK SMS traffic" 2004). However, in the Philippines people send more than six messages a day per head of population, over 500 million per day ("Cellular stats, 2004" 2004). This is in a country with only a 20 percent handset penetration. With the introduction of 3G phones, it is also becoming commonplace to use the cell phone for data, either to be kept informed by a provider or through accessing the Internet directly. Website providers are rendering their pages for cell phone access.

The cell phone has crystallized the convergence of communications technologies. It is a communications tool with various additions, which users may decide to employ or ignore, purchase or not. It is possible that in no other single gadget has there been such a convergence of technologies. As well as point-to-point telephony, cell phones have been combined with electronic games, radio, TV, photography, music entertainment, Internet access, e-mail, and texting. They are used as clocks, calculators, and memos. They may be used to shop, bank, deal in shares, or receive the latest sports scores— along with a video clip of the action. They may be used as an automatic credit card or embedded into other devices such as a palm, pocket, or laptop PC. Bluetooth[1] technology is likely to further extend these functions.

For the industry, the best thing about telecommunications is that the user by and large provides his or her own content. We speak to each other or text each other, and all the provider has to do is give us a network with which we can do this. But this can also be viewed as problematic.

The industry is very keen to lead our development of usage in mobile technologies. They are trying hard, for example, to encourage us to use MMS, or media message services, to send frivolous picture messages to each other. This has not taken off so far, but its usage is growing. In October 2004, the U.K. regulator Ofcom reported that MMS usage had doubled in the U.K., although it remained a very small proportion of messages (Ofcom 2004b, p. 8). We still text each other and call each other and say things like, "Where are you?" "I'm just walking up the path." We are very savvy as to how to use the services economically. Young people in particular will have one handset and several SIM cards that each provide free or inexpensive time, and they swap them around.

The industry is also concerned about what may be called cultural products. The issue under debate is the introduction of DRM, digital rights management. There is a fear among providers that the industry was not proactive in the development of the Internet until users had already gotten used to working out how they were going to exploit it themselves. At an industry conference in London, Ted Cohen, from EMI Music, said, "In the Internet we waited to get it right and missed it" (Cohen 2004). The music industry suffered, as they had not anticipated or been proactive in the growth of music downloading as a method of distribution and of purchase. Napster, the software that allowed Internet users to share music collections without reference to the music companies, was a severe wake-up call.

The cell phone industries are keen to use the technology to provide cultural artifacts and believe that we should be paying for this service. For example, the copyrights and sales of ring tones are now globally equal to 10 percent of the total music market ("Mobile content" 2004). This has happened in just a couple of years. In particular, the development of polyphonic ring tones has influenced this growth. Images used as wallpaper on cell phone screens may also be purchased. Homer Simpson, for example, is a copyrighted image; if you want his picture on your phone—and many people do— you will pay for that right.

Another developing market is that of downloading video clips, films, and music tracks to cell phones. Not only can we download clips of, say, a football goal, but short films and animations are being made specifically for the cell phone market. Whole music tracks may also be downloaded as MP3 files to a handset, and shortly downloads may include complete feature films. If you do not wish to watch a film on a screen of approximately an inch by an inch and a quarter, or listen to music on a cell phone headset, more realistically you can download the files again onto a computer and burn a CD or DVD so that you can use the music or film files elsewhere.

Why would you want to do this on your cell phone and not your computer in the first place? If you are a North American or Western European teenager or young adult, you may not have your own computer, but you almost certainly have your own phone. Twice as many people in the world have access to a cell phone as have access to the Internet (Internet World Stats 2005). The whole areas of distribution and distribution rights and management are suddenly up in the air. Very small companies can distribute cultural products around the world even more easily than using the Internet.

Furthermore, if you own a cell phone you have a convenient "e-wallet." A music track downloaded onto your cell phone is charged to your phone bill. You pay for it at the end of the month. However, in the U.K., more than half of cell phone users use prepaid phones. In Italy the number is about 90 percent, but in many other countries this is less common, for example in Japan, where there was an attempt to ban prepaid cell phones, as criminals could use them anonymously (Uranaka 2005). On a prepaid cell phone, you are effectively using your phone as a bank. You put money in and spend it, as you need to, on calls or downloads. In fact, regulatory bodies have to address this, as a whole set of banking regulations apply.

A cell phone may also be an "e-shopping mall," and this is where the various providers are attempting to take control and be organized. It is suggested that the cell phone mall needs "anchor stores" that people use regularly, such as news agents, as well as specialist stores for individuals, for example music shops and also what are called "daily life providers," such as sources for buying bus tickets (De Jong 2004). This service is being tested in several areas, for example in Frankfurt, Germany. In order to buy a bus ticket, you send a text and receive a "ticket" back to show the driver. The biggest headache for the industry in terms of cultural products is agreeing to share the protocols and software to let the customer access them. The Swiss company SDC is a cell phone–based music store. The company provides a music download service and then finds ways of making this provision to a host of different handsets. It is like buying a CD and having to say that you have a Samsung CD player, which is different from Sony, Phillips, and so on. Michael Bornhausser (2004), the CEO, feels that a lack of shared software among companies is the biggest problem in development at present.

Young Users

The cost of cell phone calls is comparatively more expensive than fixed line calls, but cost is relative to the value put on the device by the user, and it is the users who have defined the conventions of mobile telephony (Katz and Aakhus 2002). This is particularly noticeable among younger users, and it is in this group that the cell phone may have its greatest impact. In the U.K., over 90 percent of fifteen- to twenty-five-year-olds own a cell phone (Oftel 2003). For teenagers, its use is relatively more expensive than for an employed adult. They put a high value on being able to contact others and be instantly contactable. They make use of the text message service as a way of keeping the cost down and are responsible for a high percentage of the text message traffic, congesting the system on the day of the national school exam results and the climax to popular TV shows. In a government report, young offenders felt that "Their loss of [cell] phones in custody was one of the worst elements of the deprivation of their liberty" (Harrington and Mayhew 2001, p. 58).

Young people accept mobile telephony as a normal part of everyday living and are maturing with the technology. There is now a generation of young adults who fully expect instant communication with their friends and acquaintants, as well as having access to other services such as commercial and financial facilities and to also have personal cell phone use of the Internet. Cell phone technology has made Internet access much more available. The hardware is cheap, and although at present the phone tariff means that cell phones will not be used for surfing the Net, recent developments such as GPRS and 3G handsets will help to bring this cost down, as it means that Internet connection from a cell phone should be much briefer.[2]

Privacy and Civil Liberties

One area that has proved successful for providers and customers is location services. If you are carrying a cell phone that is switched on, your cell phone provider knows pretty much where you are. This has been converted into a useful way for companies to keep track of their staff, and if the staff are delivering goods then this service can be extended to include tracking of those products.

In the United States, phones are obliged to include an E911 device, which can give emergency services the ability to find the cell phone handset if an emergency call is made from it. Of course this does not necessarily mean that they find the person in need. There is some deliberation about these services, and not surprisingly some unease (McCullagh 2003).

It is not inconceivable that state authorities could use mobile telephony in ways that pose questions of civil liberties. On April 26, 1996, the Chechen leader Dzokhar

Dudayev spoke to an advisor in Moscow about possible peace negotiations with Russia. He used a satellite telephone.[3] Space satellites pinpointed the handset's signal, and the coordinates were passed to a Russian jet fighter. Within minutes, two laser-guided air-to-surface missiles assassinated Dudayev (Gaudin 2001).

Civil liberties and personal privacy may be seen as having a strong relationship. Jane's, the information and publishing group, gave the example of the use of cell phones to gain criminal evidence.

It has been estimated that 70 percent of Britain's population have at some time given their details, including phone numbers, to credit companies and, in this respect, criminals are no different to the rest of the population. They may think that a mobile number cannot be traced to them, but if they have used that number in any other application, or it is on any other database, it can be matched up using the same software deployed by credit agencies and market research consultants to gain access to specific customer groups.

> The new link between mobile (cell) phones and other databases will mean that detectives will also be able to use techniques normally reserved for complex fraud investigations. For example, forensic data mining is a process that combines large computer databases, neural networks and an analysis of the links between apparently random bits of information. ("Forensic telecoms" 2004)

There have been a number of cases where cell phones have been used to provide criminal evidence; for example, in a recent murder case in Britain, the location of one of the defendants at the time of the crime was traced using her cell phone ("Crucial phone evidence" 2003).

It may be felt that using data gleaned from a cell phone in this way, to convict a murderer or trace a victim, is generally beneficial to society. However, as David Lyon (2004) points out, "While this is not in principle ubiquitous, inevitable or oppressive, some aspects of mobile surveillance require careful consideration from analytical, ethical and political perspectives. . . . The key opportunity for engaging in these questions is while the technologies are being stabilized." Lyon suggests that we should apply some of the language of harm (physical and monetary) and hurt (emotional) to privacy. He identifies the notion of "personality rights" as a way of examining what we lose when another party, such as a cell phone provider, knows a great deal about us and can use and sell that information. What have we as an individual lost by that transaction? Did we give this information away or was it stolen? He expresses a concern that cell phone providers are not subject to ethical scrutiny or democratic involvement (Lyon 2004). Property rights are considered more important than privacy rights, because they are more easily priced; once privacy is viewed as being owned it becomes more valuable. We may need to be more aware of what we are giving away, such as our location or contacts, which somebody else may regard as a saleable product (Birch 2004).

An Artifact of Popular Culture and a Tool of the Public Sphere

Although in essence the cell phone is simply a tool of communications, it goes out with its user, he carries it about on his person. It has become an object by which we are known and identified, not only by those who are contacted by it but also by those who see us use our cell phone. In the U.K., there was a TV advertisement showing a young man who was more embarrassed by his out-of-date cell phone than by his soiled underwear. This is obviously encouraging the viewer to buy a more up-to-date phone, but it is also playing on the view that the young woman will judge the young man by his outmoded technology, and that this is more important than his personal cleanliness. The cell phone may be personalized, by pictures and ring tones, fascias, lanyards, holders, and styles. It has become an article of personal display. It has developed a cultural meaning beyond its use, and we have adopted it as part of our popular culture (Fiske 1989).

What was invented as a communications tool, something with a distinct use for those out of reach of a fixed line, has become a token of respect and status. Those using cell phones do so without flinching in public places, challenging conventions of discretion and coyness. They will discuss private and intimate matters in public places, so long as they do so via a cell phone. The cell phone itself has such a high status that it may demand and receive immediate attention, interrupting whatever the user is doing, even to the extent of endangering the user or those nearby.[4] A number of countries have made its use while driving illegal, following fatal motor accidents. The cell phone may take precedent over a face-to-face conversation. Even if the call is deferred, it will be acknowledged, the phone touched, glanced at, apologized for. In the contradictory ways of other popular cultural artifacts, the cell phone is paradoxical. It promises communication over distances and yet it interrupts communications between those who are right in front of us. It has required that national laws, institutional rules, and social mores be reconstructed to cope with its usage.

The cell phone is an artifact of popular culture, but it has also enhanced the public sphere. There are similarities to Internet news groups and e-mail: for example, there is no content control; content comes from users. However, the cell phone is more immediate than the Internet. When Jürgen Habermas (1989, pp. 36–37) conceived the concept of the public sphere, he used the example of the eighteenth-century London coffeehouses, where debates between individuals could take place and action could be taken without interference from the authorities. Internet newsgroups encourage debate. The technology of the cell phone enables rapid action.

John Fiske (1989, pp. 13–33) points to the social changes inherent in popular cultural texts or artifacts.[5] It may be a site for a "guerrilla sortie" by the user on the commercial world that developed it. There may be tricks and guile in the usage, which undermines and astounds the industry that produces it. The user finds ways to use the artifact that undermines the systems in place to protect it.

The cell phone has been used in just such a way. The short message service or text in particular has empowered the user in ways that were not foreseen. The text message has become a coded language in its own right. A complex subculture of codes and subtle meanings has developed by using a combination of abbreviations and phonetics:

   CU 2MORO: *see you tomorrow*
   L8R G8R: *see you later alligator*

or "emoticons":

   @—^—- *a rose*
   :-) *a happy face.* ("Joy of text" 2002)

A cell phone user who will happily and loudly hold a private phone call in a public place will encode and personalize a discreet text message; schoolchildren will text between each other in classes; text messages may be used as judicious reminders in committee meetings; or they may be used to summon or alert a group of friends and sympathizers, as happened in Manila. The cell phone as a tool has readily been adopted and adapted to new functions by its users. As Fiske would put it, "the disempowered" have developed the functions and are using them as their own.

The Philippines

The text message is where the cell phone's popular cultural aspect becomes Fiske's guerrilla warfare. At first texting was an added service offered by phone network providers at a cheap tariff or even free. It has become widely used. In the U.K., over 1.5 billion text messages are sent per month (MDA 2004). In less affluent countries such as the Philippines, where cell phone ownership outnumbers fixed line two to one, the text message has become the most common technological way of communicating. At present Filipinos send around 500 million per day ("Cellular stats 2004" 2004). It is estimated that the Philippines may account for as much as 10 percent of the world's text messages (Kaihla 2001).

The rapid increase in cell phone usage began in the Philippines in 1996.[6] By 2001, the number of handsets grew to 7 million. The country is not wealthy nor particularly developed, and the population soon discovered that the text service was much cheaper than standard voice calls, about one eighth of the cost. One commentator describes the stark disparity of watching a farmer using a hand plough and then seeing him take a cell phone from his pocket in response to a text message. The Philippines has a population of around 80 million and is a country that particularly values its close family ties and connections. By 2001, the two main cell phone operators, Smart Communications and Globe Telecom, carried around 60 million text messages a day, double the U.K. number at the time, despite having a much lower penetration of cell phone ownership. In 2001 it was 10 percent and even now it is only around 20 percent (Pepall 2003).

In January 2001 the text message is attributed with causing the downfall of the Philippine president. The SMS is able to send a "set"; that is, the sender can simultaneously send the same text message to a number of different people. In Manila, the Philippines capital, this seems to have happened among groups of friends and acquaintances. This meant that a large crowd was quickly summoned to one spot to vehemently protest about the government in a way that could have taken some weeks to organize by conventional means.

President Estrada came to power in 1998 and was at first popular, particularly with the least powerful of the Filipinos, the unemployed and less educated. At this time there were text messages circulating in the form of jokes about him, which were regarded positively by his supporters. However, in the autumn of 2000 it became apparent that the president was involved in illegal gambling, extortion, and corruption, his popularity waned rapidly, and he was impeached. On January 16, 2001, his supporters on the impeachment panel voted to disallow evidence against Estrada, which was in a sealed envelope. The news spread to the population quickly via a text message, which asked the receiver to pass on the text to others and to meet at a rallying point to demonstrate against the president. Over the following few days, the text service was used extensively to relay information and call the population to protest against their president. The operators reported a doubling of texts, many of them now derisory and rude jokes at the president's expense, which undermined what little support he retained.

Fiske could hardly have asked for a clearer example of a popular cultural artifact being used for guerrilla action against the country's establishment, and Habermas might be surprised at this newest technological "public sphere," but his criteria fit very well: first, that the participants treat each other as equals, second, that discussion is over matters of common concern, and finally that the participants are members of the public (Habermas 1989). Within a few days, the church supported Estrada's resignation; the army let its disapproval of him be known; and the deputy president prepared to take power, which she did on January 20. After which the following text message was circulated:

AFTER PEOPLE POWER 2:
CONGRATULATIONS!
THANK U 4 UR
SUPPORT N DS
HSTORICL EVENT.
ERAP WIL GO
DOWN N PHIL.
HSTORY S BEIN D
1ST PRESIDNT
OUSTD BY TXT. (Bagalawis 2001; Burton 2001)

After People Power 2 [the first being the ousting of Marcos in 1986], congratulations! Thank you for your support in this historical event. Erap [the nickname for Estrada] will go down in Philippines history as being the first president ousted by text.

September 11, 2001

The cell phone may also empower the public sphere in other ways. It allows individuals to become "town criers" to forewarn others of dangers of which they are unaware and short-circuit conventional or official channels of communication. On September 11, 2001, terrorists in the United States hijacked four commercial airliners, together with the passengers, crews, and full payloads of fuel.[7] Two aircraft were flown directly into the New York World Trade Center's twin towers; one was brought down on the Pentagon in Washington, D.C., and the fourth crashed but failed to reach its intended target.

Airline passengers are aware that the use of cell phones is generally banned on aircraft. In the United States the ban on cell phone use in the air is a dictate from the Federal Communications Commission and is based on two problems. First, if a cell phone is used from a moving aircraft, off the ground, it may connect to a number of cell phone masts almost simultaneously. It may also enter and leave the mast's area in less time than it takes to establish the "handshake" at that mast. This produces a "cascade" effect between the ground cells and could disrupt the whole cellular system. This is why the ban applies to all flying vehicles, including, for example, hot air balloons.

The second problem is the one most commonly known by passengers, which is that cell phone use inside an aircraft in flight may interfere with the plane's internal electronics. On January 10, 2000, Crossair LX 498, a Saab 340, crashed outside Zurich, with the loss of its passengers and crew. Following investigation, it appeared that the navigation system had failed following the reception of an SMS text message and a cell phone call made by a passenger (Leyden 2001). After this accident, many countries and airlines strengthened or implemented bans on in-flight cell phone use. Currently, technology is being tested to allow passengers to use their cell phones safely in the air.

On September 11, 2001, American Airlines was first contacted by a flight attendant, Betty Ong, on an air phone to alert them of the emergency taking place on flight AA11. She remained on the phone for the following twenty-five minutes, describing what was happening and what she knew. A second flight attendant, Amy Sweeney, also called her American Airlines base, from another part of the aircraft. She described the hijackers and even gave the seat numbers of three of them, starting the process of identification of who was responsible (Kean 2004).

The staff and passengers of all four aircraft made a number of phone calls, both by air phone and cell phone, some, it seems, at the instigation of the terrorists. Tragically, many calls were to say goodbye to the passengers' families. A political commentator, Barbara Olson, who was on the plane destined for Washington, phoned to alert her husband, Ted Olson, the solicitor general, what was happening, and he then endeavored to contact the attorney general. Calls to and from families of the passengers of the fourth hijacked jet informed the passengers of what was happening in New York. It appears that the passengers themselves then managed to put the plane off its course and, giving up their own lives, forced the plane to crash less destructively into open countryside in Pennsylvania.[8]

It is this last incident that must be examined more carefully in order to understand the significance of the use of the cell phone as a tool of the public sphere. It seems that none of the hijackers realized that the cell phones posed a threat to their plan. Indeed, the reports that passengers were encouraged to phone their families suggests that there was an element of boastfulness as this would be the only way that the outside world would have knowledge of what happened in the aircraft. The passengers and families were being taunted by these calls, as the hijackers believed the calls were futile and could not prevent the execution of their plan. The flight attendants, Mrs. Olson, and two passengers from the fourth plane are reported to have made their calls clandestinely, possibly from the toilets. It may be presumed that they felt that the calls could be a threat to the terrorists and they might be able to ameliorate the aircraft's situation. Their phones became defensive weapons. They were using an artifact of popular culture to try and improve and empower their position.

Clearly this was no rational coffeehouse debate on opinions of current concern. These phones were used to call for help, to warn others, to be alerted to other events, and to attempt to overcome tyrannical and cruel behavior. Although this scenario does not perfectly match Habermas's criteria for a public sphere, it shares many elements with it. The phones gave members of the public access to communication in extreme and unusual circumstances. They increased the available information in circulation about what was happening. They were a conduit for a version of events unfiltered by the authorities or the terrorists. The phone demonstrated itself to be a powerful tool of the public arena.

Perpetual Contact?

In learning to live with what James Katz and Mark Aakhus (2002) call the "perpetual contact" of mobile telephony, we are also going to have to learn to manage the negative attributes inherent in its nature. Generally the Filipinos seem to feel that the change of government helped by the text messages has been beneficial, but it is easy to imagine less positive civil unrest being managed and orchestrated in a similar way. A society that finds itself at the mercy of any pressure group armed only with cell phones will quickly become skeptical and resistant to any benefits. Rumor and gossip may also be spread using cell phone technology. How may a receiver of a text message authenticate or assess the validity of what they have been sent? Phone messages may be fabricated to give inaccurate or malicious information. Cell phone calls and text messages have been used to deceive, abuse, and simply advertise. The "junk" text message is already proving to be an irritation for many users. A third of users do not answer calls from unknown numbers and are reported as being interested in a service that would block withheld or restricted numbers (Oftel 2003).

There is a growing acceptance that immediate and constant availability for communication is a desirable and normal state of affairs. Although, as Katz and Aakhus (2002, pp. 7–11) show, the prime uses of the cell phone tend to be pragmatic ("I am at the station. Can you pick me up?") or to maintain contact with family and friends in previously inaccessible situations ("How are things? I'll see you later"), these functions mean that the caller has the mobile device and is therefore in charge of where and when it is used. However, the receiver may also be using a cell phone and where they are when the call is received is less predictable. Private and intimate calls are received in public places, sometimes in areas where silence or a hushed quiet is expected. New areas of antisocial behavior have arisen by using the cell phone inappropriately or in a situation that requires concentration, such as driving. But on occasions it is considered antisocial simply not to have a cell phone and be out of contact. When the phone system ceases to function, the frustration level is quickly high. As Nilsson et al. (2001) point out, when there is too much cell phone traffic in a small area, reception is poor or may seize up altogether. This happened in lower Manhattan on September 11. There were too many people attempting to use their cell phones, and the system stopped functioning.[9]

As with other new technologies, notably the Internet, along with new forms of antisocial behavior, new crimes have evolved. In the U.K., there appeared to be an increase in street crime directly attributed to cell phone thefts. A study published in December 2001 showed that 28 percent of all recorded robberies involved phones. Many cell phone robbers were shown to be younger than other robbers, and almost half their victims were under eighteen years old. A survey showed that 5 percent of all eleven- to sixteen-year-olds had a cell phone stolen in 2000. In all, it was estimated that 330,000 offenses involving cell phones were reported to police just in England and Wales during 2000 and 2001. Including thefts from trucks and warehouses, over 700,000 handsets were stolen during that period (Harrington and Mayhew 2001, pp. 55–61). So where do they all go?

There are a number of ways that a stolen phone may be "recycled," the simplest being to replace the SIM card for use either in the country of origin or in a new country. The handsets command a good resale value in Eastern European and third-world countries. At one point it was estimated that half of Russia's cell phone handsets were sold illegally (Seregina 2000). In addition to the illegal sale of handsets, cell phone network carriers are also very sensitive about the fraudulent use of their frequencies. Although there are increasingly more sophisticated security procedures to bar stolen phones from reuse, there are also more sophisticated dishonest unlocking measures. Following considerable losses incurred in the early 1990s by the "cloning" of cell phones, the carriers are keen to stop further illicit use, such as "rechipping." These are ways by which a handset is given a false or untraceable signature, which cannot be identified by the network. Either the phone cannot be billed or the tariff is charged to another phone's account. There is regularly publicity that the phone companies have found a final solution to prevent illicit use, but since the reports are regular it must be assumed that no one solution has been totally satisfactory.

Conclusion

The conventional fixed line telephone system is well understood as a tool for communication. It is seen as strategically important for commerce and as an indicator of the technological and social advancement of a state and its prosperity, but it is often viewed as a utility, much like the gas and electricity supply. Examinations of telephony in the terms of media and cultural studies, as opposed to the technology itself, tend to have been linked to other cultural issues, for example gender[10] or linguistics.[11] As Oliver Boyd-Barrett (2002, p. 10) and Roland Van Gompel, Hilde Van den Bulck, and Daniel Biltereyst (2002, p. 183) note it has only been quite recently that telecommunications has gained academic attention, due to the expanding digital and cable technologies and the increase in large media consortia with interests in all forms of communications.

Mobile telephony is clearly worth further academic study in its own right. Along with Nilsson et al., there are now several academic studies concerned with how individuals use their cell phones for socializing and maintaining family contacts. A study of its influence on other changing social mores may prove valuable as well. It would also be worth investigating the fraudulent and illegal cell phone markets. Without an understanding of the illicit use of the cell phone by the dishonest or the possible clandestine use by state authorities, there is a risk that regulation may undermine or not adequately uphold the civil liberties and freedom inherent in this technology.[12]

In conclusion, the importance of this small piece of technology must be stressed. The cell phone is of a significance that we are only just realizing. It is quietly and without fuss causing us to carry it about and so be locatable and be able to communicate in places hitherto unimaginable. It has forced societies to rethink laws and social mores and it has influenced our cultural forms and their distribution.

We now have the potential for every human being to be within almost immediate contact with every other, no matter where they are or what they are doing. The changes in our personal behavior and the organization of our societies have already been influenced by this extraordinary expansion of personal communication. The cell phone empowers the individual by giving access to others in situations that were not possible using a fixed line. It is a technological tool, but its use has been explored and expanded and embedded into our popular culture. It has shown itself to be an instrument of communication within the public sphere, and as the events in Manila and the United States show, these communications on occasion have a significant influence not only on personal choices and actions but also on national and international events.

Notes

1 Bluetooth is a radio protocol for connecting electronic devices to each other without using wires. For example, a cell phone can be linked to a computer. A common use of Bluetooth technology is to enable the cell phone to be used legally in a car while driving.

2 The general packet radio service allows e-mails and some Internet services to be sent and received via a cell phone network. It is said to be five times faster than a standard service. Data services are cheaper than voice traffic as they are sent and received in short packets.

3 Satellite phones rely on satellite up-links and are not the same as cell phones, but they share many of the same attributes.

4 I witnessed a woman answering a cell phone on a moving bus. She tripped and fell over, dropping her possessions. She sat on the floor and continued her conversation on the phone!

5 Fiske uses the word text to mean any area of popular culture. Artifact is my word to describe an aspect of popular culture that may be picked up, such as a cell phone. I also use the word so as not to confuse it with text messaging; that is, SMS.

6 For an interesting account of Filipino phone usage, see G. Strom, "The telephone comes to a Filipino village," in Katz and Aakhus (2002). Strom describes how one cell phone is used by many members of the same family or village group.

7 The events of September 11, 2001, are extensively recorded, but the accounts are sometimes contradictory (see the following note). For a factual account that endeavors to piece the various elements and time lines together, it is worth reading the National Commission on Terrorist Attacks upon the United States (Kean 2004). I have used a number of sources, but found the following particularly helpful: J. Baxter and M. Downing (Eds.), *The day that shook the world* (London: BBC Worldwide, 2001); T. Harnden, "Wife phoned from hijack airliner as it hit Pentagon," 12/9/2001, Washington, www.telegraph.co.uk; T. Harnden, "Hijackers reassured pilot while they stabbed stewardesses," 13/9/2001, Washington, www.telegraph.co.uk; B. Fenton, "Hijacked passengers 'go down fighting,'" 14/9/2001, Washington, www.telegraph.co.uk; A. Alderson et al., "At 8.46am, the world changed in a moment," 16/9/2001, www.telegraph.co.uk.

8 Since September 11, 2001, a number of alternative theories have been put forward as to the events that took place that day. Some versions may have some validity and some others appear fanciful and conspiratorial. Some of these theories rely on the belief that the phone calls from the aircraft cannot have taken place or that they were fabricated. Furthermore, there has been confusion in the reporting of the phone calls from the stricken aircraft as to whether the callers were using their personal cell phones or the plane's air phones. The national commission's report clarifies how some of the calls were made but not all. Having studied a number of versions and explanations, I am confident that phones calls did take place between each of the four aircraft and the ground, via both cell phones and air phones. The evidence suggests that in-flight cell phone transmission and reception might have been erratic but is perfectly possible.

9 Anecdotally, although cell phones did not operate for those attempting to evacuate the World Trade Center buildings, their BlackBerries did. These are handheld dedicated e-mail providers.

10 See L. F. Rakow, "Women and the telephone," in C. Kramarae (Ed.), *Technology and women's voices* (pp. 207–28) (London: Routledge).

11 See the work of E. A. Schegloff, in particular "On 'opening sequencing': A framing statement," republished in Katz and Aakhus (2002).

12 See the work of G. Gow (2005), "The anonymous mobile: Prepaid and location privacy," pp.

76-87; D. Tutt, (2005), "Mobile performances of a teenager: A study of situated mobile phone activity in the living room," pp. 58–75, and P. White and N. White (2005), "Virtually there: Travelling with the new media," pp. 102–112. All three articles are in *Convergence*, special issue, Mobile Phones, ed. Gordon J., Summer 2005, Volume 11, no. 2.

References

Bagalawis, J. E. (2001). "How IT helped to topple a president." *Computer World*, January 30.

Birch, D. (2004). "Managing the data trail." Paper delivered at conference on "The life of mobile data: Technology, mobility, and data subjectivity," April 15–16, University of Surrey, England.

Bornhausser, M. (Interview conducted on September 22, 2004, at the Mobile Content World Conference, London Excel Centre, London.

Boyd-Barrett, O. (2002). "Theory in media research." In Newbold C., Boyd-Barrett O., and Van Den Bulck, H. (Eds.), *The Media Book* (pp. 1–52) . London: Arnold.

Burton, S. (2001). "People power." *Time Magazine*, January 29. Accessed April 22, 2002, from www.time.com/time/asia/magazine/2001/0129.

"Cellular stats 2004." (2004). Retrieved December 27, 2004, from www.cellular.co.za/stats/stats-main.htm.

Cohen, T. (2004). "Applying DRM to mobile content." Presentation delivered at Mobile Content World, London Excel, September 22.

"Crucial phone evidence in Soham murder case." (2003). Accessed March 18, 2005, from http://archives.tcm.ie/breakingnews/2003/11/05/story120219.asp.

De Jong, M. (2004). "Keynote address: How the convergence of media and entertainment are shaping the mobile economy." Mobile Content World, London Excel, September 22.

Fiske, J. (1989). *Reading the popular*. London: Routledge. "Forensic telecoms' revolution is turning mobile phones against their criminal owners." (2004). Jane's, October 1. Accessed December 29, 2004, from http://www.janes.com/press/pc041001_1.shtml.

Gaudin S. (2001). "The terrorist network." *Network World*, November 26. Accessed April 29, 2002, from http://www.nwfusion.com/research/2001.

Gordon, J. (2002). "The mobile phone, an artefact of popular culture and a tool of the public sphere." *Convergence* 8, no. 3: 15–26.

Habermas, J. (1989). *The structural transformation of the public sphere*. Cambridge, UK: Polity.

Harrington, V., and P. Mayhew (2001). *Mobile phone theft, home office research study* 235, HMSO, December.

Internet World Stats. (2005). Accessed January 2, 2005, from http://www.internetworld-stats.com/stats.htm.l.

"Joy of text." (2002). Accessed April 4, 2002, from www.bbc.co.uk/joyoftext/facts/.

Katz, J. E., and M. Aakhus (Eds.). (2002). *Perpetual contact: Mobile communication, private talk, public performance*. Cambridge, UK: Cambridge University Press.

Kaihla, P. (2001). "The Philippines' other revolution!" May 8. Accessed April 22, 2002, from www.business2.com/articles/web/.

Kean, T. (2004). *National commission on terrorist attacks upon the United States.*

Accessed April 12, 2005, from http://www.9-11commission.gov/report/index.htm.

Leyden, J. (2001). "Mobile phone suspected in plane crash inquiry." *The Register,* January 17. Accessed May 13, 2005, from http://www.theregister.co.uk/2001/01/17/mobile_phone_suspected_in_plane/.

Lyon, D. (2004). "Why where you are matters: Mundane mobilities, transparent technologies, and the recording of time-space paths." Keynote address delivered to conference on "The life of mobile data: Technology, mobility, and data subjectivity," April 15–16, University of Surrey, England.

McCullagh, D. (2003). "Cellphones betray your every move." *CNET News,* August 13. Accessed December 29, 2004, from http://comment.zdnet.co.uk/declanmccullagh/0,39020670,39115796,00.htm.

MDA. (2004). "UK text message volume +29% to 2.2 billion in August." MDA, October 2004. Accessed February 26, 2004, from http://www.cellular.co.za/news_2004/oct/100304-uk_text_message_volume.htmSaunders.

"Mobile content." (2004). Accessed December 29, 2004, from http://cellular.co.za/news_2004/may/050104-mobile_content_shows_revenue_pro.htm.

"Mobile phone sales to beat fixed lines in 2004 says ITU." (2004). Accessed February 24, 2005, from http://www.cellular.co.za/news_2004/dec/121404-mobile_phone_sales_to_beat_fixed.htm.

"Mobile subscriber growth growth drops in China in 2004." (2004). Accessed December 27, 2004, from http://www.cellular.co.za/news_2004/sep/090504-mobile_subscriber_growth_drops_i.htm.

Nilsson, A., W. Nuldén, and D. Olsson. (2001). "Mobile media: The convergence of media and mobile communications." *Convergence* 7, no. 1 (spring): 34–38.

Ofcom. (2004a). *Market Research.* Accessed December 29, 2004, from http://www.ofcom.org.uk/research/industry_market_research/m_i_index/cm/qu_10_2004/?a=87101.

Ofcom. (2004b). *Quarterly Update* (p. 35). Accessed May 12, 2005, from http://www.ofcom.org.uk/research/cm/qu_10_2004/cm_qu_10_2004.pdf.

Ofcom. (2005). *Quarterly Update* (p. 39), January. Accessed May 12, 2005, from http://www.ofcom.org.uk/research/cm/jan2005_update/update.pdf.

Oftel. (2003). "Consumer use of mobile telephony." October. Accessed Februrary 26, 2004, from http://www.ofcom.org.uk/static/archive/oftel/publications/research/2003/q14mobres1003.pdf.

Pepall, J. (2003). "What determines ICT access in the Philippines?" November 17. Accessed February 26, 2004, from http://web.idrc.ca/en/ev-47034-201-1-DO_TOPIC.html.

Seregina, E. (2000). "Cell phone producers pushing for tighter import regulation." *St. Petersburg Times,* December 26. Accessed April 4, 2002, from www.sptimes-russia.com/secur/632/news/b_1416.htm.

"UK SMS traffic." (2004). Accessed December 27, 2004, from http://www.cellular.co.za/news_2004/may/0500404-uk_sms_traffic_continues_to_rise.htm.

Uranaka, T. (2005). "Telecom carriers' policies split on supporting prepaid cell phones." *Japan Times,* January 12. Accessed May 12, 2005, from http://search.japantimes.co.jp/print/business/nb01-2005/nb20050112a2.htm.

Van Gompel R., H. Van den Bulck, and D. Biltereyst, (2002). "Media industries." In

Newbold, C., Boyd-Barrett, O., Van Den Bulck, H., (pp. 162-211). *The Media Book*. London: Arnold.

Life in the Nomos: Stress, Emotional Maintenance, and Coordination via the Mobile Telephone in Intact Families

Rich Ling

Introduction

A central question in sociology was posed by Georg Simmel when he asked, "how is society possible?" (Simmel, 1910–11). Rephrased to some degree, we can ask, In a society where individualism is a strong element, how is it that we are able to maintain the social (Beck 1994; Beck and Beck-Gernsheim 2002; Giddens 1994; Lash 1994)?

The tension between the individual and the collective is as old as sociology (Portes 1998), and has, for example, found a new form in the dialogue around the concept of social capital (Ling 2004d). Following from this thought, there are clearly rituals and institutions that play into the structuring and maintenance of social life. We are members of various social constellations—both formal and informal—that afford us rights in exchange for our observance of the norms and rules (Ling 2004c). Participation in the Thursday-night gang means that we have to show up on time and buy a round of beers when it is our turn. In exchange we get to enjoy a few hours of social interaction with old friends. Membership in the local genealogy group means that we have to arrange the meeting on occasion, but we get access to others' research tips. A visit to the restaurant with a friend means that we have to mind our manners, but we get a good meal and a nice discussion to boot. And so it goes. We participate in various social groups, we fulfill our need for social interaction, and we contribute to the ethos of the situation. We use various forms of ritual and institutionalized interactions in our striving to balance between discord and order.

An essential element here is that in our social interaction we rely on collectively developed and understood props in order to maintain social interaction in focused social encounters. In addition, we often act in the context of what Peter Berger and Thomas Luckmann (1967, p. 54) call institutions, here defined as those situations characterized by the reciprocal typification of habitualized action. Indeed, it is our willingness to do exactly this—as well as our recognition that others are up to about the same type of wheeze—that lies at the core of our sociability.

There is an essential reflexivity in being social. We are willing to use various recognized devices in our interaction and, in turn, we are willing to allow others the use of the same—or perhaps similar—devices in their interactions with us. Further, the tighter the group is bound, the greater the strategies are elaborated and the greater the nuance one can read out of the strategies and lines that are chosen for interaction. Some social interactions are loose to the extreme, wherein we need only the broadest forms of a common parlance (for example, showing your passport to the inspector at the airport or giving the person in the tollbooth the coins for the toll). In other situations the interaction is extremely nuanced and intricate. Indeed, the subject of this paper—interaction between couples—is one situation in which the mere raising of an eyebrow can communicate volumes.

The sum of all these interactions is our ability to orient ourselves in society. Eventually we know how to deal with people at tollbooths and at passport controls. We know how to behave ourselves in restaurants or at local social gatherings. That is, we have certain socially constructed ballast with which we can weather various situations.

The material examined here looks into Norwegian parents' use of mobile communication and transportation in relationship maintenance. The interviews illustrate how the partners construct, live in, and maintain what Berger and Hansfried Kellner (1964) call a nomic situation. The interviews give us insight into the active nature of the families' lives—particularly those with smaller children—and the effort needed to keep afloat in the hectic stream of everyday life. It looks at how couples seemingly develop a stock of routines that can be used to attend to the ongoing needs of the family. These routines have a practical dimension in that they, for example, help the couple know how and when to shop for food, help the children with lessons, wash the clothes, and the like.

Technology, and specifically the automobile and the mobile telephone, are brought into this process in various ways. The comments here show that these devices are used to facilitate the tasks of the parents. They are used in order to facilitate everyday life and, in this way, to assist in the continuance of this social context. The "second" car in the family is used to deliver the children to various activities while one of the parents uses another to commute to a more or less distant job.[1] The mobile telephone is used to arrange shopping tours on the fly and to coordinate who will be picking up which child at day care. The technology is a tool that is used to facilitate the couples' responsibilities. Thus, the technology becomes a medium through which the social order is maintained.

The material examined here is a part of a larger study of transportation and communication in everyday life. The material was gathered as a part of series of twenty-five interviews carried out in the Oslo area in December 2003. The interviewees were selected based on their marital/domestic status and their parental status. We interviewed the parents of small children aged four to eight years (approximately 50 percent of the interviews) and also the parents of teens aged eleven to fifteen years (again approximately 50 percent of the interviews). This sample allowed us to examine the issues of familial coordination, since the youngest age group is completely dependent on their parents' daily care and attention, and the older group is more independent.

When considering marital or domestic status we examined both "intact" and separated families. The "intact" families made up ten of the interviews; the interviews were done with both the partners. It is this group that is in particular focus here.[2] The interviews were designed to examine the interviewees' use of transportation and communication in their daily lives:

1 How do the different families use ICT to coordinate daily activities? Which aspects of ICT are important for the different family types?
2 What characterizes the coordination of communication in the different family types? Between which persons in the family does coordination take place? How can the communication be characterized? We were particularly interested in the aspects of security/control, emotional interaction, and planning/effectiveness in this communication.
3 Which medium is used for which purpose? What are the advantages and drawbacks of texting in relation to voice or visually based ICT?
4 What types of interaction are there between the use of ICT and physical mobility? Which types of daily trips are impacted by the use of ICT? Is it such that some trips are replaced by other communication (telephone, e-mail), are they modified (the trip is changed en route), are there more trips, or is there no real interaction between the use of ICT and daily travel activity?

Aside from three homes, all households had a car. The three households without a car were all single-parent women. In addition, four of the homes in the same category did not have a land line telephone. All of the intact and eight of the distributed families had Internet access. Among those without an Internet connection were four women. The resulting interviews were taped and transcribed. The transcribed material was examined and, using a computer-based coding program, it was coded into various thematic areas. The citations used here were translated from Norwegian to English.

The Concept of the Nomos

As developed, the issues described here look into our ability to participate in social interaction. The description in this study, particularly in its focus on married couples,[3] plays on the idea of the nomos. This concept was developed by Berger and Kellner and is seen as the opposite of Emile Durkheim's notion of anomie. Looking first at anomie, in its simplest form it is the absence of norms. Anomie describes a state wherein there is a breakdown of the rules controlling behavior in society. More specifically, Durkheim saw anomie as a situation wherein social norms are confused and unclear, or possibly absent. Thus, individuals are left without a clear sense of how they should behave and interact. He felt that this could contribute to the rise of deviance and other problematic forms of behavior such as suicide (Durkheim 1997). In direct contrast to Durkheim's notion, Berger and Kellner (1964, p. 7) posit the idea of nomos as a situation in which there is an abundance of norms. "Just as the individual's deprivation of relationship with his [sic] significant others will plunge him into anomie, so their continued presence will sustain for him that *nomos* by which he can feel at home in the world."

In any group there is a need to objectify the individuals' ideas and meanings such that they become, in a sense, the common property of the group. In the words of Berger and Kellner (1964, p. 9), these common meanings need to become "massively objective." The group needs to know that it is, for example, not acceptable to smoke in the office, to wear ties on Fridays, to make phone calls during class, or to express support for one or another political position. Such considerations become the common ideology of the group. These ideologies are developed and nurtured through various forms of discipline and through their inclusion in the lore of the group. In this way, the sense of the group is defended and bolstered through the development of a common version of the world. Berger and Kellner note: "Every social relationship requires *objectification*, that is, requires *a process by which subjectively experienced meanings become objective to the individual and*, in interaction with others, *become common property and thereby massively objective*" (p. 11; emphasis in the original).

Nomos reaches one of its most developed forms in the context of the family. Their reasoning is that in modern society each family constitutes a segregated subworld, and in this way the partners, and eventually children, have a strong and relatively unmediated influence on each other. In this social situation, the familial truisms and rituals take on an importance to the members that is much stronger than it is in other social constellations.

The family, however, is a precarious institution. In other social groups there are many members who are available to help support and develop the group ideology and by extension the group identity. In the case of the couple—especially before children arrive on the scene—there are only two persons who carry this responsibility. Because of this, the couple is a particularly unstable social construction. While there are general social notions that play into the couple's sense of how to be a couple, they are also the masters of their own common ideology to a much larger degree than in other situations.

The product of both the broader social expectations and the couple's sense of their own situation is what Berger and Kellner call the coupled identity. The coupled identity is the responsibility of the two individuals to a much larger degree in modern society than in traditional society. This is because in a traditional society the couple is often surrounded by a broader extended family that has relatively free access to the couple's private sphere. In many respects this broader social sphere has a say in the nature and content of the coupled identity. By contrast, in contemporary society the private sphere is less accessible, the couple is not embedded in an extensive local society, and, further, the couple is often more mobile (Sennett 1998). Thus, the coupled identity, and the ideology supporting it, is to a larger degree the creation of the two individuals.[4]

Berger and Kellner use the metaphor of the conversation to describe the marital interaction and the process through which the coupled identity is developed and maintained. While an actual verbal interaction is a large—and perhaps the most important—part of nomos building, I would also suggest that common activities and various forms of interpersonal ritual are also a part of the nomos building (Ling 2004c). The result of the couple's interactions is a type of crystallized institution in the spirit of Berger and Luckmann (1967). "In the marital conversation a world is not only built, but it is also kept in a state of repair and ongoingly refurnished. The subjective reality of this world for the two partners is sustained by the same conversation. The nomic instrumentality of the marriage is concretized over and over again, from bed to breakfast table, as the partners carry on the endless conversation that feeds on nearly all they individually or jointly experience" (p. 13). They go on to say:

> This process has a very important result—namely *a hardening or stabilization of the common objectivated reality*. It should be easy to see how this comes about. The objectifications ongoingly preformed and internalized by the marriage partners become ever more massively real, as they are confirmed and reconfirmed in the marital conversation. The world that is made up of these objectifications at

the same time gains stability" (p. 13; emphasis in the original).

The coupled identity is a structure that provides a sense of continuity and stability in an otherwise turbulent life. These characteristics are obvious in the data considered here. To jump ahead slightly to the data, one finds in the comments of a couple I have named Tron and Tina that within the more or less fixed nomos of daily life there is the need for specific types of coordination.

> **Interviewer:** Do you call your wife often?
> **Tron (36):** We talk at any rate at least once a day, if not two.
> **Interviewer:** And you agree on getting the children and things like that? Or?
> **Tron:** That is fixed if nothing unexpected has happened.
> **Tina (39):** We agree...What we are going to have for dinner . . . (laughs)
> **Tron:** ...we agree on that . . . (laughs)
> **Tina:** ...shopping and . . .
> **Tron:** ...small things, practical messages like that.
> Interviewer: What is going to happen and who is going to do what?
> **Tina:** Yeah.
> **Tron:** Otherwise, the taking and getting the children is fixed. We have our fixed days in order to make it function.
> **Tina:** It is always like one will take them and the other will get them. It is like . . . it is rare that one does both on the same day.
>
> *(Couple with a six- and a nine-year-old child)*

The practical work of deciding on the evening's menu and what is needed from the store constitutes a part of the ongoing need to coordinate within the family. As with Tron and Tina, the cycles of job, day care, or school and various evening free-time activities all mean that the families are bounded into certain regular daily rounds. These are formulated into a quasi-institutionalized routine of calling each other.

Different things arise that break out of these routines. A child can be sick, the car can break down, one or the other partner might have to work late or travel to a business meeting, or they can run out of milk at a critical point when making dinner. There are many large and small threats to the stability of the coupled identity. It is in these situations that the resilience of the institution is brought into play. One can see this in the comments of Hans and Marianne, a couple who both work in relatively well paid administrative positions. They talk about how they try to take the needs of the other partner into account when they have to rework a schedule because of sickness.

> **Interviewer:** Are there things [that mean a change of plans during the day]?
> **Marianne (36):** . . . Not too often.
> **Hans (40):** If there is sickness, with the children for example.
> Marianne: Yeah, that can happen but it is not so often that we throw out . . . what we have agreed on. We do that as a rule, it is usually work. We respect each other's work and if something comes up we

really try to . . .
Hans: have understanding.
Marianne: Yeah, understanding, right. Beyond that, we usually don't, it is not like I jump on every chance to go out with friends or things like that because I already have some things at home that I need to do. That doesn't happen too often.
Interviewer: Is it like that with you also?
Hans: Yeah as a matter of fact, there is not too much spontaneity.

(Couple with two children under seven years old)

The partners describe a rather stable, routinized daily life that is rarely disturbed by irregular events. They both work, and the children have their regular daily routines. The partners' careers are important and so, as they note, they are careful about making demands on the other. Thus, ad hoc scheduling—be it done over the telephone, e-mail, or in another form—is not simply a mechanical process, but indeed involves interaction between the partners and a willingness to set oneself into the position of their partner. The reader sees this in Hans's and Marianne's comments on being understanding toward one another. Their agreement here brings to life Berger and Kellner's notion of a "common objectivated reality."

Beyond the comments of these couples, the sequences are interesting for the staging of their talk. The way that they fill in the words for each other provides insight into their common sense of coupled identity. There is the sense here of a well-oiled interaction between two adults. There is a type of gracious interweaving of interaction. The woman seems to pause slightly when trying to think of a word and the man provides her with an adequate suggestion that she accepts, confirms, and uses in further comments. Two people are talking but only a single sentence is being uttered. While Berger and Kellner speak of the marital conversation in metaphorical terms, one sees it being concretely practiced here. The couple is filling out and embroidering the common version of reality being presented to the interviewer. In doing so, they help each other and collectively present a rounded, if perhaps somewhat selective picture of the coupled identity. This illustrates, at a rather specific level, the nomos-like aspects of their interaction.

Along the same lines is the use of laughter. As we will examine below, beyond the simple functional aspects of familial interaction, the interviews point to the need for expressive interaction as a type of social lubricant within the family. The laughter in the citation from Tron and Tina also helps to carry the discussion here. In a social sense, laughter is used to assist the conversation past difficult shoals (Duncan 1970). The fact that deciding on the evening's menu was the cause of such mirth may point to the fact that the couple also chats about other matters during these calls that are ostensibly for the instrumental act of deciding on dinner. In this case, it is difficult to tell if the intention here is to protect the couple's inner life or to, in essence, ask for the indulgence of the interviewer for relating the undramatic humdrum of their lives. It may indicate that beyond the simple need to coordinate, the couple shares a type of expressive interaction in these calls. Nonetheless, the fact that both partners use it in telling about their daily phone call(s) indicates that the conversational device is being used in presenting the gloss of the familial situation, and again we see the mechanisms of the coupled identity at play. The work of Berger and Kellner helps us to set a broader context around the discussion of family life and the role of technology, a discussion of which follows.

Complex Reduced by Flexible Routinization

Complex and Less Complex Life Phases

A common theme that came out in the interviews with the intact couples was that everyday life is full of various activities and demands. This is particularly true for those with smaller children. While it is clear that single parents also have complex life situations, the demands of life in the intact families also mean that there is a certain amount of stress in daily life.

> **Toril (44):** Everyday life is often quite hectic. Especially in relation to work. It isn't often that I sit and [cannot hear] during a weekday. It is really nice to relax and do something else.
> **Bjørn (40):** It is stressful with the social things sometimes. It can be a little "Yikes," Christmas comes and then there is New Year's and then it all starts up again. We are doing too much!
> **Toril:** You have to do everything. You have to do everything you can't manage in daily life.
>
> *(Couple with two small children both under three years of age)*

This couple with younger children describes the pressure to carry out all the diverse activities that having children involves. The fact that both partners work and must commute (the husband must commute seventeen kilometers and the wife commutes forty-seven kilometers) means that it is even more difficult for this family to make their time budget stretch to cover all the issues that come up.

Another mother of two (one in day care and another in school) describes her life as continually having to plan various logistics.

> **Inga (36):** Now we have gone to the other extreme where we feel like we plan all the time. Who is doing what, where you are, and who you are. (laughs) I was about to say. It is clear that there is a lot more stress and we both work and that means that we are there more than the normal eight hours a day. So it is clear that it has been a big change. The children have started in day care. They were not in day care until...then they don't go to the same place you know. They don't go to the same day care, so there is a lot more organizing of daily life. First I have to deliver there and then I have to deliver there and then I have to go to work by a certain time and the opposite for the person that gets them you know. Yeah, it is a lot of planning. Food for dinner. Endless planning. An endlessly returning theme you know. Who will make dinner today and what it is going to be and who will go shopping and...Yeah!
>
> *(Mother in an intact family with a four- and a six-year-old child)*

To be constantly on the run seems to be an aspect of having children, particularly younger children. In the case of older children, there is also stress, but it seems that the growing independence of the children provides a buffer. While the parents in the following citation comment on the relative level of activity, they seem to have a more relaxed attitude toward it.

> **Interviewer:** You manage at any rate to make the ends meet?
> **Kjetil (45):** I think that it goes pretty well.
> **Mona (41):** But there is almost never a day when there is not something or other.
> **Kjetil:** If you have teens then . . .
> **Mona:** They are so active.
> **Kjetil:** But I would rather drive to practice than drive around looking for them.
>
> *(Couple with three children five, fourteen, and eighteen years of age)*

Their less troubled attitude toward planning family life perhaps reflects the fact that the children in this family are somewhat older, and that the distances the parents commute are shorter. This family had had two major changes. First, the wife has started to work. This has meant the need for more telephoning to cover all the different aspects of the family's coordination. In addition, they have also purchased a new car that has helped to facilitate the interaction in the family such that there were not as many demands for the use of the single car.

The Need for Flexibility vis-à-vis Work and Family

The working situation of some couples adds an element of irregularity to family life. The families also indicate that mobile communication and second cars helped to resolve some of the complexity of everyday life.

In those cases where both partners work regular hours this is less of a problem. However, in those families where one or eventually both of the partners have shift work, planning is more complex. It becomes even more intricate when, for one reason or another, a partner trades shifts with other coworkers. This means that the other members of the household need to reorder responsibilities for, for example, food making, transport of children, the arrangement of affairs, and so on.

> **Kjetil (45):** With [soccer] practice and things like that it is me. She has night shift quite often so I take her with me and drive to practice.
> **Interviewer:** Is this agreed upon during the day or when you come home?
> **Kjetil:** It is often during the day I have to say. We never know when she is going to work. She trades shifts [with other colleagues] and changes things.
> **Mona (41):** It is often agreed on the day before.
> **Kjetil:** ...but I have most certainly forgotten it the next day.
> **Interviewer:** Who is it that calls and reminds or asks?
> **Mona:** We girls [sic] normally have control over everything so I call and remind him about it.
> **Kjetil:** We men, we think about so many other things you know.
>
> *(Couple with three children five, fourteen, and eighteen years of age)*

In this family the wife is a nurse who has various evening and night shifts along with a day job at a medical center. The husband is a contactor. In this citation one sees that the daily routines are irregular. However, in this fluid working situation it is the woman who has the role of making sure that her husband receives reminders as to when she will be away working. The fact that the couple has irregular aspects to daily scheduling along with the more regular issues of training, purchasing food, and the like means that they have developed routines that provide a structure within which their activities can take place. Beyond the more structural changes in schedule based on shift work, there are other exigencies that arise in daily life. These can also result in changes in the way that they organize the mundane activities of the family.

> **Interviewer:** How do you change agreements if something comes up? Do you use SMS, e-mail?
> **Inger (34):** Telephone, mobile. A lot of mobile.
> **Robert (33):** If I find out at 3:30 that I cannot come home at 4, then I just call and say that I cannot come home to dinner and that I cannot get the children.
>
> *(Intact family with a nine- and a five-year-old child)*

In the cases in which there are irregularities in the daily schedule, the parents spoke of using e-mail, the traditional telephone, and the mobile telephone to reschedule their affairs. In the case of the following family, the man describes how they use the telephone to rework their familial responsibilities in the case of new exigencies.

> **Toril (40):** The only [changing of routines] that has happened is there is suddenly tennis practice for the children on Saturdays and not on weekdays and that they have practice with an hour's break. It is a little impractical. The one is from twelve to one and the other is from one to two, right in the middle of Saturday.
> **Bjørn (44):** That has meant a little more calling. Trading driving with the other parents. There are probably more agreements ("Can you get them, can you . . .?"). I usually use the mobile or the regular telephone when I am home. Otherwise we would have had a huge telephone bill, it would be. You can do things more on the spur of the moment than you could before. The mobile is either a blessing or a curse.
> **Toril:** Yeah, quite often he goes to the store right after work and so he calls and says "Is there anything we need?"
>
> *(Couple with a ten- and a thirteen-year-old child)*

The families described the need to find flexibility within the broader regularities of daily life. Some of the situations were predictable (shift work), while others (sickness) were less so. In these cases, the need to quickly change the staging of life was accomplished with the use of communication between the partners.

Flexible Routinization of Activities

The material here points to a full life for the parents as they go through the routinized and the irregular events that make up everyday life. They have full lives and they use various strategies to fulfill their various responsibilities. As we will see, there are various ways that they develop strategies for dealing with these issues. These strategies include both techniques for dealing with these issues and various technologies for assisting in their execution.

The material from the interviews also points out that the parents in intact families seemingly have a repertoire of routines that they draw upon in order to maintain the family. These routines can be rearranged on a modular basis, and one can step in for the other as the need arises. The routines can be viewed as Berger and Luckmannian institutions in that they are reciprocally developed between the partners (Berger and Luckmann 1967). They are also often imbued with various types of ideological veneers such that the task has to be carried out in a certain manner in order to be seen as being well executed. They are also a part of the stuff of which the relationship is made. There is a consistency in the activities that characterizes the ongoing mainte-nance of the partners' nomic identity (Berger and Kellner 1964). It is perhaps wrong, however, to say that the tasks must be performed in a fixed order, or that one or the other partner needs to carry out certain portions of the process. Rather, there is flexi-bility here.[5]

There are rules or understandings that are used as to who does the shopping, who cleans house, who delivers the children to activities such as day care or after-school activities, and so on. It seems that there is a basic template that governs these types of activities and helps the couple (and by extension the children and other family members) to come through the day. However, the pattern is never exactly the same. One day, it is one partner who does the shopping and the other cleans up. The following day the first partner does both, since there is a parent-teacher meeting at school. The dishes are cleaned and put in the cupboard in about the same way. The children's lunches contain roughly the same elements, and they arrive at their scouting meeting at about the same time via about the same route. All the while, the couple is drawing on a common stock of routines.

> **Tron (36):** It is like the first one that comes home makes dinner.
> **Tina (39):** And he washes and cleans up also…(laughs)
> **Tron:** The one that does not make food cleans up…(laughs)
> **Tina:** Yeah.
> **Tron:** It is a little like that. It manages itself after fourteen years…(laughs)
>
> *(Couple with a six- and a nine-year-old child)*

The dinner may be spaghetti or it may be hamburgers. The person doing the shopping may fancy one type of bread as opposed to another. However, these small variations take place within a larger context of the ongoing sense of the family, in that the essential tasks are carried out and the inner ethos of the family is burnished. A mother of two describes her family's "rule-based" system for managing the evening activities as well as providing the space for the other partner to deal with the demands of his or her job.

Marianne (36): The one that gets the children is responsible sort of from when they come home, or from when we come home, with making dinner, with lessons and play and all of that there. And then the others are free to come home when it is convenient. If the other doesn't come home then the one at home has responsibility for everything. That is how we do it. So the one that takes the children in the morning is, in some ways, done and the one that gets them has that part.

(Mother in an intact couple with a four- and a six-year-old child)

The routines are developed and refined over time. They will necessarily change as the family moves from the stage of having newborn children to when the nest is empty (or the partnership ends). However, when interviewing these families who are in intact situations, one is struck by the fact that the routines are in place and that they form the tools with which the family tackles the demands of everyday life.

The routines also involve various uses of technologies. Of special interest here is the role of the automobile and other forms of transport and that of telecommunication. In the process of addressing the various requirements of daily life, the couples discuss how there is a need for effective (that is, time effective) and flexible transport and the need for coordination over broader areas that is afforded by mobile communication.

Kjetil (45): My wife and I talk during the day. It can be that I get stuck and have to be late.
Mona (41): Get stuck in traffic.
Kjetil: Yeah, you know. Suddenly there is a crash on E18, and you wait there a couple of hours.
Mona: It is generally about agreeing who will get the child at day care. They close the door at 4:30.

(Couple with three children five, fourteen, and eighteen)

In the spirit of Berger and Luckmann, there is a crystallized habitual nature to the routines that families develop. Informants spoke of the "natural" spheres of responsibility. A lot of the things that need to be agreed upon in a family fall into the sphere of one or the other partner. This habitualized division of tasks is referred to here as a "natural" phenomenon, but it is in all likelihood quite embedded in the history of the relationship and in the gendered assumptions of what is done by whom. In the context of this work, in an intact family that is functioning, the division of tasks is only partially discussed. In general it is habitual. Only when it becomes problematic for the one or the other is there the need for discussions.

Klaus (33): ...we have areas that are naturally hers and naturally mine. Aside from that, we agree in the evening...and we are in agreement the next day and longer into the future also. [Agreeing via] telephone, that is not too often.
Ylva (34): ...no that is not too often...That would have to be if there is perhaps something that we have forgotten and then we suddenly remember it right there.

Klaus: You mean tasks? Yeah, washing clothes, cleaning the house and those things, Yeah.
Interviewer: Yeah, they are completely normal things that you are...
Klaus: Yeah, it is like...
Ylva: That is agreed on by us....
Klaus: Yeah, there is little high technology here...
Interviewer: Do agreements about who is going to do what change during the day?
Ylva: Yeah, that can happen.
Klaus: Yeah, that is like...it can change. But there are things that can be delayed and depending on what it is . . .
Interviewer: What are you thinking about?
Klaus: I am thinking about the daily tasks like only to, like to get...deliver and get the kids and to feed them and to take care of them. That has to be done. And food in the refrigerator. You have to agree on that if there is something. Generally, if there is an agreement then it is OK and there are not too many changes. That was a little surprising, actually, I don't know if I have any examples, but if you have to change then there is always the telephone.

(Couple with two children ages two and four)

The comments of Klaus and Ylva are in line with the notion of flexible routinization. They show that the couple has routines, but that they are practiced in a flexible manner. The couple seems to have their "natural" spheres of responsibilities in the home. However, there is also the flexibility to adjust these as various situations arise. The wife here is a flight attendant and commutes sixty kilometers from their home west of Oslo to the airport northeast of town. The husband commutes twenty kilometers to his job as an engineer. This family has worked out various ways of shuttling between public transport and their use of the family's single automobile.

Interviewer: Are there many telephone calls between you during the day?
Ylva: Actually our commuting is agreed on beforehand...If I am going to work, then either I leave so early that I take the bus or whatever, either that or he uses public transport and I come later with the car. If I start later.
Klaus: The only transport we need to agree on is if we should get you on the train. If you don't take the bus and otherwise the telephone...Our telephone calls are more exchange of agreements and other information.

(Couple with two children ages two and four)

As with Ylva and Klaus, other couples also generally made agreements face-to-face and supplemented them by using other media. SMS is an addition to the agreements that are made over the breakfast table. Thus, SMS does not seem to be at the core of the system, but it is a technology that allows the partners flexibility. In other situations—notably among teens and young adults—SMS is probably more central (Ling 2004a;

Ling 2004b). In this case, however, it seems to be a useful but secondary medium used to modify interaction.

> **Interviewer:** How do you agree on who will do which tasks in the family?
> **Ola (47):** It is like: "Do you have the time, do I have the time?"
> **Interviewer:** Is it verbal, in the morning?
> **Ola:** Yeah.
> **Interviewer:** Do you send SMS to each other?
> **Ola:** Yeah, we send SMS to each other.
>
> *(Father in an intact couple with children thirteen, sixteen, and nineteen years old)*

These comments indicate that these couples have a repertoire of routines at hand with which to address the different exigencies of life. There are certain basic activities that need to be addressed such as work, child care, shopping for food, and the like. As noted in the quotation above, these routinized tasks are agreed upon face-to-face and there is little need for the use of technology. In the words of a thirty-six-year-old father of two, "My day is pretty much (laughs) to work, get the kids from school, and like that..." Even within this matrix of "work, picking up the children, et cetera," there is the need to plan at a more specific level.

Shopping as a Flexibly Routine Institution

One can see the particular way that various families develop flexible routines when examining the way that routine food purchases are made. There are many alternative approaches that include, for example, one (or perhaps both) doing the purchasing, preparation, and cleanup, turn taking, ad hoc arrangements where the tasks are taken by one or the other partner as they arise. Purchasing of food can either be off-the-cuff trips to the store as the need arises (perhaps including calls on the mobile telephone during the actual shopping) or the structured development of a shopping list.

In the case of intact families, and in particular those families that have been intact for longer periods of time, the material shows that these tasks are more or less routinized. There is a type of division of labor here. The way they make food has been included in the flexible routinization described above. That is, one partner does something and the other lives with the assumption that the one will be doing it. In spite of this routinization, there is still the need for interaction in the logistics of, for example, food making. If it is the man that makes the lunches, and the woman who shops for food, then information about what is needed and what is in the house has to be communicated between them. The specific coordination often comes through face-to-face conversations. However, mobile telephony is often used as a supplement.

In some cases it can be the person who has the main responsibility for making the food who does the shopping. In these cases, that person has a sense of what is needed and he or she can act in a relatively independent way.

> **Tron (36):** I am the one [who buys the food] (laughs), because I have the car.

> **Tina (39):** Yeah…he has the car and so generally he does it. I can get small things on the way home, but in general it is definitely him that shops.
> **Interviewer:** When do you agree on this?
> **Tron:** We really don't agree on that much. I am self-sufficient (laughter from both). If there is something or other that you want, then you tell me.
> **Tina:** Otherwise we shop together in the weekends…
> **Tron:** …and then I shop during the week and I am the one that makes the food.
> **Tina:** Yeah, he is the chief for making food.
> **Interviewer:** So there are no real telephone calls?
> **Tron:** No. You know there is.
> **Tina:** Oh, he has been known to go around in the store with the mobile telephone.
> **Tron:** …yeah, that has happened.
> **Tina:** It happens and I have to tell him what he needs (laughs).
>
> *(Couple with a six- and a nine-year-old child)*

In this example it comes out that the man is the one who both purchases the food and is generally responsible for making food for the family. The interesting thing is that in the process of discussing this, it comes out that they use the mobile telephone while he is in the store to check on certain types of purchases. This is a type of microcoordination, or perhaps it also concerns having access to the wife on an "as needed" basis. This allows for more effective interaction, since both can be carrying out certain activities while still coordinating purchases.

In other cases one person usually does the ad hoc shopping while another does the more basic shopping. In the case of the following family, there is a type of division of labor in which the wife does the daily shopping and the man does the larger shopping trips.

> **Ylva (34):** I have, eh . . . do the daily [shopping], what should I say? For a couple of days. While he is a lot better at the major shopping, so he often makes . . .
> **Klaus (33):** We shop one time a week, usually, and otherwise we make small purchases. But make the big trip on Saturdays, with a list. Otherwise there are small things…like, but for dinners. I don't shop on the way home. I have thought about it beforehand and it is available.
> **Interviewer:** Just small things but larger trips are planned?
> **Klaus:** Yeah, it is planned.
> **Ylva:** …It is such that, eh, when I am at home, then I have the responsibility for getting things. But he does the same if I am at work or if he thinks it is necessary.
>
> *(Couple with two children under four years of age)*

In other cases there is an almost unspoken system of assembling the materials that the family needs to make food. This is seen in the following citation that comes from a family with two children and where the responsibility for making food is divided between the partners.

> **Inger (34):** I am the one who actually has the main responsibility for [grocery shopping]. But I am not always here and it is happing all the time, so he must do some of it.
> **Interviewer:** How do you agree on this?
> **Inger:** We don't talk about it. It is just done when there is the need.
> **Robert (33):** It takes care of itself.
> **Interviewer:** How do you know when there is the need?
> **Robert:** ... [to Inger] Now you can just keep quiet. Here is my big point: I am the one that makes all the lunches here. So I am the one that knows that we need lunch meat, and milk and things like that. But she is better with dinners.
> **Interviewer:** ...but how do the makings for these lunches come into the house?
> **Robert:** If she is going to the store I say, "Get some lunch meat!"
> **Inger:** You say it to each other.
> **Robert:** Or: "Can you go to the store? We need lunch meat and bread." And we know that we buy cheese...We know what we need and we don't need to say it.
> **Interviewer:** The main part of the shopping list is done verbally but is any of it done via the telephone?
> **Inger:** Yeah.
> **Robert:** "Stop by the store when you are driving by."
>
> *(Couple with two children under ten years of age)*

The comments here point to a rather informal system for shopping. In the case of this family there are the advantages of propinquity, a seemingly mutually supportive relationship, institutionalized routines, and an economy that does not demand discipline.

There are also situations in which the coordination is quite explicit. In the following case, the family seems to have quite routinized forms of shopping in that they have a list system that seems to be respected by both partners.

> **Hans (40):** Both [of us shop for food].
> **Interviewer:** How do you agree on it?
> **Marianne (36):** We write a list during the week, some things we remember and other things are on the list and then we write the list on the day that we really *have* to shop. It can be on Thursday or Friday or Monday. That is not as important.
> **Robert:** The one of us who has the time goes shopping.
> **Marianne:** Not too often, or maybe pretty often, the one who is not shopping finds out that we need a little of this or that and then we call via the mobile phone and tell the one who is shopping.
> **Robert:** And order home delivery of food. (laughs)
>
> *(Couple with a four- and a six-year-old child)*

The degree to which the system is integrated into the couple's lives can be seen in the way that they both fill out each other comments in the description of their system. Their routinized system of developing the list, the general agreement that the least encumbered person does the shopping, and at the same time the flexibility to add items to the list points to the way that this is a common task. There is clearly a common focus on the maintenance and a well-understood mechanism for the purchase of food.

One sees here the workings of what Berger and Luckmann would call an institution. These various couples have developed reciprocal understandings of how food comes into the home. This process did not simply arise fully formed, but rather it resulted from the various exigencies that the family had to confront. The accessibility to a car, the time to shop, an interest in making food, and a willingness to contribute to the welfare of the family are all elements that come into play. With time, the couples have developed taken-for-granted routines for the purchase of food. This often involves various forms of the division of household labor, with one partner, for example, doing the ad hoc shopping and the other doing the more basic shopping.

The point that is of interest to this study is the way that access to various technologies play into the picture. In at least one case, access to a car is seen as the deciding factor as to who should do the largest portion of the shopping. There is certain logic in this, since the car allows for a greater range of movement and for larger loads of goods.

The other technology that was named here, the mobile telephone, provides flexibility to shopping. Items that should have been included on the shopping list can be added while the shopping is in progress and clarifications can be made by the shopper who, for example, is unsure if the recipe calls for cream or for skim milk. Thus, the mobile telephone comes into this institution in that it allows the couples a certain flexibility when purchasing food.

The final point here is that the interviews quoted above point to a willingness to contribute to the general welfare of the family, something that is not necessarily a part of the picture in divorced families. The comments here point to a set of mechanisms that contribute to the successful maintenance of the household. As these mechanisms fall away—through, for example, divorcement or estrangement—the simple task becomes more and more complex and difficult.

The Second Car and the Mobile as Elements of Flexibility

As we have seen, the material indicates that there are different transportation and communication needs for family during the various life phases as well as different uses of technology in the face of these issues. The period when children need to be driven to all activities perhaps gives way to a period when the children are more independent and can manage their own transportation and coordination needs.

The material indicates that there is also a need for the parents to employ various technical fixes during the period when the children are youngest. Second cars are purchased, telephones are used to coordinate, and levels of interaction between the couple are complex. This is particularly the case if it is a dual-career couple. In addition to the care of the children, the couple is each pursing a career and must observe the potentials and constraints contained therein.

In the following sequence, the family is just coming out of the most intense "small child" phase. They live in one of the more remote suburbs of Oslo. The man commutes seventeen kilometers, while the woman commutes thirty-two kilometers. The oldest child has started at school, and the youngest child is still in day care, and the woman has just begun working again.[6]

> **Interviewer:** Have there been any changes in the family that have changed the daily routines, for example changing jobs, new home, purchase of a car, or children beginning a new school or day care?
> **Hans (36):** [...] You have started to work.
> **Marianne (40):** Yeah, OK, if you go so far back as six months ago then that was a big change. To go from being at home to having a full-time job.
> **Interviewer:** Can you tell me about that?
> **Marianne:** Yeah, it was a big change so it is clear that we had to organize ourselves in a completely different way in the way that we laid out plans for our days. There was a lot more calling and that type of thing to find out who should do what. But it was not just via the telephone, we talked about it in the evenings. Much more driving around on my part. So we already had two cars, and I was glad for that, and we had to plan out routines in a completely different way, but that didn't have anything to do with communication. We had to plan in a much more structured way than when it was just him working.

(Couple with two children under seven years old)

This woman's return to the workforce meant that there was a need to reorganize and rework everyday patterns. The couple needed to call each other more often to coordinate activities, and there was more driving here and there with the children. It seems that access to the second car was an element that facilitated the wife's return to the working world. It provided a type of cushion in the planning of various activities.

One finds some of the same themes in the comments of another family with two children, both of whom were still in day care at the time of the interview.

> **William (36):** We bought our second car not too long ago.
> **Interviewer:** What were the consequences of that?
> **Jorid (32):** We have more time in the morning for example and...it made it easier for me to go food shopping. Before it was on the way home from work and that was difficult. We save a lot of time and I feel that I am more flexible in some ways when I have my own car.
> **Interviewer:** Have there been any changes that have resulted from that?
> **William:** For example, you do more like practical things in daily life, you get more time.
> **Jorid:** Yeah, for example, so you can make a quick trip to the post office or some other small errand that you need to do, it is suddenly much easier.
> **William:** And it means that I do less.
> **Jorid:** Or that he doesn't have to do all these small things on Saturday.

(Couple with two children under seven years of age)

As with the previous couple, the use of a second automobile helps in completing all the tasks that arise in the course of the day. The man commutes sixty kilometers each day, and the woman works four kilometers from their home. The fact that each has a car provides certain efficiency. The wife reports being able to attend to various geographically distributed tasks that otherwise would have to wait.

Maintenance of the Emotional Balance

Up to this point we have been generally discussing the instrumental activities of the family and the ways in which various technologies play into their completion. Beyond these types of activities, there is also a need to maintain an emotional balance within the family and between the partners. Indeed, this is an aspect of the general maintenance of social order.

The stress of everyday life can provide challenges to the emotional balance of the family. The following quotation came in the context of how stressful daily life can be. The woman, who works full time and who has two "day care" children, speaks of how the stresses of daily life can have consequences for the maintenance of a relationship.

> **Toril (44):** That about being burnt out and all that. I cannot see that you get status for that.
> **Bjørn (40):** I have worked as a personnel leader for five years. I have seen a lot of that and I have seen it directly. We both work a lot. I wound up with a hundred hours of overtime. I like to work such that I have some highs and some lows. I like to have a little pressure, not because it is status, but because that is how it always has been. When I am in between projects, I feel a little empty.
> **Toril:** I don't see that you get status by being busy. I think that more and more people want to have free time and more time for their children. There are many who slide away from each other because they don't have time together.
> **Bjørn:** But I think that it is difficult to come out of a situation with a conscious decision.
> **Toril:** You have responsibilities also. It is difficult to suddenly one day . . .
> **Bjørn:** I hear a lot about people that are pushed into jobs that they actually don't want.
>
> *(Couple with two children aged ten and thirteen)*

In this context, the potential for universal and omnipresent communication can contribute to the stress. One is never really free from telephonic intrusions. However, the very omnipresence of mobile telephones also means that there are various gaps in daily life that can be used just for the maintenance of the emotional balance. The mobile telephone was mentioned as a way to help avoid worrying about other family members who were out and about. It is used to tie together the social network and it is used, in some cases, to repair small spats that had arisen between the couple. With reference to the first of these, one woman describes how she uses the mobile telephone to calm herself when her husband is away.

Marianne (36): We don't use it to check where the other is, generally we know that, like only between us, even though I called yesterday since I was curious when he hadn't come at the time he said he would. Generally I call if it will be later than he has said or to know where he is, so it is to calm myself because I have trouble sleeping before I know that he is OK, you know. So sometimes I use it as a type of control, just so that you are OK. Then I can sleep. That is the way it is if somebody is out late to in some way say that everything is OK.

(Mother in an intact family with a four- and a six-year-old child)

A second theme, one that was surprisingly common, was that the interviewees describe the practice of having what Norwegians call a *hyggeprat*, or a good chat. This type of interaction, usually between family members, was seen as a common activity when one was not otherwise occupied with demanding tasks.

Interestingly, these types of conversations were common while driving. This type of use was not only to microcoordinate the tasks facing the couple, but also to simply have a good chat. Many of the interviewees reported using the car as a type of portable telephone booth wherein they could have an expressive conversation with their partner, or perhaps another member of their social network. While the dangers of driving and talking on the phone are well documented (Burnes et al. 2002; Cain and Burris 1999; Recarte and Nunes 2000; Redelmeier and Tibshirani 1997; Strayer and Johnston 2001; Strayer et al. 2003), the impulse to use what is seen as otherwise unused time for the emotional maintance of one's social sphere seems to be quite strong. Indeed, this concept was discussed in five of the ten intact families as well as several of the divorced or separated interviewees. Many of the interviewees reported *hyggeprat* while driving back and forth to work. It fits into the idea that sitting in the car is empty time that allows one to engage in other activities. This open space is a good time to contact one's partner or other person in the intimate sphere for simple chatting and social interaction. It is an arena in which one can maintain the emotional elements of a relationship. In this way the mobile telephone provides a new communications channel and the opportunity to exploit what Leopoldina Fortunati calls the "folds" of daily life in order to interact with significant others. In the words of one couple:

Toril (44): [...] I generally don't call so much in the afternoon. I don't call from the home (land line) telephone in the afternoon. Sometimes I call my mom or dad when I am in the car on the way home. That is not every day but sometimes, on the way home in the car, since I am sitting quietly and I have time to think . . .
Bjørn (40): It is often on the way home that you make calls...It is pretty common. That is the only time that you have.
Toril: It isn't every day, but you think of a friend that you haven't talked to. It is strange that you call a friend on the way home from work.
Interviewer: Is it a new trend?
Toril: When you come home there are so many other things that happen. Dinner, homework. To sit down and call friends is a real

effort. In addition, I have a half-hour commute. You don't call on the
way to work, but on the way home, when you know that they have
come home.

(Intact couple with a ten- and a thirteen-year-old child)

The telephone, for course, has a long history of facilitating expressive interaction.
Teens have flirted, lovers have courted, and couples have maintained their relationships
over the telephone almost as long as the device has been available (Fischer 1992). In
addition, friends have kept up and deepened friendships at least partially via the
telephone. However, it seems that the mobile telephone has opened up a new area in
which this can take place. To play on Fortunati, it is a new fold in our daily lives that is
being used for social interaction. In other work it has come out that the mobile phone
has been used in the car to deal with small instrumental tasks such as making dentist
appointments and the like (Ling 2004b). The sense that comes out in the comments here
is that it is also used for more expressive tasks. The couple describes the use of the time
in the car as a type of open space in which they can call friends and do some of the work
associated with maintenance of their social networks. The time used to commute is seen
as a period of free time during the day.

Robert (33): When you are sitting in the car, with the hands-free in
your ear, it is easy to chat [with friends].
Interviewer: Do you also call more to friends?
Inger (34): I don't call so much at home. It is more when driving to
and from work in the car. Actually a lot in the car. I call my sister,
friends, parents.
Interviewer: What do you usually talk about?
Inger: It is about daily life. How we are doing right then and there.
Interviewer: Pleasant conversations?
Inger: Yeah.
Interviewer: The conversation you had with your mother, can you
summarize that for me?
Robert: It was a pleasant conversation while I was on my way
home. After thirteen kilometers we ended the call. It was just
"Hello, how are you?" and "Why didn't you take the phone when I
called earlier in the week?"

(Intact family with a nine- and a five-year-old child)

Another couple described how the mobile telephone in the car provided the opportunity for a good chat and also made the time of driving go more quickly.

Interviewer: Do you call to family and friends?
Tron (36): It is usually friends...I talk on the telephone on the way
home. I talk not only with you (to wife) and not just to make agree-
ments, but just to have a nice talk.
Tina (39): Wasting time!
Tron: Yes...(laughs)
Tina: You have one friend you usually call.

Tron: Yeah, he calls all the time.
Tina: He calls on the way home from work…and he calls, and he talks and talks all the way from Oslo to Ski (approximately forty kilometers). (laughs)

(Intact couple with a six- and a nine-year-old child)

Beyond simple maintenance of relationships, it seems that the combination of mobile telephony and the private space afforded by a car allows other types of repair work for partners. In the following example, the couple seems to have had a small disagreement.

Interviewer: Your log book says you had a mobile call in the car in Lommedalen?
Robert (33): I could have written mobile callback…I have thought to admit that, OK!
Inger (34): Oh, you called? Today. You!
Robert: You don't remember that? You have not written it down [in your log book]?
Interviewer: That was at?
Robert: About quarter to 10.
Inger: That is right. It was an apology. Sorry… (laughs)
Interviewer: SMS or a conversation?
Robert: I have a free telephone so I don't bother sending SMS, I call.
Interviewer: From Lommedalen?
Robert: Yeah.
Inger: …Say "I am sorry."
Robert: No, I wrote to say "hi."
Inger: Also to agree, it was an agreement conversation.
Interviewer: Did it lead to anything?[7]
Inger: No.
Robert: Yes, that we were both happy!

(Intact family with a five- and a nine-year-old child)

As the sequence develops, the reader sees that the man had used the opportunity of driving in his car to call his partner and to smooth over a disagreement they had had. It is interesting in that it takes place in the car and it involves the use of the mobile telephone. The car provides a type of mobile telephone kiosk, and the mobile means that he can actually employ the time in a secure private sphere to deal with an issue that is slightly touchy. It would be more difficult to do this at work, where others might hear or at a telephone booth that is partially open.

Conclusion

This chapter started by dealing with the broader question of social organization. Within this broader issue I have focused on the more specific issue of familial interaction. The point of departure here is the idea that the family provides one with a well-crystallized social arena. Particularly after the arrival of children, the family often represents a basic realm in our social orientation.

Indeed, the family is often the resource that we draw on when storms seem to be raging in other parts of our lives. It is an area where we can draw on both instrumental and expressive reserves. For many people this is the center of the nomos, and its dissolution means that we need to strive to reestablish these points of orientation in other ways.

There are norms and rituals associated with the maintenance of the family. The intense and close nature of the family means that these are perhaps more elaborated and internalized than in other social groups. Indeed, couples seemingly speak with one voice in some instances.

This is not to say that the coupled identity is inflexible. On the contrary, there seems to be a willingness for flexibility among the interviewees. They report on how they have developed a common understanding of what the familial context will include, and general notions as to how they—or their partner—can fulfill these needs. There are more or less ritualized interactions and ways of dealing with the needs of the family. The partners fill in for each other in a more or less elegant pas de deux, in which one partner makes dinner or washes up while the other drives the oldest child to a birthday party and will return in order to help the younger child with his or her homework, or to put away the laundry. Each of them draws on a stock of routines that attend to the ongoing needs of the family. By making the mashed potatoes in just a certain way, or by folding the underwear and placing it in a particular corner of the drawer, the individuals are celebrating the coupled identity in some small way while at the same time contributing to its massiveness.

These issues are not new. The things that are new, perhaps, are the technologies that we use in order to support the broader goal of nomos. The interviews quoted here describe how the second car is often seen as a way to facilitate the daily chores, because it buys time and flexibility. It allows one partner to do small tasks such as shopping and the ferrying of kids in the broader urban landscape while the other commutes to a job that may be on the other side of the city. The mobile telephone is seen as a way to microcoordinate the interactions between the partners on the fly as various exigencies arise. It allows the partners to know when they should come or where it is most convenient to meet (Ling and Yttri 2002). These technologies assist the couple in their daily activities.[8] The technology is a tool that affords flexibility in the couple's routines.

The technologies also seemingly give the individuals the space for the expressive maintenance of their lives. The talk on the telephone is not just "what kind of cheese do we need from the grocery store." It also allows the individuals to talk about daily life with each other and with members of their social sphere. The interesting twist here is that the automobile has become today's phone booth, only we don't have to limit our conversations because of another insistent person who needs to make a call.

Thus, we are playing out our interactions through the use of a repertoire of ritual and institutional devices. We balance between discord and order. The interaction can be more or less elaborate, but we rely on collectively developed and understood ritual strategies to maintain the social order within the encounter.

Notes

1 Among the ten intact families, the men commute a longer distance than the women, 29.9 kilometers versus 20.1 kilometers. Interestingly, among the separated interviewees the women commute a slightly longer distance to work than do the men. In this case the women commute 9.1 kilometers versus the men's 7.7 kilometers. The differences between groups do not appear to be statistically significant in either case.

2 Marital status of the interviewees include both married, cohabiting, or, as in one case, a "reconstituted" family. According to Statistics Norway, approximately 15 percent of adults between the ages of twenty and seventy-nine are cohabiting, 51 percent are married, and 34 percent are living alone. The data material also included fifteen interviews with divorced or "place separated" families that are described in other material produced by the project (Hjorthol et al. 2004; Ling 2004a). In five of the couples, each of the partners was interviewed individually. The distributed sample consisted of nine women and six men.

3 I use "married" couples out of literary convenience here. Many of the couples in the study were cohabiting. This is a relatively common familial form in Norway. According to Statistics Norway, approximately 40 percent of children are born to parents who are cohabiting but not married (SSB 2004).

4 When a relationship ends, this structure needs to be dismantled. In many respects it is the opposite process; that is, the replacement of an individual identity where a coupled identity was previously in place (Vaughn 1983).

5 This is not to say that the tasks in the home are equally shared. Many studies have shown that women are often the ones who spend the most time doing housework. In 2000, women in Norway reported using slightly more than three and a half hours per day, as opposed to men, who used just over two and a half, for housework (SSB 2001).

6 In Norway, there is a universal one-year maternity leave of absence that can be divided between the mother and father. In this case it seems that the family extended this period somewhat using private means to finance the mother's staying at home with the younger child.

7 The specific question was as to whether it led to any new trips, but the woman is willfully misinterpreting the question.

8 This is not to say, of course, that they are socially neutral. The car pollutes and the mobile telephone can also "pollute" the public sphere with seemingly inane conversations.

References

Beck, U. (1994). "The reinvention of politics: Towards a theory of reflexive modernization." In U. Beck et al. (Eds.), *Reflexive modernization: Politics, tradition, and aesthetics in the modern social order.* Cambridge, UK: Polity.

Beck, U., and E. Beck-Gernsheim. (2002). *Individualization: Institutionalized individualism and its social and political consequences.* London: Sage.

Berger, P., and H. Kellner. (1964). "Marriage and the construction of reality." *Diogenes* 45: 1–25.

Berger, P., and T. Luckmann. (1967). *The social construction of reality: A treatise in the sociology of knowledge.* New York: Anchor.

Burnes, P. C., et al. (2002). "How dangerous is driving with a mobile phone? Benchmarking the impairment of alcohol." Transport research laboratory, Crowthorne.

Cain, A., and M. Burris. (1999). "Investigation of the use of mobile phones while driving." vol. 2003: Tampa: Center for Urban Transportation Research, University of South Florida.

Duncan, H. D. (1970). *Communication and the social order*. London: Oxford.

Durkheim, E. (1997). *The division of labor in society*. New York: Free Press.

Fischer, C. (1992). *America calling: A social history of the telephone to 1940*. Berkeley: University of California Press.

Giddens, A. (1994). "Living in a post-traditional society." In U. Beck et al. (Eds.), *Reflexive modernization: Politics, tradition, and aesthetics in the modern social order*. Cambridge: Polity.

Hjorthol, R.J., et al. (2004). "Virtuell og fysisk mobilitet i hverdagslivets organisering: En studie av samspill mellom ikt og transport blant barnefamilier i Oslo-området." TØI, Oslo.

Lash, S. (1994). "Reflexivity and its doubles: Structure, aesthetics, and community." In U. Beck et al. (Eds.), *Reflexive modernization: Politics, tradition, and aesthetics in the modern social order*. Cambridge, UK: Polity.

Ling, R. (2004a). "'I have a free telephone so I don't bother to send SMS, I call": The gendered use of SMS among adults in intact and divorced families." In J. Höflich (Ed.), *Qualitative analysis of mobile communication*. Erfurt, Germany: Universität Erfurt.

Ling, R. (2004b). *The mobile connection: The cell phone's impact on society*. San Francisco: Morgan Kaufmann.

Ling, R. (2004c). "Where is mobile communication causing social change?" In S. D. Kim (Ed.), *Mobile communication and social change* Seoul: Hallym University.

Ling, R. (Ed.). (2004d). "Report of literature and data review, including conceptual framework and implications for IST." EU, Brussels.

Ling, R., and B. Yttri. (2002). "Hyper-coordination via mobile phones in Norway." In J. E. Katz and M. Aakhus (Eds.), *Perpetual contact: Mobile communication, private talk, public performance*. Cambridge, UK: Cambridge University Press.

Portes, A. (1998). "Social capital: Its origins and applications in modern sociology." *Annual Review of Sociology* 24: 1–24.

Recarte, M. A., and L. M. Nunes. (2000). "Effects of verbal and spatial-imagery tasks on eye fixations while driving." *Journal of Experimental Psychology: Applied* 6: 31–43.

Redelmeier, D. A., and R. J. Tibshirani. (1997). "Association between cellular-telephone calls and motor vehicle collisions." *New England Journal of Medicine* 336: 453–58.

Sennett, R. (1998). *The corrosion of character: The personal consequences of work in the new capitalism*. New York: Norton.

Simmel, G. (1910–11). "How is society possible?" *American Journal of Sociology* 16: 372–91.

Statistisksentral Byrå (Statistics Norway). (2001). "Tidsbruk til ulike aktiviteter blant personer 9-79 år, alle og etter kjønn og alder. Tidsbruk blant alle og andel som har utført aktiviteten. 2000." Oslo: SSB

Statistisksentral Byrå (Statistics Norway). (2004). "Å gjete kongens harer." Oslo: SSB.

Strayer, D., and W. A. Johnston. (2001). "Driven to distraction: Dual-task studies of simulated driving and conversing on a cellular telephone." *Psychological Science* 12: 462–66.

Strayer, D., et al. (2003). "Cell phone induced failures of visual attention during simulated driving." *Journal of Experimental Psychology*: Applied 9: 23-32.

Vaughn, D. (1983). "Uncoupling: The social construction of divorce." In H. Robby and C. Clark (Eds.), *Social interaction* (pp. 405–422). New York: St. Martins.

Tsunami Mobilizations: Considering the Role of Mobile and Digital Communication Devices, Citizen Journalism, and the Mass Media

Wendy Robinson and David Robison

Introduction: 'Citizen Journalism' via Mobile Communication Devices

Like many people across the world, I was transfixed by the mainstream news during the 2004 holiday season. I watched as the enormity of the Sumatra-Andaman earthquake and tsunami disaster unfolded. Every day the casualty count rose and receding waters revealed still more affected areas. From the standpoint of media research, I was struck by the fact that the news did not directly come from and was not wholly controlled by the "media giants" (Croteau and Hoynes 2003), the conglomerates that own most U.S. mass media. The reporting instead came from the proverbial man in the street, residents and tourists, as well as local reporters who operated outside the Western mainstream media.

They gathered and shared news through mobile gear, and sent information on the go (for example, from shops with Internet or wireless access). Survivors' tales were related via e-mail, mobile texting, and digital cameras. Vacationers phoned in from cellphones and transmitted images through cellphone cameras and attached e-mail files. Locals and amateurs captured stories and remarkable video with camcorders. Bloggers and rescue workers published online on a regular basis, establishing Internet-based missing persons' networks. Ten days after the earthquake struck, a reporter with the *Straits Times* in Singapore, Shefali Srinivas (2005), discussed where the news of 12/26 was coming from:

> The answers [regarding the tsunami have been] in text messages, jerky amateur footage and online. Everyday technologies like digital cameras, mobile phones and weblogs have become the source of riveting accounts of survivors all the way from Aceh, Indonesia—the epicentre of the quake—to the ravaged coastal towns of Thailand,

Malaysia, Sri Lanka, India and the Andaman and Nicobar islands. . . .

For the first time, hundreds of ordinary people produced powerful coverage of a huge news event, along with traditional media. This army of citizen journalists continues to grow, connecting those who want to help with those who need it.

The efforts of ordinary "citizen journalists" were first noticeable during and after 9/11. It was thought then that this type of informal reporting and publishing primarily took place in the northeastern United States—although 9/11, like the tsunami disaster, was of international scope. Late 2001 marked a moment of change for the cross-cultural practices of newsgathering, signified by average people who carried ordinary portable electronic equipment but were able to cover important news stories before, alongside, and after the professionals. Three years later and oceans away, far from the home base of the mainstream news and political interests that resoundingly sought to own 9/11 (McChesney 2002), 12/26 signifies an important moment of change in the ways that news is gathered, reported, and disseminated through mobile communication devices. Writing for the Poynter Institute, columnist Steve Outing (2005a) said:

The earthquake and tsunamis in South Asia and their aftermath represent a tipping point in so-called "citizen journalism." What September 11, 2001, was to setting off the growth and enhanced reputation of blogs, the December 2004 tsunamis are to the larger notion of citizen journalism (of which blogs are a part).

If you think about it, this worst natural disaster in a lifetime is an amazing media story. (And that's not to discount the horrible human tragedy of it, only to focus here on the media angle.) . . . What's amazing is how many of the people who experienced and survived the disaster—spread across several countries and thousands of miles—were able to share their heart-wrenching stories, photographs, and videos with the rest of the world.

Digital technologies—the Web, e-mail, blogs, digital cameras, camera phones—have evolved to the point where people on the scene share with professional journalists the ability to reach a wide audience. . . . Where once disaster eyewitness photographs and videos turned up for widespread viewing only on news programs and in newspapers, today [the electronic mobile ad hoc] infrastructure . . . spreads amateur news quickly and efficiently, they often find large audiences without the help or need of mainstream news outlets.

This chapter similarly is concerned with post-9/11 citizen journalism and disaster eyewitnesses who take news reporting into their own hands, such as through mobile and wireless devices, and through on-the-go electronic and networked access, with emphasis on the former. Likely operating independently of mainstream news outlets, nevertheless the outlets may rely on their efforts. The events of 12/26 offer an opportunity to foreground the shifting practices of citizen journalism taking place outside and within the West.

This chapter focuses on: (1) the use of mobile and digital communication devices for information gathering and dissemination during the tsunami crisis; (2) mobile device–enabled eyewitness testimony and credibility as contrasted with and as relied on by the traditional mass media with its deep pockets and established resources; (3) assumptions about encroaching electronic surveillance and creeping westernization to explore some implications of mobile development within the tsunami-affected regions; and (4) woven throughout, beyond its natural causes, 12/26 compared with other recent politically and technologically disruptive events, significant for mobile device–enabled newsgathering and significant because the mobilizing events cut across technologies, politics, individuals, and institutions. I specifically compare the media coverage of 12/26 with that of 9/11 and the exposé of prison abuse in Iraq. I conclude with thoughts on 12/26 as a "tipping point" for citizen journalism, on some challenges that may complicate the relationship between citizen journalists and the mass media, and on the mass media's treatment of the tsunami.

Background: Sumatra-Andaman Earthquake and Indian Ocean Tsunami

On December 26, 2004, a greater than 9.1-magnitude earthquake, lasting nearly ten minutes, struck at approximately 7 a.m. EST (0000 GMT). The epicenter was one hundred miles from the western coast of Indonesia's Sumatra island. The quake triggered powerful tsunami waves that rolled imperceptibly below the surface of the Indian Ocean. On the quiet Boxing Day morning, a Sunday, tourists from around the world and local residents enjoyed the tropical beaches and weather. There was no tsunami warning system—although some people in areas later affected received warnings via telephone and e-mail, on an individual basis, from those struck earlier. The tsunami arrived so stealthily and with such velocity that people were swept off their feet, conversations were interrupted in midsentence, and people with cameras were swiftly overcome while photographing the shoreline that receded before the arrival of the first wave (KATC3.com 2005). "All of a sudden you could hear the water coming in. It sounded like a hundred jets," Berkeley, California, resident Sandi Thompson, who caught the impact of the waves on her Thai resort on videotape, said (CBS5.com 2005, ¶¶ 1–3). Although the waves directly affected twelve countries on two continents and a subcontinent that border the Indian Ocean, due to its severity the quake and waves were felt across the globe. Casualties approached 250,000, of which nearly one third were children.

The fourth largest earthquake since 1899 (according to NPR's *All Things Considered*, perhaps the second largest; Joyce 2005) brought about the greatest loss of life from a tsunami in modern times. In deep water, the waves traveled at three hundred to six hundred miles per hour and took ninety minutes to two hours to recede (Wikipedia). In some locations, the waves were described as "rising to at least the second floor of buildings" (Associated Press 2005a), reaching one hundred feet high in Aceh (Wikipedia). Although aid from around the world arrived relatively quickly and the tourism industry quickly set out to rebound, it will take years to rebuild, at astronomical expense. The enormous human toll of the event, and its socioeconomic and geologic significance, make the story of the tsunami and its survivors "a huge news event" and "an amazing media story," as Srinivas (2005) and Outing (2005a) note.

But bureaucracies sometimes move slower than tsunamis. Like other large organizations, television networks and newspapers have systems in place to ensure regularity. The natural disaster hit during what generally is a "slow news" week of top ten lists, reruns, and family fare. The holiday period from Christmas to New Year's is the one sustained break during the fiercely competitive twenty-four-hour news cycle, a time to regroup and make changes for the coming year. Media organizations function with skeleton crews, saving money during the last week of the fourth quarter. Staff members take time off. The Internet, however, and those who interact with it through electronic devices, never sleep. The news broke online shortly after the first waves struck. People affected by the tsunami were informally reporting from cellphones within an hour.

The media giants had been caught with their collective guard down during the annual nadir of the business cycle. Citizen correspondents, who could sprint, who were more adaptable, who traveled lighter, who needed less, soon would outrun the dinosaurs. Some citizen journalists had the advantage of already being there, on the other side of the world. They were able to gather and record the emerging news through portable gear available to almost anyone. In the developing world, a sizable market exists for secondhand and inexpensive disposable cellphones and digital cameras, which means that cost and size need not be deterrents (Critical Friends of Technology 2003). Like digital cameras, use of cellphones does not require knowledge of English or QWERTY, and the devices are gender- and age-neutral. Cellphone users can communicate in their own language, speaking immediately, without having to learn anything new for basic functionality.

Within a half-day, the BBC, CNN, *New York Times,* and wire services were the first major news organizations to respond to the event. In the United States, there was some coverage on the evening news and in newspapers the next day. Given the global breadth of CNN's resources, its television journalists nearby on vacation, such as Dr. Sanjay Gupta, could be summoned to work, and personnel from regional news offices, such as Christiane Amanpour, the cable network's chief international correspondent, who often is on assignment in the Mideast, could be dispatched.

But these established professionals and their organizations had been scooped by bloggers and other citizen journalists who used spontaneous mobile, networked infor-mation to share the news as it happened—and to which the mainstream news sources turned to complement and bolster their coverage. Through the last days of December 2004 and into January 2005, the borrowing and repurposing could be seen on the news organizations' websites, Yahoo!, and elsewhere through links to and cited eyewitness reports, photographs, and video. Clips were provided by citizen journalists, who sometimes sold their work without necessarily receiving a byline or acknowledgment unless he or she became part of the story (Glaser 2005). Online and in print, URLs were provided to blogs, such as to the South-East Asia Earthquake and Tsunami Blog (2004–5) that was up and running within hours (Associated Press 2004; Coren 2005; Schwartz 2004a). Srinivas (2005) writes, "Mainstream news organisations also set up pages to document the first-hand accounts that were pouring in. By the end of the first week, the BBC Online Web site, which dedicated an entire page to first-person e-mail accounts of the disaster, had received about 50,000 e-mails. Its message board saw over 400,000 visitors." During broadcasts, people in the Indian Ocean area called in through cellphones. Tourists and residents located online access, such as cybercafés, through which to send messages back home and to post descriptions of their ordeals. Their help was essential to the professional media back home, since the devastation produced logis-tical challenges to flying in correspondents.

The dependence on amateur and eyewitness news reporting, enabled by personal electronic devices and the Internet, had been developing incrementally since 9/11. But 12/26 marks a much greater degree of reliance on bottom-up, digital- and mobile-enabled reporting by the mainstream media, and a much greater assumption that the bottom-up service was there for the taking. New media no longer was a bright shiny object to wave as proof of keeping up with the times. Most advantageously from news management's perspective, most of the on-site reporting was provided for free or at low cost, there for the framing. The media giants regained and reestablished their disaster-coverage credibility by piggybacking on the efforts of amateurs, who acted on their own, bore witness, and disseminated news during of the heat of the moment. Citizen journalists acted in a spirit of cooperation, wanting to help, volunteering out of personal conviction, and for other reasons. For the media giants, on the other hand, news is business. However much they worked in unequal accord to share news of 12/26, the objectives of citizen and professional journalists differed.

On-the-Scene Device-Enabled Reporting: Smooth Transitions and Disruptions

Little disruption to newsgathering occurs when a cellphone is grabbed instead of a land line phone, or text messaging, a PDA, or wireless access is used instead of e-mail from a desktop computer, or, to go low-tech, instead of simply picking up pen and paper. The tools are just one factor. Differences come when reporting and transmission take place remotely, away from the news bureau or forms of censorship. For more than 150 years, war photographs, for instance, have served as witness testimony (for example, in the Crimean War and the American Civil War), and the printed word has been sent via wire services. The Daguerreotype and telegraph, however, required specialist skills and equipment; they were not personal technologies. But in the early twenty-first century, reporting from the field takes place with greatly enhanced ease. So great is the ease and so low are the barriers to entry that the widespread use of mobile devices within the traditional news reporting system is taken for granted in many parts of the world.

For instance, it is unthinkable today that Western reporters on assignment would not carry cellphones, probably with integrated cameras, along with laptops and other wireless personal gear. For years within broadcast media, the separation between those who write and those who shoot video has been dissolving. Discussing the broadcast coverage and downsizing that came before 12/26, *Denver Post* television commentator Joanne Ostrow (2005) writes, "CNN . . . caught a break . . . [having] invested heavily in video news phones (16 are in use in the affected region) to produce instant pictures." Since the downsizing of news organizations—partially enabled through the availability of smaller, lighter, converged consumer electronics devices—there has been increasing reliance on content provided by amateurs or local professionals working outside the mainstream. These individuals sometimes risk life and limb and that of their families to capture stories.

For example, Bedu Saini, a photographer in Banda Aceh, Indonesia, who works for the local daily *Serambi*, captured the incoming waves and destruction that washed away most of the city and its population. His eyewitness shots were carried by the Associated Press (2005b) and disseminated across the world with captions in many languages. Putting his camera down, he left to find out what happened to his relatives, later discovering that much of his personal news was unfortunate. A few days later, his camera was found and returned to him. Saini's work was saved, thereby documenting what had happened in one of the hardest hit areas. He was referred to by name in the filed AP news report because his survivor story had interest, although often when mainstream news organizations picked up the report, he was identified incorrectly as an amateur.

Similarly, a cameraman named Hasyim, who normally shoots weddings in Aceh, began videotaping immediately after the earthquake, capturing people milling about the rubble, unaware that a sea surge was headed directly at them (Associated Press 2005a). He told the AP that fifteen to twenty minutes later the wall of water hit with such force, carrying so much debris, that the water could hardly be seen. He taped from atop a domed mosque, but nevertheless the water almost touched his feet.

Elaine Young, a colleague of Srinivas's (2005, ¶ 28) at the *Straits Times,* who "was on holiday near Phi-Phi Island with her husband James when the tsunami struck . . . survived only because they were able to clamber up the side of a hill as waves engulfed the beach." Managing to get back to her hotel in Phuket, Thailand, eight hours later, she

> found a computer with an internet connection that was still working in a lobby at her hotel. "I just sat down and wrote what happened. Everything was so fresh in my head and James was helping me along. I was really stressed though and kept shouting at him to just let me concentrate. . . . There were all these people behind me who were waiting to use the computer," she said. Young's story—the story of a survivor, not a journalist—made it into the next morning's newspaper. (Srinivas 2005, ¶ 29)

The evolving use of citizen and multiracial journalism to cover 12/26, which anyone could recognize as a major news story, comes in sharp contrast to the disruption caused by the revelation of U.S. prison abuse in Iraq. News was leaked partially because images were captured with digital and cellphone cameras and through soldiers corresponding with friends and family members on e-mail. Soldiers sent photos as attached files, and notoriously shot several video journals, ran webcams, and kept written diaries. In one of her last important articles, Susan Sontag (2004, ¶ 2) wrote:

> The pictures taken by American soldiers in Abu Ghraib reflect a shift in the use made of pictures—less objects to be saved than messages to be disseminated, circulated. Most soldiers possess a digital camera. Where once photographing war was the province of photo-journalists, now the soldiers themselves are all photographers—recording the war, their fun, their observations of what they find picturesque, their atrocities—and swapping images among themselves, and e-mailing them around the globe. There is more and more recording of what people do, by themselves. . . . And one wonders how much of the sexual tortures inflicted on the inmates . . . was inspired by the vast repertory of pornographic imagery available on the internet, and which ordinary people now webcasting themselves attempt to emulate.

Collecting the images for their own purposes, the soldiers—men and women—unwittingly became citizen journalists who documented torture in which, in some cases, the photographer or videographer was complicit. Apparently the abuses were well known within the armed forces; they took place at other military installations, such as Guantánamo Bay, in Cuba. The mistreatment of prisoners was not the work of marginal elements as later claimed by President Bush (Hersh 2004; Sontag 2004). Since the interrogation methods were common knowledge, apparently there was not a clear sense on the part of those who leaked the story, later picked up by CBS's 60 *Minutes*, that the tortures were newsworthy. Nevertheless, the mainstream news followed the lead of inadvertent reporters: troop members and their families who used mobile devices and who accessed the Internet, who shared images among themselves.

After the infamous images from the Abu Ghraib prison were shared across the world, Defense Secretary Rumsfeld called for the confiscation of cellphone and other digital cameras, which were then banned from all U.S. Army installations in Iraq (Hersh 2004; Sontag 2004). "It's hard to censor soldiers overseas who don't write letters home, as in the old days, that can be opened by military censors who ink out unacceptable lines, but, instead, function as tourists," Sontag wrote (2004). Citing Rumsfeld, she continued, they've been "'running around with digital cameras and taking these unbelievable photographs and then passing them off, against the law, to the media, to our surprise.'" After their release, the U.S. government sought to classify the compromising images as evidence for criminal prosecution. The military, some legal, and other environments, such as where there is much classified or highly competitive commercial information (for example, celebrity and sports marketing, toy and game manufacturing), are known for disallowing the use of mobile devices, or requiring that the IR ports be covered, in an effort to ensure that information is not surreptitiously exchanged. Therefore, safeguards already have been implemented to impede citizen journalism—although with Abu Ghraib the news leaked out despite governmental containment efforts.

As Outing (2005a) notes, the marked shift in citizen journalism came with 9/11. In the World Trade Center that morning, the situation was dire. When every moment counted, difficult life-or-death decisions were made by people who considered what to take as they fled, literally from burning buildings. Escaping office workers grabbed cellphones, BlackBerries, and similar mobile devices, leaving behind photographs of loved ones, handbags, briefcases, and important documentation (Romero 2001a, 2001b). Their cellphones were deemed indispensable, since they provided a portable means to reach friends and relatives during the crisis. Out on the sidewalk, the devices offered a crucial lifeline, as did air phones in the ill-fated planes (Romero 2001a, 2001b). In the weeks following 9/11, blogging began in earnest, through eyewitness accounts, message boards dedicated to the missing, and Web-based memorials. Although the mainstream news moved swiftly to frame and semiotically contain 9/11 (Carey 2002, pp. 74–75), to some people who received their news online the reputable or trusted journalism—news that had not yet been "hijacked" for various political and marketing purposes (Jhally and Earp 2004)—came from average people bearing witness. They shared their stories, images, and clips on the Internet, available to all at any time, not tied to the business cycles or interests of news organizations.

Setting the precedent more than three years before 12/26, after the collapse of the twin towers, when cellphone and cable television access was spotty in the metropolitan area, people with ties to lower Manhattan turned to the Internet for news. The Internet also was a source used by the mainstream media. As later with 12/26, the efforts of citizen journalists were assimilated, becoming part of the way that information was obtained by virtually all the major news outlets: for example, represented through amateur photographs of the planes' impact, the raging fire, the wounded skyline, the collapse of the buildings, and panic on the narrow streets, followed by ash and destruction. Iconic images and clips since, their testimony has become part of the public record and cultural memory of 9/11 (Zelizer 2002, pp. 63–64).

Also as with 12/26, the content generally was provided with no or small commercial compensation to bloggers, average people with camcorders and cameras, and other citizen journalists. While in many cases it would be inappropriate to pay for the use of the material, there are costs—such as for server space and access fees—that can spiral upward when there is a surge of interest. Server activity sharply increases after a link is provided from a major news website. After 9/11 all the major U.S. networks displayed banners carried over from television, such as "America under Siege" or "America Strikes Back" (Schudson 2002, p. 43). Information provided by citizen journalists may not be wholly in the public domain, although it is often treated that way, amateur conflated with anonymous. Or, given the exigency of the moment, a major news source's online publishing staff may link first, perhaps asking permission later. The links probably are appreciated, though incidental costs are not.

In this light, it should be remembered that am press reaped significant benefits from 9/11 coverage in the form of branding, market share, and journalism awards, which translated into financial gain and expanded influence. For several months afterward, the major television networks reestablished their relevance and gained governmental favor. They repeatedly aired 9/11 footage, and still find occasions to repurpose the content. It is unlikely that for-profit considerations and political connections, however, had the same importance for citizen journalists, since they are not accountable to corporate interests in anything approaching the same degree, nor do they have equivalent clout. Their and the traditional media's stories and images have been used in exploitative ways, and there are always disreputable elements in both traditional and new media, but it stands to reason that there generally was less exploitation on the part of individuals working alone on news stories during the fall of 2001 and the winter of 2004–5.

Rousing the Sleeping Giants

Despite the correlations, there are important ways in which citizen journalism and mainstream news coverage of the Sumatra-Andaman earthquake and resultant tsunami differ from 9/11 and the Iraq prison abuse scandal. First of all, in the case of 9/11, offices or headquarters for much of the mainstream news and wire services are located only a few blocks uptown from Wall Street, and their Washington bureaus are located not far from the Pentagon. As James W. Carey (2002, p. 71) brought out, the helicopters that reported morning traffic in New York City were sent to the scene immediately, providing television and radio coverage of the second plane's collision at eye level. Events unfolded close to home, often with direct personal involvement on the part of news personnel.

But with 12/26, events took place halfway across the world from those same news organizations, during the slow holiday week. The situation was not shaped by the American mainstream media and could not be. The mainstream media fumbled and lost the opportunity to capture the most significant geologic disaster likely to strike in most contemporary lifetimes. Assistant editor of the *Guardian Unlimited* Neil McIntosh refers to a "'growing army of citizen journalists'" who did "'an amazing job in the last nine days'" (Srinivas 2005, ¶ 20): "'It has reported and reassured, breaking the news in words, photographs, sounds and video. Then it moved the story on—at the point much of the mainstream media was only beginning to catch on to the full scale of the disaster—to tell more of the human tale of the tragic aftermath, and help the rest of us donate towards the aid effort,' he said." From the beginning to the end of its cycle as a major news story, the tsunami story largely was told from the point of view of average people with personal electronic equipment.

Secondly, by the time the mainstream media landed in Southeast Asia and nearby locations, the news had gone stale. The "hard news" had been covered by citizen journalists a week to ten days before. The established media elbowed in to own the relatively soft follow-up stories, providing supplementary content for special television programming, newspaper sections, and bannered websites devoted to coverage (for example, CNN's "Turning the Tide" and ABC's "Wave of Destruction"). Reporters sent to cover the tsunami aftermath focused on the plight of orphans, survivor tales (more reliance on eyewitness accounts collected independent of the mainstream media), and Western relief efforts. Not to detract from their human importance, these were not the headline news stories that will be of historic importance. The moment had resoundingly slipped through their fingers, but by God the pros had arrived. Looking very much out of their element, anchors, rising network stars, and their crews set up shop.

ABC's Diane Sawyer volunteered for the assignment. During her five to six days in Thailand, she was reported to have gone without sleep (Shister 2005). Brian Williams manifestly was prompted to use his time in Indonesia to establish himself as Tom Brokaw's replacement at NBC. Having come to prominence at CNN during its 9/11 coverage, Aaron Brown looked distinctly uncomfortable on air in his postcolonial khakis, swatting flies, coping with heat, and otherwise dealing with makeshift conditions and the gritty reality of the situation. The arrival of his younger, hipper colleague at CNN, Anderson Cooper, was delayed because of a prior commitment to host the live New Year's Eve celebrations in New York City, plans for which had been made well in advance and which CNN did not alter in the face of natural disaster. The ratings race with MTV came first, then Cooper was sent to Sri Lanka. Perhaps drawing on his professional experience with juvenile news at Channel One, Cooper was assigned the "Tsunami Disaster: The Children" features that ran for a week online and as broadcast, for which he won a National Headliners Award.

But their sanctioned presences largely were irrelevant, since the news event had long since passed. What was relevant were the stark images and stories the networks aired, often prefaced with warnings about graphic content, obtained from locals and tourists who had genuinely suffered, who had gone through the calamity and recorded their experiences, and who could speak from a first-person perspective.

Thirdly, the tsunami was not photogenic in the way that 9/11 and the shocking images from Abu Ghraib were. As Sontag (2004) pointed out about the Iraq prison photographs of torture and humiliation, the digital cameras and cellphone cameras bore witness. The appetite for disturbing or arresting photographs has been ratcheted up by everyday atrocity, arguably beginning with the Rodney King videos. The continual flow of roughly shot images of terrorism has grown numbingly familiar: for example, news photos of bombings in Madrid and London; images released by the press and online of beheadings, kidnappings, warfare, and other bloodshed in the Mideast; Al-Qaida videos.

Yet there is an assumed appetite for more. Over and over again, reporters from the mainstream press asked leading questions about big waves. Over and over again, those interviewed replied that the waves were more like an enormous crashing splash, followed by a bathtub overflowing. Despite media demand and the paradisiacal setting in better times, there were no images of awesome, curling surfing waves and no witness testimony that described them as living up to cinematic expectation. The tsunami rolled silently along the ocean floor, struck through several waves, swept over everything in its path, looking more like swollen floodwaters than an ocean, and much more slowly retreated, dark with debris and evidence of wounded life.

The devastation did not lack visual interest, but amazing shots of the moment of impact failed to materialize. The locations were muddy and unfamiliar, lacking the resonance of the twin towers and planes or appealing to prurient interest. Before and after near-travelogue shots were provided so that readers and viewers could comprehend the devastation. Nevertheless, the longing for views of enormous waves persisted. Eventually the images were manufactured online, appearing as well-circulated hoaxes (Sreenivasan 2005; Tsunamis.com). Digital photographs had been altered to meet demand. When the fraudulent images were discovered, the mainstream media took the moral high ground, debating the ethics of those rogue Internet publishers and amateurs—who had been the bedrock of serious news reporting during the unfolding crisis, but whose voice was muted after the arrival of mainstream news in early 2005. The desire for the images arguably had been fed through the televisual interests of the professional news organizations. The thirst nevertheless was quenched: the media establishment had its shocking big waves, simultaneous with its shocking story of the spurious credibility of new media sources.

Finally, in order to own the news story and make it visually compelling, an appalling callousness toward non-Western bodies was shown by the mainstream press. The exploitation came in marked contrast with the treatment of 9/11, as observed by Barbie Zelizer (2002, pp. 64–65), for which there was a noted absence of bodies, although people from around the world perished, literally vanishing before our eyes on television. We watched, while simultaneously the major media organizations averted their gaze from the bodies. The World Trade Center came to symbolize and displace the people within (Zelizer 2002, p. 65), the twin towers becoming mythic in the Barthesean sense. Zelizer compared the treatment of 9/11 with bearing witness after the Holocaust sixty years earlier, when piles of bodies appeared in photographs that gained iconic significance (p. 53). The emaciated bodies connoted suffering, toward which the viewer was supposed to feel compassion and pride in Allied liberation, tacitly being promised that such horrors never would be repeated.

The camera's gaze of early 2005 had more in common with 1945 than 2001, but with less empathy. The piles of brown bodies were seen through unflinching Western eyes, in the manner of a closed-circuit camera, rather than as if a compassionate human being were looking through the lens. Comparing the treatment of bodies during 9/11 with 12/26, Ostrow (2005) observes: "Footage of distended bodies being plowed into mass graves testified to the undeniable inequity: Dead foreigners are somehow deemed fit spectacles for the camera, whereas dead Americans are generally off-limits." In the mass pyres and graves of tsunami victims and in the faces of traumatized children, the mass media found the powerful secondary news images that had been sought. The subjects were not European tourists who lost their lives or their families' private grief. Those survivors' tales, particularly the celebrity casualties, were integrated sympathetically within mainstream coverage and received disproportionate attention. When panning the drowned human beings, the visual inventories discreetly avoided white bodies. The wide shots that further objectified the loss of human life were justified on the grounds of capturing the "magnitude of the disaster." In contrast with the blurry or jerky images captured by citizen journalists with low-resolution equipment that bore witness to the initial devastation in late 2004, the funeral bodies of evidence were professionally crisp and clear.

In a neat representative inversion, as the burning towers displaced unseen bodies on 9/11, post-12/26 bodies displaced the unseen tsunami waves for the scooped media giants. And after the images had been captured and the sensational story had been told, the crews packed up. Mainstream reporting on the Indian Ocean disaster pretty much was over, except for some photo ops associated with the fundraising efforts of former U.S. presidents Bush and Clinton, and a tsunami summit attended by heads of state from Japan, the United States, India, and Australia during the winter of 2005. Online, however, there continue to be blogs, regular reports on rebuilding efforts and on the multifarious political ramifications, proposals for a tsunami warning system, and on many other topics, since people from around the world and different walks of life contribute. Recently the six-month anniversary of the earthquake and tsunami was observed quietly by Western media, although it served as an important marker of recovery in Southeast Asia.

Mobilizations: The Weedy West, Mobile Development, and Benighted Neglect

James Rule (2002, pp. 252–54) speaks of "weediness" to describe the incursion of the cellphone into public areas and to connect up its private-public encroachment with expanding Western and corporate interests into most areas of contemporary, globalized life. Mark Andrejevic (2004) draws on the metaphor of reality television and the webcam to discuss the willing surrender of privacy for public consumption, which cooperates with the ceaseless monitoring of marketing and governmental interests. Exploring political and technological mobilization, James Hay and Jeremy Packer (2004) analyze "the mobilization of a citizenry for a 'war on terrorism'" (p. 215), and the role of the "auto-mobile" and "technologies of the self" that include personal, electronic gear (p. 217). Sontag (2004) considered the normalized personal mediation of webcasts, "in which people record their day, each in his or her own reality show," ordinary people empowered to share "unstoppable" snapshots and videos that can partially fill the traditional media's watchdog role, thereby influencing the political process.

These media analysts take the panoptic view to its next logical step of assimilation, extending but not unrecognizably stretching Michel Foucault (1979/1975): citizens cooperate with governmental-commercial interests by using mobile communication (and other electronic mobilizing) devices that are part of a transparent—"wireless," "free," "handsfree," "automatic"—surveillance grid within capitalist society, all that is solid melting into air (Marx and Engels 1983/1848, p. 207). A cellphone is not "just a cellphone"—obviously not, since without a wireless system installed it is nearly useless. Anthropologist Gertrude Stotz (2001) considered the introduction of a Toyota within an aboriginal community in Australia. She wrote that the SUV—which was shared within the Warlpiri community, affecting the community in myriad ways—was "like a Trojan horse: it appears simply to be a vehicle of transport, but actually it is an agent of colonization which allows Western notions . . . to penetrate almost imperceptibly into

Warlpiri society" (2001, p. 236). Technological artifacts as taken for granted as cellphones and cars carry with them considerable Western baggage: from infrastructural, such as the electrical grid, wires, towers, satellites, roads, and gas stations, to socioeconomic, such as finance and credit, globalized cultural use and exchange practices, and a matrix of political and marketing interests. Eventually all technologies result in refuse and bring environmental changes, since nearly all technologies are intended to be disposable (Critical Friends of Technology 2003, "Disposable cell phones" section and "Conventional cell phones and other wireless devices" section).

Generally dismissed as anachronistic, it is for good reason that the Amish of the central United States are cautious about the introduction and use of cellphones (Rheingold 1999), which is in accord with their communal, intentional approach to technology. The Amish culturally resist yet accept limited Western mobilization. The use of personal technologies is political, whether potentially subversive from Sontag's standpoint; hegemonic from the standpoint of Rule, Andrejevic, and Hay and Packer; or cautious, open-eyed, with measured acceptance, with regard to the Amish. No matter what, electronic mobility is not value-neutral; the use of the devices carries an ideological kernel that can germinate and spread like weeds.

It is striking that personal consumer electronics are used around the world, that citizen journalism is not solely a Western phenomenon, and that its actualizing potential is within reach of people in developing areas. Nevertheless, the garden (presupposing a time unsullied by Western imperialism, which has not been true in Southeast Asia for centuries) need not be overrun by weeds. There are surprising moments of counter-hegemony or cultural reinterpretation to be found adjacent to and within the citizen journalism of the tsunami. Globalizing interests are not quite as omnipotent and scary as they would seem to be from a perspective that assumes the media giants, with their alliances and resources, already have won (McChesney 2000, 2003), before agency even can be expressed. A few moments of slippage follow. The slippages represent cultural practices and a moment of omission too below-the-radar even for Western, capitalist hegemony: it seems that there just was not enough at stake in late 2004 to bother—a form of benighted neglect perhaps.

Many countries and cultures within Southeast Asia and beyond were affected by the tsunami, well beyond those commonly mentioned in the press. From a business standpoint, the region is divided into country-based markets and demographic micromarkets, with advertising and subscription plans geared accordingly. Although features and functions vary widely among locations and subcultures, in contrast with Western private ownership and cyclical obsolescence, in some markets there is greater tolerance for older and shared devices. Southeast Asia is a media-rich area that includes multicultural Bollywood, cosmopolitan Singapore, and developing-world labor for electronics engineering and manufacturing that attracts international interest. The tourism industry is important, with many regular visitors traveling from Scandinavia, an area with one of the world's most highly developed cellphone markets (Ling 2004; as is Singapore, where there is nearly 100 percent cellphone penetration), and other parts of Europe and the world. Therefore, some of the affected cultures are not necessarily "backward," and the tsunami devastation was not necessarily monolithic.

The local uses are negotiated, and in some areas are more communal or spiritual than personal or business: for example, cybercafés in India, "telephone ladies" in Bangladeshi villages, "Mecca indicators" on cellphones for Muslims, cellphones given blessings by Buddhist monks (*Economist: Technology Quarterly* 2005; see also Katz and Aakhus 2002; Ling 2004; Nyíri 2003; Plant 2001; Rheingold 2002; see also Campbell, this volume). Additionally, there are considerable differences between neighboring countries because of different penetration rates: for example nine cellphones per one hundred people in Indonesia, compared with twenty-seven per one hundred in the Philippines (*Economist Leaders* 2005), reflecting disparities in capital, wireless access, and other factors.

Cellphones can offer a means for women, the elderly or physically challenged, and the illiterate to earn income, for all the mixed blessings that outside exposure and competition can bring. For example, a poor fisherman can continue the work of generations of his family in the Indian Ocean, with a cellphone on board for business transactions and ship-to-shore information (*Economist: Technology Quarterly* 2005, p. 25). Mobile access could offer considerable beneficial results with less environmental and economic costs than other development solutions (that is, the intrastructure, lifestyle change, and retraining required for manufacture of the deskbound Internet), possibly being able to "leapfrog" over earlier industrial development cycles and their known problems (Critical Friends of Technology 2003, "Developing countries" section).

Citizen journalism is a type of empowerment that Rheingold (2002) calls "the power of the mobile many." Great enough is the area's overall cellphone penetration that the devices have been proposed as the basis of a tsunami warning system, which would rely on ring tone alerts, texting, distributed sirens, or other ways to broadcast warning messages to a disparate populace, including residents and tourists, scaling language, religious, and other cultural barriers (Schwartz 2004b, 2004c). Mobile connectivity already was used in a cooperative way during the 12/26 crisis: for forty-eight hours, mobile calls were free in Sweden and Denmark so that vacationing survivors could reach families (Associated Press 2004), the Czech government sent text messages to close to one hundred missing tourists, and in Italy a mobile phone number was used for donations through text and voice messages (Yahoo! News 2004b), while in Sri Lanka cellphone signal patterns were used to trace missing Britons and workers from Hong Kong (Yahoo! News 2004a). These examples of cross-cultural cooperation suggest further opportunities for positive outcomes, if not without escaping some of the negative effects of Western influence.

Regarding insularity and venerable ways of life, it is worthwhile to consider that among the Southeast Asian residents there are populations of aboriginals. The mainstream news reported on "stone age" cultures that escaped the tsunami's devastation by attending to nature rather than technology. Members of the Jarawa tribe, located on the Andaman and Nicobar islands, watched the movement of birds and fled to the forest, all surviving intact—but later telling an AP cameraman that they would "fall sick if . . . photographed" (CBSNews.com 2005a). A nude member of the Sentinelese tribe of the South Indian archipelago shot an arrow at a U.S. Coast Guard relief helicopter (CBSNews.com 2005c). Known as the "sea gypsies," upon instructions from their village chief a group of Thai fishermen fled to the mountains after seeing the surf recede (CBSNews.com 2005b). Not aboriginal but remote, in southern India Veerapatinam was spared the tsunami's wrath because the temple well behaved strangely before the waves struck, distracting thousands of villagers from the beach that morning (*Economist: Technology Quarterly* 2005, p. 25). These cultures largely are protected by their insularity and the preservationist efforts of friendly government agencies. While in the greater scheme of things the Indian Ocean's aboriginals are incidental, their resilient cultures represent slippage in Western hegemony and its assumed assimilations.

Another slippage truly was so below-the-radar that it escaped attention, yet is as plain as a nose on the global face. Few objective moment-of-impact photographs of the waves crashing ashore exist. Despite the magnitude of the earthquake, seismologists sent out few warnings. Overall, 12/26 had no more aerial monitoring than 9/11. If it exists, where was the all-seeing panoptic gaze? It seems that 12/26 was another "massive failure of intelligence" (Carey 2002, p. 76), and that the media giants were not the only institutions asleep at the wheel. Although the economic incentive to publish big wave images was enormous, there were some satellite images, astronauts took digital photographs with a handheld camera ninety minutes after the waves struck Sri Lanka, and some radar images were taken two hours later, but that was pretty much it for omniscient views from the heavens (Viren 2005; Wikipedia).

Considering that the Indian Ocean area is not small or far from regions known to support anti-West insurgents, and the United States, the U.K., and allied nations were engaged in a nasty second war in Iraq a subcontinent or so away, the lapses are quite odd. Also missing in action was Prime Minister Blair throughout the tsunami episode, despite his country's legacy of colonial interests in the area and the loss of life to Britons.

A number of explanations could be offered for the gaps, from political and economic disinterest to covert operations and withheld information. But at the very least, the gaps suggest that the net of global detection is less fine than often is supposed. With the West's ubiquitous surveillance cameras, perhaps it is easy to project that experience and assume the rest of the world follows suit. Telephony scholar James Katz (2003), however, has flatly stated that there is no cellphone-enabled global surveillance network: over his years of research into cross-cultural cellphone adoption, he has found no concrete evidence that a spy network exists. Since the physical network of poles and satellites is in plain view and inextricably bound with political and corporate interests, GPS capabilities, and easy cellphone interception, this seems an ingenuous, or at least incurious, position to take. But perhaps Katz is not dissembling, and the conspiracy theorists have overstated their case.

Since the first war in Iraq, the tools of military surveillance increasingly have been turned on citizens in the West (Robins and Levidow 1995). One of the implications of the military-citizen journalism of Abu Ghraib is that average people acted in willing panoptic ways, flaunting behavior that surely could cost their careers. This is one of Andrejevic's (2004, p. 206) observations about public participation through webcams and reality television: the government and marketers are voluntarily given access. But outside the West, with its capital for infrastructural monitoring and unending interest in watching itself, including through cellphone cameras, home video, satellites, and other means, monitoring may not be quite so pervasive. The Western gaze that has been generalized as panoptic also may be narcissistic—endlessly fascinated with its own reflection, assuming its problems are the world's problems, oblivious to the different circumstances of Others, who really may be coming from a different place.

Conclusion: Tipping Point of What?

Interviewed by the *Toronto Star* about the citizen journalism signified by 12/26, Liss Jeffrey, of the McLuhan Global Research Network, said:

> We had the Rodney King video, even 9/11 videos, or even more recently the beheadings on the internet. . . . Amateur video isn't new.

And people will go to them, especially if they don't trust conventional news sources for their slants, or conspiracy theories. But the amount of videos on the internet, and the ease with which you can upload and download them, that is something new. . . .

These blogs are helping raise money, and finding and connecting people affected by this tragedy.

There are so many video blogs because the scale of the disaster was huge. And it happened at the beach, where camcorders are pervasive. There's easy access to internet. . . . All this has raised some very, very interesting questions about new media. These (video-blogs) show things you don't see on the news. For example, on one site you could see the waves coming. Then someone commented you couldn't see the tide going out. Immediately someone posted a link, where you could see it. There's interactivity. That's new technology. (Bhandari 2005)

Citizen journalism will continue to influence and interact with mainstream news, particularly when large stories break. Cooperative newsgathering will further blur the line between amateur and professional, which never has been clear in journalism.

The rights of video bloggers have been touched on only in passing, although an alliance, the Media Bloggers Association, was formed after the tsunami to deal with bandwidth, royalties, and other issues involving ownership and compensation (Glaser 2005; Outing 2005b). The association launched a tsunami video hosting initiative, which worked with Washingtonpost.com to ensure that legitimate clips were available, as was bandwidth. Citizen journalists have been creating their own policies and alliances to bridge traditional and new media, hoping to forge positive working relationships.

This chapter does not address Podcasting, which arose after 12/26 and which already has reshaped blogging, just over the past few months. Regarding consumer electronics gear, continual convergence in smaller devices means that the artificial division between cellphone, videophone, camera, camcorder, webcam, DVD player, MP3 player, Podcast, webcast, blog, texting, e-mail, and online or offline has been dissolving, also markedly since 12/26. The iFilm Network, for example, "has its sights set on mobile platforms, where short-form videos would make sense as next-generation cell phones become audio- and video-friendly. So . . . an on-the-scene amateur might shoot something right on her videophone and forward the clip on to hundreds of thousands of others with videophones, just as SMS messages spread after the tsunamis" (Glaser 2005). There will be new ways to bypass the media giants and commercial and governmental censorship through Podcasting, blogging, and short-form cellphone-enabled video.

While the primary concern of this chapter has been the American mainstream press, its shortcomings and lapses in comparison with citizen journalism, many complaints were lodged about the local media in areas near the Indian Ocean. People in neighboring countries had direct need for information and reason to worry about family, after-shocks, socioeconomic, and other effects. During the intra-holiday week, the Malaysian mass media too continued its regularly scheduled programming, despite the suffering nearby and anxious public awaiting reliable news (Aliran 2005). Although there was far less distance to cover, official bulletins and answers often did not appear in publications or on television until early January 2005, no sooner than that provided by the BBC and

American mainstream press. Filling the gap, survivors spontaneously told their stories and served as international foreign correspondents.

These are among the reasons why 12/26 serves as the tipping point mentioned by Outing (2005a): during the crucial week after the earthquake and tsunami, the news came from citizen journalists who substantially kept the world informed, calmed, and helped to mobilize aid efforts. The citizen journalism trend is developing as a fusion of traditional and new media, with nonspecialists enabled by evolving, converging electronic gear and the Internet. The frustration with TV3 was such that, on the website for Aliran (2005), a Malaysian human rights organization, an editorial said, "Sounds like ordinary folks know better how to do journalism or serve the public than this supposedly number one TV station in the country." Aliran went on to accuse the Malaysian government of censorship and incompetence, including dozing on the job when it should have been providing news, as well as falling down with earthquake preparedness and relief efforts. Echoing across the globe, Aliran's anger was shared by many who observed that 12/26, not unlike 9/11, largely was bungled by the authorities. Such frustration fuels the citizen journalism trend, contributing to political mobilization that is enabled through the use of mobile and digital communication devices.

With regard to the island cultures of Southeast Asia and their mass media representations, I could not help but think of *Survivor* while watching the tsunami coverage. Later it emerged that reality-television producer Mark Burnett had scouted the area for future show locations (Brioux 2005). I wondered how Burnett and his staff would manage the next season, set on Palau, in Micronesia, since the premise of the series was now in appalling taste. Or perhaps someone at CBS would call on Burnett as a commentator to help contextualize the real-world *Survivor* that was no game. But instead, with deplorable insensitivity—particularly when considering the media's careful handling of anything associated with downtown Manhattan for more than a year after 9/11—less than two months after 12/26, the tenth season began without even an opening screen acknowledging the tsunami victims or sharing a website for donations. It was back to hyperreal normal. Aspiring Americans scrambled and backstabbed for a chance at winning a jackpot. Dark-skinned natives made cameo appearances as hunters and gatherers in exotic dress. In between product placements and commercial breaks, contestants frolicked before video cameras in the tiki-hut theme park, while bongos and animal calls played on the soundtrack. There is much about 12/26 and its media representations that confound. But if that sort of reality-television beach scene met classic Hollywood spectacle (think Edward G. Robinson and the golden calf), it would end with a giant wave wreaking biblical destruction.

References

Aliran. (2005). "The official gatekeepers of the breaking news." *Malaysian Media Monitors' Diary*, January 10. Retrieved August 3, 2005, from www.aliran.com/charter/monitors/2005/01/official-gatekeepers-of-breaking-news.html.

Andrejevic, M. (2004). "The webcam subculture and the digital enclosure." In N. Couldry and A. McCarthy (Eds.), *MediaSpace: Place, scale, and culture in a media age* (pp. 193–208). London: Routledge.

Associated Press. (2004). "Search for tsunami survivors goes online." December 29. [Not retrievable August 3, 2005, from www.ap.org.]

Associated Press. (2005a). "Newly released video shows tsunami sweeping through Indonesian town, engulfing busy street." January 9. [Not retrievable August 3, 2005, from www.ap.org.]

Associated Press. (2005b). "Through the lens of catastrophe." January 13. [Not retrievable August 3, 2005, from www.ap.org.]

Bhandari, A. (2005). "Tsunami videos break the mould on morality." *Toronto Star*, January 3, p. D1. [Not retrievable August 3, 2005, from www.thestar.com.]

Brioux, B. (2005). "Canada on Survivor radar." *Calgary Sun*, January 21. Retrieved August 3, 2005, from www.calgarysun.com/perl-bin/niveau2.cgi?s=films&p=91788.html&a=1.

Carey, J. W. (2002). "American journalism on, before, and after September 11." In B. Zelizer and S. Allan (Eds.), *Journalism after September 11* (pp. 71–90). London: Routledge.

CBS5.com. (2005). "Berkeley couple takes dramatic tsunami pictures." January 3. [Not retrievable August 3, 2005, from www.cbs5.com.]

CBSNews.com. (2005a). Ancient tribe survives tsunami. January 6. Retrieved August 3, 2005, from www.cbsnews.com/stories/2005/01/04/world/main664729.shtml.

CBSNews.com. (2005b). "Sea gypsies' tsunami rebuild curse." January 14. Retrieved August 3, 2005, from www.cbsnews.com/stories/2005/01/14/world/main667167.shtml.

CBSNews.com. (2005c). "Ancient tribes touched by tsunami." January 17. Retrieved August 3, 2005, from www.cbsnews.com/stories/2005/01/14/world/main667173.shtml.

Coren, M. (2005). "Internet aids tsunami recovery." CNN.com, January 5. Retrieved August 3, 2005, from www.cnn.com/2005/TECH/01/05/tech.tsunami.

Critical Friends of Technology. (2003). "A social ecology of wireless technology." *First Monday* 8, article 8. Retrieved August 3, 2005, from www.firstmonday.org/issues/issue8_8/critical/index.html.

Croteau, D., and W. Hoynes. (2003). "The new media giants: Changing industry structure." In G. Dines and J. M. Humez (Eds.), *Gender, race, and class in media*, 2nd ed. (pp. 21–39). Thousand Oaks, CA: Sage.

Economist Leaders. (2005). *Economist* 374, no. 8417 (March 12): 11.

Economist: Technology Quarterly. (2005). [Special section]. *Economist* 374, no. 8417 (March 12): btwn. 54–55.

Foucault, M. (1979). *Discipline and punish: The birth of the prison.* (A. Sheridan, Trans.). New York: Vintage. (Original work published 1975.)

Glaser, M. (2005). "Tsunami video alliance portends future distribution for amateurs." *Online Journalism Review*, January 11, Annenberg School for Communication. Los Angeles: University of Southern California. Retrieved August 3, 2005, from www.ojr.org/ojr/stories/050111glaser.

Hay, J., and J. Packer. (2004). "Crossing the media(-n): Auto-mobility, the transported self, and technologies of freedom." In N. Couldry & A. McCarthy (Eds.), *MediaSpace: Place, scale and culture in a media age* (pp. 209-232). London: Routledge.

Hersh, S. (2004). *Chain of command: The road from 9/11 to Abu Ghraib.* New York: Harper.

Jhally, S., and J. Earp. (Eds.). (2004). *Hijacking catastrophe: 9/11, fear, and the selling of American empire.* Northampton, MA: Olive Branch.

Joyce, C. (2005). "December Indian Ocean quake was larger than thought." *All things considered* [Radio broadcast], March 30. Washington, D.C.: National Public Radio. Retrieved August 3, 2005, from www.npr.org/templates/story/story.php?storyId=4568150.

KATC3.com. (2005). "New home video captures tsunami." January 6. [Not retrievable August 3, 2005, from www.katc.com.]

Katz, J. E. (2003). Keynote address given at Mobile communication: Social and political effects. Sixth Communications in the 21st Century Conference, April, Budapest, Hungary.

Katz, J. E., and M. Aakhus. (Eds.). (2002). *Perpetual contact: Mobile communication, private talk, public performance.* Cambridge, UK: Cambridge University Press.

Ling, R. (2004). *The mobile connection: The cell phone's impact on society.* Amsterdam: Morgan Kaufmann.

Marx, K., and F. Engels. (1983). "Manifesto of the communist party." *The portable Karl Marx.* (E. Kamenka, Ed. and Trans.). New York: Penguin. (Original work published 1848.)

McChesney, R. (2000). "So much for the magic of technology and the free market: The World Wide Web and the corporate media system." In A. Herman and T. Swiss (Eds.), *The World Wide Web and contemporary cultural theory* (pp. 5–35). London: Routledge.

McChesney, R. (2002). September 11 and the structural limitations of US journalism. In B. Zelizer & S. Allan (Eds.), *Journalism after September 11* (pp. 91–100). London: Routledge.

McChesney, R. (2003). "The *Titanic* sails on: Why the Internet won't sink the media giants." In *Gender, race, and class in media*, 2nd ed. (pp. 677–83). Thousand Oaks, CA: Sage.

Nyíri, K. (Ed.). (2003). *Mobile democracy: Essays on society, self, and politics.* In K. Nyíri (Series Ed.). Vol. 6. Communications in the 21st Century. Vienna: Verlag.

Ostrow, J. (2005). "Tsunami tests TV journalism." *Denver Post*, January 10. [Not retrievable August 3, 2005, from www.denverpost.com.]

Outing, S. (2005a). "Taking tsunami coverage into their own hands." Poynter Institute, January 6. Retrieved August 3, 2005, from www.poynter.org/content/content_view.asp?id=76520.

Outing, S. (2005b). "The finer points of amateur tsunami videos." Poynter Institute, January 12. Retrieved August 3, 2005, from www.poynter.org/column.asp?id=31&aid=76877.

Plant, S. (2001). *On the mobile: The effects of mobile telephones on social and individual life.* New York: Motorola.

Rheingold, H. (1999). "Look who's talking." *Wired* 7, no. 1 (January): 128–31, 160–63.

Rheingold, H. (2002). *Smart mobs: The next social revolution.* Boston: Perseus.

Robins, K., and L. Levidow. (1995). "Soldier, cyborg, citizen." In J. Brook and I. A. Boal (Eds.), *Resisting the virtual life: The culture and politics of information* (pp. 105–13). San Francisco: City Lights.

Romero, S. (2001a). "The simple BlackBerry allowed contact when phones failed." *New York Times*, September 20, p. G1.

Romero, S. (2001b). "Using a cellphone signal to hunt for a victim in desperate need." *New York Times*, September 20, p. G6.

Rule, J. (2002). From mass society to perpetual contact: Models of communication technologies in social context. In J. E. Katz & M. Aakhus (Eds.), *Perpetual contact: Mobile communication, private talk, public performance* (pp. 242–254). Cambridge, UK: Cambridge University Press.

Schudson, M. (2002). What's unusual about covering politics as usual. In B. Zelizer & S. Allan (Eds.), *Journalism after September 11* (pp. 36–47). London: Routledge.

Schwartz, J. (2004a). "Blogs provide raw details from scene of the disaster." *New York Times*, December 28, p. 17.

Schwartz, J. (2004b). "Sounding the alarm on a tsunami is complex and expensive." *New York Times*, December 29, p. 8.

Schwartz, J. (2004c). "Text messaging pushed for use as disaster warning systems." *New York Times*, December 31, p. 12.

Shister, G. (2005). "ABC's Sawyer hasn't slept since reporting tsunami." *Philadelphia Inquirer*, January 10. [Not retrievable August 3, 2005, from www.philly.com.]

Sontag, S. (2004). "What have we done?" *Guardian*, May 24, p. G2. [Not retrievable from www.guardian.co.uk; retrieved August 3, 2005, from www.commondreams.org/views04/0524-09.htm.]

South-East Asia Earthquake and Tsunami Blog. (2004–5). [Web site]. Retrieved August 3, 2005, from tsunamihelp.blogspot.com.

Sreenivasan, S. (2005). "Watch before you hit 'forward.'" Poynter Institute, January 11. Retrieved August 3, 2005, from www.poynter.org/column.asp?id=32&aid=76760.

Srinivas, S. (2005). "Online citizen journalists respond to South Asian disaster." *Online Journalism Review*, January 7, Annenberg School for Communication. Los Angeles: University of Southern California. Retrieved August 3, 2005, from www.ojr.org/ojr/stories/050107srinivas.

Stotz, G. (2001). "The colonizing vehicle." In D. Miller (Ed.), *Car cultures* (pp. 223–44). Oxford: Berg.

Tsunamis.com. (N.d.). [Web site]. Retrieved August 3, 2005, from www.tsunamis.com/tsunami-pictures.html.

Viren, S. (2005). "Photos from space show tsunami's wrath." *Galveston County Daily News*, January 14. [Not retrievable August 3, 2005, from galvestondailynews.com.]

Wikipedia. (N.d.). "2004 Indian ocean earthquake." Retrieved August 3, 2005, from http://en.wikipedia.org/wiki/2004_Indian_Ocean_Earthquake.

Yahoo! News. (2004a). "Mobile phones save stranded Britons, Hong Kong workers in Sri Lanka." December 28. [Not retrievable August 3, 2005, from http://news.yahoo.com.]

Yahoo! News. (2004b). "Mobile phone plays valuable role in wake of tsunami disaster." December 31. [Not retrievable August 3, 2005, from http://news.yahoo.com.]

Zelizer, B. (2002). Photography, journalism, and trauma. In B. Zelizer & S. Allan (Eds.), *Journalism after September 11* (pp. 48–68). London: Routledge.

Section Two

Identity Politics and/of/in the Cell Phone

Cstng A pwr4l spLL: D evOLshn f SMS

(Casting a Powerful Spell: The Evolution of SMS)

Collette Snowden

Among the many applications now available to the millions of cell phone users is the simple text-based format known as SMS, or texting. The use of short message services (SMS) to send and receive messages is undoubtedly one of the cell phone's most successful applications, and is now a significant, even characteristic element of communication by cell phone, but tracing the development of SMS and its subsequent adoption and diffusion tells us as much about the nature of the social construction of technology as it does about the specific conditions of forms of communications.

The first official SMS transmission, simply saying (somewhat early), "MERRY CHRISTMAS," is understood to have been sent in Britain on December 3, 1992, from the computer of engineer Neil Papworth to the cell phone of Richard Jarvis at Vodaphone (Saunders 2002; BBC News 2002). While it took several years before the service found favor with cell phone users in Europe, and eventually elsewhere, it took less than a decade for SMS applications to become a major component of mobile communication traffic on cellular networks.

While the adoption of SMS was initially constrained by technical and business barriers, the use of SMS is now a popular phenomenon there. Wherever it is available, SMS has become a popular communication application and its use for person-to-person communication and for broadcasting short messages has proliferated. In April 2005 the Vatican press office sent an SMS alert to thousands of registered media representatives about the death of Pope John Paul II (Oaks 2005; Allen 2005). Days later, as hundreds of thousands of people crowded into Rome for the pope's funeral, Italian cell phone operators used SMS broadcasting to inform millions of cell phone subscribers about traffic conditions and accommodations (Oaks 2005; CWNews.com 2005). Later the same month, Chinese authorities sent 30 million text messages to discourage anti-Japanese protests (Dickie 2005).

Such examples illustrate the extent of the mass communication potential that SMS now has, but the use and popularity of SMS also differentiate cell phone communication from traditional telephony by integrating two related but quite different forms of communication, text and orality, in one appliance. While it is now possible, with the use of VoIP (voice over Internet protocol), to do this via the Internet, it was the cell phone that first introduced large numbers of people to this convergent aspect of communications technology. The widespread use and acceptance of SMS communication has therefore increased the potential, for both users and developers, to use cell phone technology with other forms of communication media. The phenomenon of SMS also encompasses both cultural and technical dimensions of the technology of the cell phone to remind us that it is human intervention and action that ultimately shape and direct communication technology use and its consequences. However, the case of SMS also serves to illustrate that human responses to technology are influenced by a number of different factors, from national economic and political interests to the micromanagement of the culture and social practices of small social groups. To fully appreciate the dimensions of SMS and its position in the culture of communications technology it is necessary to consider the complex social construction of the overarching technical system that makes SMS possible.

In developing the technical protocol for the digital mobile communications system for Europe, or the GSM system (initially the general system for mobiles or *groupe spéciale mobile*, but now global system for mobiles), engineers planned and allowed for the transmission of text messages of up to 160 characters, or 140 bytes (or only 70 characters for languages not based on the Latin alphabet, such as Chinese, Arabic, Japanese, Korean), when designing its data services. Seeking to maximize the technical potential of the GSM system, they anticipated that SMS would be used to provide short messages similar to those sent and received on pagers, to notify consumers of voice mail messages or network faults. In planning these specific applications, they created a simple communications technology that became a multibillion-dollar income earner for telecommunications operators, spawning new and unanticipated means for people to communicate.

Once SMS became available, its use increased at a phenomenal rate. New and ever more inventive uses were developed. The remarkably inventive and ingenious applications of SMS demonstrate the capacity of human beings to apply creative power to a technology and make more of it than initially imagined by its inventors. The seeming limitations of the SMS system became one of its strengths, while the network structure of the mobile communication systems meant that these uses were quickly adopted. From the mundane messages of teenagers passing "notes" in class to dramatic rescues from remote and isolated places made possible by SMS messages, from the organization of political rallies and demonstrations to the transmission of news headlines, sports results, and traffic updates, from ring tones and interactive television voting to the monitoring of vital health conditions, the story of SMS is a compelling example of how the curiosity and playfulness of human beings, combined with technical ingenuity, shrewd policy initiatives, political and business machinations, and the global network of telecommunications have combined to extend the communication capacity of the cell phone.

Unexpected, Not Accidental

Social analysis of the development and use of SMS is dominated by the perspective of the individual user or more lately by consideration of it as a mass-market medium, especially by the media and telecommunications industries. However, this perspective does not fully account for the political, economic, and technical foundation on which the social practices and uses of SMS are based.

In the emerging social history of the cell phone the notion that SMS was an "accidental" technological innovation is being propagated (Rheingold 2004; Schutz 2001; Chan 2001). The difference between accidental and unexpected or unanticipated may seem like little more than a semantic argument, but the distinction is worth emphasizing. If the myth of "accidental" success persists to become the received story of SMS, then its complex evolution as a socially constructed success story becomes trivialized and distorted, as does our subsequent understanding of both the nature of technological development and communication more generally.

Framing SMS as an accidental success conforms to a recurrent narrative theme in the history of technology, which positions a specific technological development as the result of fortuitous or unplanned events, seemingly beyond human control or intervention. While conceiving technological invention from this Promethean perspective is rather romantic, it is, in the case of SMS, also inaccurate. Suggesting that the invention of SMS was accidental denies and even denigrates the innovation and ingenuity of the engineers, technicians, and policymakers involved in developing the technical architecture for SMS and industry standards for digital mobile communications. More important, it denies the sophisticated industrial and business capacity of the telecommunications industry and depoliticizes what has become one of the major applications in the global telecommunications sector. The preparedness and willingness to use both the technical capabilities of technology and the considerable promotional capacity of the telecommunications and media sectors to exploit and co-opt the curiosity of human beings in a novel and useful communication form for economic benefit can be seen as "accidental," but only from a strictly technological determinist view. Such a view would requires us to look only at the technology itself, rather than, as Brian Winston (1998) argues, to situate the technology centrally in the social sphere, where understanding the position of a particular communications technology in our culture requires a considered examination of all the factors that produce the conditions in which a technology is conceived, invented, developed, adopted, and diffused.

Far from being accidental, the inclusion of SMS in the digital mobile communications system was planned and deliberate. The scale of its success was, however, unexpected, as were the cultural consequences of its popularity, but SMS is not the first communications technology that has proved to have different capacities for communication than those imagined when it was first conceived. The successful global diffusion of SMS as a communication application is more a salient example of how the success of a technology is dependent on a coalition of social, political, and economic factors and how those factors are harnessed and redirected to increase the success of a technology when its early popularity is identified and exploited by a voracious market. While the eventual success of SMS may be regarded as *surprising*, its invention and eventual success must be considered in the context of its origins in socially situated decision-making apparent at every stage from invention to mass diffusion.

The technical genesis of SMS is based in the entire scientific and technological complex involved in the development of the global telecommunications systems over more than a century and a half. More specifically, SMS is based in the more recent development of mobile communications systems for general consumer communication, particularly in Europe, where an analog system was successfully planned and developed in the 1980s. Despite technical limitations and relatively high prices, the early analog cell phone networks established in Europe, and particularly in Scandinavia, were remarkably successful in attracting users. Even if the consequences of the new technology were not immediately apparent, or even interesting, to most social analysts (Snowden 1999; Katz and Aakhus 2002), the early mobile communications networks demonstrated both the appeal and utility of mobile communications and alerted network designers and industry insiders to the potential market for mobile communications. By the mid-1980s, a move to digital systems was considered essential to meet demand, and to provide improved and new services in Europe. The European Community was concerned about how to manage capacity constraints, technical problems, and the associated issue of spectrum access and allocation in the crowded European airspace. The move to a digital system for mobile communications in Europe was therefore considered critical to servicing the burgeoning market for cellular services. Building a digital communication system that was compatible and consistent across Europe at the same time was seen to offer an opportunity to develop a system that would allow users to access services across national borders, while also providing additional services, with potential for future development. It was also seen as an opportunity to consolidate the disparate European markets into one larger, more efficient market that would offer competitive advantages to suppliers, equipment manufacturers, and operators.

The introduction of GSM was thus a complex, planned process that took place over more than a decade and that involved European governments, the European Community, telecommunication companies, equipment manufacturers, technical standards bodies, and regulatory and policy organizations, as Jacques Pelkmans (2001) has documented. Mike Short, chairman of the GSM Memorandum of Understanding Association from 1995 to 1996, has said, "I think that what we've done with GSM is equivalent to putting a man on the moon ten times over—that was the level of complexity " (GSM Association 1997). In discussing the evolution of SMS as a cultural and social phenomenon, it is therefore necessary to acknowledge its genesis as a socially constructed technology contingent upon political and economic decision-making in relation to technology research, innovation, and adoption.

One of the compelling features of the development of the digital mobile communications system, which incorporated SMS, was that it was in fact developed with a deliberate and conscious view of the market it was designed for. While an understanding of which specific applications would succeed was not immediately apparent, the system was designed with the knowledge and awareness that the technology was being developed for a mature and burgeoning communication market within the context of the expanding global information, communications, and telecommunications industries. To that end, an enormous wealth of technical knowledge, economic and political power, and understanding of communications markets was heavily invested in developing a system for digital mobile communications technology designed with potential for growth and market domination. Such deliberate action and focused intent could hardly be seen as "accidental." Pelkmans argues that the success of the GSM system adopted in Europe was especially reliant on a process of cooperative standardization, which required strict governance of "an array of actors, private and public, at different levels" (2001, p. 449; see also Harrison and Holley 2001; Bekkers, Duysters, and Verspagen 2002; Mina 2003; Trosby 2004). Factors critical to the development of the standardization process include control of policy and regulatory regimes, intellectual property rights, and international agreements. The application of Brian Winston's (1998) model of technological innovation, diffusion, and suppression to the case of SMS suggests that its development conforms to a pattern that has emerged over the entire history of communications technology.[1]

While recognition of the critical importance of the socially situated and determined political, economic, and business decision-making may account for the development of the entire system, the inclusion of SMS within the digital mobile system was also clearly a result of social decision-making. Finn Trosby's (2004, p. 193) personal account of how SMS was developed when the technical standards for data services for GSM were designed categorically states, "the birth of SMS was definitely not due to a mishap or accident." He records that in the mid-1980s the research and development department of the Norwegian telecommunications company Telenor established the Mobile Networks for Special Purposes (*Mobilt spesialnett*) survey group "to explore the potential of mobile communications for other services than telephony" (p. 187). Among its findings, the survey group established that mobile communication and messaging services were highly compatible, particularly where mobile users were out of coverage areas or had their handsets turned off. The survey group's conclusion that mobile messaging services should be offered simultaneously to private and corporate sections of the market, based on the premise that the services that SMS offered were more likely to be adopted in the mass market than in the corporate sector, proved to be particularly prescient (p. 188). Trosby's account of the development of SMS is especially useful for its recognition of the "extensive market analysis" (p. 187) involved. Substantial cultural and social knowledge was recruited at the earliest stage of the development of SMS and other mobile data services to shape and direct mobile communications technology formation. It is significant and important to recognize that the social construction of technology involves far more than the everyday use of specific applications, and that the important stage of technology invention and development is integral to the eventual social use of a technology, and its subsequent analysis.

The Social Penetration of SMS

Building the potential for SMS messaging into the architecture for digital mobile communication networks, however, was not enough by itself to guarantee successful adoption and diffusion. A major obstacle was the problem that messages could only be sent between users on the same network. Here again the mobilization of governments, regulators, and telecommunication operators influenced the diffusion of the technology. The introduction of network interoperability enabled seamless communication between different operators and introduced global roaming, both of which were critical in expanding SMS use.

With greater freedom to use their cell phones, people found many uses for SMS. Some current applications include: person-to-person messaging, voice mail and fax notifications, unified messaging, Internet e-mail alerts, ring tones, chat, news and information services, mobile banking, vehicle positioning, job dispatch, remote point of sale and remote monitoring, and moblogging. But listing the applications gives no hint of the enormous variety of situations in which SMS is used, and which vary not only according to individual preference and culturally defined modes of communication, but also to network accessibility and the cost of use.

The marketing and promotion of SMS, and other cell phone applications, was also significant in developing the network of users. Initially, cell phones were marketed specifically to the corporate sector of the communications market, and promotional effort was directed at this sector of the market. This strategy did not deliberately aim to restrict the diffusion of the technology, but the early technical limitations and initial high costs were barriers to other sectors of the market. Reappraisal of the potential of the consumer market, especially for SMS services, proved to be an important strategy, as did developing charging systems that encouraged both adoption and use of the available applications. This reappraisal was again a result of deliberate and directed organizational and system planning, in which market assessment and evaluation were critical. The considerable investment in establishing digital mobile communications networks had not only to be recouped, but protected and made profitable. Consequently, innovative uses for SMS were monitored and, when identified, deliberately and consciously encouraged through the use of market control mechanisms and intense promotional activity.

To this end, an important factor in the rapid escalation of the use of SMS was price sensitivity. One of the most influential factors that encouraged SMS use was its initial low price, which in turn influenced who adopted it and what they did with it. The usability problems of SMS, such as the need to press multiple keys, small screen size, asynchronous communication, and the perceived superiority of voice for person-to-person communication, were factors in making SMS communication inexpensive. In some cases SMS was even provided as a free additional service. Many cell phone users found this an incentive to use SMS and also identified situations in which it was a preferred means for communication. When network operators identified patterns of use, they introduced new payment methods and tariff structures to take advantage of user preferences as they emerged, and began to charge for SMS use.

The enthusiasm of people for finding their own purposes and reasons for the use of cell phones is a critical aspect of the sociology of the cell phone, and is the one area in which its designers were unable to anticipate the scale of enthusiasm and subsequent use. In this sense, the success of cell phones—and SMS applications in particular—could be regarded as "accidental" in that many of the initial uses and conventions of SMS use were not specifically controlled or driven by industry but arose from the creativity of users with access to the technology. However, at each new moment in the evolution of SMS, industry has responded rapidly to user innovation to capture these new uses and repackage them as fee-producing services or applications.

SMS's capacity for asynchronous silent communication was especially attractive to users because it extended the places in which their cell phones could be used and the types of communication affordances available. This aspect of SMS use was especially attractive to young people, for whom cell phones in general had quickly become desirable (see Haddon 1998; Ling and Helmersen 2000; Ling 2001; Plant 2001). In its early stages, young people were not considered to be a significant market for cell phones, but the industry quickly saw and responded to young people's enthusiasm for the new technology by switching its promotion, marketing, and pricing strategies (Saunders 2002; Kavassalis et al. 2003; Andersson, Foros, and Steen 2004). Kjetil Andersson, Øystein Foros, and Frode Steen argue that this created a "bandwagon" effect that assisted in expanding the use of cell phones generally and SMS in particular. The extent of social science analysis of teenage or adolescent use of cell phones and SMS reflects the industry focus on the youth market, with a substantial research literature emerging on cell phone use (including SMS) that identifies the deeper social meanings of its use among many, if not all, of its users (Ling and Helmersen 2000; Ling 2001; Taylor and Harper 2002, 2003; Aoki and Downes 2003). Social science research on cell phone use by young people has been strongly allied to industry aims and objectives, and in some cases has been commissioned and then co-opted to further enhance industry objectives in promoting cell phone use and diffusion.

Alex Taylor and Richard Harper's work on the use of cell phones by teenagers found that the capacity to transmit communication in a variety of different circumstances, including times when it was understood that communication was difficult or problematic, was a major attraction of cell phone use, and of SMS use in particular. They argue that cell phone use by teenagers can be best understood as a complex ritual of exchange with particular rules and prescribed actions and responses. The practice of SMS or texting as a social practice involving gift exchange is also related to the ability of the messages sent and received being seen as tangible. Unlike voice communication, the messages sent and received by SMS have the additional property of possessing concreteness because the text produced is visible on the cell phone screen and can be retained. While the capacity to store messages is limited, this quality adds a dimension to text messages that increases its value to the communication affordance for users. Information sent by SMS can be stored, even archived, while more personal messages take on the value of keepsakes or mementos. Other research has indicated an important "social grooming" function of cell phone communication and SMS exchange in order to create or maintain a "sense of connection and community" (Fox 2003, p. 2).

There is a more sinister side to this aspect of SMS use, with the recognition of such ritualized "gift exchanges" and "social grooming" for negative as well as positive social purposes. The rise of text-bullying and other forms of harassment is now recognized (NCH 2005; Colman 2004; Charlton, Panting, and Hannan 2002). Such uses demonstrate the transfer of existing social practices, including those of hierarchical domination, to a new mode of communication rather than the development of a new form of behavior, with Internet "flaming," telephone crank calls, and poison pen letters and stalking all examples of the malicious use of communication technology. Other negative consequences of the use of SMS include increasing financial debt among young people (Weekes 2004).

The turn to the use of SMS, especially as an adjunct to voice services, marked a departure in the perception and use of the cell phone as a mobile version of the fixed phone. As long as the capability of cell phones to provide other applications was constrained by business and technical limitations, so too was the potential for people to use them. Consequently, in the beginning voice applications were most important, and even continue to be the most used. The promise of the cell phone as a device that could deliver multiple communication applications was first revealed to users by SMS use. The playfulness inherent in SMS was critical in accelerating its adoption and diffusion, and in innovation in its use.

SMS users, especially in the youth market, once familiarized with the mechanics of SMS, began to explore and play with the technology. This element of playfulness, expressed in a fascination with either the mechanical functions of the appliance or with any of its applications, or both, can be characterized as "enchantment" (McCarthy et al. 2004). Enchantment with technology is influenced by "the specific sensuousness of a thing; senses of play, paradox and openness; and the potential for transformation" (p. 1). Enchantment with texting can become so intense that "addiction" has been identified, and anecdotal accounts claim that addicts can spend hours each day sending text messages and scanning their cell phones for incoming messages (Biddlecombe 2003). Empirical studies of the alleged syndrome are not yet documented, although Adriana Bianchi and James.G. Phillips (2005) have developed a mobile phone problem use scale based on the addiction potential scale and overall mobile phone usage levels.

In playing with the technology, users radically expanded and transformed its use. It was here that the flexibility of the technical standard was critical in allowing the innovation and creativity of individual users to be transferred to the larger system and distributed through the networked nature of mobile communications. At every moment in the innovation phase, new SMS applications that developers thought might be moderately successful, or that might even struggle to find a viable market, have become wildly successful. Ring tones, for example, which use the SMS technical protocol, have become a major source of revenue for telecommunication companies, with billions downloaded annually (Halper 2004; Reuters 2004; Hanman 2005). The "Crazy Frog" (a.k.a. "the Annoying Thing"), which was originally spun off from a home recording to become an Internet joke, reformatted as a ring tone and heavily promoted on television, became a global cultural phenomenon that generated a range of related media products, including recorded music, screen logos, and games (Mills 2005; Downie 2005). In November 2004 the American music magazine *Billboard* introduced a new chart category for ring tones (Associated Press 2004) and weeks later awarded rapper and hip hop star 50 Cent the first *Billboard* Ringtone of the Year Award.

While the success of SMS ring tones was significant in generating income for cellular operators, so too was its impact on related industries. Telecommunications companies and handset manufacturers initially may not have appreciated the potential for such a seemingly trivial "service," especially given the limitations of the sound quality provided. Users were not so critical, privileging the individuality and quirkiness of their personal choice of ring tone over audio fidelity. Operators quickly realized both the revenue-raising potential and the importance of providing similar personalized consumer content. For the music industry, smarting from its seeming inability to counter music downloading over the Internet, it demonstrated that there was another avenue through which they could reach consumers, and, more important, that consumers were willing to pay for music in nontraditional formats. The potential for cell phones to be used as personalized music devices was shown to be not only realistic, but logical.

The ability of SMS to provide and deliver tangible attributes of individuality and personalization has been important in developing the cell phone as more than a purely utilitarian device. Applications such as ring tones and screen logos, with either audible or visual characteristics that set them apart, have been especially important and has led to other applications that are now being exploited, including mobile marketing delivered by SMS.

Responses to SMS

Responses to the use of SMS or texting have been mixed, ranging from those who have embraced its use as yet another positive sign of a "revolution" in communication to those who regard it as another step toward the destruction of human civilization, beginning with written language. The production of SMS requires the disruption and manipulation of conventions of grammar and syntax and is regarded by critics as a contributing factor in the debasement of text, and of the social and cultural importance of text associated with information and communications technology. SMS thus joins the list of communication technologies that in their early stages were deemed to be threats to established communication practices and norms.

Disquiet about SMS and language appears to be based more on the visible structure of text messages and their brevity, rather than the communication content or intention.

Such structural criticism of texting arises because efficient use of the text messaging system is enhanced by use of a truncated form of spelling and grammar. The use of this truncated language is regarded by its critics as damaging to writing and to literacy. Development of an SMS-specific lexicon (for a variety of languages) that conforms to basic conventions and rules has produced a recognizable "language of text" with a special English texting dictionary produced by Collins (2005; see also Knight 2001). Familiarity with this lexicon, and dexterity in the use of the cell phone keypad, allows users to quickly and conveniently communicate and offers specific communication affordances.

However, the practice of texting also met with hostility and claims that the widespread use of SMS by young people would result in a (further) deterioration of language use, and thus of communication. The basis of this argument is that SMS use constituted a completely new way of using language, but such interpretations of the application of SMS overlook previous related technologies. Long before SMS, the requirement to cut and truncate text in order to transmit it electronically had been developed into an art form by early telegraph operators, especially by journalists. James W. Carey (1983) argues that the requirement of telegraphy to use brief, concise language was an important influence on the writing conventions and style of modern journalism. The efficient use of telegraphy required messages to be reduced to the smallest number of words or characters to increase the speed and reduce the costs of transmission (Pierpont 2001). Similarly, the efficient use of the limited format of SMS is maximized by truncation and abbreviation. Elements of the language of SMS can also be traced to the use of telegraphy's Morse Code, with some of its common terms and abbreviations residually used in SMS. It is perhaps no coincidence that the Morse Code system was officially retired on January 31, 1999 (Smith 1999), as SMS was reaching the communication consciousness of cell phone users. Furthermore, the use of e-mail had also become quite widely established by the late 1990s, when SMS became successful, and the language of e-mail, the Internet chat room, and instant messaging services, all of which also preserved elements of telegraphese while introducing additional abbreviated terms, were transferred seamlessly to the SMS platform, thanks to the malleability of text. Prior to cell phones and SMS, electronic pagers had been used for short messages, and the success of handheld electronic gaming devices among young people had familiarized many with the practice of game playing, which producing SMS messages with the small keypad and screen resembled. Nonetheless, warnings about the destruction of language were considered seriously, and many media reports reflected public concern. When the Scottish Qualifications Authority expressed concern about the use of SMS text–style spelling by students (North 2003), global media attention was focused briefly on the issue, although millions of cell phone users blithely ignored their concern and continued to increase their SMS use. Research into the use of language has also been influenced as scholars turn to examining SMS for what it reveals about literacy.

The argument about the capacity of SMS to negatively influence language reprised the debate relating to the Internet several years earlier, which framed digital communications technology as a threat to text-based language and to the social fabric of text-based cultures. New communications technologies were positioned as a threat to literacy (Birkerts 1994; Postman 1999), even where they were heavily reliant on the use of text. That SMS use actually requires language use, in a way that voice-based communication systems does not, was mostly overlooked by its critics. The use of language as SMS authorship requires can be seen as similar to the wider play with language embedded within existing culture, and within the culture of literacy in particular. We see this language play in word puzzles, in code, in word games, and in literatures; for example, in the poetry of e.e. cummings. With its preference for lowercase letters, sparse prose, playful manipulation of syntax and text symbols, cummings's poetry is an evident cultural precursor to the kind of text use that SMS favors and allows. Cummings's (1923) well-known poem "Grasshopper" even resembles a text message. Norman Friedman (1960, p. 123) argues that cummings's work demonstrates "a style of constant emphasis: since he relishes each phrase, word, and letter of a poem, he wants the reader to relish them too, and many of his devices are aimed simply at slowing down the reader's intake of the poem."

In a similar way, the construction of SMS messages can be seen as a deliberate and playful manipulation of the text to serve different purposes. On a purely functional level, playing with the text makes the medium more efficient; on a linguistic level it "relishes" the text while also codifying the content so that only others who share an understanding of the conventions and meaning of the language style can understand the message transmitted. And, like cummings's poems, an SMS message slows the recipient's intake of the message, as its tangible form requires attention to its detailed textual context—even where it is a simple instruction, such as, "mt me n 30, rng lt"—or, "Meet me in 30 [minutes, I'm] running late." This play with language is an element of SMS communication that is essential to understanding its attraction. Marshall McLuhan may even have approved of the playful literacy of SMS, especially if his own love of language play is considered, especially as seen in *Counterblast* (1970), with its playful textual representation of ideas. McLuhan notes that "The children of technological man respond with untaught delight to the poetry of trains, ships, planes, and to the beauty of machine products. In the school room officialdom suppresses all their natural experience; children are divorced from their culture" (p. 50). The technology of SMS places a new kind of literacy in the hands of individuals, in which the official rules of the classroom have been dispensed with in favor of a unique culturally created language.

The similarity between SMS messaging and poetry was also noticed more widely. The *Guardian* newspaper in the U.K. established an SMS poetry competition in 2002 that received more than five thousand entries (Wilson 2002). Emma Passmore's (2002) winning entry read:

> I left my pictur on th ground wher u walk
> so that somday if th sun was jst right
> & th rain didnt wash me awa
> u might c me out of th corner of yr i & pic me up

Second-prize winner Sharon Mann (2002), used a slightly different form:

> Awokewashedcoffeetoast
> trainworklunchworktrain
> homepasta.putbinout.
> the lightofthesun,reflectedbythe
> surfaceofamoonfleckedwith
> thegreyshadowsofmountains,
> littheyard

New text-based, literary-rich use of SMS continues to emerge and includes serialized SMS novels, which have been produced in Japan, Korea, China, and India. A number of Internet-based translation services are now available to translate messages into standard languages, and vice versa. TrnsL8it (Translate It), for example, suggests:

> jst typ n yor SMS o TXT lingo & lt transL8it! cvert it 2 pln eng o typ
> n a frAze n eng & cvert it 2 TXT lingo!

> [just type in your SMS or TXT lingo and let transL8it! convert it to
> plain English OR type in a phrase in English and convert it to TXT
> lingo!] (TransL8it.com 2005).

The use of acronyms has also proved to be popular and efficient, although familiarity with their meaning is fundamental to understanding, for example, the message "PLZ 4GV ME G2G Tm 2 PUKS CUB L8R," uses a combination of common SMS acronyms to construct the message "Please forgive me, I've got to go, it's time to pick up kids, I'll call you back later."

A more recent forerunner of SMS text style is seen in the work of recording artist Prince, who from the early 1980s used abbreviations in song titles and lyrics that can now be commonly seen in SMS texting and in e-mail. Prince was enormously popular in Europe, and the cultural impact of his *Sign o' the Times* album (1987) should not be underestimated. As a critical and commercial success in a number of media, including recording, video, and in live touring, it reached millions of people. British music journalist Sean O'Hagan (2004) argues that "Prince was the most prodigiously gifted singer-songwriter and multi-instrumentalist to emerge in the Eighties." Critically, Prince demonstrated to a mass audience that text was media malleable; for example, he used text heavily in the music video of the song "Sign o' the Times" to deliver a highly political, and highly danceable, message. Prince further positioned the issue of symbolism and text prominently in popular culture by changing his name in 1993, in response to a dispute with his recording company, and replacing it with an unpronounceable symbol (De Curtis 1999).

Drawing on the examples of e.e. cummings or Prince is not to claim that they or any other artists—and there are more: William Burroughs, for example—are *directly* responsible for the language use adopted widely by SMS users. However, these notable and visible examples from popular culture prior to the success of SMS point to practices in language use that SMS reflects and amplifies. They also remind us, as McLuhan (1964, p. 75) suggests, that "the artist picks up the message of cultural and technological challenge decades before its transforming impact occurs."

The generation that first embraced SMS eagerly and, for the most part, effortlessly also was one accustomed to the concentrated messages of the promotional culture of marketing and advertising, but also of newspaper headlines, the running news bar of satellite television news, and music video. The existing use of language and the brevity of existing forms of communication already normalized within everyday culture and familiar to members of contemporary media-rich societies was perfectly adaptable to SMS use. With SMS, users of the technology were also not only passive recipients of messages, but could construct and create messages to share with a number of people simultaneously. This supposed empowerment assisted in pushing the use of SMS and cell phones more generally.

The cell phone interface requires an element of concentration and an understanding of both everyday language and the SMS conventions for a user to succeed in creating a message—although conventional spelling can also be used. Once mastered, the use of SMS is not only a practical means of communication, but can also be entertaining. The most successful applications of communications technology are frequently those that may be considered slight, frivolous, and fun—for example, portable music devices and handheld games. The roots of technology for industrial applications detract from the importance of the joy of technology, but the playfulness associated with SMS is a critical feature in understanding its social meaning and value. However, it was recognized and understood as a critical "push" factor by industry, especially in emphasizing the youth market for SMS. The ability to charge for services through the cell phone tariff system was an important factor. The experience of early Internet entrepreneurs who struggled to obtain a fee for services served as a warning to the mobile communications industry that maximizing payments for services was critical to survival. The inbuilt payment system, which was part of the technical system for SMS, thus further assisted in driving the technology.

While the fear that the use of SMS, especially by young people, would destroy thousands of years of human communication practices, preliminary research, both academic and industry based, indicates that SMS use is a rational form of communication that extends and maintains social communication and social networks. Pioneering analyses of cell phone culture specifically examining the use of SMS, such as the work done by Taylor and Harper (2002) and Rich Ling (2001), identified the importance of SMS for particular communication affordances that support and maintain established social relationships and networks. In this sense, SMS becomes another useful means of communication, even a better and more efficient means in some situations. For example, in 2001 a woman aboard a boat sinking in the ocean off Indonesia sent an SMS to her boyfriend in England and set in motion a rescue mission involving the British Coastguard and Australian and Indonesian authorities (Batista 2001).

In other situations, SMS has been used to communicate with people outside of social networks, but in a way that elicits a distinctly social response. For example, in India when "doctors told Harinder Choudhary his father's life would be saved if he arranged for two units of rare A-negative blood each day, he turned to wireless carrier Airtel for aid. Within a half hour of meeting with Choudhary, Airtel agreed to send out text messages to thousands of subscribers, pleading for blood. In a matter of hours, Choudhary received dozens of calls from willing donors" (Ankeny 2003). In Australia, a thief who stole a car returned it after receiving—and, more important, responding to— a series of text messages sent to the mobile phone in the car (O'Shea 2004). Such examples illustrate the way in which communication applications can be recognized and used when a particular communication intention is identified.

For some people with speech and hearing disabilities (see Goggin and Newell's chapter in this volume), SMS makes the functionality of the telephone available without the need for an intermediary operator. However, people who use sign language as their first language of communication do not necessarily find SMS any more useful or easy to use, possibly indicating that a facility with both spoken and written language is necessary to get the best use of SMS (MORI Social Research Institute 2004).

The communication affordances of SMS are as broad and as differentiated as all communication among human beings. The many different situations in which SMS has been used in the brief period of its rise to popularity indicate that people are extraordinarily adept at adapting communications technology to meet their communication needs. But, as with other communication technology, especially those associated with the telephone, almost every use has produced its opposite. So, while teenagers may use SMS to sustain social friendships and networks, they can also use it to harass and bully each other, or to communicate exclusion or ostracism from the group by the absence of communication. Similarly, SMS text messages can be used for mass political mobilization in a quite democratic way (see Gordon's chapter in this volume; also Rheingold 2002). At the same time, it has become yet another avenue for political marketing and advertising in election campaigns in many countries, prompting the California assembly of California in the United States to vote to introduce a ban on unsolicited political advertising sent via SMS (Associated Press 2005).

The quality of interactivity of SMS is attributed as a factor in the appeal and successful diffusion of SMS. "Interactivity" is said to be operational in SMS use at the level of person-to-person communication, but also between broadcasters of messages and their audiences. SMS interactivity is apparently directly related to the degree of responsiveness that it provides an individual, particularly when prompted to act, for example to vote, to buy, to reply, or to make selections of one option over another. Incorporation of SMS voting into television programming has been spectacularly successful, prompting producers, broadcasters, and telecommunication companies to explore further possibilities for generating responsiveness in audiences to stimulate SMS activity and its associated income. Numerous ways to integrate SMS into television programs quickly developed throughout Europe, from SMS voting, to the production of special ring tones, competitions and text-to-screen functions, and inevitably SMS advertising. In the U.K., there is even a unique television Text Channel. The advent of m-commerce applications is also heavily reliant on the use of SMS, and here again interactivity is said to be irresistible to consumers. But is SMS interactivity what it is claimed to be? There is little evidence that SMS audiences are fully engaged agents in the production process, but rather are positioned as customers paying for the passive consumption of mass-produced media content. The director of content and marketing for MTV Networks in the Netherlands, Joris van Heukolem, is reported to have told an industry conference at the Second SMS Meets TV Seminar that interactivity should give viewers "only the illusion of controlling content, but not actually controlling content" (Phillips 2003). It would perhaps be more accurate then to use the term *participatory* rather than *interactivity*, for it is developing and exploiting a sense of participation in a particular media-related act that is encouraged and sought.

Just as the use of the term *accidental* in relation to SMS can be seen to disguise a more complex history, the term *interactivity* has its own problematic definition (see Rafaeli 1988; Jensen 1998). Interactivity between individuals using SMS has been shown to be essential in complex social relationships, but the supposed interaction between cell phone users and the producers of television programs and other commercial entities ignores substantial differences in the communication taking place. The ritual aspect of gift-giving identified in SMS communication between known individuals is quite different from the interaction that occurs when SMS is used in other contexts, such as television voting. However, the process of exchange is exploited, with the appearance or possibility of gifts or rewards considered vital to sustaining consumer interest and use. Such gifts take the form of perceived power to influence the outcome of an event in the form of voting, privileged access to information or other content, or opportunities to benefit through competitions with attractive prizes. In this sense, a level of engagement, and even of enchantment, is required to attract and sustain audience interest, becoming a promotional act, which plays with and demands consumer participation. To suggest that this is a form of interactive communication ignores the commercial transaction that is at its heart, which is primarily a one-way communication between the sender of the SMS and the producer of content. Understanding why people are prepared to spend time and money on communication that appears to return little to them is likely to give us new insights into how all forms of media "work," but that knowledge is likely to be co-opted to produce even greater efficiencies in developing services that consumers are required to pay for. But we have been warned before about allowing media organizations to acquire too much control over communication technology. As early communication theorist Harold Innis (1949, p. 37) noted long before the current range in modern communication technologies had been developed, "Technological advance in communication implies a narrowing of the range from which material is distributed and a widening of the range of reception in which large numbers receive, but are unable to make, any direct response. Those on the receiving end of material from a mechanized central system are precluded from participation in healthy, vigorous and vital discussion."

While the initial fun, playfulness, and creativity of SMS persists in the construction of private and personal messages between individuals or members of closed social groups and its simple utility remains for many purposes, the increasing penetration of the forces of the media and telecommunications industries is becoming more pervasive. The rapacious desire to manage and control SMS and other applications is now limiting the degree of responsiveness, or interactivity, in consumers. Perhaps the need for those industries to maintain and support the system that makes SMS and other forms of communication possible renders any other path impossible. The initial fun and creativity of innovation is replaced with business as usual or the same old mass-media, mass-marketing massaging of the audience, or, as Winston (1998) would have it, the radical potential of the technology is suppressed through the inevitable exertion of the power of existing social formations.

Note

1 The development of radio "broadcasting" is one example of a similar phenomenon, in which the communications potential of a technology was inherent, but only realized after early adopters of the technology began to use and develop it. Even though early radio technology was seen primarily as a means of "point-to-point" communication, it was amateur radio operators with an understanding of the technology who developed its capacity to send single signals to many listeners. The history of broadcasting, however, often relates the development of broadcasting to "accidental," rather than deliberate, development of the capacity of the technology of radio by its users. See Winston 1998, pp. 67–87; Sterling and Kittross 2001; Walker 2001.

References

Allen, J. L. (2005). *Pondering the first draft of history: Reflections on covering one pope's funeral and another's election.* Retrieved April 30, 2005, from www.nationalcatholicreporter.org/word/pfw042605.htm.

Andersson, K., Ø. Foros, and F. Steen. (2004). *The SMS bandwagon in Norway: What made the market?* Retrieved February 12, 2005, from www.nhh.no/sam/cv/paper/sms.pdf.

Ankeny, J. (2003). *A weird, unwired world.* Retrieved June 7, 2003, from telephonyonline.com/mag/telecom_talk_broadband_economy_37/.

Aoki, K., and E. J. Downes. (2003). "An analysis of young people's use of and attitudes toward cell phones." *Telematics and Informatics* 20, no. 4: 349–64.

Associated Press. (2004). "Ringtones get their own Billboard chart." Retrieved April 15, 2005, from www.msnbc.msn.com/id/6354430/.

Associated Press. (2005). "Calif. to ban political ads on cell phones." Retrieved May 22, 2005, from news.findlaw.com/ap/o/632/05-20-2005/917b0008c9612fdb.html.

Batista, E. (2001). "SMS provides SOS lifeline." Retrieved February 12, 2005, from wired-vig.wired.com/news/technology/0,1282,41621,00.html.

BBC News. (2002). "Hppy bthdy txt!" Retrieved April 30, 2005, from http://news.bbc.co.uk/1/hi/uk/2538083.stm.

Bekkers, R., G. Duysters, and B. Verspagen. (2002). "Intellectual property rights, strategic technology agreements, and market structure: The case of GSM." *Research Policy* 31: 1141–61.

Bianchi, A., and J. G. Phillips. (2005). "Psychological predictors of problem mobile phone use." *CyberPsychology and Behaviour* 8, no. 1: 39–51.

Biddlecombe, E. (2003). "Tech Addicts Need Textual Healing." Retrieved April 6, 2004, from http://www.wired.com/news/print/0,1294,60936,00.html.

Birkerts, S. (1994). *The Gutenberg Elegies: The fate of reading in an electronic culture.* Boston: Faber and Faber.

Carey, J. W. (1983). "Technology and ideology: The case of the telegraph." In J. W. Carey (Ed.), *Communication as culture: Essays on media and society.* Boston: Unwin Hyman.

Chan, T. (2001). "Those i-mode/mobile data blues." *Telecom Asia* 12, no. 4: 56.

Charlton, T., C. Panting, and A. Hannan. (2002). "Mobile telephone ownership and usage among 10- and 11-year-olds: Participation and exclusion." *Emotional and Behavioural Difficulties* 7, no. 3: 152–63.

Collins (2005). *Collins Texting Dictionary.* London: Harper Collins.

Colman, A. (2004). "SMS bullying." *Youth Studies Australia*. 23 (2): 3–4.

CWNews.com. (2005). "Rome strains as millions arrive for funeral." Retrieved April 30, 2005, from www.cwnews.com/news/viewstory.cfm?recnum=36339.

De Curtis, A. (1999). "The artist is back - but don't call it a comeback." Retrieved June 10, 2005, from http://perso.wanadoo.fr/antoine.house/prince_interview_1999.html.

Dickie, M. (2005). "Chinese police send text messages to head off anti-Japan protests." *Financial Times*, April 29, p. 2.

Downie, S. (2005). "Crazy for the frog." Retrieved June 11, 2005, from http://entertainment.news.com.au/story/0,10221,15576249-7484,00.html.

Fox, K. (2001). *Evolution, Alienation and Gossip: The Role of Mobile Telecommunications in the 21st Century*. Oxford: Social Issues Research Centre.

Friedman, N. (1960). *e. e. cummings: The art of his poetry*. Baltimore: Johns Hopkins University Press.

GSM Association. (1997). *History of GSM: Setting the standard*. Retrieved November 13, 2004, from www.gsmworld.com/about/history/history_page9.shtml.

Haddon, L. (1998). *The experience of the mobile phone*. XIV World Congress of Sociology, Social Knowledge: Heritage, Challenges, Prospects. Montreal, Canada. 26 July–1 August.

Halper, M. (2004). "The sweet sound of success." Retrieved September 27, 2004, from www.time.com/time/europe/magazine/article/0,13005,901040816-678568,00.html.

Hanman, N. (2005). "The ring of success." Retrieved February 6, 2005, from www.guardian.co.uk/online/mobilematters/story/0,12454,1404149,00.html.

Harrison, F., and K. A. Holley. (2001). "The development of mobile is critically dependent on standards." *BT Technology Journal* 19, no. 1: 32–37.

Innis, H. (1949). *The press: A neglected factor in the economic history of the twentieth century*. London, New York, and Toronto: Oxford University Press.

Jensen, Jens F. (1998). "Interactivity: Tracking a New Concept in Media and Communication Studies." *Nordicom Review* 19 (1): 185–204.

Katz, J. E., and Aakhus, M. (Eds.). (2002). *Perpetual contact: Mobile communication, private talk, public performance*. Cambridge, UK: Cambridge University Press.

Kavassalis, P., et al. (2003). "Mobile permission marketing: Framing the market inquiry." *International Journal of Electronic Commerce* 8, no. 1: 55–79.

Knight, H. (2001). *Total texting*. Melbourne: Penguin Books Australia.

Ling, R. (2001). *Adolescent girls and young adult men: Two sub-cultures of the mobile telephone*. Unpublished manuscript.

Ling, R., and P. Helmersen. (2000). *"It must be necessary, it has to cover a need": The adoption of mobile telephony among pre-adolescents and adolescents*. Paper presented at the the Social Consequences of Mobile Telephony conference, Oslo, Norway.

Mann, S. (2002). "SMS poem." Retrieved February 15, 2005, from http://books.guardian.co.uk/textpoetry/story/0,12586,853760,00.html.

McCarthy, J., P. Wright, J. Wallace, and A. Dearden. (2004). *The Experience of Enchantment in Human-Computer Interaction*. Paper presented at the CHI'2004 Fringe conference.

McLuhan, M. (1964). *Understanding media: The extensions of man*. London: Sphere Books.

McLuhan, M. (1970). *Counterblast*. London: Rapp & Whiting.

Mina, A. (2003). "The creation of the European market for mobile telephony: Overview of an instituted process." *International Review of Sociology* 13, no. 2: 435–54.

Mills, D. (2005). "Ad hoc: Crazy Frog reaffirms power of TV." Retrieved June 14, 2005, from http://www.telegraph.co.uk/money/main.jhtml?xml=/money/2005/06/14/ccadh14.xml&menuId=242&sSheet=/money/2005/06/14/ixcoms.html.

Mori Social Research Institute. (2004). *Universal Service Obligation: Deaf and hearing impaired consumers and text phone services*. London: Ofcom.

NCH—The Children's Charity. (2005). Putting U in the picture. Retrieved May 1, 2005, from www.nch.org.uk/uploads/documents/Mobile_bullying_%20report.pdf.

North, M. (2003). "My summer Hols wr CWOT. B4, we used 2 go 2NY 2C my bro, his GF & thr 3:-@ kds FTF." *Times Higher Education Supplement*, September 19, p. 22.

Oaks, T. (2005). "Pope a champion of new technology." Retrieved April 8, 2005, from http://edition.cnn.com/2005/WORLD/europe/04/08/pope.technology/.

O'Hagan, S. (2004). "Fifty years of pop." Retrieved May 3, 2005, from http://observer.guardian.co.uk/review/story/0,6903,1207579,00.html#80s.

O'Shea, F. (2004). "Thief follows text as car returns to sender." *Daily Telegraph* April 8, p. 5. Sydney.

Passmore, E. (2002). "SMS poem." Retrieved February 12, 2005, from http://books.guardian.co.uk/textpoetry/story/0,12586,853760,00.html.

Pelkmans, J. (2001). "The GSM standard: Explaining a success story." *Journal of European Public Policy* 8, no. 3: 432–53.

Phillips, L. (2003). *Mobile industry looks to SMS/TV interactivity*. Retrieved February 24, 2003, from www.europemedia.net/showfeatureasp?ArticleID=14997.

Pierpont, W. G. (2001). *The art and skill of radio-telegraphy: A manual for learning, using, mastering, and enjoying the international Morse Code as a means of communication*. Retrieved February 27, 2005, from http://break.org/gisle/HamRadio/binaries/TASRT.pdf.

Plant, S. (2001) *On the mobile: The effects of mobile telephones on social and individual life*. Retrieved January 7, 2002, from http://www.motorola.com/mot/documents/0,,296,00.pdf.

Postman, N. (1999). *Building a bridge to the 18th century: How the past can improve our future*. New York: Knopf.

Rafaeli, S. (1988). "Interactivity: From new media to communication." In R. P. Hawkins, J. M. Wiemann, and S. Pingree (Eds.), *Advancing communication science: Merging mass and interpersonal processes, vol. 16* (pp. 110–34). Newbury Park, CA: Sage.

Reuters. (2004). "Mobile ringtone sales hit $3.5bn." Retrieved January 15, 2004, from http://www.itweb.co.za/sections/business/2004/0401140920.asp?S=Reuters&A=R EU&O=FPW.

Rheingold, H. (2002). *Smart mobs: The next social revolution*. Cambridge, MA: Perseus Books.

Rheingold, H. (2004). "Why mobile services fail." Retrieved April 15, 2005, from www.jensondesign.com/Feature1.pdf.

Saunders, C. (2002). "SMS, Ten Years Later." Retrieved February 11, 2005, from http://www.instantmessagingplanet.com/wireless/article.php/10766_1553321.

Schutz, A. (2001). "What is SMS?" Retrieved April 15, 2005, from http://50.lycos.com/071201.html.

Smith, T. (1999). *Morse: The end of an era?* Retrieved April 9, 2005, from www.unesco.org/courier/1999_08/uk/connex/txt1.htm.

Snowden, C. (1999). *Hello! The future is wireless.* Paper presented at the Exploring Cybersociety conference, September, University of Northumbria, Newcastle, England.

Sterling, C. H., and J. M. Kittross. (2001). *Stay tuned: A history of American broadcasting.* Mahwah, NJ: Lawrence Erlbaum Associates.

Taylor, A., and R. Harper. (2002). "Age-old practices in the 'New World': A study of gift-giving between teenage mobile phone users." Proceedings of the SIGCHI conference on Human factors in computing systems: Changing our world, changing ourselves: 439–446. Minneapolis, Minnesota, USA.

Taylor, A., and R. Harper. (2003). "The gift of the gab? A design oriented sociology of young people's use of mobiles." *Computer Supported Cooperative Work* 12, no. 3: 267–96.

TransL8it.com. (2005). "SMS LINGO dXNRE & gloSRE." Retrieved April 23, 2005, from www.transl8it.com/cgi-win/index.pl.

Trosby, F. (2004). "SMS: The Strange Duckling of GSM." *Telenor Telektronikk* 3: 187–94.

Walker, J. (2001). *Rebels on the air: An alternative history of radio in America.* New York: New York University Press.

Weekes, P. (2004). *Children of misfortune.* Retrieved September 8, 2004, from www.smh.com.au/news/Money/Children-of-misfortune/2004/09/23/1095651449010.html.

Wilson, A. (2002). "Windows on Life." Retrieved February 10, 2005, from http://books.guardian.co.uk/textpoetry/story/0,12586,834749,00.html.

Winston, B. 1998. *Media, technology and society. A history: From the telegraph to the Internet.* London: Routledge.

Can You Fear Me Now?: Cell Phones and the American Horror Film

Allison Whitney

In Wes Craven's 1996 film *Scream*, the teenage heroine Sidney Prescott (Neve Campbell) answers the telephone, and the male caller, who she believes to be one of her friends, starts asking her questions about her favorite horror movies. After explaining that she has no interest in horror films, she asks the caller to identify himself.

> Man: The question isn't who am I, the question is where am I?
> Sidney: So, where are you?
> Man: Your front porch.
> Sidney: Why would you be calling me from my front porch?
> Man: That's the original part.

As Sidney later discovers, the caller and his accomplice are her boyfriend Billy (Skeet Ulrich) and classmate Stu (Matthew Lillard), who are in the midst of a grotesque killing spree, attacking their victims according to the conventions of American horror films. Such conventions often include telephone-based scenarios in which victims are subjected to harassing calls, killers thwart their victims' attempts to call for help, and people are forced to listen to acts of violence while being powerless to intervene. The strategy of calling Sidney from her front porch is "original" in that it involves a new technology—the cell phone—a medium whose mobility affords the killers new powers to confuse and torment their victims, and to avoid detection by authorities. In this essay I will argue that in *Scream* and its two sequels, *Scream 2* (1997) and *Scream 3* (2000), the filmmakers use the unique contingencies of cell phone communications in order to propose thematic revisions to the horror genre, particularly regarding gender roles, sexual identity, and shifting understandings of the public and private spheres.

In the late nineteenth and early twentieth centuries, as telephones became a commonplace feature of modern infrastructure, they began to appear with some regularity in theatrical productions and in cinema. It is no surprise that the telephone's everyday uses, such as relaying information over great distances, coordinating simultaneous activities in disparate spaces, or calling for help in emergencies, were all integrated into dramatic narratives. In the case of cinema, widespread familiarity with the telephone may even have contributed to developments in film style, for, as Tom Gunning explains in "Heard over the Phone: *The Lonely Villa* and the De Lorde Tradition of the Terrors of Technology" (1991), by 1908, crosscutting had become the standard strategy for representing both phone calls and other simultaneous actions in disparate spaces. Gunning suggests further that the similarity between the spatiotemporal form of the telephone call and that of crosscutting (where the film cuts back and forth among different spaces to denote simultaneity) may have contributed to audiences' understanding of what is now a common editing strategy (p. 188).

In most cases, telephones' narrative functions were essentially benign, but some of the more grotesque dramatic traditions seized upon the technology's potentially disturbing qualities, such as its estrangement of the voice from the body. For example, as Mel Gordon explains in his study *The Grand Guignol: Theatre of Fear and Terror* (1997), André de Lorde and Charles Foley's 1902 play *At the Telephone* centers on a husband who leaves his family at their remote country home while he travels to the city on business. While en route, he speaks to his wife by telephone numerous times, and tries to allay her fears of strange noises she hears outside. During their final conversation, intruders break into the house, and the horrified husband is forced to listen as his family members are murdered (p. 53). The telephone's distancing of the voice from the body's physical presence not only brings the husband closer to his wife's suffering, but also underlines the physical distance between them, and the ineffectiveness of anything but co-presence. A similar scenario is played out in D. W. Griffith's *The Lonely Villa* (1911), in which a husband discovers over the telephone that his home is being invaded by thieves, overhears his wife and children screaming, and then, once the robbers cut the telephone wire, rushes home to the rescue. The film cuts back and forth among the narrative agents: the panicked husband, the imperiled family, and the robbers. Finally, these lines of narrative converge at the dramatic climax, when the husband and his companions rescue the family and trounce the villains. In this film, and the many that followed this pattern, the telephone motivates the convergence of disparate spaces through the transmission of auditory information in a way that plays on the perceived vulnerability of the bourgeois home.

On one level, the use of the telephone in this type of scenario seems little more than a narrative premise—without it, the husband would not know that anything was wrong, and there would be no suspenseful "ride to the rescue." However, telephones, like all technologies, carry significant cultural connotations emerging from both their intended uses and actual functions in society. Considerable social anxieties accompanied the introduction of the telephone into private homes, resulting in a correspondence between the drama of home invasion and the very presence of the technology. While the first telephone companies envisioned their machines as business tools, and initially had little interest in offering services in domestic spaces, by the late 1890s women of means began to use the telephone on a regular basis for social purposes (Martin 1988, p. 94). Consequently, questions arose about the telephone as a potential threat to the strict distinctions of public and private spheres that were so essential to Victorian social norms, since women could now access a broad spectrum of society with little supervision or control. As Carolyn Marvin explains in her study of nineteenth-century communications, *When Old Technologies Were New* (1988), public discussion of the telephone noted its capacity to "unsettle customary ways of dividing the private person and family from the more public setting of the community" (p. 6). While the telephone was recognized as a safety device, allowing one to summon emergency help, it was also regarded with trepidation for its ability to override the elaborate conventions that had controlled interpersonal communication and outsiders' access to private areas of houses.

The telephone line quite literally penetrated the perimeter of the bourgeois home, and thereby posed a threat to the women who both inhabited and embodied the private sphere. It is no coincidence, therefore, that in films like *The Lonely Villa* home invaders break through a succession of barriers, moving from the public exterior to the increasingly private interior of the house, each time coming closer to the imperiled woman and her daughters. Other films that use a similar premise, such as Lois Weber's *Suspense* (1913), show the invader breaking into the bedroom—the threatened woman's last refuge. This violation is a clear evocation of rape, and the successive movement through the house continues to be a trope of the horror genre—one that has been theorized in gendered terms in feminist theories of the horror film. In Carol Clover's study of gender and the horror genre, *Men, Women, and Chain Saws* (1992), she describes this process of penetration in terms of the iconic horror film scenario in which "the victim locks herself in (a house, room, closet, car) and waits with pounding heart as the killer slashes, hacks, or drills his way in" (p. 31).

While people grew to appreciate the telephone's efficacy in supporting personal and public safety, modern societies' growing dependence on this technology also aroused larger anxieties about the system's potential contingencies and failures. Just as in real life, there are many instances in cinema where, for example, the telephone is used as a means to violate one's privacy, as a tool of harassment, or where the telephone fails to allow one to summon help. For example, in Anatole Litvak's 1948 film *Sorry, Wrong Number*, an adaptation of Lucille Fletcher's radio play, *Leona* (Barbara Stanwyck) tries to make a call, but due to a switching error overhears two men plotting a murder. She spends the rest of the film trying to convince authorities to investigate—continually calling the operator, the police, her doctor, her husband's business colleagues, and her father, to no avail. Leona calls her husband, Henry (Burt Lancaster), and says that she is frightened to be alone in the house, but he assures her that she has no reason to worry because she is in the middle of New York City and has a telephone by her side. Leona realizes too late that the murder the men were planning is her own, and that Henry himself conspired to have his wife killed so that he might collect insurance money. The killer enters Leona's bedroom while she is on the phone with Henry, who is forced to listen to her screams before she is strangled.

Sorry, Wrong Number clearly draws upon earlier traditions where callers overhear violent or disturbing events, but Leona's inability to get effective assistance from authorities and family members alike indicates certain doubts as to the telephone's reputation as a protective technology. In her analysis of *Sorry, Wrong Number*, Ann Lawrence (1986–87) suggests further that not only does the infrastructure fail to protect Leona, but she is actually punished for trying to use the telephone to enhance her own agency. Lawrence points out that most of the conversations in this film consist of "women talking behind men's backs," usually exchanging information about the "secret" activities of their husbands and employers (p. 24). These activities correspond to another key fear that accompanied the spread of the telephone, namely that women might use it to create communities or share ideas in an unsupervised context. Women's socializing by phone came to be denigrated as "gossip," or as a trivial use of a necessarily serious communications technology. Indeed, at the beginning of *Sorry, Wrong Number*, Leona differentiates gendered ways of using the telephone when she asks the operator to trace the killers' call. The operator explains that this can only be accomplished if the parties are still talking to one another, and Leona exclaims "of course they've stopped talking now . . . they weren't exactly gossiping."

Many narratives exploit women's social attachment to the telephone, either punishing them for unauthorized use or placing women in jeopardy by perverting the telephone's powers of personal connection. For example, in the horror film *Halloween* (John Carpenter, 1979), teenage girls who are babysitting on Halloween night continually call one another, not only to gossip, but also to make arrangements for trysts with their boyfriends. During one of these calls, Laurie (Jamie Lee Curtis) overhears her friend Lynda (P. J. Soles) being strangled, but interprets the sounds as sexual rather than violent, and initially assumes that it is a prank call. Furthermore, Laurie believes that the caller is a different friend, Annie (Nancy Loomis), who is supposed to be babysitting in the house across the street. Laurie becomes suspicious that something is amiss, but rather than calling the police, she goes across the street to investigate, only to discover her friends' murdered bodies and narrowly escape being stabbed herself. The constant telephone contact among these teenage girls not only facilitates their illicit sexual behavior—behavior that arouses the killer to commit murder—but also serves to draw the heroine into harm's way. Without overhearing the mysterious noises of her friend's strangulation, Laurie would not have felt compelled to investigate, and would not have confronted the killer.

In another horror film from the same year, *When a Stranger Calls* (Fred Walton, 1979), a babysitter (Carol Kane) receives disturbing calls from a man who continually asks if she has gone upstairs to "check the children." She reports these calls to the police, but they initially dismiss her fears because the caller neither uses obscene language nor threatens specific action. The babysitter tries to protect herself by securing the perimeter of the house—checking the lock on the front door and closing the living room curtains to deter Peeping Toms. However, her strategy works against her, for when the police finally trace the call, they realize that the man is calling from an extension inside the house. Her efforts to protect herself by locking the doors only make it more difficult to escape, and indeed, a common trope in horror films is for containers, usually houses, to quickly transform from safe havens into traps, where "the same walls that promise to keep the killer out quickly become . . . the walls that hold the victim in" (Clover 1992, p. 31). While the babysitter in this film manages to open the door in time to save herself, the children under her care have already been murdered.

When a Stranger Calls is based on an urban legend, titled in folkloric studies as "The Baby-sitter and the Man Upstairs," and Jan Brunvand suggests in *The Vanishing Hitchhiker* (1981) that the story of the babysitter being harassed by telephone has currency among teenage girls because this technology is their favorite means of communication (p. 56). It seems, therefore, that in *Sorry, Wrong Number, Halloween,* and *When a Stranger Calls*, women's dependence on the telephone for both their personal security and their social networks leaves them particularly vulnerable to attack. Furthermore, the notion that women's talk is unauthorized, subversive, and worthy of punishment lends to the misogynistic subtext of these scenarios. In films in which the telephone is used as a weapon to harass, frighten, manipulate, or isolate a potential victim, the scenario always begins with the killer's contacting the victim by telephone, a technology whose penetrative power is more insidious than other weapons because the material of telephone contact is invisible, nearly impossible to deter, and, in some cases, not tangible enough to warrant police action.

When a Stranger Calls' revelation that the caller is inside the house is particularly frightening because it violates the traditional spatial logic of telephone communications that a caller is in a fixed and distant location. Here, the drama of home invasion moves a step further, for not only does the killer threaten the private sphere, but he also manipulates the woman's movements within that sphere. Furthermore, one of the things that makes this film disturbing is that while we see shots of the babysitter speaking into the receiver, and portions of the interior and exterior of the house, we never see who is on the other end of the line. Since film viewers are accustomed to crosscutting in telephone scenes, with equal screen time for each speaker, it can be disconcerting if only one side of the conversation is shown, particularly if the interlocutor poses a threat. Not only does the lack of visual information disguise identity, but, often more important, it disguises physical location. The film therefore creates suspense by playing against viewers' assumptions about communication technology, assumptions based on both their personal experience of using the telephone and their experience of its narrative function in other films.

Viewer expectations are a crucial component of films' intelligibility, particularly in genre cinema, where filmmakers operate on the premise that their viewers will recognize and anticipate the narrative structures, character types, iconography, and emotional responses associated with a given tradition. This truism is particularly relevant in the *Scream* films, where the killers conspire to commit murder according to the generic conventions of horror films. Not only do *Scream's* audiences come to the theater with preconceived notions about how the film will proceed and how they are expected to respond (usually with laughter and a measure of disgust), but the characters within the film also become aware of their generic expectations, even going so far as to discuss the "rules" of horror films as a way of avoiding attack. Meanwhile, the killers differentiate themselves from their generic predecessors by making cellular telephones a critical part of their murder techniques. Since the contingencies of telephone communication are an important part of the horror genre both structurally and thematically, it is interesting that the *Scream* films judiciously employ the cell phone to demonstrate contemporary social fears. First, the cell phone's primary feature, mobility, comes to be loaded with anxieties about the mutability of identity and social structures, particularly sexual and gender identity. These fears are enhanced by the cell phone's close connection to the body of its user, rather than the fixed location of a land line. The cell phone also facilitates the further breakdown of public and private distinctions, but now in an opposite direction, where the private realm comes to intrude upon the public sphere. I will explain each of these issues in relation to exemplary sequences in the *Scream* trilogy.

The very first image in *Scream* is a shot of a telephone. The telephone rings, and Casey (Drew Barrymore), a teenager who is home alone, answers. The caller refuses to identify himself, and yet he continually calls back, hoping to talk more with Casey, who gradually obliges and admits that she is planning to watch *Halloween* on video. Casey walks through the house with her cordless phone, and she and the anonymous caller chat for a while about their favorite horror film, *Nightmare on Elm Street* (Wes Craven, 1984). Although we see Casey casually locking one of the exterior doors of her house, she clearly believes that this is little more than a harmless flirtation; that is, so she thinks, until the caller asks her name, explaining that "I want to know who I'm looking at." Much like the babysitter in *When a Stranger Calls* (a film that is clearly referenced in this sequence), Casey initially assumes that the caller is in a distant location, but when she realizes that he is using a cell phone and is just outside the house, she hangs up, turns on the house's exterior lights, and latches the patio doors in an effort to protect herself. When he calls back and threatens to kill her if she hangs up again, she runs through the house, locking doors and looking out windows, trying to ascertain his location. He asks, "Can you see me?" while shots representing Casey's point of view indicate that she cannot. He torments her further by ringing the doorbell, calling her "blondie" (she has blond hair), and repeating things that she said while not on the phone, indicating that he is close enough to both see and hear her. When she threatens to call the police, he says that they will never arrive in time, since the house is "in the middle of nowhere." She counters that her boyfriend Steve (Kevin Patrick Walls) will arrive shortly to protect her, but her hopes are dashed when she looks outside and sees Steve gagged and tied to a chair. The killer tells her that the only way she and Steve can survive is for her to correctly answer some horror-film trivia questions.

First, he asks her to name the killer in *Halloween*, and she correctly answers Michael Myers. He then asks the name of the killer in *Friday the 13th* (Sean Cunningham, 1980), but her answer, "Jason," is incorrect, since the killer in that film is actually Jason's vengeful mother. The killer says, "poor Steve, I'm afraid he's out," and when Casey turns on the patio lights, she sees that Steve has been disemboweled. The killer's final question is "What door am I at?"—the front door or the patio door. Before Casey has a chance to guess, he throws a chair through the patio door, and she runs to the kitchen, grabs a knife, and, still clutching the cordless phone, sneaks outside just as the killer enters the house. The following shot is of her parents' car coming over the hill—a nod to the "ride to the rescue" tradition of films like *The Lonely Villa*—although they do not yet realize that their daughter is in danger. By the time they arrive home, the killer has already emerged from the house and is stabbing and strangling Casey on the lawn. While she manages to fight back, she can neither move fast enough nor cry out to attract her parents' attention as they enter the house. Realizing that something is terribly wrong, her mother picks up the telephone extension, only to overhear her daughter's final gasps as she is stabbed to death. The sequence ends when the parents see Casey's eviscerated body hanging from a tree.

This sequence clearly calls upon each of the key uses of the telephone in horror and suspense films, including harassment of the victim, perversion of the telephone's protective qualities (that is, the killer occupies the line constantly, giving Casey no opportunity to call police), the killer's use of the telephone in close proximity to the victim, and the horrified listener who overhears violence while being powerless to intervene. This fairly comprehensive referencing of telephone narratives is partly a well-devised homage to generic conventions, but the sequence also capitalizes on the fact that a cell phone user has no fixed location. While confusion about physical location does have precedents in the *When a Stranger Calls* scenario, the mobility that is inherent to the cell phone allows the *Scream* killers to further violate the material boundaries of the private sphere, and to torment their victims in explicitly spatial terms by controlling their movements within and outside their houses, and by making them fearful of possible escape routes.

Obviously, the physical and auditory boundaries of houses are constantly at issue in the *Scream* films, and the killers are heavily invested in violating the interior/exterior distinction of both the houses and bodies of their victims. For example, in *Scream*, Casey and her boyfriend are not only killed, but disemboweled. Indeed, when Casey asks the killer what he wants, his response is "to see what your insides look like." Later, when

Casey's classmates are discussing her murder, they refer to her "insides on the outside." Similarly, in *Scream 3*, the killer taunts one of his victims by saying "how much fun it's going to be to rip your insides out" as he stabs through a door. While grotesque murders are to be expected in horror films, it is important to note that the interest in "what your insides look like" is substantially different from the killer's statement of purpose in a similar dialogue in *When a Stranger Calls*. In that film, the babysitter asks the caller what he wants, but his response is "your blood . . . all over me"—a threat that is certainly as terrifying but does not explicitly map the invaded house onto the murdered body.

In each of the *Scream* films, the killers' physical mobility gives them a strategic advantage over land line users. In his article "Mobile Communications in the Twenty-First Century City," Anthony Townsend (2002, p. 70) comments on users' conception of their cell phones in explicitly bodily terms, referring to the idea of relying entirely on a cell phone for one's personal communications as "cutting the cord." This umbilical metaphor for the land line corresponds to a larger conceptualization of the home in gendered and indeed explicitly maternal terms, and in the horror film, where bodily metaphors abound, the land line's physical attachments are readily equated with the female body. Several of the *Scream* murders are constructed in a way that shows land lines literally tying their users to the domestic spaces they occupy, while cell phones allow freedom to move freely between the interior and the exterior. For example, Cici (Sarah Michelle Gellar), the third victim in *Scream 2*, receives calls from the killer while she is alone in her sorority house. She begins to suspect that there is someone upstairs, so she takes her cordless phone to the front porch to call campus security. However, her receiver's range is too limited to operate outdoors and her message cannot get through, so she is forced to reenter the house. When the killer calls back, she picks up a different telephone (not a cordless model) directly outside the closet where the killer is hiding. The land line not only confines her to the house, but its physical connection to the wall places her directly in the killer's sights. Moments later, at another sorority house down the street, Sidney is about to leave with her boyfriend, but she returns to the house to answer a ringing phone—also a telephone with a cord. Sidney's picking up the receiver allows the killer just enough time to confine her to the house, where she narrowly escapes his attack. Meanwhile, in *Scream*, although most of Casey's conversations take place using a cordless phone, she initially answers using a telephone with a cord—and thus, from the outset, she is represented as having a direct physical attachment to her house.

It is significant that the killers' capacity to trap and overpower their victims is contingent on conversations between a cell phone and a land line, in what is literally a dialogue between two technologies and the identity formations that accompany them. The cell phone's mobility and public presence serves to overdetermine the land line's identification with the private sphere, and in each of these sequences the land line physically traps the woman inside the home, while also penetrating the home's protective boundaries. Although each of these female victims fights back with a measure of success (particularly Cici, whom audiences would identify with Sarah Michelle Gellar's lead role in the horror television series *Buffy the Vampire Slayer*), the killers manage to literally put these women in their place and thereby exploit the physical isolation of the house to commit murder.

In both *Scream* and *Scream 2*, there are two killers, but they appear to be one person because they wear matching costumes, use digital devices to make their voices sound identical, and share a single cell phone to harass their victims. Meanwhile, in *Scream 3*, the killer uses a device to simulate individuals' voices, tricking victims into believing that they are conversing with loved ones or coworkers. Of course, concealing one's identity over the telephone is by no means unique to the cell phone, and even from its beginnings the industrial infrastructure has relied on a level of auditory deception. In her study "The Making of the Perfect Operator," Michele Martin (1991, p. 59) explains how in the 1880s, telephone companies hired women as operators because women's patience, dexterity, courtesy, and moderate tempers were considered ideal for the role, not to mention the "clear feminine quality of voice" that apparently suited the sound-trans-mission technology. However, the majority of operators were not in fact middle-class Victorian matrons, but rather young working-class unmarried women who received extensive training in diction and deportment so as to disguise their social origins. Some nineteenth-century commentators even ascribed ethnic qualities to the ideal operator, singling out the American-raised daughters of Irish immigrants as having the best voices and manners (Maddox 1977, p. 268). From the beginning, the telephone infrastructure has incorporated a form of class- and ethnicity-based ventriloquism, making the notion of deliberately hiding one's identity by altering the quality of one's voice a necessary component of the system's public persona.

In the case of the *Scream* films, it might seem that voice modification is the most crucial component in the killers' strategies to confuse their victims. However, it is important to consider how the cell phone's capacity to disguise location also contributes to uncertainty about personal identity. In *Beyond Mobile*, Mats Lindgren, Jörgen Jedbratt, and Erika Svensson (2002, p. 27) explain that postmodern society offers "a dizzying array of identities and roles" where one "gets accustomed to dipping in and out of roles and structures in a way that has not been possible at other times in history," and mobile technologies greatly facilitate these rapid transitions of identity. At the same time, cellular phones generally belong to, and are often used by, a single individual and are therefore closely associated with the owner's body. Indeed, by the late 1990s many users had come to perceive their phones as "an extension of the body . . . a tool linked to the owner on the most basic level" (Townsend 2002, p. 69). Conversely, a land line in a private home, although usually listed in an individual's name, is anchored to its immovable physical location such that if you receive a call from a land line and the call is traced, you know where the caller is located, but not necessarily his or her identity. Meanwhile, knowing who a cellular phone belongs to tells you little or nothing about the user's location, but supposedly offers you a bodily referent. By using a single cell phone, *Scream*'s killers make their victims believe that multiple users occupy a single body, thus exacerbating the spatial confusion that is so integral to their murder strategies, such that when one killer asks, "What door am I at?" Casey fails to consider that the answer could be "both." By speaking with one voice and sharing a single cell phone, the killers' personal identities become functionally interchangeable, and in a sense, they become one body. Indeed, as the killer explains to Sidney when he calls her from her front porch, "who am I" is no longer a relevant question, since for the killers, the distinction of *I* and *We* has collapsed. Just before Casey is fatally stabbed, she reaches up to unmask her killer, but since we do not share her point of view, his identity remains a mystery. While we might attribute this withholding of information to the filmmakers' need to maintain suspense, it is also true that in a way, the killer's identity is immaterial, since Billy and Stu's individual identities have become mobilized, destabilized, and homogenized via the cell phone.

Given that gender is so clearly mapped onto telephone technology, it is important to consider how the cell phone's destabilization of traditional communication might correspond to shifts in gender norms. Distortion of gender is standard material in the horror film (consider Norman Bates's relationship with, and as, his mother in Alfred Hitchcock's 1960 film, *Psycho*), and the genre's continual evocation of castration directly relates monstrosity with sexual ambiguity, but the *Scream* films call on this tradition in particularly significant ways. First, in *Scream*, the killer's horror-film quiz is structured in such a way that Casey is likely to lose the game because of gender confusion, or rather, presumption of gender. Their dialogue about horror film villains such as Freddy Krueger and Michael Myers sets up a particular model of male killers whose films generate a cult following. Therefore, when the killer asks Casey to name the villain in *Friday the 13th*, she mistakenly identifies him as Jason, while the killer is actually a woman—Jason appears only in the sequels. Realizing her mistake, Casey says, "you tricked me"—an interesting response given that, technically, the error is hers. The next question that Casey is doomed to answer incorrectly is of course "Which door am I at?" I believe that the sequencing of these questions suggests a correlation between gender confusion and spatial confusion. When Casey's classmates are discussing her murder, Tatum (Rose McGowan) insists that the killer could be a woman, and indeed, in *Scream 2*, one of them is. In this case, however, the female killer disguises her voice to sound like that of her male counterpart. Meanwhile, in *Scream 3*, the killer's voice-modification technology allows him to change genders at will. While threats to the feminine and to the private sphere are a standard part of the telephone traditions, I believe that this element of the *Scream* films points to an anxiety about masculinity, and a corresponding threat to the integrity of the traditionally male-dominated public sphere.

Academic studies of the social impact of the cell phone consistently comment on how this technology compromises public/private distinctions by allowing private speech and behavior to intrude into the public realm. For example, in *The Mobile Connection: The Cell Phone's Impact on Society*, Rich Ling (2004, p. 140) describes the often embarrassing phenomenon of "forced eavesdropping" wherein cell users carry on intimate conversations in public spaces, compelling those within earshot to listen to personal information they would rather not hear. Meanwhile, the fact that a user can remain in perpetual contact with friends, family members, and coworkers means that many people spend much of their public time on the telephone, making it less likely that they will interact socially with the people around them. For example, if one has the option of talking to a friend on the telephone, then one is less likely to strike up a conversation with a stranger on a train. Furthermore, cell phone calls often interrupt public interactions, and in their analysis of cell phone adoption in the United States, Kathleen Robbins and Martha Turner (2002, p. 91) note that these interruptions frequently disrupt traditional forms of dyad communication. Meanwhile, women sometimes use the pretense of interruption to their advantage, deterring unwanted public interactions by pretending to be engaged in a phone conversation (Ling 2004, p. 45). As James Katz and Mark Aakhus explain in their introduction to *Perpetual Contact: Mobile Communication, Private Talk, Public Performance* (2002, p. 9), prohibitions against cell phones in places such as restaurants "dramatize how public space is destroyed, and even colonized, by private talk that interferes with ongoing interactions or that prevents spontaneous public interaction." Furthermore, many of the dangers associated with the cell phone have to do with its tendency to distract users from their public responsibilities. For example, studies on driving safety indicate that the distraction of cell phone conversations greatly increases rates of driver error (Ling 2004, p. 49).

As explained above, Victorian anxieties about the telephone had much to do with a public intrusion into the private sphere, threatening the very notions of femininity that relied on a clear definition of the private. Now it would appear that the cell phone threatens the social order by inserting the private into the public realm, and if the private sphere is identified with femininity, it follows that a compromised public sphere could jeopardize the integrity of masculine identity. While attacks on women in the *Scream* films involve conversations between cell phones and land lines, telephone-based murders of male characters involve cell phones exclusively. For example, in *Scream 2*, which takes place on a college campus, Randy (Jamie Kennedy), Dewey (David Arquette), and Gale Weathers (Courteney Cox) are standing in the quadrangle discussing the murders when the killer calls Gale's cell phone. Randy answers it, and the killer asks, "I'm not interrupting anything, am I?" Randy announces to his companions that he is talking to the killer, and they decide to disperse, hoping to locate the caller in the quadrangle. During their conversation, the killer makes a point of insulting Randy's masculinity, taunting him that he'll never be "the leading man" and never "get the girl." Randy counters that the killer will never be one of "the big boys . . . Manson, Bundy, O.J.," and mocks him for trying to emulate Billy and Stu, describing them as a "homo-repressed mama's boy" and a "pussy-ass wet rag," respectively.[1] While it would seem that the open and emphatically public space of the college quadrangle would be safe, particularly from a killer who wears a costume and typically stabs his victims, the cell phone compromises the public sphere just enough to subvert its protective functions. In "The Challenge of Absent Presence," Kenneth Gergen (2002, p. 238) observes that cell phone conversation in public spaces "typically establishes an 'inside space' ('we who are conversing') vs. an 'outside space' constituted by those within earshot but prevented from participating." By interrupting public conversation, the killer in *Scream 2* manages to trap Randy in the "inside space" of private conversation, and, as the killer suggests, this feminizes him in a way that makes him vulnerable to attack, not unlike the female victims who found themselves trapped inside houses. The cell phone isolates Randy from the "outside space" that might have afforded him some protection, and therefore the killer is able to manipulate his movements and lure him toward Gale's television van, where he pulls Randy inside and stabs him to death. It follows that if women are threatened by the telephone's penetration of the private sphere, then public masculinity is threatened by the cell phone's imposition of private talk into public space, and indeed Randy and the killer devote most of their conversation to the issue of compromised masculinity.

In *Scream 3*, the killer also conspires to lure a male victim into a private space, but in this case the threat is not one of emasculation, but rather an appropriation and distortion of the victim's masculine identity. In the film's opening sequence, television personality Cotton Weary (Liev Schreiber) is driving in Los Angeles, talking to his agent on his car phone, when he is interrupted by another call on his cell phone. Cotton believes that the caller is one of his female fans, and they engage in a flirtatious conversation until the caller mentions Cotton's girlfriend. When he denies having a girlfriend, the caller suddenly takes on a male voice, and informs Cotton that he is standing outside his girlfriend Christine's (Kelly Rutherford) bathroom door. He threatens to kill her if Cotton does not tell him how to find Sidney, who is living in seclusion after the numerous attempts on her life. Cotton drives home in a panic, hoping to rescue his girlfriend, all the while trying to call 911, but hearing only a message saying that all operators are busy. He also tries to call Christine, but the killer has severed her land line. Meanwhile, the masked killer uses a voice-simulation device to convince Christine that he is Cotton in disguise, and by the time the real Cotton arrives home, Christine believes that he has gone mad and is trying to kill her. Cotton is unable to convince her that he means her no harm, so she attacks him with a golf club, giving him no opportunity to defend her from the killer. After a final struggle, the killer murders Cotton as well, but not before taunting him one last time with the voice simulator, speaking to Cotton in Cotton's own voice.

Just as in Randy's murder in *Scream 2*, the killer interrupts Cotton's conversation, and uses the forced intimacy of the cell phone to draw him into a private space to be killed. In addition, by convincing Christine that it is Cotton who is attacking her, the killer perverts Cotton's traditional protective role in the household. While Cotton goes through the motions of a "ride to the rescue" much like the husband in *The Lonely Villa*, he arrives home to discover that his identity has been stolen and has been replaced with a demonized version of masculinity. While Cotton intends to protect the private home and the woman within, the killer instead casts Cotton as a perpetrator of domestic violence. For Randy and Cotton alike, the cell phone interrupts their public interactions and colonizes the public spaces they occupy to the extent that their masculine personae come under deadly attack.

It might seem that the *Scream* films assume a conservative attitude toward both the cell phone and the shifts in gender roles and identity that seem to correspond to this technology. However, it is also important to consider that the *Scream* films actually position themselves in opposition to the often misogynistic logic of the horror genre, particularly concerning women's sexual identity. When Randy delivers a speech to his friends about the "rules" of the horror film, his first statement is that "you can never have sex," and he goes on to say that the only guarantee of survival in a horror film is to remain a virgin. Indeed, Carol Clover explains that "killing those who seek or engage in unauthorized sex amounts to a generic imperative in the slasher film" (1992, p. 34). Meanwhile, the villains are usually thwarted by a "final girl" whose virginity and, in many cases, masculinity (as expressed through her independence, mechanical skills, sexual reluctance, and in many cases masculine-sounding name) offer her a level of immunity (p. 48). In *Scream*, the killers take such distinctions seriously, and Sidney's virginity is the main topic of conversation when we meet her character. Early in the film, Billy crawls in through Sidney's bedroom window, and they have a playful discussion about their relationship in terms of film ratings, where her desire for a relatively chaste PG-13 scenario contrasts with his NC-17 agenda. Sidney eventually decides to sleep with Billy, and it is only after losing her virginity that the killers consider her fair game, for as Stu explains during their final confrontation, "now that you're no longer a virgin, you gotta die—those are the rules." Stu and Billy explain further that a year previously they had murdered Sidney's mother as a punishment for her sexual promiscuity.

Scream is not sympathetic to the killers' puritanical reasoning, and instead the film represents Sidney's change in sexual identity in more positive terms. For example, while Sidney had long suspected Billy of being involved in the murders, it is immediately after having sex with him that she begins to realize, for instance, that he had threatened her by telephone while in police custody. While the tradition is that the virgin girl is the lone survivor, Sidney instead loses her virginity and enters a new realm of wisdom. During the final confrontation in Stu's kitchen, where Billy and Stu plan to murder Sidney and her father, Gale enters the house and threatens the killers with a gun. Sidney uses this distraction to appropriate the killers' cell phone, voice-modification device, and their identity-concealing costume, using them to taunt her tormentors and eventually kill them, but not before calling the police. On a practical level, Sidney does not really need to modify her voice, disguise her identity, or even speak to the killers at all in order to defeat them, so it is clearly of great symbolic import that she becomes capable of defeating Billy and Stu once she takes on the mutability of identity and bodily location afforded by the cell phone.

It is important to note that while this is transpiring, the film *Halloween* is playing on the television in the living room, and in the background we can hear the soundtrack—Michael Myers is breaking into the closet where the virginal final girl Laurie is hiding. It is at this moment that Sidney bursts out of a closet to stab Billy with, of all things, an umbrella. She then struggles with Stu, and when he makes a comment suggesting sexual violence, "I always had a thing for you, Sid," she retaliates by biting him and finally electrocuting him by smashing the television onto his head. The sequence in *Halloween* is clearly in the tradition of the home-invasion scenarios described above, and, indeed, Sidney had rehearsed this trajectory of attack herself earlier in the film when she was attacked in her own house. In that instance, Sidney, not unlike the family in *The Lonely Villa*, runs from the front porch to the main hall, up the stairs, into the bedroom, and finally opens her closet door to barricade herself in. Therefore, when Sidney now breaks out of a closet wearing the killer's costume she literally reverses the trajectory of violence, emerging from the enclosed space to defend herself and take control of the scene. Indeed, Sidney makes her relationship to the genre's gender traditions clear by defending herself by both biting and penetrating—forms of attack associated with violent fantasies about female and male sex organs, respectively, and by smashing the television while it is showing a close-up of Laurie's terrified face. Just as Billy and Stu had used the cell phone to collapse their identities into what was, in effect, a single body, Sidney uses the cell phone to defy traditional categories of sexual status by retaining the self-containment and resourcefulness associated with virginity while also internalizing the awareness and power of mature womanhood.

I would suggest that Sidney's use of the cell phone distances her from the elaborate and retrograde symbolic systems that serve to both isolate and violate the female body, and she does so by transforming her prescribed role within the horror genre. No longer affixed to the private sphere by a land line, and no longer willing to acknowledge the virgin/whore dichotomy that underlies patriarchal visions of femininity, Sidney's strategy is even more "original" than the killers', as she enhances her own agency by taking on the cell phone's mobility and mutability. When Sidney first appears in *Scream 3*, we see her activating her home's elaborate safety devices, including a gate with an access code, multiple locks on the doors, and an electronic security system. However, by the end of the film, even though Sidney has been attacked by a succession of killers over a period of many years, she makes the conscious decision to let the boundaries between the interior and exterior fall away. In the final scene, she refuses to lock the gate, chooses not to turn on the alarm system, and when the wind blows open her front door, she smiles and turns away, leaving it ajar. Sidney is indeed an original kind of heroine, for while her society has historically relied on distinctions of public and private, inside and outside, and, in the case of female virginity, penetrated and not penetrated, in order to maintain the social order, she decides to deny such distinctions outright. Realizing that in the era of mobile communications traditional boundaries are so readily violated that they become almost meaningless, Sidney chooses to embrace this new openness, whereby she becomes victorious.

While cell phones were widely used in North America when the first *Scream* film was released in the mid-1990s, changes in technology and in user behavior have been so rapid that, in many ways, these films appear dated to a twenty-first-century viewer. Consider, for example, that James Katz's 1999 book *Connections: Social and Cultural Studies of the Telephone in American Life*, includes a chapter on caller ID, raising questions as to whether it constitutes a threat to privacy. Such a debate might well seem inconceivable to contemporary telephone users who are now accustomed to text messaging, picture and video phones, Internet access, and ever more complex and versatile mobile technology. As more of us rely on mobile communications for our business and social lives, we also become more aware of cellular systems' fragilities. For example, in *Cellular* (David R. Ellis, 2004), a kidnapped woman uses a damaged land line to contact a stranger's cell phone, and once she convinces him to help her, much of the film's suspense arises from contingencies that are now familiar to anyone who has used a cell phone, or received a call from a cell user. As the hero tries to rescue the caller's family and solve the mystery of her kidnapping, there is a constant danger that his battery will run out of power, or that he will lose the signal—indeed, the film's promotional tagline is "If the signal dies, so does she." Here, the social impact of the cell phone is, in a sense, a fait accompli, and rather than fearing the destabilization of social spheres or traditional forms of communication, the viewer fears only that the cellular infrastructure will curtail the hero's mobility. For example, he finds that he cannot drive through tunnels, nor can he make his way to the upper floors of a police station to report the kidnapping lest he lose the cellular signal.

While the scenarios presented in *Cellular* present the cell phone as an established part of everyday life, and tap into possible fears that emerge from our near-constant reliance on such technology, we might regard the *Scream* films as an artifact of a particular moment in late-twentieth-century culture when communications systems were undergoing a radical change. All the films I have discussed, from *The Lonely Villa* to *Cellular,* provide us with clues as to the social impact of the telephone in its various manifestations, but they also provide us with a form of cultural memory, allowing us to contemplate what it was like when old technologies were new. It is fair to say that any shift in technology may be viewed with both promise and trepidation, and while the *Scream* films express anxiety at the gradual dissolution of the traditional social order, they also embrace technological change and the social progress that may accompany it, as evinced in Sidney's heroic assumption of the powers of mobility to flesh out the humanity of her Final Girl.

Note

1 I would suggest that there is indeed a queer element to Billy and Stu's relationship, or at least a suggestion of bisexual attachment. While they are never reluctant to express desire for women, they do conspire to murder one another's girlfriends, and their alibi culminates in a bizarre ruse where they repeatedly and ecstatically stab one another in the abdomen to make themselves look like victims.

References

Brunvand, J. H. (1981). *The vanishing hitchhiker: American urban legends and their meanings.* New York: Norton.

Clover, C. J. (1992). *Men, women, and chain saws: Gender in the modern horror film.* Princeton, NJ: Princeton University Press.

Gergen, K. J. (2002). "The challenge of absent presence." In J. E. Katz and M. A. Aakhus (Eds.), *Perpetual contact: Mobile communication, private talk, public performance* (pp. 227–41). Cambridge, UK: Cambridge University Press.

Gordon, M. (1997). *The grand Guignol: Theatre of fear and terror.* New York: Da Capo.

Gunning, T. (1991). "Heard over the phone: *The Lonely Villa* and the De Lorde tradition of the terrors of technology." *Screen* 32: 184–96.

Katz, J. E. (1999). *Connections: Social and cultural studies of the telephone in American Life.* London: Transaction.

Katz, J. E., and M. A. Aakhus. (2002). "Introduction: Framing the issues." In J. E. Katz and M. A. Aakhus (Eds.), *Perpetual contact: Mobile communication, private talk, public performance* (pp. 1–13). Cambridge, UK: Cambridge University Press.

Lawrence, A. (1986–87). "Sorry, Wrong Number: The organizing ear." *Film Quarterly* 40, no. 2: 20–27.

Lindgren, M., J. Jedbratt, and E. Svensson. (2002). *Beyond mobile: People, communications, and marketing in a mobilized world.* New York: Palgrave.

Ling, R. (2004). *The mobile connection: The cell phone's impact on society.* San Francisco: Elsevier.

Maddox, B. (1977). "Women and the switchboard." In *The social impact of the telephone.* Cambridge, MA: MIT Press.

Martin, M. (1988). "Rulers of the wires?: Women's contribution to the structure of mass communication." *Journal of Communication Inquiry*, no. 12: 89–103.

Martin, M. (1991). "The making of the perfect operator." In *"Hello, Central?": Gender, technology, and culture.* Montreal: McGill Queens University Press.

Marvin, C. (1988). *When old technologies were new: Thinking about electric communication in the late nineteenth century.* New York: Oxford University Press.

Robbins, K. A., and M. A. Turner. (2002). "United States: Popular, pragmatic, and problematic." In James E. Katz and Mark A. Aakhus (Eds.), *Perpetual contact: Mobile communication, private talk, public performance* (pp. 80–93). Cambridge, UK: Cambridge University Press.

Townsend, A. M. (2002). "Mobile communications in the twenty-first century city." In B. Brown, N. Green, and R. Harper (Eds.), *Wireless world: Social and interactional aspects of the mobile age* (pp. 62–77). London: Springer-Verlag.

Texting the Faith: Religious Users and Cell Phone Culture

Heidi Campbell

The cell phone has become a symbol of the emerging information economy, an icon of global information culture representing the trademark characteristics of mobility, interconnection, and multiple functionality. In many ways it represents a technology that is embedded in the daily lives of its users. Cell phone technology meets a perceived need for connectivity, the ability to connect with anyone, at anytime, on one's own terms. It serves as a connection point in the formation of contemporary social networks, allowing users to manage and maintain their different networks of relationships with more individualized control. Yet the cell phone is not only a tool for communication; through added accessories and features it can come to represent your personal style and even beliefs.

George Myerson, in *Heidegger, Habermas, and the Mobile Phone* (2001), argues that the mobilization of the phone is not simply a technological process; it is a cultural one changing the very nature of how and why we communicate. He suggests that communication has become a concept linked to devices, and "talk" is increasingly taking place through networks of media-steered interactions. In this process, people seek to establish personal systems that can control and manage the increasing flow of information. A strength of mobile culture is new technology's ability to be both personal and networked at the same time. The cell phone serves as a tool for self-expression, as users personalize their technology through ring tones, fashion phone covers, or screen wallpaper. Cell phones also serve as a corporate communication tool, supporting new and traditional social networks through messaging services and caller plans that encourage communication within dedicated groups.

One unexpected area of life the cell phone is empowering is people's personal and corporate religious sensibilities. Just as research has shown that the Internet has become a technology used to enhance and express ones spirituality (Hoover, Clark, and Rainie 2004; Dawson and Cowan 2004), the cell phone is becoming a device used to integrate religious practices into the mobile lifestyles of its users. With the ability to configure your phone to access who and what you value, the cell phone enables users to create a private-public space for religious expression. From religious ring tones to services that provide religious texts, cell phone users are being given increasing options to make their faith mobile.

The embrace of cell phones by religious groups and the debates that surround this appropriation provide important insights into the social shaping of technology. The process by which a cell phone becomes an extension of religious life raises questions of how and why a distinct community of users must negotiate a new technology in order to make it compatible with the life of that community. The social shaping of technology is an area of research that considers the social use and socialization of technology in public and private spaces. While much work has been done on how and why different groups of users make certain choices at each stage of the innovation and design process, religious groups on the whole have been overlooked within these studies. Yet as religion still plays a key role in the social construction of cultural spaces within society, it is an area that needs to be explored within a global information society.

This chapter explores how religious user communities have responded to cell phone culture, looking at how different groups have adopted and adapted cell phones for use in their patterns of religious life. First, an overview is given of various ways cell phones are used by different religions, with special consideration being given to religious groups' reaction to this mobile technology. Next, studies of religious user communities' interaction and perception with communication technologies are noted. This is done in order to identify characteristics of the technological negotiation process, which religious user communities undergo when engaging with new technologies. Then a case study is presented on the emergence and development of the "kosher phone." This provides a unique example of how a distinct religious user community, the ultra-Orthodox in Israel, have reacted and responded to cell phone technology. Finally, reflections are given on how to approach religious user communities' negotiation of communication technology, especially cell phones.

Religious Use of Cell Phones

Since Samuel Morse communicated the famous words "what hath God wrought" in the first telegraph conversation, communication technology has been infused with an element of mystical and spiritual undertones. The idea of a disembodied voice speaking across time and space has echoes of an otherworldly quality that remain in reflections on this technology (see "A spiritual connection" 2005). Religion and technology is not always an easy alliance. Some religious communities are hesitant to use certain technologies, seeing them as tools of secular culture. However, since the Gutenberg printing press revolutionized the spread of Christianity in Europe in the fifteenth and sixteenth centuries, many religious groups have been willing to consider the potential use of technology for the spread of their beliefs. In the same way, many religious groups have embraced the cell phone and even encouraged the development of features that support religious life and daily spiritual reflection. One of the first examples of religion meeting cell phone culture was an SMS-mobile church service conducted via cell phone in 2001 by an evangelical youth church in Germany. Over two thousand people across Europe participated in this one-off event, with prayer and the sermon being sent in text message segment with pauses in between to allow time for reflection (Connolly 2001). Since then, numerous experiments and established examples of religion via SMS have surfaced.

One common way religion interacts with cell phones is through the numerous daily Bible text messaging services that are available around the world. An Italian priest in Milan birthed the idea in 2002 to send daily texts to his parishioners, which featured a prayer, thought for the day, or information on saints (Zwartz 2003). His efforts inspired others in counties such as Australia, the United States, the Philippines, and the U.K. to offer similar services, culminating with the pope offering a service of daily inspirational SMS messages or prayers ("Pope spreads the word by SMS" 2003). Pope Benedict XVI also seems set to carry on the same "thought for the day" text service, sending out his first SMS just days after his induction: "Let us go forth in the joy of the risen Lord and trusting in his permanent help." This service was also used to inform subscribers of John Paul II's death, funeral details, and the new pope's election ("'Let us go forth'" 2005).

But Christianity is not the only religion to embrace technology to text the faith. Muslims using a special handset launched by LG Electronics of South Korea and features provided by Ilkone Mobile Telecommunications of Dubai can use their cell phones to help remind them of prayer times. These services also include a "Mecca Indicator" that presents a digital compass aiding them in finding the direction of Mecca for prayer (Biddlecombe 2004). Also, Indian spirituality promoter Deepak Chopra's "seven spiritual laws" have gone mobile with the help of Airborne Entertainment. Followers of Chopra can download "The Mobile Deepak Chopra" and access daily texts based on his writings, success tips, and inspirational images, which provide a mobile "lifestyle enhancement program."

Many examples exist of cell phones and their associated features being designed specifically to facilitate believers' ability to carry out traditional religious rituals, in harmony with mobile culture. Catholics in the Philippines were the first in the Christian tradition to offer mobile rituals. The "Mobile Way of the Cross" was launched in time for Lent 2004. This Java program contains a series of reflections and images of the traditional Stations of the Cross that takes the faithful through a reflective journey on Jesus' pilgrimage to the cross. It can be downloaded and run on a cell phone. It is meant to help Catholics to participate in this traditional Easter ritual, without having to walk through the fourteen stations in a church setting. "Most people download games and play them on their cell phones, usually when they are bored or have time to kill . . . our idea was . . . if you have time to kill . . . why not pray instead of just playing games?" stated project director Dr. Luis F. G. Sarmenta, executive director of Ateneo Java Wireless Competency Center in Manila. Similarly, the "Mobile Rosary" was developed, a program that, once installed, allows users to move through this traditional prayer by highlighting "the proper sequence of prayers . . . it shows you which bead you are on and helps you count" (personal correspondence from Luis F. G. Sarmenta, April 6, 2004).

A British company, MS Wireless Marketing, offers Muslims a "TXT & Donate Islamic Prayer Alert" service. Subscribers pay a small fee, and not only do they receive daily prayer times and verses from the Koran, but subscription costs go directly to Muslim charities, helping the faithful fulfill their religious duties to give donations to the poor. According to managing director Saaid Hussain, "The mobile phone is a perfect solution because it allows you to do micropayments. Over the year people are spending 70 pounds ($128), but they don't realize it because they are spending 25 pence (46 cents) a day" (Biddlecombe 2004; "A spiritual connection" 2005). Other religious groups have also discovered the cumulative value of the micropayment, allowing religious users to subscribe to services that generate funds for religious organizations or make direct donations or tithes to charities via SMS. These cases highlight not only how mobile believers are using the cell phone to enhance or supplement traditional religious practice, but how designers of technology can allow their religious convictions to shape their technological innovations.

Cell phones are also being designed in ways that reflect the ability of technology to be transformed into a sacred object or spiritual tool. A Taiwanese handset maker, Okwarp, has capitalized on local religious belief and designed a limited-edition phone featuring Matsu, the Chinese goddess of the sea and popular religious icon. The phone contains a holograph of the goddess, special religious chant ring tones, and Matsu wallpaper for the display screen. However, the key selling point appears to be that each phone is reportedly blessed in a special ritual at a Matsu temple ("Phones have been blessed" 2004).

A British youth prayer organization, 24-7, is using cell phone networking to create a national prayer chain for young people. WOW (Watchman on the Walls) is a SMS service linking young people from around the U.K. with like-minded prayer supporters. Prayer text alerts, news, or Bible verses are sent to subscribers to encourage them to pray at the same time for different needs expressed through the site www.24-7prayer.com/wow. A typical message reads as a "call to prayer": "Sept 11- As u go2 bed 2nite, pray 4 those mourning 2 years on = 4all the victims of wars since. 'Blessed r those who mourn...Blessed r the peacemakers' Mat 5" (SMS sent from WOW to subscribers, 9:18 p.m., 11/9/03). These instances illustrate cell phone technology being set apart for religious use and purposely designed so that the cell phone can be conceptualized as a tool for the sacred by certain users.

Yet while numerous cases of religious use and design of cell phones exist, the technology has not been without controversy. New-generation mobile phones with Internet access, video- and photo-messaging capabilities, and greater susceptibility to spam texting means that cell phones begin to cross the line into promoting secular content, which makes the technology more dubious to some religious groups. For instance, Muslim leaders in Malaysia have ruled that SMS-based contests containing elements of chance are *haram* (or unlawful for Muslims), as they are considered gambling (Sharif and Yapp 2004). Also, SMS greetings during Ramadan that replace traditional custom of visits or even phone calls from friends and family during this holy month have also received public criticism. An editorial in *Al Jazeerah* described this new practice as an outworking of "capitalist culture," highlighting SMS as a symptom of a larger problem, the disappearance of Arab hospitality due to the economic and time pressures of modern life (Qusti 2003). These reactions by religious communities to cell phone use show that it may encroach on religious boundaries and ways of life. When a technology moves from being a helpmate to reflecting an unwanted shift in cultural values, members are more likely to unite and speak out against the technology.

Acceptable use of technology often varies depending on the cultural context of religious users and the way in which the technology is incorporated. Hindus in Bombay readily embraced the option to send their prayers to Ganesh via SMS thanks to a mobile cellular operator, allowing them to avoid queues at temples during religious festivals ("Hindus make their offerings" 2003). However, public outrage occurred in Malaysia among Hindus around the same time at the appearance of imported statues of Ganesh talking on a mobile phone. The altering of the traditional object of worship by incorporating a contemporary technological artifact was deemed "offensive," giving "a distorted depiction of Lord Ganesha" ("Hindu God not allowed to use a cell phone" 2003). Comparing these two instances highlights a key point about the use of technology by religious communities. The religious user communities are willing to accept technology that augments or supports traditional rituals. However, cell phone design elements or technological practices that challenge or recontextualize religious traditions or beliefs are often viewed as problematic and are heartily resisted.

Another area of conflict has been certain types of religious text message services that have sprung up. Especially controversial are the several SMS confession services that exist. One example is the "Sin to Win" service that was offered by Virgin Mobile in the U.K. that encouraged people to use the service to confess their sins—with the best confessions receiving prizes. The Catholic Church has spoken out against these wireless confessional services; the Catholic bishops conference of the Philippines publicly denounced accepting confessions and offering absolution by SMS as "unacceptable" in 2003 ("Virgin mobile users confess" 2004).

Within the tension and embrace of the cell phone by religious groups lies an interesting exploration of how communication technology is socially shaped by its users. In the next section examples of research on religious user communities associated with a social shaping approach to technology are considered. The aim is to identify characteristics that can lead to a framework for studying the shaping of cell phone technology by religious users and the process of technological negotiation occurring within religious communities.

Religious User Communities and Technology

Studies of the social shaping of technology explore technological change and user innovation as a social process. This can include looking at issues relating to sexual divisions of labor and use, how technology is used in everyday life, the role of the user in design, anticipating social effects of users to provide feedback into the design stage, or consequences of technology within institutional and cultural contexts. While many of these factors could be considered, attention is given here to studies that highlight how values or beliefs influence technology negotiation in religious user communities and how these determinants can be identified.

Many recent studies of cell phone use have explored various factors of the social and cultural effects of mobile technologies on culture. James Katz and Mark Aakhus (2002) argue that people's choices concerning technologies are often overlooked or taken for granted. In their collection of studies of cell phone use around the world they argue that technology is the primary influencer of human life. In light of this, they suggest an approach called *apparagiest*, is meant to refer to the "spirit" behind a technology, or meaning behind individual and collective societal behaviors within a given culture. They state that it is "the spirit of the machine that influences both the design of the technology as well as the initial and subsequent significance accorded to them by users, non-users and anti-users" (p. 305). Through this perspective, they attempt to highlight the importance of user "evaluations and choices [that] are based not only on the function of the technology but on their own social roles, status and values" (p. 315).

They identify three aspects of the current *apparatgeist* of our mobile-networked age. First, mobile technologies facilitate a "perpetual contact" that reshapes public-private boundaries. Second, when humans embrace a technology they also embrace the values and symbols that surround the technology. Third, it recognizes that everyone in society, even nonusers and antiusers, are affected by technology. They go on to present a matrix that can be used to outline desirable characteristics that drive design, adoption, and use of a technology by user communities. However, a problematic in their approach is the unspoken assumption that technology imposes itself in a uniform way on all peoples and cultures.

While the social shaping of technology tradition has given much attention to questions of how and why groups negotiate new technologies, little work has been done on the unique intersection of religious communities and communication technologies. Choices made by religious users about technology, especially those within traditional religions (such as Islam, Christianity, and Judaism), are negotiated in distinct ways. This is because choices within religious groups not only are guided by needs and desires, but occur within a distinct worldview, laden with spiritual meanings and values, that guides their interpretation of the world. Traditional religious groups often see the world as composed of that which is sacred and that which is profane or secular. Their desire is to engage and interact with the sacred and shun, or at least distance themselves from, the secular. For many conservative religious groups this means the rejection of modernity and its tools, which are seen as secular. Technology becomes a problematic area, as it is so often equated with modernity. If technology is not rejected outright for this reason, it must undergo negotiation within the community so it can become acceptable for use or shaped in ways that allow it to be included within community life.

Studies of the social shaping of technology must identify which values and beliefs influence how a technology is designed or redesigned, in order to allow it to sit conformably within the cultural boundaries of that group or meet specific needs of that community. One approach that has been employed is "domestification," which studies how technology becomes encultured or embedded in everyday life, especially the life of the home. Roger Silverstone, Eric Hirsch, and David Morley (1992) pioneered this approach, arguing that technologies are conditioned and tamed by users in ways that enable them to fit more neatly into the routines of daily life or "the moral economy of the household." Moral economies are spaces where symbolic meaning transactions occur. Domesticating a technology or artifact means making choices about the meaning and practice of a technology within this sphere. Thus a technology is shaped by the setting in which it lives and by the agents who utilize it. The domestication approach can be used to study religious user communities by identifying how they create a "moral economy," be it physical or ideological, that guides judgments about the technologies, whether they will appropriate or reject them, and sets rules of interaction with them. As a "family of users," these communities transfer symbolic meaning to these choices, thus highlighting the fact that this process can provide valuable insights.

Diane Zimmerman-Umble's (1992) study of the Amish use and relationship to the telephone provides a key example of how this approach can be applied to studies of religious user communities. She highlights how the Amish community resists certain patterns of life they see as being reinforced through the use of certain technologies. Instead of rejecting the use of the telephone, the Amish choose to resist how its use may interfere with valued patterns of family life by privatizing communication. The telephone is domesticated by becoming a communal rather than an individual resource, phones being shared by a number of families and located in a central location, such as in a shed at the intersection of several farms. In this way they reconstruct technology by situating it in the community, thus allowing use while still affirming their values about maintaining distance from secular society. Through the domestification approach, Zimmerman-Umble highlights that the social shaping of technology must consider the unique culture of a religious user community along with its history and general ideological approach to technology in order to fully explain its engagement with new technologies.

Recent examination of religious user reaction to new technology can be seen in research on the Internet and religion. In the past ten years numerous studies have considered how religious users have responded to and used the Internet for a variety of religious rituals and to form spiritual communities. Beginning in the mid-1990s, researchers such as Stephen O'Leary and Brenda Brasher (1996) have investigated how religion is being influenced by and manifested in online environments in ways that increase public advocacy of faith and create new acts of ritual communication. Some studies have attempted to categorize religious use of the Internet through describing different narratives of technology religious users subscribe to (Bauwens 1996; Helland 2000; Campbell 2005). Others, such as the Barna Research Group (2001) and the Pew Internet and American Life Project (Larsen 2000, 2001; Hoover et al. 2004), have sought to provide more quantitative analysis of the variety of uses of the Internet by "religion surfers." Still, little attention has been given to identifying key characteristics within religious user communities that point toward identifying the process of technology negotiation within these distinct groups.

A recent study that does provide helpful insight into this area is the work of Karine Barzilai-Nahon & Gad Barzilai (2005) on how religious groups "culture" technology so that use is shaped in ways that preserve, rather than subvert, their unique culture. They argue that "cultures modify technologies and endow them with a communal context" (p. 26). Through their examination of the ultra-Orthodox religious community in Israel, a highly conservative sect of Judaism, and its interaction with the Internet, they found several dimensions of tension between religious users and religious leaders. While ultra-Orthodox rabbis had initially condemned Internet use, many community members wanted to use the Internet for economic purposes and self-expression. Investigating *Hevre*, an Israeli website that helps friends from the past reconnect, they found that the Internet became a "cultured technology." Users, especially females, shaped and conceived of the Internet in terms of needs. The Internet was used to meet particular needs within the community, such as enabling women to work at home. This led to a change in official views within the community about the technology.

For Barzilai-Nahon and Barzilai, "cultured technology" emerges as a social discourse that recognizes that religious cultural spaces are affected by both complex social and distinct value-construction processes. They state, "the internet becomes a set of various cultured technologies with a variety of cultural contexts" (p. 26), and suggest that the concept of "cultured technology" provides a way to address the framing of technologies with specific cultural or religious traditions. Culturing a technology involves making the technology acceptable with a communal context by reshaping it so it is in line with valued ideals of the group. The extent to which a religious group can culture the Internet indicates the extent to which it can be incorporated into the community and provide opportunities for self- or group expression within these boundaries.

In their exploration they highlight two key processes that occur within the culturing of a technology: cultural modification and localization. Cultural modification refers to the reshaping of a community's culture in order to engage with a particular technology. It recognizes that it is user communities, and not only technologies, that undergo a culturing process when a technology is shaped by its users and bound to a specific communal context. A technology's use and associated meaning changes when it is brought into a new culture. Therefore, Barzilai-Nahon and Barzilai argue, "the extent to which technology can be culturally modified creates opportunities for community members to express themselves" (p. 26)

Localization refers to "adapting a technology product or service (including its software, documentation and related material) to a specific culture" (Barzilai-Nahon and Barzilai 2005, p. 371). This can involve altering the design, display, advertising, and legal procedures associated with a given technology so that it is "culturally appropriate" (p. 25). Within religious communities, localization means that a technology that is viewed as useful by the community, but deemed a secular medium, must be adapted so that it fits within the spiritual practices and values of that community. Together, cultural modification, the reshaping of a specific community, localization, and the reshaping of a specific technology create a cultured technology. For Barzilai-Nahon and Barzilai this is especially true within religious fundamentalist communities that have a distinct hierarchy and structure marked by patriarchy, rigid discipline, and seclusion from general society. "While the community localizes the technology, the community itself is reshaped to become part of the globalized world. Cultured technology becomes a requirement for religious fundamentalist communities in order for them to exist within their traditional internal and external boundaries" (p. 26).

The process of a culturing of technology can be identified in three aspects of a religious community. It can be seen in the social structures within a given community, or a distinct network of the community. It is noted in the specific behaviors, or discipline, the members commit to. It is also seen in community regulations, internal and external controls set by leadership to regulate and govern community practices. By carefully studying the networks, discipline, and regulation of a religious community, we can identify how cultural modification and localization occur. Thus, we can describe the process of how a specific community negotiates and "cultures" a specific technology.

The cultured technology approach, which addresses religious user communities' interaction with new media technology, provides a fruitful way to examine religious communities' engagement with cell phone technology and culture. This approach, along with considering a religious group's general rhetoric concerning technology, will now be used to investigate a specific example of the religious culturing of cell phone technology: the kosher phone.

Case Study: The Kosher Phone

It has been said that Israel has a love affair with talk—and with technology. Amit Schejter and Akiba Cohen (2002, pp. 35–36) explain part of the reason for Israel's exponential cell phone use growth as "an infatuation Israelis have with new technologies in general and communication technologies in particular." They claim that Israelis' love of talk and gossip has made them one of the world's usage leaders of mobile technologies, with estimates that the average Israeli cell phone user spends 450 minutes per month talking on their cell (p. 30). Israeli wireless operators have been quick to promote new features and marketing schemes to encourage this use. They have also been leaders in developing service options specifically for religious users.

Schejter and Cohen recount that in early 2000 the Israeli cellular company Cellcom introduced a special club for religious Jewish cell phone owners with features designed to meet members' needs. By dialing 613—a significant number, as it indicates the number of *Mitzot* or requirements an observant Jew is to perform—a user can find out daily prayer times and when to light Shabbat candles (p. 28). Since this innovation, other cellular phone providers have developed similar services to target religious cell phone users. This recognition that religious user communities represent an important market has led to a unique example of how beliefs can direct the design, or redesign, of a cellular technology to meet the particular goals and desires of religious users.

In March 2005 MIRS Communication, an Israeli wireless company, announced the launch of a phone specifically designed for the ultra-Orthodox Jewish community in Israel. The idea for such a phone began when religious authorities and members of this community became concerned that mobile phones might be serving as a conduit for unacceptable content. This led to an official, lengthy, and interesting process of value and need negotiation between the community and several mobile phone providers in 2004 and 2005. The result of this was the launch of the "kosher phone."

"Kosher" (meaning approved or acceptable under rabbinical, religious law) phones are first-generation Motorola handsets that have been modified to disable Internet access, SMS text messaging, and video and voice mail application. These are services that many rabbinical authorities felt would expose members of this conservative religious community to unmonitored secular content. These phones are visibly marked with a stamp signifying approval by rabbinical authorities. *Mobiledia*'s online reports describe MIRS efforts as a decision "to cater towards [a] demographic largely neglected by major cell phone companies; the . . . ultra-Orthodox Jews," where these features are "deemed threatening to their conservative way of life, particularly with the young" ("Kosher phones for ultra-Orthodox Jews" 2005).

Ultra-Orthodox Judaism in Israel represents a small conservative segment of the overall religious community in Israel. Also refereed to as haredi (or charedi), the community is characterized by their rejection of the values of modernity, following a strict rule of life and wearing the dress and head coverings of their ancestors of eighteenth-century Europe (Heilman and Friedman 1991). It is important to note that ultra-Orthodoxy differs from other form of Judaism (Stadler 2002), such as the more liberal expressions of conservative and reformed Judaism, or Orthodox Judaism, which is the most prevalent expression in Israel. The ultra-Orthodox have been described as a "culture of the enclave," a community that follows strict religious rule along with an isolated lifestyle (Stadler 2005, p. 217). These communities typically take a concerned and reflective, but less reactionary, approach to technology. In ultra-Orthodox communities, technology is often seen as a symbol of modernity and secular values, from which they consciously distance themselves. Thus the use of technology is a point of great debate and subject of law making. Discussions about technology use are often framed in terms of possibilities and danger. Common issues of discussion relate to the boundaries of use of certain modern technologies, from how electrical appliances might be used on Shabbat, the Jewish sacred day (lasting from sunset to sunset, Friday to Saturday), to reasons for forbidding televisions in homes, as TV is a device that symbolizes the epitome of secular values and seen to promote moral seduction (Stadler 2005).

Ultra-Orthodox religious leaders in Israel lauded the launch of the kosher phone as a success and demonstration of "consumer power of the charedi community" ("Opinion and comments" 2005): "Rabbonim and public figures said *maran verabonon* (masters and sages) defined the battle for kosher communication as an existential battle, a battle for the soul, and that every effort must be made to insure its success" (Kahn 2005). The kosher phone represents a unique negotiation between a distinct religious user community and a cellular phone company, resulting in the culturing of technology toward specific desires and religious ideals. However, this is not simply the story of a service provider responding to some consumer demands; it is a story of cultural beliefs guiding the hand of the designer toward distinct social-religious ends. By carefully considering the processes of cultural modification and localization within the development and launch of the kosher phone, we can see how the cell phone became a cultured technology.

Cultural Modification

User communities undergo a culturing process when a new technology is introduced. Each technology brings with it a set of meanings and expectations built into the design of that technology. Cultural modification means that the culture of the community must in some way adapt to these meanings, or it must negotiate these technological expectations in order to engage with it. In the case of the kosher phone, the haredi community had to undergo a definite culturing process in order to accept cell phone technology into its rules of religious life. This was especially evident in the network or social structure that emerged within the community to oversee the concerns and potential hazards flagged around cell phone technology. It was also seen in the regulations created by religious leaders to ensure that acceptable use of the technology was carried out within the boundaries of the community.

Months before the kosher phone became a reality, a distinct network arose within the ultra-Orthodox community to deal with conflicting issues being raised by cell phone use. It began in 2004, when public outcry became more distinct. An article in *Yated Ne'Eman*, a haredi newspaper in Israel, reported on a movement among some ultra-Orthodox calling for the partial ban of cell phones and the blocking of phone signals in religious communities (Tzippori 2004). Concerns were voiced about the amount of time community members were spending on their cell phones and the financial strain this was putting on some families. Cell phones were also described as a "dangerous weapon" attacking the morality of the community and should be battled against, because of some of the content it allowed members access to. "Today trials comes with us into the holy places [that is, yeshivas]. . . . [T]he main reason resources are being channeled to sound the warning for cell phones which, unlike computers, follow us wherever we go, and even kosher channels are liable to turn into spiritual disaster through an incidental flashing message or another" (Tzippori 2004, p. 15).

According to a report in the Orthodox newsletter *Dei'ah veDibur*, the birth of the kosher phone began when a special committee of ultra-Orthodox rabbis was formed in 2004. The committee's focus was to address concerns raised within segments of the community about the "spiritual and educational pitfalls resulting from content services accessible using most cell phones" (Kahn 2005). This committee represented a select network of leading ultra-Orthodox rabbis, formed specifically for the task of evaluating and making official community policy on the issues of cell phone use. The committee met regularly for several months to discuss issues such as SMS content and phone access. One of the committee's first actions was to instruct haredi newspapers to stop carrying all advertisements by cellular companies until an official course of action was agreed upon. This demonstrated the committee's influence with and regard within the community.

In the months that followed, the committee consulted a variety of communication and technology experts throughout the country on aspects of the cell phone issue. With the help of a Jewish attorney, they entered into negotiations with all of the major cellular companies in Israel to voice their concerns and needs. In the end, MIRS was the only company that "demonstrated a readiness to meet the haredi's public demands" (Kahn 2005). The committee approved and then signed a contract stating that MIRS would provide specially designed kosher phones for community members. MIRS also opened three special service centers specifically for the ultra-Orthodox community in Ashdod, Bnei Brak, and Jerusalem. They also specially trained religious sales representatives to market these unique phones to the public in haredi communities across Israel.

The committee, a distinct network of religious authorities, represented a strong organized and focused hierarchical structure. Their arduous process of evaluating the cell phone in light of their community's life and practices caused them to change how their community engaged with this technology. They not only altered official community policy on cell phone use, but also promoted a distinct rhetoric about the technology that sought to guide public reaction to the technology.

Before the launch of the kosher phone, religious rhetoric about the cell phone focused around proper or acceptable use, and make and model of the phone was a nonissue. However, after the launch of the kosher phone, attention was placed on the type and features of the phone one used. This is a clear indication of how cultural regulation plays a key role in the cultural modification of a technology. As the community established official regulations around cell phones, it also created rigid boundaries around community engagement with technology.

In a statement issued by *gedolei Yisroel* (the chief rabbinical council of ultra-Orthodox rabbis), directives were given instructing those "who must use cellular devices" to choose only those that have been authorized by the rabbinical committee. According to *Dei'ah veDibur*, the statement read:

> The great spiritual danger inherent in the development of high-tech communications is widely known and we can not longer stand quietly and watch the resulting spiritual decline.
>
> We hereby state our opinion, *daas Torah*, that whoever needs a cellular device (but not those who were instructed not to use any type of cellular device whatsoever, e.g. yeshiva students Bais Yaakov students and seminary students) may possess and use only this device approved by the above committee and marked with a special imprint. The possession and use of any other types of devices not approved by the rabbinical committee is strictly prohibited, as are advertisements for any unapproved company or device. And let this not be breached and all who heed will be rewarded with pleasantness and will merit *nachas* [happiness] for all of their offspring. (Kahn 2005)

"Setting a fence around Torah" is a Jewish phrase used to describe the setting of strict limits in relation to a new innovation so that its use will not violate Torah law until it can be fully understood or observed. The council's statement represents an example of clarifying and setting firm guidelines around a technology that clearly tighten the boundaries around the community itself.

Yet it was not only the religious leaders who were calling for increased regulations. In the *Yated Ne'Eman* article "Put up the Phoneblocks!" a religious journalist suggested the idea for "charedi-only cell phones" that would be specially marked as a way to supervise users and separate them from unapproved content. It was a call by community leaders to have control over the technology and its content, and ultimately over the users themselves. The proposed phone would presumably indicate religious commitment: "Show me your cell phone and I'll tell you what you're made of. Whether a young man is from our ranks, or whether he is connected to the internet will be apparent" (Tzippori 2004, p. 15). Thus the kosher phone becomes a symbol of religious devotion and affirmation of community affiliation. The rhetoric that technology use can indicate religious commitment is a powerful tool to create community cohesion through unifying around specific policy decisions made by the community.

The public decision to confirm the use of cell phone technology into the community boundaries required a cultural renegotiation within the community. This also went hand in hand with the call to change the technology.

Localization

Often, to become part of the religious context, a new technology must also change. Localization occurs when the technology itself is adapted in some way so that it meets community requirements—and is in line with the values—of the specific culture that is adopting it. This technological negotiation means that the user community must highlight beliefs that are challenged by, supported by, or in conflict with the technology. If use of the technology is deemed important, they must decide what essential changes need to be made in design or use in order to accept it into the community's boundaries.

The haredi community clearly identified those values that were being challenged by cell phone technology and highlighted the changes necessary to make the technology acceptable within the bounds of the community. According to a *Times Online* report, "rabbis say they are not against technology as a matter of course. But they fear that the latest feature packed telephones coming into the market will provide the opportunity to access corrupting influences" (MacKinnon 2005).

The problematic aspects of the cell phone involved certain features that could be associated with secular media and entertainment culture. Deleting these features and shaping the cell phone simply as a communication tool enabled it to be deemed an acceptable technology. In light of this, MIRS agreed to provide the ultra-Orthodox community phones stripped of all content services, with a special seal, and that these devices would all begin with the same dialing code and prefix. This agreement and adaptation of the technology would make acceptable phones easier to spot. Special calling plans offered by MIRS would encourage calling within the newly established network. The ultra-Orthodox community felt it was vital to change certain phone features such as having access to secular content and clear identification about adherence to this policy. These desires highlight a cultural and religious commitment to certain disciplines. A cultured technology can be seen as one which promotes and reinforces specific behaviors that religious members are committed.

The ultra-Orthodox have a concern that media technologies often expose members to unnecessary temptations through the content they display. The fear of allowing images into the home that might lead community members into sin, and concerns for personal purity, have led to official bans on television within the community, and strict guidelines on acceptable use of the Internet. The cell phone represented another technology that, while providing useful communication capabilities, also promised to introduce unnecessary hazards for those already committed to limiting their exposure to secular content. However, culturing the cell phone so it becomes a simple communication device would solve this problem. Therefore their desire not to be exposed to secular values, along with recognizing the value of the technology, promoted the community's push for the redesign of the cell phone to provide communication capabilities without the other content. "Without fanfare, the entire community quietly joined the struggle to protect ourselves from the encroaching tide of filth. Our demand was a simple consumer request: we want new phones that provide basic phone service. We want voice communication and nothing more" ("Opinion and comments" 2005).One noteworthy aspect in some haredi reports of kosher phones was the deep displeasure voiced about other cellular providers that were unwilling to work with the community on this issue. Frustration was directed toward companies that claimed they were unable to provide the minimalist services the community was requesting. However, a few commentators noted that it was not the "technological breakthrough" that was the stumbling block but companies unwilling to forego revenue that might be generated from content services. "There is no way that the issue can be cast as having to so with progress, technological or otherwise . . . but rather a business need for higher profits. Nowadays, the easiest path to profits is through providing soul-destroying content" ("Opinion and comments" 2005). By highlighting the secular values of the service providers, the community framed the push for the kosher phone in terms of a battle with secular culture. Thus it was not just a demand for special treatment but a moral imperative to pursue this cultured technology. "All too often the modern world is proving to be *chachomim lehora*—smart people who use their talents destructively. It is up to us to defend ourselves and to take only what is truly beneficial—until the day comes when the whole world is filled with the knowledge of Hashem" ("Opinion and comments" 2005).

By emphasizing the discipline or values of the community, a distinct rhetoric of technology was employed by the haredi community. Technology is to be a helpmate, to help one live life in light of a strict commitment to faith. In this way the creation of the kosher phone represents the emergence of a cultured technology. The culture of the ultra-Orthodox community was affected by having to create an official network and regulations to deal with the community use of the technology. Also, the cell phone itself was affected, as it was redesigned with the help of a mobile service provider in order for it to fit within the religious values and rule of life of the community.

Conclusion: Approaching Religion and Cell Phone Culture

While the kosher phone represents a particular community's tension and mediation with technology, it highlights several key aspects of the negotiation process that can occur between religious groups and cell phone culture. First, it emphasizes that most religious groups are not ultimately against communication technology. Rather they are willing and often eager to embrace technologies that will support their community life or religious practices. Second, when concern is expressed about a given technology it is usually in relation to specific features or uses that may allow unauthorized information or inappropriate practices into the community. Third, decisions on whether a specific technology can be accepted into a community are based on the group's official ideology about technology, and whether it can support or come in line with the values and religious discipline of that community. Fourth, if a technology with questionable features is deemed valuable to the community, a "culturing" process must take place.

The culturing of a technology involves change in both the culture of the community and the technology itself. Finally, once technology is cultured and welcomed into a religious community it often may be accompanied by an official rhetoric about the device that guides community use and perception of the new technology.

The numerous examples of religious engagement with the cell phone offered in this chapter illustrate how religiosity and religious cultures are being transformed in our global information age. From encouraging mobile religious practices to creating spiritual interconnection through SMS, and supporting simultaneous communicative and spiritual functions, the cell phone represents a technology that can be used to supplement traditional religiosity in unique ways. This survey also points to a new area of potential exploration, the social-religious shaping of technology. By uncovering the social processes that emerge during technological change and user innovation within religious user communities, we can begin to see how traditional communities themselves become transformers of technology. The ways religious groups use and respond to the cell phone offer insights not only into the social construction of these communities but also into the ideological negotiation that must occur in any fixed social group that tries to adopt a new technology. When religion meets the cell phone it creates a new private-public space for religious expression, and a unique microcosm in which to examine how traditional social networks are being transformed through interaction within a global information culture.

References

Barna Research Group. (2001). "More Americans are seeking net-based faith experiences." In *Barna Research Online*. Retrieved January 28, 2003, from www.barna.org/cgibin/PagePressRelease.asp?PressReleaseID=90&Reference=D.

Barzilai-Nahon, K., and G. Barzilai. (2005). Cultured technology: Internet and religious fundamentalism. *Information Society* 21, no. 1: 25–40.

Bauwens, M. (1996). "Spirituality and technology: Exploring the relationship." *First Monday*. Retrieved January 28, 2003, from www.firstmonday.dk/issues/issue5/bauwens/index.html.

Biddlecombe, E. (2004). "Cell phone users are finding God," *Wired*, August 19. Retrieved April 24, 2005, from www.wired.com/news/culture/, 1284,64624,00.html.

Campbell, H. (2005). "Consider spiritual dimensions within computer-mediated communication studies." *New Media and Society* 7, no. 1: 110–34.

Connolly, K. (2001). "German gspel according 2 txt msg." *Guardian Online*, May 2. Retrieved April 27, 2005, from www.guardian.co.uk/Print/0,3858,4179188, 00.htm.

Dawson, L., and D. Cowan. (Eds.). (2004). *Religion online: Finding faith on the Internet*. New York: Routledge.

Helland, C. (2000). "Online-religion/religion-online and virtual communitas." In J. K. Hadden and D. E. Cowan (Eds.), *Religion on the Internet: Research prospects and promises* (pp. 205–23). New York: JAI.

Heilman, S. C., and M. Friedman. (1991). *The haredim in Israel*. New York: American Jewish Committee.

"Hindu God not allowed to use a cell phone." (2003). *Cellular News*, October 1. Retrieved April 24, 2005, from www.cellular-news.com/story/9830.shtml.

"Hindus make their offerings by SMS." (2003). *Textually.org*, September 3. Retrieved April 24, 2005, from www.textually.org/archieves/001803.html.

Hoover, S., L. S. Clark, and L. Rainie. (2004). "Faith online: 64% of wired Americans have used the Internet for spiritual or religious information." *Pew Internet and American Life Project*. Retrieved April 12, 2004, from www.pewinternet.org/reports/toc.asp?Report=119.

Kahn, B. (2005). "New 'kosher' cell phones free of content services." *Dei'ah veDibur: Information and Insight*, March 7. Retrieved March 7, 2005, from http://charedi.shemayisraek.com/VRK65amirs.htm.

Katz, J., and M. Aakhus. (Eds.). (2002). *Perpetual contact: Mobile communication, private talk, public performance*. Cambridge, UK: Cambridge University Press.

"Kosher phones for ultra Orthodox Jews." (2005). *Mobiledia.com*, March 7. Retrieved March 21, 2005, from www.mobliedia.com/news/27118.html.

Larsen, E. (2000). "Wired churches, wired temples: Taking congregations and missions into cyberspace." *Pew Internet and American Life Project*. Retrieved April 12, 2004, from www.pewinternet.org/reports/toc.asp?Report=28.

Larsen, E. (2001). "CyberFaith: How Americans pursue religion online." *Pew Internet and American Life Project*. Retrieved April 12, 2004, from www.pewinternet.org/reports/toc.asp?Report=53.

"'Let us go forth,' new pope says in first text message." (2005). *Yahoo-Agence France Presse*, April 21. Retrieved April 24, 2005, from http://news.yahoo.com/s/afp/20050421/tc_afp/vaticanpopephonetext&printer=1.

MacKinnon, I. (2005). "Kosher phone taps into new market for mobiles." *Times Online*, March 3. Retrieved April 24, 2005, from www.timesonline.co.uk/article0,,251-1508115,00.html.

Myerson, G. (2001). *Heidegger, Habermas, and the mobile phone*. Cambridge, UK: Icon Books.

O'Leary, S., and B. Brasher. (1996). "The unknown God of the Internet." In C. Ess (Ed.), *Philosophical perspectives on computer-mediated communication* (pp. 233–69). Albany: State University of New York Press.

"Opinion and comments: Kosher cell phones." (2005). *Dei'ah veDibur: Information and Insight*, March 16. Retrieved March 16, 2005, from http://charedi.shemay-israek.com/VRK65ocellphn3.htm.

"Phones have been blessed in ritual at a Matsu temple." (2004). *Textually.org*, July 1. Retrieved March 20, 2005, from www.textually.org/textually/archieves/oo4381.htm.

"Pope spreads the word by SMS." (2003). *Ananova*, January 14. Retrieved March 20, 2005, from www.ananova.com/news/story/sm_739682.html.

Qusti, R. (2003). "Ramadan: Saudi society under the influence of capitalist culture." *Al Jazeerah*, October 29. Retrieved March 24, 2005, from www.aljazeerah.info/Opinion%20editorials/2003%20Opinion%20Editorials/October/29%200/Ramadan%20Saudi%20Society%20Under%20Influence%20of%20Capitlaist%20Culture%20Raid%20Qysti.htm.

Schejter, A., and A. Cohen. (2002). "Israel: Chutzpah and chatter in the holy land." In J. Katz and M. Aakhus (Eds.), *Perpetual contact: Mobile communication, private talk, public performance* (pp. 30–41). Cambridge, UK: Cambridge University Press.

Sharif, R., and E. Yapp. (2004). "SMS contest based on chance declared haram." *Star Online*, July 27. Retrieved March 24, 2005, from http://star-techcentral.com/story.asp?file=/2004/7/27/technology/8537769&sec=technology.

Silverstone, R., E. Hirsch, and D. Morley. (1992). "Information and communication technologies and the moral economy of the household." In R. Silverstone and E. Hirsch (Eds.), *Consuming technologies: Media and information in domestic spaces* (pp. 15–31). London: Routledge.

"A spiritual connection." (2005). *The Economist*, March 10. Retrieved March 24, 2005, from www.economist.com/science/tq/displayStory.cfm?story_id=3713855.

Stadler, N. (2002). "Is profane work an obstacle for salvation? The case of the ultra Orthodox (haredi) Jews in contemporary Israel." *Sociology of Religion* 64, no. 4: 455–74.

Stadler, N. (2005). "Fundamentalism." In Nicholas de Lange and Miri Freud-Kandel (Eds.), *Modern Judaism: An Oxford guide* (pp. 216–27). Oxford and New York: Oxford University Press.

Tzippori, R. (2004). "Put up the phoneblocks!" *Yated Ne'Eman*, June 4, pp. 14–16.

"Virgin mobile users confess their sin." (2004). *Textually.org*, December 6. Retrieved March 20, 2005, from www.textually.org/textually/archieves/006286.htm.

Zimmerman-Umble, D. (1992). "The Amish and the telephone: Resistance and reconstruction." In R. Silverstone and E. Hirsch (Eds.), *Consuming technologies: Media and information in domestic spaces* (pp. 183–94). London: Routledge.

Zwartz, B. (January 22, 2003). "Has Don Paolo got a line for you." *The Age*. Retrieved April 7, 2004, from www.theage.com/articles/2003/01/21/1042911381612.html.

Disabling Cell Phones

Gerard Goggin and Christopher Newell

The cell phone has enjoyed an extraordinary rise to prominence. It is now owned and used by more people worldwide than its fixed line counterpart. A common motif of discussions of the cell phone around the world is the new communicative possibilities it has opened up for millions of people. The cell phone is characteristically identified with new modes of mobility, personalization, identity, and individual and group relations. (We note at the outset that names for the technology itself vary across culture, and so we will use the terms *cell phone* and *mobile phone* interchangeably.) Such contentions have been critically examined and interrogated with quite a number of useful studies of the cell phone, including book-length accounts and collections (Brown, Green, and Harper 2002; Fortunati, Katz, and Riccini 2003; Katz 2003; Ling 2004). Much work still remains, and is unfolding—for instance, understanding the cell phone in non-Western countries (Lin 2005), and in low- and middle-income countries rather than just the high-income countries well represented in the mobiles literature (Donner 2005).

Surprisingly, however, very little has been written about disability and the cell phone. Estimates of people with disabilities in population vary, but figures of between 15 and 20 percent are often cited in many countries (ABS 2004; Metts 2000; on the difficulties and politics of defining and measuring the incidence of disability see Abberley 1992; Altman 2001). While people with disabilities have had problems with accessibility of many technologies, especially mobile telecommunications, they have also as a group been avid and often pioneering users. Yet in the history, culture, and technology of this mobile device, disability has played a crucial yet overlooked role. Such an overdue recognition of this topic is not only important in its own right, but also suggestive for a general account of cell phones.

Our approach is informed by several disciplinary sources. As yet the new ways of studying disability as an integral part of humanities and social sciences are still not well understood—especially when it comes to the still rarely theorized area of disability and technology. In our work, first, we are informed by the social studies of science and technology, especially the key insight that technology is socially and cultural shaped (MacKenzie and Wajcman 1999; Wajcman 2004), and, a radical response to and extension of this, that society and technology are mutually constituted as suggested by actor-network theory (Law 1999). Second, we draw upon critical disability studies (Albrecht, Seelman, and Bury 2001; Snyder, Brueggemann, and Garland-Thomson 2002). Diverse and interdisciplinary in its constitution, critical disability studies critiques the dominant understanding of disability via the medical model, where disability is believed to be located in the individual's deficient, sick, or abnormal body. It also opposes the allied, and historically anterior, charity discourse of disability, according to which the person with disability is to be pitied and controlled by benevolent institutions (Stiker 1999).

As it has emerged in the United States, Canada, the United Kingdom, Europe, and Australia, critical disability studies theorists typically propose a sociopolitical approach to disability. For instance, British theorists of the social model propose a distinction between an individual's impairments (the bodily dimension) and disability that is socially produced (as in the barriers society unfairly creates for the person with impairments, for instance) (Barnes and Mercer 2003). Our approach seeks to go beyond classic social model accounts by recognizing the wide range of disability; by acknowledging the interaction among gender, sex, race, class, and age in the social relations of disability; by seeking to understand the important cultural dimension of disability; and in proposing the importance of technology in the contemporary social relations of disability.

To date there has been little scholarly work at the intersection of the literatures of social study of science and technology, on the one side, and those of critical disability studies on the other (noteworthy studies on disability and technology include Cornes 1991; Goggin and Newell 2003; Roulstone 1998; Seelman 2001, 2005; papers in Goggin and Newell 2005c, 2006). Yet such a rapprochment is called for because of the "intimate relations" between technology and disability:

> Whether in the home, at work or leisure, technology plays an important role in the lives of people with disabilities, and also in the way that disability is conceived, experienced, and framed in society. A wide range of technologies are adopted, consumed, and used by people with disabilities. We do so, moreover, in unexpected and innovative ways, often unforeseen by the designers and promoters of such technologies. (Goggin and Newell 2005b).

This is the case also, we would suggest, with regard to networked digital technologies now so pervasive and ubiquitous in many countries.

Accessibility for people with disabilities is often now a focus of discussion yet still more often honored in the breach (Goggin and Newell 2003). Important initiatives have been taken in the area of the World Wide Web to make the Internet accessible, yet the overlapping cluster of software, hardware, and networks associated with online communications is proving far more intractable. As the Internet merges with mobile and wireless devices, inclusive and accessible technologies for text, video, and voice communications have been overlooked or only slowly eventuated. As the National Council on Disability has noted,

> There are limitations that make cell phones either inaccessible or difficult to use (and, therefore, possibly undesirable). People who have visual impairments may have the most difficulty reading the display and accessing visual information. People who are deaf or hard of hearing may have difficulty carrying on a verbal conversation and

detecting auditory alerts. People with a mobility disability may have difficulty making accurate inputs and simultaneously handling the phone and manipulating the controls. People who have cognitive disabilities may have difficulty understanding metaphors that are used and remembering how to access information. (NCD 2004, pp. 102–3)

The topic of access generally, and accessibility for people with disabilities specifically, has been much ventilated over the past decade, not least under the not-especially-helpful rubric of the "digital divide." We are certainly interested in access, but reframing the concept and placing it within a general account of technology, culture, and the social. In this chapter, however, our focus is squarely on disability as an intriguing, perplexing, and revealing site of the cultural dialectics of the cell phone. In what follows, we first discuss the incompatibility of second-generation digital mobiles for hearing aid users and Deaf people using teletypewriters. Then we turn, second, to users' cultural and social innovation, exploring Deaf people's use of short text messages (SMS). Third, we contrast Deafness and mobiles with Blind people's nonuse and use of SMS. Finally, we conclude with some remarks on the implications of disability for general accounts of the cell phone.

Designing Disability: The Case of Digital Mobiles

Mobile cellular phones were commercially introduced around the world beginning in the late 1970s, commencing with in-car phones. This system was based on analog technology, which we now call first-generation mobile technology, implemented in various standards (the most prevalent standard being the US AMPS) (Agar 2003; Steinbock 2003). When handheld mobiles became available these were very bulky, and even the lighter, more portable models were cheerfully referred to as a "brick." Obviously, at this stage the mobile phone was difficult for many people with disabilities to hold and use.

With advances in miniaturization, computerization, and manufacturing, mobiles were made smaller and lighter. This made them easier to use for some consumers, but more difficult for others because of the dexterity and nimbleness demanded by tiny buttons and interfaces. Many people with disabilities did use mobiles for a range of purposes, including safety, security, and mobility assistance. There is much further to say on first-generation mobiles and people with disabilities (for example, see Von Tetzchner 1991; Roe 1993), but we will leave this topic and now turn to second-generation digital mobiles.

Second-generation mobiles were introduced around the world starting in the early 1990s, promising better voice quality, data transfer rates, more efficient use of the scarce radio spectrum, and security from interception of calls. The three dominant systems implemented were the global system for mobiles (GSM) system (in Europe, parts of Asia, and Australia), the code division multiple access (CDMA) system (in the United States, Australia, and other countries), and the time division multiple access (TDMA) system (Agar 2003; Hillebrand 2002).

New features of second-generation mobiles opened up new possibilities but also created new forms of exclusion:

> The present trend of marketing mobile phones that are smaller but with an ever-increasing number of features, ranging from memory store to

calculator functions, is good for many people—but not for everybody. Blind people cannot use text-based information on the screen at all [including phonebook maintenance and use], while those who are partially-sighted have great difficulty with very small displays. Voice outputs are of no use to deaf people and may be difficult for those who are simply hard of hearing. The extensive range of network based facilities like automatic answering and voicemail: functions, text messages and call progress announcements require either useful vision or useful hearing, if not both. The internet-based applications, such as sending and receiving emails, surfing the net and engaging in e-commerce, are all visually oriented and so exclude blind consumers. Manufacturers and service providers seem to give low priority to solving these problems, for example by offering alternative output modes. (Shipley and Gill 2000)

Here mobiles illustrate the general proposition that when technology is reshaped it is because of other sorts of imagined users and markets than people with disabilities: "Yet some problems are being overcome: hands-free operation is now offered on some models, not in response to demand by disabled people who have difficulty in using a very small keypad, but because it is wanted by drivers who wish to use their mobile phones in a moving vehicle" (Shipley and Gill 2000).

For people with disabilities there were also significant difficulties with second-generation mobiles, overlapping other sites of conflict over the technology (such as fears that electromagnetic emission from phones or towers might cause cancer). Not long after the new digital mobile system had been developed and was starting to be introduced commercially in a number of countries in the early 1990s, it was revealed that this technology emitted a high level of electromagnetic interference (Berger 1997; Burwood and Le Strange 1993; ETSI 1993; Joyner et al. 1993; NTAD 1994; Roe 1993). Such interference had the potential to cause a buzzing sound in people's hearing aids, as well as actually making the phones difficult to use for people with hearing aids. Phone companies internationally, governments, and regulators put much effort into "managing" the public outcry. In doing so, they appeared to be motivated by a concern that this new, expensive technology might not be adopted by consumers, despite widespread support from governments.

What was intriguing here was that for quite some time hearing aids *rather* than mobiles were conceptualized as the principal problem by providers of mobile telephony. Attention was directed to the need for hearing aids to cope with higher levels of electromagnetic emission, something that was seen as important given the wide range of technologies emitting such signals—not just mobile phones. A European standard was introduced in 1990 requiring hearing aids to be immune to emissions from mobile phones. Research was also conducted on removing the source of emission further away from the hearing aid, and eventually "hands-free kits" were designed for hearing aid users as a solution. Even this solution did not provide assistance for many, and other tactics were required on the part of the disability movement.

In Australia, for instance, resort to human rights and antidiscrimination law was needed in order for the matter to be successfully addressed: the Human Rights and Equal Opportunity Commission (HREOC) conducted a public inquiry into the matter, which resulted in a conciliation some eighteen months later (HREOC 2000). Despite such interventions and measures such as "hands-free kits," the problem remains, and is only partially solved in some countries with the availability of an alternative digital mobile technology (namely CDMA).

In early 1996, the U.S. Federal Communications Commission (FCC) convened a summit of the wireless industry, hearing industry, and consumers in an effort to resolve the hearing aid and mobile phone compatibility matter (Berger 1997; Victorian 1998). This precipitated the formation of a dedicated task force under the aegis of the American National Standards Institute (ANSI) to develop a standard on immunity and emissions requirements and test protocols, which devices are required to meet (Victorian 2004). This work culminated in an American standard (namely ANSI C63.19—for details see ANSI 2001; see also Victorian and Preves 2004). In July 2003, the FCC reopened hearings into the issue. It gave federal imprimatur to the ANSI C63.19 standard, and also ordered a rolling timetable and further accessibility improvements. Other requirements included that within two years every major handset manufacturer and service provider must offer at least two mobile telephones that reduce interference to a level defined in the standard; and that by early 2008 half of all mobile telephone handsets have interference down to these levels or less (FCC 2003; Victorian 2004).

A related and further illustrative aspect of the construction of disability in digital mobile telephony lay at the intersection of a newer technological system and an older one with their overlapping yet distinctive cultural practices. Deaf people in a number of Western countries, especially the United States, had developed a rich repertoire of communications and cultural practices using an early form of text communications. Devised in the early to mid-1960s, this technology was variously called in different countries the telecommunications device for the Deaf (TDD), teletypewriter (TTY), Deaf telephones, or just text telephone (Lang 2000). TTY communication involves two keyboard devices connected to the telecommunications network that are then capable of sending and receiving text messages. Many Deaf people own their own text phones, and, to meet the requirements of legislation such as the 1990 Americans with Disabilities Act, TTY pay phones may be found in public places such as airports. From its inception, this form of text phone communication by Deaf people relied on the Baudot standard developed for telexes. With the advent and growing popularity of computers and online communication in the 1990s, devices and standards were developed such as V.18 that used the ASCII standard but also incorporated the Baudot standard (Hellström 2002).

Three Deaf men were instrumental in the technical breakthrough that made the TTY possible: a coupling device that allowed sounds transmitted over the telephone to be translated into data and, eventually, alphabetic letters (Lang 2000). Like modems, this meant that TTYs functioned compatibly (within limits) over the telecommunications work. TTYs also worked satisfactorily with first-generation analog mobiles: "Analog systems work fairly well with teletype devices (TTYs). Some phones have built in modular jacks into which a TTY can be plugged; other phones can be used with an adapter" (NCD 2004, p. 103). However, the much vaunted second-generation digital mobiles threatened this interworking or knitting together of technologies: "Initially, digital systems did not work well with TTYs. Digital wireless transmissions inherently contain errors, but error correction techniques can reduce the problem for speech. Digital networks are less forgiving in the case of the tones generated by TTY devices, however, and the transmission errors can cause characters to be lost or changed, resulting in unintelligible messages" (NCD 2004, p. 103.)

In his account of Deaf people and telecommunications in Australia, Phil Harper observes that "When the government decided to move from an analog to digital telecommunications system in 2000, on the premise that it would improve the wireless network access to a wider range of the Australian people, it did nothing to find a solution for those who were losing a service—Deaf people using TTYs on an analog mobile service" (Harper 2003, p. 156–57).

The consequences of second-generation cell phones for the Deaf community were quite significant. In Australia, for instance, as the national relay provider, Australian Communication Exchange, argued,

> In the late 1990s, telecommunications access for people with a disability made a tremendous leap forward and the future looked positive. . . . However, in three short years since 2000, more than half of the telecommunications network is now not accessible to people who are Deaf or have a hearing or speech impairment despite the existence of the disability discrimination and telecommunications legislation [due to shut-down of the analog network in 2000, and complete switch to digital mobile networks]. (Quoted in Goggin and Newell 2004, p. 416)

The Australian experience was one shared by Deaf people around the world, underscoring the "glocal" nature of mobile telecommunications, the workings of this eminently global technology back and forth through local arenas.

Internationally, it took concerted pressure from the Deaf community and their supporters, with alliances of users, scientists and technologists, academics, and interested industries across national, regional, and international settings, and also the invocation of general disability discrimination legislation in various countries, before the mobile phone manufacturers and telecommunications carriers took this problem seriously.

In the United States, for instance, the Federal Communications Commission, which played a central role in the reshaping of telecommunications and disability through the 1990s (Goggin and Newell 2003), issued a requirement in 1996 that carriers were responsible for ensuring connection of 911 (emergency) calls over digital wireless networks for callers using a TTY (FCC 1996). Certainly this was only the beginning of the process: "The deadline for compliance was extended repeatedly as various wireless carriers worked to provide a solution" (NCD 2004, p. 104). An industry group, the TTY Forum, comprising carriers, wireless handset and infrastructure manufacturers, TTY manufacturers, telecommunications relay service providers, and disability consumer organizations, worked from 1997 on to ensure that the networks would be able to carry 911 calls via TTY by the mid-2002 deadline set by the regulator (Harkins and Barbin 2002; NCD 2004). A number of larger providers met this deadline and implemented wireless TTY compatibility: AT&T Wireless Systems, Cingular Wireless, NexTel, Sprint PCS, T-Mobile (formerly Voicestream), Verizon Wireless, and others (TAP 2002). A number of carriers petitioned the FCC for an extension.

There were certainly some genuine difficulties faced in making cell phone networks and handsets compatible with TTY devices. These included redesigning to accommodate the speed and tone of TTY Baudot signals and "setting standards for the interface between TTY devices and digital wireless mobile phones operating with several different digital standards" (TTY Forum 2002; NCD 2004, p. 105). At the end of the process, however, there is evidence to suggest that in the United States reasonable compatibility has been reached between cell phones and TTYs in nonemergency situations, though difficulties still remain with wireless 911 TTY calls (especially related to some of the equipment used by operators or emergency services answering calls) (NCD 2004, p. 105). However, not all cell phones are compatible with TTYs, and consumers have been urged to test their TTY with their wireless provider (TAP 2002). Elsewhere, too, the problems of TTY and mobile compatibility remain, without such initiatives to offer some consumer information.

Seeing Telephony: Deaf People and Text Messaging

We have seen how the needs and desires of hard-of-hearing and Deaf cell phone users were not initially understood or envisaged as part of the design of second-generation digital mobile networks, and that this set of design and consumption issues has not been widely noticed and discussed. To explore these issues further, we now turn to a case that has received significant publicity: Deaf people's invention of text messaging.

Deaf people have long used text communications. As we have seen from the 1960s on, Deaf people had established a set of communicative and cultural practices around the TTY. Coupling TTYs with mobile cellular devices, something attempted by some users with analog mobiles, offered new telecommunicative possibilities for Deaf people. While the introduction of digital mobiles rendered mobile TTY communications fraught with difficulties, another unexpected possibility was gradually opened up—text messaging.

While engineers, designers, and marketing and business people saw the potential for mobiles to go beyond mere voice communication to become a data medium (not least with the rise of the Internet in 1993–94), early applications were not successful. Textual communication through mobile phones was an unexpected use of the technology (see Snowden's chapter in this volume; also Agar 2003; Trosby 2004). Technology designers, manufacturers, and mobile phone companies had been preoccupied with transferring telephone capabilities and culture to the mobile phone platform. With the growth in data communications from the 1960s on, consideration had been given to data capabilities of mobile phones. One difficulty, however, had been the poor quality and slow transfer rates of data communications over mobile networks, especially with first-generation analog mobiles. SMS was built into the European global system for mobile (GSM) standard, as an insignificant, additional capability (Trosby 2004). The character sets were limited, the keyboards small, the typeface displays rudimentary, and there was no acknowledgment that messages were actually received by the recipient. Yet SMS was cheap, and it offered one-to-one, or one-to-many, text communications that could be read at leisure or, more often, immediately. By 1999–2000, text messaging had been adopted in a number of countries, especially by young people (on the history of SMS, see Goggin 2005; Taylor and Vincent 2005; Snowden's chapter in this volume).

Text messaging was also adopted by the Deaf community. While a definitive history of the Deaf adoption of SMS has yet to be written, this story has now become widely known: "The deaf have taken to this technology as an answer to their prayers. As texters in countries like Australia, Britain, and Israel, where the mobile phone service providers have agreed to interconnect their networks, they can take their means of communication with them as far as they can go and reach anyone who has a mobile phone" (Power and Power 2004, p. 334).

Detailed studies of Deaf people's adoption and use of text messaging are still to be undertaken, but one central theme in accounts to date is that users can now communicate with other Deaf and hearing people without the intermediary of a human TTY relay operator. Des Power and Mary Power point out that abbreviating text has "long been familiar to [Deaf people] because it is used in TTY conversations," and that the characteristics of the SMS genre "suit the sometimes-limited English of Deaf people" (2004, p. 335). There is some evidence to suggest that the rate of use of SMS among Deaf people is higher than it is among their hearing counterparts (Harper 2003; Power and Power 2004).

Certainly Deaf people's creative use of mobiles caught the attention of mainstream media: "Over the last few years, the mobile phone has emerged as a popular device for what at first may seem an unlikely user group: the deaf and other people who are hard of hearing. This usage shows how a group of people can take up a technology that was not initially designed or marketed to them, and adapt it to suit their own needs and purposes" (Wurtzel 2002). Service providers in a range of areas, including emergency services, law enforcement, and education institutions, began to realize the potential to reach Deaf people via SMS.

Just like the rise of text messaging in general, once mainstream mobile phone companies noticed the Deaf community's avid use of text messaging, they were keen to market to Deaf consumers, and also publicize this use for wider, public consumption. In September 2001, for example, Vodafone New Zealand sponsored 2001 Deaf Awareness Week:

> Text messaging is more than just a youth craze turned mainstream—
> it also gives deaf people the chance to communicate via mobile phone.
> . . . Vodafone New Zealand's GM Company Communications, Avon
> Adams said it was good to see text messaging providing options for
> the deaf community. "Text messages are free to receive and only 20c
> to send to anywhere in the world. They open up a realm of possibil-
> ities to deaf and hearing impaired people who can't make use of voice-
> based communications," said Ms Adams. (Vodafone NZ 2001)

Specific reworking of the technology in light of such use was slower in coming: "As the technology was not developed with this community in mind, operators and manufacturers have been slow to tailor offerings for the deaf and hard of hearing" (Wurtzel 2002). Problems include SMS not offering asynchronous rather than real-time interaction (Harper 2003) as it is a store-and-forward technology resembling e-mail in this respect—despite the often very fast communication it can often afford; textual messages need be written in hearing languages such as English rather than native sign language; and the high cost of the frequent text messaging required by Deaf users.

Deaf users have also avidly taken up devices such as text-messaging pagers and portable digital assistants, with the T-Mobile Sidekick becoming a cult object among some communities of users (Kilner 2005). Mobile devices are also being used with Internet protocol relay services, for instance with America Online and MCI's "My IP-relay" service launched in 2004 (AOL and MCI 2004). This enables Deaf people to have their phone calls transcribed by relay operators and sent to them over the Internet, and then to have their instant message replies read back to the hearing person by the relay operator (LaVallee 2005).

The implications of these new networking of Deaf culture are still being registered and debated. Certainly, as a new textual media, the cell phone, and associated technologies, are deeply involved in significant transformations in Deaf identity and community: "These technologies have begun to alter how Deaf people contact and communicate remotely with each other" (Harper 2003, p. 160). As in wider debates on mobiles, there are those who praise the utility, function, freedoms, intimacies, and sociability such technology brings to Deaf people and others who lament the decline of older social forms. For example, face-to-face contact and gatherings have been much prized by Deaf communities, not least as a way to communicate via the visual and tactile medium of native sign language. In this respect, Deaf clubs have been an important social and cultural institution, and fears have been expressed that the mediated communications offered by SMS, instant messaging, and the Internet will led to an attentuation of social ties and cultural norms, and the disappearance of important customs (see Kunerth 2005; and response from the blog of Laird 2005). These fears have been more generally raised regarding mobiles, and have a long history in the reception of new media (Marvin 1988; Winston 1998). Such emotions, or what in their raw form cultural theorists call "affect," need to be recognized, taken seriously and examined.

We would also suggest that these technologies are being socially and culturally shaped by the innovations of these users, though this is much less widely grasped. Thus SMS takes its place in a historical ensemble of technologies and communicative and cultural practices, including TTYs, fax machines, and, more recently, electronic mail and instant messaging (Bowe 2002; Lang 2000; Power and Power 2004).

Blinded by SMS

From the celebrated Deaf use of SMS, we now move to a contrasting case, in which a disability culture and its desires and needs regarding a technology have not been reflected in values, design, or narratives of use. In doing so, we are mindful of the problematic, dynamic, yet intensely invested categories of "Deaf" and "Blind," and the entire vexed taxonomic enterprise of knowing the truth of a person via an impairment label (for a discussion of this see the opening chapter of Goggin and Newell 2005a).

As with people with disabilities in general, and Deaf users in particular, we propose the thesis that for Blind users the cell phone has gone hand in hand with new personal and collective possibilities. As William Jolley notes, "People who are blind have enjoyed the flexibility that results from mobile communications. Using their mobile phones they can find each other more easily in public places, and they have the added security of being able to make a phone call if they are lost or feeling endangered" (Jolley 2003, p. 27).

Yet, to propose an antithesis, the technology has not been imagined or designed with Blind users in mind. Jolley usefully summarizes a number of taken-for-granted features of mobile phones that Blind people most often cannot use:

> People who are blind have very limited access to the standard features of mobile phones. In general terms they can only make calls by manually entering the number to be called, and they can receive calls if the phone rings or vibrates. But they do not know the battery strength, the signal strength, if the PIN has been wrongly entered, if calls are missed, if the phone is accidentally on divert, or anything else that is shown on the screen. They cannot use the menu system, the telephone directory system, or anything but the most elementary speed dialing features. And, of course, they cannot use SMS. These features have been introduced gradually, as network services have been enhanced, and as new models of mobile phones have been released. (Jolley 2003, p. 27)

People with low vision also face problems: "However, [m]any people with low vision find it difficult to find a mobile phone with a large enough, brightly lit screen that they can comfortably read. So if they cannot read the screen, people with low vision face the same denial of access to the features of their mobile phones as do people who are blind" (Jolley 2003, p. 27).

The author of a comprehensive series of articles on cell phone accessibility for Blind users for an American Federation of Blind publication (Burton 2004, 2005a; Burton and Uslan 2003, 2004a, and 2004b; Burton et al. 2003) offers this account:

> In the early days of cell phones, when they were used only to make and receive calls, accessibility was not a major issue. As long as visually impaired people could tactilely identify the control buttons on the cell phone, it was no problem to make and receive calls. However, they were left out of the loop when the evolution of cell phones brought display screens and other new advances, such as phone books, text messaging, and e-mail, into the mix. Although people who are visually impaired were still able to perform the basic functions of making and receiving calls, the manufacturers did not design these new phones in a way that would allow them to independently access the new, more advanced features. There was no text-to-speech functionality to accommodate cell phone users who are blind, and there were no display screens with the visual characteristics, such as large fonts or highly contrasting colors, that would accommodate users who have low vision. (Burton 2005b)

As mobile phone manufacturers and mobile service providers did not collectively envisage and design mobile technological systems with affordances and capabilities for Blind users, it has been largely left to specialist disability technology providers to design purpose-built workarounds. This was only possible, however, when it became possible for third parties to add software programs and applications to mobile phones: "With the advent of high-end mobiles (such as the Nokia Symbian Series 60), blind and vision-impaired users can install software to allow speech-enabled access to text messages, appointment calendars and contact lists" (Molloy 2004).

The company Cingular Wireless, for example, has licensed for the United States a software application called TALKS. TALKS is able to read screen-based menus, instructions, and content and convert these into synthetic speech, either using the phone's speaker option or plug-in earphones or a headset. Another application is Mobile Speak. It is designed to work with the Symbian series 60 operating system, to be carrier independent and to access "most of the functionality of the device," and is offered in a number of language (to date mostly English and European languages but also Turkish, Arabic, and Chinese). As well as a number of Nokia phones, it also works with the Siemens SX1 (Mobile Speak 2005). Mobile Speak is offered by Code Factory, a Spanish developer of "software solutions for the blind and visually impaired" (www.codefactory.es). Code Factory also offers a related product, Mobile Accessibility: "a complete mobile phone solution for the blind and vision-impaired. . . . All of the essential phone features are right at your fingertips, in a way specially designed to provide complete accessibility" (Code Factory 2005).

There is much to be said about the politics of artifacts here, and the inscription of the boundaries between mainstream and specialist technology, that we are able only to note here for reasons of space. However, one index of these matters is the prohibitive price of adaptive software: "the screen reading packages Talks and Mobile Speak cost several hundred dollars, are locked to a single hand-set, only work on GSM phones and are difficult for some to use" (Noonan 2005).

Not surprisingly, in 2003 Spanish technology company Owasys saw an opportunity and announced the world's first mobile phone specifically designed for Blind people. (After all, producing a *national* mobile phone has been an important project for some countries, so why not a *disabled* mobile?) When the phone was exhibited in Britain, a company representative explained the thinking behind the product's development: "We thought there were parts of the consumer market whose demands were not very well covered by the big players. . . . From our conversations with ONCE (the blind people's organisation in Spain) and RNIB here in the UK, it was clear that there was a need among blind people for a product like this" (Adams-Spink 2003). It is not clear to what extent Owasys's dedicated product has been taken up by Blind users, or whether most are more comfortable with a screen reader or application option (at least those who can afford it, and have the skills and training to use it). One difficulty may be slow and costly progress on approvals in different countries. In addition, the Owasys phone has fewer features than a phone running a screen reader, and is priced similarly to a high-end phone plus screen-reading software (Noonan 2005).

Motorola has recently announced a software upgrade for one of its phones that would enable text-to-speech reading of menus, messages, and other screen-based phone features. As the capabilities of mobile devices are rapidly expanding at this time, so too are creative options beginning to emerge, extending the capabilities of the cell phone for Blind people. A technology company called voICE—"See with your ears!: Wearable Bionics used by the Blind Aim: Vision through Brain Plasticity"—has developed an aural camera phone designed for Blind users (The voICE 2005), which translates images into soundscapes that are transmitted to the user via headphones (Sandhana 2003). The company has a utopian vision for its innovationa: "Within a decade, second-hand camera phones could become an affordable platform for use of The voICe by blind people living in developing countries! These phones can at the same time serve many general communication, Internet access and computing needs for the sighted poor, while doubling as a digital camera" (The voICE 2005).

There are other software programs now available that allow a person to use a phone camera to identify colors of objects (via a "talking color identifier"). These are ingenious, if relatively untested, reinterpretations and redeployments of the visual cultural and multimedia features that now ship with the majority of mobile phones.

As our discussion of the development of mobiles for Blind people suggests, there are now some feasible, if more expensive, options available. Significant numbers of Blind people are indeed now using text messaging and other data features on mobiles, as they are dedicated portable digital assistants, wireless laptop computers, and other devices. These innovative uses of mobile and wireless technologies build on and complement other media innovations of Blind users, such as Braille, radio, Internet, audio recording, Podcasting, talking books, and new digital publication standards such as Daisy (www.daisy.org). Outside Blind community and cultural lists, websites, journals, and circles, there is little recognition in other audiences of innovative uses of mobiles (or perhaps these other technologies). Not surprising, perhaps, progress in reshaping cell phone technology for Blind users is still slow at the time of writing: "To date, little real progress appears to have been made in this area, and people who are blind remain largely excluded from all but the most basic features of mobile telephony. We strongly encourage all stakeholders to discuss and implement strategies for improving accessibility in this important area" (HREOC 2005). Tim Noonan's 2000 explanation of this situation still applies:

> there are only two significantly developed zones of [blindness] accessibility momentum—PC access, predominantly via Microsoft's Windows32 operating systems; and Web accessibility, predominantly driven by the WAI (Web Access Initiative). . . . This is important to consider when we note recent projections in the IT industry that more than half of the internet connections by 2002 (or 2005 in other estimates) are expected to be from non-PC devices. This means that they will be from technologies which, currently, have no means of accessibility to their visual output. This raises the important question as to how people will be able to access set-top-boxes, WAP-capable mobile phones, personal organizers, smart domestic appliances and the like, which are solely visual (and non-textual) in output. (Noonan 2000)

The implications of such an impasse in technology are far reaching. SMS is now intensively used around the world, especially by young people, and is often pivotal to cultural participation and social membership. Such emergent norms mean that Blind people's lack of access to SMS, and neglect in the design and shaping of mobile technologies more broadly, can lead to significant social exclusion.

Cell Phones and Next-Generation Disability

As the sources cited in the course of the chapter make clear, study and discussion of disability and the cell phone is largely to be found in the specialized technical literatures of scientists and health professionals devoted to disease and disability categories such as hearing or vision impairment journals; in the newsletters, websites, e-mail lists, journals, or other publications of disability service provider, advocacy, or self-representative organizations; in reports, policy, regulation, and legislation pertaining either to telecommunications or disability discrimination; in e-mail lists, websites, and publications of information and communication technology specialists; and, occasionally, in mainstream media or technology supplements. Only rather haltingly is discussion of disability beginning to be found in telecommunications, new media, or Internet studies literature, and there has been very little scholarly discussion of social and cultural aspects of mobile communications technologies.

In seeking to stimulate such inquiry, we have been able to only briefly sketch three different case studies in disability and the cell phone. There is a great deal of empirical work that remains to be undertaken to establish, first, the histories of disability and technology touched upon here, and, second, to debate and theorize these. It is our view that this is an important research agenda, not only as a matter of human rights and justice but also because these narratives unsettle our taken-for-granted theories of technology. From a different perspective, we would note that Internet, games, and new media studies have made much of the role of the user in appropriating, domesticating, developing, and actually producing networked digital technology and the cultural forms and content that circulate through it. There is much interest among mobile phone scholars in questions of use and consumption. As people with disabilities, we are mostly overlooked as users, consumers, and audiences. Accordingly, our third recommendation for research is that people with disabilities be credited as do-it-yourself consumer-producers of mobile phones and media, and that their narratives be taken seriously and their uses appropriately studied and analyzed. That is, as people with disabilities we too are everyday users of mobiles.

To adequately understand cell phones and disability, one needs to confront some deeply ideological notions (or myths) of technology. The term *ideology* is appropriate because it marks the operation of power. We have long contended that the social construction, or shaping, of disability in technology has decisively to do with relations of power (Goggin and Newell 2003). It is often very puzzling to those dedicated to the pursuit of accessible technology for people with disabilities that, time and time again, new technology brings not the much vaunted benefits (indeed salvation), but instead insidious new forms of exclusion, regulation, and control. Why, the proponent of accessible technology asks, if accessibility and "universal design" are such simple, fruitful, and potentially profitable principles (NCD 2004), do we nearly always find that technologies are designed without imagining that people with disabilities will be among their users?

Hopeful answers to this question include more education, clearer guidelines, embedding accessibility in all stages of innovation and design, standards, fairer laws and regulation, and economic incentives such as procurement policies. And yet, we suspect that such stubbornly resistant aspects of achieving inclusive technologies form part of a larger project of dismantling the oppressive power relations of disability in our societies, in which, mutatis mutandi, people with disabilities have long been seen as *other*, indeed, all too often still, as inhuman (Goggin and Newell 2005a). Discourses of access and universal design have become a cogent, forceful, and recurrent response to the paradoxes of disability and technology. A representative instance is found in the excellent National Council on Disability report on how to interest the market in accessible technology: "Despite their popularity and their capabilities, cell phones are not accessible to everyone. . . . Each of these problems can be overcome, to some extent, through proper design" (NCD 2004, pp. 102–3). Here we see much faith invested in the corrigibility of disabling technology, especially in design as an overarching and pliable practice for accessibility. This is indeed a vital undertaking, but it is neither sufficient nor will it succeed without a wider and deeper rethinking of the entire question of disability and technology, starting with a recognition of the fundamental question of power.

This is why we call the cell phone disabling, and believe that this is actually a richly productive and ambiguous thing to do. The cell phone, like other contemporary technologies, is implicated in the macropolitics and micropolitics of the regulation of contemporary lives. As an artifact, it is shaped in its turn by social relations and cultural dialectics. Seizing the phone from a different angle is what people with disabilities have perhaps managed to do, opening up new modes of being and becoming, and tools of freedom, and new ways to frame their world with technology. The cell phone intersects with crucial aspects of identity, community, and politics in the lives of people with disabilities. It is a fitting example not (only) of the woes of a narrowly conceived, pathologizing notions of access and divide—but rather of an eminently cultural dialectics.

Our thanks to Tim Noonan for invaluable information and comment on mobiles and blind people.

References

Abberley, P. (1992). "Counting us out: A discussion of the OPCS [Office of Population, Censuses, and Surveys] surveys." *Disability, Handicap, and Society* 7: 139–56.

Adams-Spink, G. (2003). "UK debut for 'blind mobile.'" *BBC News*, November 21. Available at http://news.bbc.co.uk/1/hi/technology/3226314.stm.

Agar, J. (2003). *Constant touch: A global history of the mobile phone.* Cambridge, UK: Icon Books.

Albrecht, G. L., K. D. Seelman, and M. Bury (Eds.). (2001). *Handbook of disability studies.* London and Thousand Oaks, CA: Sage.

Altman, B. M. (2001). "Disability definitions, models, classification schemes, and applications." In G. L. Albrecht, K. D. Seelman, and M. Bury (Eds.), *Handbook of disability studies* (pp. 97–122).Thousand Oaks, CA: Sage.

American National Standards Institute (ANSI). (2001). *Method of measurement of compatibility between wireless communication devices and hearing aids, C63.19.* Washington, DC: ANSI.

America Online (AOL) and MCI. (2004). "America Online and MCI enable deaf and hard-of-hearing individuals to receive incoming calls anywhere, anytime using their own, unique phone number." *Media release,* December 13. Retrieved June 24, 2005, from www.timewarner.com/corp/newsroom/pr/0,20812,1007089,00.html.

Australian Bureau of Statistics (ABS). (2004). *Disability, ageing, and carers: Summary of findings.* Canberra: ABS.

Barnes, C., and G. Mercer. (2003). *Disability.* Cambridge, UK: Polity.

Berger, M. S. (1997). "Hearing aid compatibility with wireless communications devices." *Proc. IEEE Int. Symp. Electromagnetic Compatibility,* 123–28.

Bowe, F. (2002). "Deaf and hard of hearing Americans' instant messaging and e-mail use: A national survey." *American Annals of the Deaf* 147: 6–10.

Brown, B., N. Green, and R. Harper (Eds.). (2002). *Wireless world: Social and interactional aspects of the mobile age.* London and New York: Springer.

Burton, D. (2004). "The signal gets stronger: Three cell phones with speech output." *AccessWorld 5,* no. 4. Available at www.afb.org/afbpress/pub.asp?DocID=aw050406.

Burton, D. (2005a). "Two more approaches: A review of the LG VX 4500 cell phone from Verizon Wireless and Microsoft's Voice Command Software." *AccessWorld 6,* no. 3. Available at www.afb.org/afbpress/pub.asp?DocID=aw060308.

Burton, D. (2005b). "You get to choose: An overview of accessible cell phones." *AccessWorld 6,* no. 2. Available at www.afb.org/afbpress/pub.asp?DocID=aw060206.

Burton, D., and M. Uslan. (2003). "Answering the call: Top-of-the-line cell phones, part 1." *AccessWorld 4,* no. 3. Available at www.afb.org/afbpress/pub.asp?DocID=aw040302.

Burton, D., et al. (2003). "Answering the call: Top-of-the-line cell phones, part 2." *AccessWorld 4,* no. 4. Available at www.afb.org/afbpress/pub.asp?DocID=aw040404.

Burton, D., and M. Uslan. (2004a). "Do cell phones equal software equal access? Part 1." *AccessWorld 5,* no. 1. Available at www.afb.org/afbpress/pub.asp?DocID=aw040606.

Burton, D., and M. Uslan. (2004b). "Do cell phones equal software equal access? Part 2." *AccessWorld 5,* no. 1. Available at www.afb.org/afbpress/pub.asp?DocID=aw050106.

Burwood, E., and R. Le Strange. (1993). *Interference to hearing aids by the new digital mobile telephone systems, global systems for mobile (GSM) communications standard.* Sydney: National Acoustic Laboratories.

Code Factory. (2005). "Mobile accessibility." Retrieved June 24, 2005, from www.codefactory.es/mobile_accessibility/maccessibility.

Cornes, P. (1991). "Impairment, disability, handicap, and new technology." In M. Oliver (Ed.), *Social work, disabled people, and disabling environments.* (pp. 98–115). London: Jessica Kingsley.

Donner, J. (2005). "Research approaches to mobile use in the developing world: A review of the literature." In A. Lin (Ed.), *Proceedings of the International Conference on Mobile Communication and Asian Modernities* (pp. 75–97). June 7–8, City University of Hong Kong, Kowloon.

European Telecommunications Standards Institute (ETSI). (1993). Technical report, GSM 05.90, GSM EMC Considerations, January. European Telecommunications Standards Institute.

Federal Communications Commission (FCC). (1996). E911 First Report and Order, CC Docket No. 94-102, 11 FCC Rcd 18676 (1996), adopted June 12, 1996. Available at http://ftp.fcc.gov/cgb/dro/e911tty.html.

Federal Communications Commission (2003). "FCC acts to promote accessibility of digital wireless phones to individuals with hearing disabilities." Media release, July 10. Available at http://hraunfoss.fcc.gov/edocs_public/attachmatch/DOC-236430A1.pdf.

Fortunati, L., J. Katz, and R. Riccini. (Eds.). (2003). *Mediating the human body: Technology, communication, and fashion.* Mahwah, NJ: Lawrence Erlbaum.

Goggin, G. (2005). "Mobile phone culture and the love of text messaging." Proceedings of Communication at Work, the 2005 ANZCA conference, Christchurch, New Zealand, July 4–7. Available at www.anzca.net.

Goggin, G., and C. Newell. (2003). *Digital disability: The social construction of disability in new media.* Lanham, MD: Rowman and Littlefield.

Goggin, G., and C. Newell. (2004). "Disabled e-nation: Telecommunications, disability, and national policy." *Prometheus: Journal of Issues in Technological Change, Innovation, Information Economics, Communication, and Science Policy* 22, no. 4: 411–22.

Goggin, G., and C. Newell. (2005a). *Disability in Australia: Exposing a social apartheid.* Sydney: University of New South Wales Press.

Goggin, G., and C. Newell. (2005b). "The intimate relations between technology and disability." Introduction to the "Technology and Disability" special issue of *Disability Studies Quarterly* 25, no. 2/3. Available at www.dsq-sds.org/_articles_html/2005/spring/intro_goggin_newell.asp.

Goggin, G., and C. Newell. (2005c). Special double issue of *Disability Studies Quarterly* 25, no. 2/3. Available at www.dsq-sds.org/_articles_html/2005/spring/.

Goggin, G., and C. Newell (Eds.). (2006). "Disability, identity, and interdependence." Special issue of *Information, Communication, and Society.* Forthcoming.

Harkins, J., and C. Barbin. (2002). "Cell phones get smart—and more accessible." *Silent News,* May. Retrieved May 12, 2005, from http://tap.gallaudet.edu/WirelessTelecom/AccessibleCell.htm.

Harper, P. (2003). "Networking the Deaf nation." *Australian Journal of Communications* 30, no. 3: 153–66.

Hellström, G. (2002). "Standardization of text telephony." Retrieved March 15, 2002, from www.omnitor.se/english/standards.

Hillebrand, F. (Ed.). (2002). *GSM and UMTS: The creation of global mobile communication.* Chichester and New York: John Wiley.

Human Rights and Equal Opportunity Commission (HREOC). (2000). *Inquiry on mobile phone access for hearing aid users.* Sydney: HREOC. Available at www.hreoc.gov.au/disability_rights/inquiries/MP_index/mp_index.html.

Human Rights and Equal Opportunity Commission (HREOC). (2005). *Access to telecommunications: Status report.* Sydney: HREOC. Available at www.hreoc.gov.au/disability_rights/communications/update05.htm.

Jolley, W. (2003). *When the tide comes in: Towards accessible telecommunications for people with disabilities in Australia.* Sydney: Human Rights and Equal Opportunity Commission. Retrieved June 20, 2005, from www.hreoc.gov.au/disability_rights/communications/tide.htm.

Joyner, K. H., et al. (1993). "Interference to hearing aids by the new digital mobile telephone system, global system for mobile (GSM) communication standard." Sydney: National Acoustic Laboratory.

Katz, J. (Ed.). (2003). *Machines that become us: The social context of personal communication technology.* New Brunswick, NJ: Transaction.

Kilner, K. (2005). "The latest: Not just trendy, T-Mobile Sidekicks are more than a fashion statement for the Deaf community." *Web @ devil,* April 28. Available at www.statepress.com/issues/2005/04/28/arts/693124?s.

Kunerth, J. (2005). "Deaf culture fades." *Sun-Sentinel* (South Florida), January 27. Reprinted at Deaf Chat Coffee website. Retrieved June 27, 2005, from www.deafcoffee.com/cgi-bin/dada/mail.cgi?flavor=archive&id=20050 130191808&list=dcc.

Laird, G. (2005). "Deaf culture fades - misleading?" Blog of Grant W. Laird, Jr. http://grantlairdjr.com/b2evolution/index.php/all/2005/02/01/p149.

Lang, H. G. (2000). *A phone of our own: The deaf insurrection against Ma Bell.* Washington, DC: Gallaudet University Press.

LaVallee, A. (2005). "For the Deaf, instant messaging reaches out and touches." *Columbia News Service,* March 1. Available at http://jscms.jrn.columbia.edu/cns/2005-03-01/lavallee-deafmessage.

Law, J. (Ed.). (1999). *Actor network theory and after.* Oxford: Blackwell.

Lin, A. (Ed.). (2005). Proceedings of International Conference on Mobile Communication and Asian Modernities, June 7–8, City University of Hong Kong, Kowloon.

Ling, R. (2004). *The mobile connection: The cell phone's impact on society.* San Francisco: Morgan Kaufmann.

MacKenzie, D., and J. Wajcman (Eds.). (1999). *The social shaping of technology,* 2nd ed. Buckingham, UK: Open University Press.

Marvin, C. (1988). *When old technologies were new: Thinking about electric communication in the late nineteenth century.* New York: Oxford University Press.

Metts, R. L. (2000). *Disability issues, trends, and recommendations for the World Bank.* Washington, DC: World Bank.

Mobile Speak. (2005). "The screen reader made for you." Retrieved June 24, 2005, from http://mobilespeak.codfact.com/.

Molloy, F. (2004). "Scene and heard." *The Age* (Melbourne), October 30.

National Council on Disability (NCD). (2004). *Design for inclusion: Creating a new marketplace.* Washington, DC: NCD. Retrieved May 12, 2005, from www.ncd.gov/newsroom/publications/2004/publications.htm.

National Telecom Agency Denmark (NTAD). (1994). "Interference with hearing aids caused by GSM digital cellular telephones and DECT digital cordless telephones."

Conclusive report by the working group on GSM and DECT telephones and hearing aids.

Noonan, T. (2000). Blind Citizens Australia submission to the Human Rights and Equal Opportunity Inquiry into Electronic Commerce. Retrieved July 12, 2005, from http://www.hreoc.gov.au/disability_rights/ inquiries/ecom_subs/bca1.htm.

Noonan, T. (2005). Personal correspondence, June 22.

Power, M., and D. Power. (2004). "Everyone here speaks TXT: Deaf people using SMS in Australia and the rest of the world." *Journal of Deaf Studies and Deaf Education* 9, no. 3: 333–43.

Roe, P. (Ed.). (1993). "Telephones and hearing aids." Proceedings of the COST 219 Seminar, The Hague, March 17, XIII/61/94-EN.

Roulstone, A. (1998). *Enabling technology: Disabled people, work, and new technology.* Buckingham, UK: Open University Press.

Sandhana, L. (2003). "Blind 'see with sound.'" *BBC News*, October 7. Available at http://news.bbc.co.uk/2/hi/science/nature/3171226.stm.

Seelman, K.D. (2001). "Science and technology policy: Is disability the missing factor?" In G.L. Albrecht, K. D. Seelman, and M. Bury (Eds.), *Handbook of disability studies* (pp. 663–92). London and Thousand Oaks, CA: Sage.

Seelman, K. D. (2005). "Universal design and orphan technology: Do we need both?" *Disability Studies Quarterly* 25, no. 3. Available at www.dsq-sds.org/.

Shipley, T., and J. Gill. (2000). *Call barred? Inclusive design of wireless systems.* London: Royal National Institute of the Blind. Available at www.tiresias.org/phoneability/wireless.htm.

Snyder, S. L., B. J. Brueggemann, and R. Garland-Thomson (Eds.). (2002). *Disability studies: Enabling the humanities.* New York: Modern Language Association of America.

Steinbock, D. (2003) *Wireless horizon: Strategy and competition in the worldwide mobile marketplace.* New York: American Management Association.

Stiker, H.-J. (1999). *A history of disability.* (W. Sayers, Trans.). Ann Arbor: University of Michigan Press.

Taylor, A. S., and J. Vincent. (2005). "A SMS history." In L. Hamill and A. Lasen (Eds.), *Mobile world: Past, present, and future.* (pp. 75–91). Vienna: Springer-Verlag.

Telecommunications Access Program (TAP). (2002). "Wireless telephones and TTYs." Washington, DC: TAP, Gallaudet University. Retrieved May 12, 2005, from http://tap.gallaudet.edu/WirelessPhoneTTY0902.htm.

Trosby, F. (2004). "SMS, the strange duckling of GSM." *Telektronikk* 3: 187–94. Available at www.telenor.com/telektronikk/ volumes/pdf/3.2004/Page_187-194.pdf.

TTY Forum. (2002). "TTY Forum consensus statement for the FCC." TTY Forum, June 27, sponsored by Alliance for Telecommunications Industry Solutions. Retrieved June 20, 2005, from www.atis.org/atis/tty/ttyforum.htm.

Victorian T. (1998). "Update on digital cellular telephone interference and hearing aid compatibility." *Hearing Journal* 51: 53–60.

Victorian, T. (2004). "Hearing aid compatibility: Technical update." *Audiology Online*, June 12. Available at www.audiologyonline.com/articles/pf_arc_disp.asp?id=1263.

Victorian, T., and D. Preves. (2004). "Progress achieved in setting standards for hearing aid/digital cell phone compatibility." *Hearing Journal* 57, no. 9: 25–29.

Vodafone New Zealand. (2001). "Txt messaging provides a world of mobility for the deaf." Media release, September 21. Available at www.vodafone.co.nz/aboutus/media_releases/12.4_20010921.jsp.

The voICE. (2005). "The voICe MIDlet for mobile camera phones." Retrieved June 24, 2005, from www.seeingwithsound.com/.

Von Tetzchner, S. (Ed.). (1991). *Issues in telecommunication and disability.* COST 219. CEC-DGXIII (EUR 13845 EN). Brussels: COST 219.

Wajcman, J. (2004). *Technofeminism.* Cambridge, UK: Polity.

Winston, B. (1998). *Media technology and society, a history: From the telegraph to the Internet.* London: Routledge.

Wurtzel, J. (2002). "Deaf go mobile phone crazy." *BBC News*, February 8. Available at http://news.bbc.co.uk/1/hi/sci/tech/1808872.stm.

"Do You Know the Importance of a Skypager?": Telecommunications, African Americans, and Popular Culture

Davin Heckman

To consumers of popular culture texts, the pager plays a prominent role in both positive and negative depictions of inner-city youth. Since their establishment as a widely available and relatively inexpensive piece of telecommunications technology in the early 1990s, such devices have developed from their more rudimentary origins of simple numeric display into integrated wireless communications devices, which muddle the borders between cellular phones and PDAs and traditional pagers—the result being a vast array of small, portable, and relatively inexpensive machines that provide a variety of features like e-mail, Internet browsing, voice mail, and telephone service for people on the go. This type of portable communications technology is quickly becoming a standard feature of the American cultural landscape, much like the standard telephone or wristwatch, securing it as a relevant topic of study for years to come.

While the title of this paper makes reference to a song by A Tribe Called Quest, and professes to be about these new technologies and their relationship to African Americans as expressed in popular culture, it has a great deal more to do with issues of class than race. I chose to link my topic to race because many class issues that deal with urban poverty are brought to the forefront via rap music—what Chuck D calls "the black CNN." Although rap music plays a crucial role in this study, I also include film and newspapers in my catalogue of texts to provide a clearer picture of the ways in which issues of technology play themselves out across the American landscape in the form of stereotypes and promises—dreams and nightmares about what our technological future might hold.

While it may come off as insensitive for me to deal with race and popular culture, which inevitably leads me into the dangerous realm of stereotypes and generalizations, I would like to remind my readers that I am dealing with ideas about technology and class that are attached to race by way of popular culture texts. In my other writings, I deal with the ways in which privileged classes gain access to power through technology in what Manuel Castells has dubbed "the Network Society." In this chapter, I hope to deal with the ways in which this network is being foisted upon those who lack the means to participate fully in the global economy—the result being ambivalent views toward technology, which may prove to be both a blessing and a curse.

The Dream: A Hip-Hop Fantasy

A sampling of rap music reveals a variety of references to portable wireless technology. Perhaps the earliest and most notorious reference appears NWA's 1989 hit, "Fuck tha Police," in which a young Ice Cube booms, "Fuckin' with me 'cause I'ma teenager/ with a little bit of gold and a pager/ Searchin' my car, lookin' for the product/ Thinkin' every nigga is sellin' narcotics." A passionate response to police brutality, the song draws attention to what has become a fairly universal equation: fear and ignorance manifested in a spirit of general police harassment targeting African-American people. In this equation, a pager, a chain, or an article of clothing is interpreted as a secret signifier for criminal activity, regardless of the activities of the person wearing it. The less intelligible the sign, the more panicked the response. In the case of "Fuck tha Police," the pager exists alongside gold as a marker of status, but it also points to an information exchange that is mobile, unspecified, and difficult to police. It certainly could be used for dealing drugs, but it is only a consequence of the drastic cultural shifts brought out in the "War on Drugs" (and now the "War on Terror") that we have come to expect our legal system to operate on a presumption of guilt that targets people who fit certain social profiles.

Another early example is the enormously popular Tribe Called Quest's anthem to the pager, which focuses on a more positive depiction of the device as a marker of success. As Q-Tip explains,

> Those who don't believe, see you're laid behind
> Got our skypagers on all the time
> Hurry up and get yours cuz I got mine
> Especially if you do shows, they come in fine
> If you're with a G and you're sippin' wine
> Eatin' cacciatore with a twist of lime
> Gotta meet your lover at a quarter to nine
> (Tribe 1991)

In other words, the skypager serves an important communicative function for a young professional with a full calendar. The pager serves as a means to negotiate a flexible work schedule, preventing missed opportunities and avoiding wasted time. More important, as Phife adds later in the song, "The 'S' in skypage really stands for sex," making the pager an emblem of masculinity, as if to say that while he is successful at everything, he is most successful in the sack. The song ends on an abrupt and ironic note, with Q-Tip explaining, "My shit is overflowin, they won't allow/Another page, so I'll just end this now" — pointing to the ways in which this sort of twenty-four-hour availability can also serve as an inconvenience for someone who is in such high demand.

Numerous other artists make references to wireless technology. E-40's (1996) "Ring It" circulates around cell and pager use, explaining, "If it's major, hit me on my pager/Rang it, ring it, rang it, ring it, ring my telephone, ring my telephone." E-40 focuses on the use of the pager in social and business relationships, but also ends with his "pager on the overflo'," and complaining of drained batteries. Other songs, like Master P's (1992) "I'm Going Big Time," Ice Cube's (1991) "Steady Mobbin'," Method Man's (1998) "Elements," Will Smith's (1997) "Just Cruisin'," Lil' Romeo's (2001) "Don't Want To," and Kool Keith's (2001) "I'm A Tell-U" (to name a few examples from a broad cross-section of artists), mention pagers and cell phones as just another feature of everyday life. In other words, this sort of mobile technology has become a standard weapon in the player's arsenal.

A number of female artists also make references to wireless communications, which often revolve around romance and romantic problems. Pop stars 3LW (2000) turn to the pager as evidence of too many attachments that detract from the relationship in the song "No More," which proclaims, "I'm getting a little tired of your broken promises, promises./Looking at your pager seeing different numbers and numbers." In Mya's (2000) song "Lie Detector," the pager reveals female infidelity, "Picked up the pager numbers/Said who's called sixty-nine/She said don't be surprised/Cause it's your best friend." Missy Elliot's (1997) "Beep Me 911," which is also directed at a male lover, streamlines the breakup process in the chorus:

> Beep me 911
> Or call me on my cell phone
> I'll call you back
> And see what you gon' tell me
> You don't wanna date
> No if's ands or waits
> It's over babe

The impact that this technology has had on day-to-day things such as relationships is brought to light in such songs. This phenomenon attests not only to widespread technology use, but to the proliferation of uses that conform to gender stereotypes and suggests that it is an adaptable technology that resists uniformity and lends itself readily to everyday use—and thus fulfills technology guru Niel Gershenfelds's (1999, p. 7) observation that "invisibility is the missing goal in computing." In other words, the goal of truly popular technology is paradoxical in that it strives to "improve" form while leaving content relatively intact.

It is only in our era of rapid technological shifts that we can see new technologies unfold in symbiosis with culture in such dramatic ways. In less than twenty years, pagers have gone from a tool for technocratic elites to something adopted by kids living in the projects. Police have developed a response to the device, hip-hop artists have integrated it into lyrical narratives, middle-aged segments of the middle class have learned to associate it with criminality, while middle-class kids have embraced it as a fashion item. The technology itself has mutated from a one-way numeric device to a two-way alphanumeric platform, from a phone to a hybrid telephone/Internet browser/camera/game console/PDA. And, finally, hip-hop artists have gone from singing about wireless devices to being featured on the devices themselves.

But it would be a mistake to credit the technology alone for its rapid deployment and innovation. As Tricia Rose (1994) explains in her groundbreaking discussion of hip-hop music, "North American blacks, Jamaicans, Puerto Ricans, and other Caribbean people with roots in other postcolonial contexts reshaped their cultural identities in a hostile, technologically sophisticated, multiethnic, urban terrain" (p. 34). In other words, the communities that have given rise to hip-hop have developed in part through frequent and often mandatory cultural and technical changes. George Nelson (1998) confirms this assertion in the context of the history of music:

> We [African Americans] love to take things that were once out of reach—the saxophone, the sampler, the pager—and reinvent the technology in our own image. The sax was invented by Adolphe Sax in the mid-nineteenth century, yet it didn't become a valued instrument until brothers got their hands on it in the '30s. The sampler was invented by sound scientists in the 70s, but it was via the ears of hip-hop producers that this technology found its deepest use. The pager, long a tool of doctors on call, became a staple of American culture because of the curiosity and vision of black young people. It started as a tool for drug dealers, spread to the rest of the community, and, ultimately, has entered the everyday life of the nation. (pp. 52–53)

The cultural roots of innovation and adaptation that have been crucial to the development of hip-hop create an ideal situation for the rapid ascent and development of wireless technologies as a site for imagination and cultural production. In fact, it would be difficult to even imagine the everyday use of wireless technology without the powerful push that it took from the hip-hop community.

The Reality: Telecommunications for the Inner-City Poor

The spreading use of wireless technology, especially by those who live in the inner city, is easy to understand. A 1999 marketing study by Nancy McGuckin entitled "Analysis of Households with Interrupted Telephone Service Using 1995 NPTS," which uses data from the Federal Highway Administration's *Nationwide Personal Transportation Survey*, explains that the inner-city poor (especially blacks) who have household telephones are more likely to experience interruptions in telephone service. Furthermore, a 1999 study by the National Telecommunications and Information Administration entitled *Falling through the Net* revealed that only 78.1 percent of African-American households with an income under $15,000 had telephone service, compared to 89.1 percent of white Americans (chart I-6a). The reasons for the wide gap most likely have to do with the ghettoization of impoverished minorities, which amplifies the effects of poverty through increased competition for scant resources and jobs, decreased tax revenues for education and basic services, and the complex problems of drugs, crime, and violence—a phenomenon described by William Julius Wilson in *The Truly Disadvantaged* (1987). In such a context, it is not difficult to imagine how lapses and gaps in telephone service can be clustered around race.

Neither government study accounts for cellular phone or pager use, but as McGuckin notes, "Previous research shows that many people who live in households without telephones use pagers or cell phones, or at least have telephones available at their place of work" (1999, p. 1). Faced with problems such as an uncertain future and family instability, and lacking many of the comforts of the suburban home, residents of such communities often look for alternatives—one alternative being the street gang, which Dwight Conquergood (1994) astutely describes as "preeminently a communication phenomenon" (p. 52), which as an association of "bonded communitarians" tries to compensate for the harsh realities of urban life (p. 26). For a community that must rely on communications for survival, it is not surprising that cellular phones and pagers would present the best of both worlds, allowing citizens to remain plugged into both public life and electronic communication. The pager and the cell phone help to extend the vital network, and thus represent exceptional tools for inner-city residents. They also have the additional benefit of keeping the user online even if he or she has to change addresses or commute great distances to work via public transportation. As a result, wireless technology, in improving physical mobility, can help to improve economic mobility.

The Silver Screen: Ambiguous Technology

While the promise of wireless technology leads an exciting life in rap and R&B videos, new technology enjoys a much more detailed and developed discussion in film. Several films in recent years deal with wireless technology and African Americans, painting a more ambivalent and complicated view than those that are only hinted at in the more mainstream hits, which seek to link this technology with opulent lifestyles. While many films produced by African Americans or featuring African Americans, like D.J. Pooh's *3 Strikes* (2000) or *Def Jam's How to Be a Player* (Martin 1997), feature uses of cell phones and pagers, I would like to turn toward more loaded examples of technology use that will help to bring my discussion into sharper focus and reveal deeper cultural issues. *I Got the Hook Up* (1998), written by and starring the founder and CEO of No Limit Records, Master P; *Bait* (2000), starring black comedian Jamie Foxx; and *Enemy of the State* (1998), starring rap pop star Will Smith all present a grim underside to this technology in varying ways and degrees, positing, at the very least, that technology is something to be wary of, especially when it can reveal things about a person's whereabouts and allow eavesdropping.

I Got the Hook Up tells the story of two friends, Black (Master P) and Blue (A.J. Johnson), who in the course of running a used electronics business in the ghetto acquire (through a bit of hustling) a shipment of cellular phones that are delivered to the wrong address. With help from a friend, the two get the phones outfitted with new microchips. Black's girlfriend Lorraine (Gretchen Palmer), who works for a telecommunications company, helps the two to hide all of the calls that are being made illegally. Making loads of cash by hooking their neighborhood up with cell phones, Black proclaims himself "the first wireless cellular phone CEO in the hood." As the business grows, the volume of calls attracts the attention of Lorraine's boss, who is concerned about discrepancies in the company's records. At the same time, local crime lord Roscoe orders a slew of phones. But when a problem with the pirate chips in the cell phones causes a series of misdirected calls, culminating in Roscoe's broadcast of a secret telephone call over the radio, things take a turn for the worse. As a result, Roscoe loses $70,000 and seeks revenge on Black and Blue. With Roscoe, Lorraine's boss, and the FBI in hot pursuit of Black and Blue, their dreams of unlimited growth quickly crumble. By the end of the film, the two avoid arrest and death by playing the various parties off against one another.

The film *Bait* tells the story of small-time criminal Alvin Sanders (Jamie Foxx), who gets arrested for stealing shrimp from a seafood warehouse. He finds himself imprisoned with John Delano Jaster (Robert Pastorelli), an accomplice responsible for a heist from the National Treasury. Jaster, suffering from a bad heart, gives Sanders clues as to the whereabouts of the stolen gold, which is being sought by government agent Edgar Clenteen (David Morse) and Jaster's partner in crime, the ghoulish super-hacker Bristol (Doug Hutchinson). In a bid to catch the super-hacker, who presents a threat to national security, Sanders is secretly implanted with a high-tech bugging device and released from prison in the hopes that Bristol will track him down, hence the film's title. With the implant in his jaw, Sander's every word is monitored and his location is tracked by satellite, all in the hopes that the agents can learn the whereabouts of Bristol. Needless to say, this exploitation presents a serious threat to Sanders, his son, and girlfriend. In the end, Sanders manages to outsmart and kill Bristol, becoming a hero and earning the reward for the returned gold.

Enemy of the State, the most menacing of the three films, is a conspiracy film that tells of events revolving around the fictitious "Telecommunications Security and Privacy Act," which has parallels to a number of issues of privacy and national security currently being hashed out by the U.S. government. Robert Dean (Will Smith) is a successful attorney who finds himself at the center of an NSA assassination cover-up. After crossing paths with an old acquaintance (Jason Lee) who secretly slips him a digital video copy of the assassination of a senator, Dean's life quickly falls apart. The NSA, eager to avoid scandal, seeks to discredit Dean by sifting through his records and fabricating stories about mob ties and an extramarital affair in an elaborate smear campaign. Dean is fired from his job, has his credit cards cancelled, and loses his wife's confidence. He crosses paths with the reclusive Brill (Gene Hackman), a former NSA employee and electronics expert, who informs Dean that he is being bugged by the NSA. Dean's pen, pager, cell phone, watch, pants, and shoes all contain bugs. Dean is forced to remove all of the markers of his success in order to avoid surveillance, and Brill suggests that Dean live the rest of his days in hiding, totally stripped of his identity. Dean and Brill eventually decide to fight back, using technology of their own to wage a war of resistance. Dean is eventually vindicated, and the government agents responsible for the conspiracy are brought to justice.

For middle-class and upwardly mobile African Americans, the films tell of the need for control over technology, a concern that is reflected in the popular press. A 1996 article by Staci Bush in the *Sacramento Observer*, entitled "African-Americans and Technology," reports on the promises of technology:

> Alfred A. Edmond, Jr., executive editor of Black Enterprise, and vice president of editorial operations, added, "This is all so new, but if we take it for granted we will (fall behind). . . . African-Americans and the nation as a whole are being reluctantly dragged into this. We're not falling behind—everything is at square one. This is a chance to get on the ground floor of something revolutionizing the industry." (p. F3)

Bush adds, "African-Americans stand to lose more from their hesitancy to ride the techno wave" (1996, p. F3). Similarly, a 1999 article by Anthony Walton from *The Atlantic Online*, which provides a detailed history of the ways in which African Americans have been blocked out of technological advancement, offers a warning:

Mastery of technology is second only to money as the true measure of accomplishment in this country, and it is very likely that by tolerating this underrepresentation in the technological realm, and by not questioning and examining the folkways that have encouraged it, blacks are allowing themselves to be kept out of the mainstream once again. This time, however, they will be excluded from the greatest cash engine of the twenty-first century.

The possibility of being burned by technological lag and the "digital divide" looms large in the minds of upwardly mobile African Americans, if the abundance of articles expressing sentiments similar to those voiced above are to be believed.

In addition to anxieties over the prospect of being left behind, the films depict the tensions upwardly mobile blacks face by being a hot demographic group, targeted by marketers for disposable income. One report on Internet trends highlights this explosion: "According to figures from Nielsen/Net Ratings, the African-American online population increased by 44 percent to 8.1 million between December 1999 and December 2000," which is a substantially higher growth rate than the 33 percent growth for the general population (Nua 2001). Offline, "African-Americans are the largest minority segment in the U.S., with nearly 33 million consumers. They will grow at an astounding rate, doubling to 62 million consumers by the year 2050" (McLean 1998–99). With telecommunications companies like Sprint[2] and Windwire[3] eagerly seeking penetration into what is clearly a hot (and hopefully lasting) market, it's not hard to see how technology can generate anxiety. As marketers strive to provide an increasing number of services (as they continue to do for white Americans), it is possible that many longstanding cultural values might erode as more and more blacks opt for suburban life and its accoutrements, much like European ethnic immigrants have made the transition to their status as white suburbans, shedding the problems of the inner city along with rich cultural heritage. One only has to turn an eye toward the suburban middle class that has long been critiqued for its insularity, isolation, and excessive consumption to find examples of the potential problems communities in transition might face.

While this discussion has primarily focused on the more affluent members of the black community who have the means to access the latest technological toys, for lower-class blacks the anxieties expressed in the films present a different set of concerns. As mentioned above, the maintenance of communication and networks makes wireless technology especially desirable. The possibility of being available at all hours of the day is one way to help secure social bonds, making wireless communications even more practical and important than it is for those citizens who have more money, security, and resources. Concurrently, this technology serves an additional social and communicative purpose as a marker of a certain level of success. Gadgets and conveniences have long been a sign of affluence, but communications technology has the benefit of making the holder available via media. A phone number is a mark of existence in an era when so much of human communication and interaction takes place electronically. In effect, it is a way of saying, "I am here." It means something to have a cell phone in the inner city.

Marketers, aware of this reality, have been quick to offer financing and credit options to soak up expendable income and secure continued payment over long periods of time, making technology available even to those who can't quite afford it. The social promises and advantages of wireless technology coupled with the expansion of credit in the new economy have made the cellular phone and pager, as relatively small and inexpensive purchases, much easier to justify even if they do present users with the prospect of debt and financial crisis down the road. And since these technologies constitute a certain vital presence once adopted, to discontinue their use is tantamount to disappearing. During flush times, a consumer may purchase a cell phone or pager to facilitate work and social activity, but any failure to pay that would result in an interruption in service discontinues the benefits that technology brings, but it also does deeper damage by causing the user to miss appointments and lose credibility in social and professional spheres. As a result, such technology is difficult to sacrifice, and its continued payment becomes a basic necessity for the user, especially during economic hard times when this technology becomes the standard means to compete in a scarce job market.

Along with the social and practical benefits and liabilities of new technology, however, there is a more menacing side. Wireless technology's dangers can also be seen as just one more development in a long history of state antagonism toward people of color. Seen in the context of slavery, pre–World War II American eugenics, the Tuskegee experiment, the African AIDS epidemic, the Norplant controversy, the rumored CIA-crack connection, anti-gang ordinances, COINTELPRO, the War on Drugs, and so on, the menace of electronic surveillance looms large as another site of torment.

While the songs cited present only small-scale social surveillance as a threat (a lover finds someone else's number on a pager), it is significant that both *Bait* and *Enemy of the State* deal specifically with the menace of state surveillance. Although both were presented as mainstream films (whereas *I Got the Hook Up* was a black-controlled project), it is interesting that both films' protagonists were cast as African-American males, an acknowledgment of the historic relationship between African Americans and the state and a critique of current trends toward surveillance, especially the surveillance of marginalized groups. The wireless technology in *Bait* clearly mirrors the wireless surveillance technology currently used to monitor convicts in house arrest programs. The tracking technology in *Enemy of the State* foreshadows the impending inclusion of GPS technology into all wireless communications devices, coupled with the proliferation of surveillance cameras and eye-in-the-sky technologies already in place in urban areas across the nation. With this cunning combination of panoptic technologies in place, the possibility of converting inner cities into prisons is a scary possibility.

Similar to watching, listening plays a profound role in all three films, turning the promise of communication into a threat by making all mediated conversations accessible. This possibility is further inflected in the African-American community, which has relied on intracommunity communication coupled with a certain level of secrecy since the days of slavery in order to survive the numerous obstacles thrown into its path. The overhearing (intentional and accidental) that takes place in all three films represents invasions of both personal and professional privacy, generating mayhem and danger for the films' protagonists.

Aside from electronic surveillance, the symbolic status of the pager and cell phone also feed into white moral panics over gangs and drugs. The connection between gangs and pagers and cells is certainly realistic. Conquergood (1994, p. 49) notes, "In the section of the gang with which I have worked most closely, influential members all carry these paging devices," reinforcing the notion that gangs are a communication phenomenon. This connection becomes problematic when it is employed in profiling efforts. For example, a recent article reports, "any two of the following may still constitute gang membership to the local police: 'slang,' 'clothing of a particular color,' 'pagers,' 'hairstyles,' or 'jewelry,'" and continues, "nearly eighty percent of Aurora's [a suburb of Denver] list is African-American" (Pintado-Vertner and Chang 2000, p. 9). Furthermore, an organization called the Nonprofit Risk Management Center (2000) issued a report entitled "Perspectives on Gangs and Gang Violence," which cites Pepperdine safety specialist Ronald D. Stephens, who includes "Beepers, pagers, and cellular phones" in a list of warning signs that include graffiti, shootings, and tattoos. As previously mentioned, pagers and cell phones are not peculiar to African-American communities, but the fact that the possession of such technologies by members of this group can lead to arrest or being identified as a gang member by local police certainly testifies to force of symbolic power contained in such technology.

Reach Out and Touch Someone: A Cell for Everyone

The rapid incorporation of wireless technologies into the fabric of daily life has a great deal to do with their pervasiveness in many spheres: culture, economics, and repression. From music to film, from grim economic realities to the brutalities of punishment, wireless technology appears as a constant presence, both as form and as content. And ultimately, this is what makes an institution different from a novelty. Where wireless communications technologies are exceptional is that they normalize surveillance, much in the same way that a person has a name that links them to a body that ties them to a set of actions and ideas, and they reflect unprecedented opportunities for discipline and control.

The image of the pager and cell phone and how this image intersects with ideas and realities concerning race and class is certainly a complex picture. This intersection, with all of its positive and negative potential, has no ready and clear-cut answers. It seems natural that such potentially powerful technology would play a prominent role in the realm of discourse; thus it is important to further analyze how the discourse that circulates around wireless technology is itself a vehicle of ideological power. To repeat Marshall McLuhan's familiar phrase: "The Medium Is the Message" (1966, p. 23). Wireless technology is certainly functional, but, as Baudrillard (1996, p. 63) writes, "'functional' in no way qualifies what is adapted to a goal, merely what is adapted to an order or system: function is the ability to become integrated into an overall scheme." In other words, the functionality of wireless technology and all the discourses about it must be situated within a political context in order to understand what a cell phone or pager really is.

The emergence of the African-American community as a hot demographic and the explosion of rap music as a hot commodity are very much linked to the availability of wireless technology, the rise of global capitalism, and the expansion of credit toward segments of the population normally denied access. Within this constellation, an interdependent web of forces is at work to construct an idea of the world and an image of reality within which new economic models can find their purchase, offering a prime example of hegemony at work. Gramsci (1971) describes this process: "Undoubtedly the fact that hegemony presupposes that account be taken of the interests and the tendencies of the groups over which hegemony is to be exercised, and that a certain compromise equilibrium should be formed—in other words, that the leading group should make sacrifices of an economic-corporate kind" (p. 161). The rise in cell phone use is accompanied by corrections and interruptions, promises and penalties to ownership.

A complex of forces is hard at work to secure the place of wireless technology, especially for the most marginalized elements of society. Profit promises to deliver cell phones, along with a popular culture that will debate its values and liabilities. But because popular culture is also reliant on providing benefits like relief and happiness, these debates must not be too dire. All three films discussed in this paper conclude happily, with a reassertion of the protagonist's mastery over the situation. *Enemy of the State* and *Bait* add to this mastery the paternalist support of a government that is able to cope with the risks and dangers contained within it. Rather than providing cautionary advice, the films ultimately assert that while technology can be scary, in the end it is OK.

Althusser's ideological state apparatuses and repressive state apparatus offer another angle to the high stakes of the wireless game. Althusser (1971, pp. 142–43) answers the question, "What are the ideological State apparatuses (ISAs)?":

> They must not be confused with the (repressive) State apparatus. Remember that in Marxist theory, the State Apparatus (SA) contains: the Government, the Administration, the Army, the Police, the Courts, the Prisons, etc., which constitute what I call the Repressive State Apparatus. Repressive suggests that the State Apparatus in question "functions by violence"—at least ultimately (since repression, e.g. administrative repression, may take non-physical forms). I shall call Ideological State Apparatuses a certain number of realities which present themselves to the observer in the form of distinct and specialized institutions.

The ISAs are those institutions that remain independent of centralized control, yet still function to promote the ideological interests of the state. These institutions, often at odds with one another, play the game of hegemony that Gramsci proposes by replicating the logic of the centralized state within and scattering it throughout the culture.

As the economy becomes more and more deterritorialized, the role that these peripheral institutions play becomes the carrier of the logic of the new marketplace. As Fredric Jameson (1991) maintains, the bundle of concepts known as "postmodernism" is indeed the "cultural logic of late capitalism." And as new institutions emerge, institutions take new forms, often redefining what the term means. While "institutions" are normally considered to be large structures that embody a clear mission and values, in its own way the cellular phone is quickly becoming an institution itself, embodying a decentralized logic that strives to construct a network that can contain all members of society.

If one grants that an informal informational network can exist as an institution, then quite literally the cellular phone and its kin are ideological apparatuses. As Althusser (1971, p. 173) explains, "*all ideology hails or interpellates concrete individuals as concrete subjects.*" Since communications technology does nothing but call out and expect an answer, it is plain to see how a network can interpellate subjects and enforce ideological uniformity. When one considers the efforts made to improve market penetration, and the ease with which communications technology facilitates market penetration, the ideological strength of the wireless network is obvious.

The futures of technology and African Americans are uncertain, but in a strange way intimately linked. While there seems to be a persistent anxiety about whether or not we will see an end to racism and its effects, great strides have been made in race relations, and economic gains have certainly been made by middle-class African Americans. But the prominence of representations of African Americans is more ambiguous. Because the economic boom of the 1990s had largely to do with the rapid growth of communications and information technology, to extend technology toward all levels of society does not necessarily represent good intentions. As films like *Bait* and *Enemy of the State* demonstrate, it is especially important for the marginalized to be put into the network. As a conspicuously disproportionate number of blacks have discovered, the state is more than happy to provide wireless technology in the form of electronic house arrest. The combination of surveillance and communication results in a form of "hegemonic panopticism"—a form of surveillance that is not only normative in its effects, but normative in its causes, calling forth subjects that actively seek out the means of their own surveillance, often in positive terms. Unlike food, clothing, shelter, medicine, and other commodities, communications technology is very much a two-way street, both liberating subjects to participate in new mediated interaction and increasing control of subjects by circumscribing these networks of discourse.

Postscript

Originally, I had intended this chapter as a sort of jeremiad, a word of caution for the potential threats that were forming on the horizon. Unfortunately, it has been reduced to a mild critique by real-world innovations in fear, technology, and legislation. Even before September 11 ignited a big push for government surveillance, the FCC had mandated that all cell phones be equipped with GPS technology (Crouch 2001). As I write this, the U.S. Department of Homeland Security is running an eight-city pilot program that will require seventeen hundred immigrants who have not been charged with any crimes to wear electronic ankle bracelets twenty-four hours a day; if it is a "success," Homeland Security will consider expanding the program to all aliens (Zwerdling 2005). Schools in California and Texas have implemented RFID name tags (Zetter 2005), a logical advance considering the metal detectors, surveillance cameras, barbed-wire fences, and locker searches that are already commonplace to many students. Auto rental agencies, delivery services, and police departments are already making ready use of GPS in automobiles, to track driving habits and travel patterns. One can only imagine that this will only become more pervasive as GPS comes equipped as a standard feature. In a post-9/11 world, terror provides a powerful pretext for expanding such technologies even further.

If the potential government abuses of these powers aren't enough, perhaps the commercial abuses that these technologies enable are just as bad. GPS can also be used to harvest detailed and individualized consumer profiles, much in the way that cookies are used to monitor web navigation. Or consider the controversies surrounding the use of databases compiled by ChoicePoint, Inc., which was paid to provide a "scrub" list of felons for use by Florida elections officials, and accidentally included eight thousand eligible voters—an error that disproportionately affected minorities and some believe could have influenced the outcome of the 2000 election (Palast 2000). As ChoicePoint and LexisNexis database services have been awarded large contracts to monitor individuals under the guise of Homeland Security, these companies have accidentally released hundreds of thousands of personal files to hackers (Krim and O'Harrow 2005).

Certainly, the War on Terror has diverted much attention away from policing the American underclass—while they are scary to many, the thought of waging war against the very salt-of-the-earth folks that do all the hard work simply isn't heroic. And as real

wages decline for most Americans, the popular support for a crackdown on broke
Americans as a "crackdown on broke Americans" is eroding quickly. It is much easier
to support a rise in police power if done to defend against foreign invaders.[4] The implementation of profiling, for example, is discussed in the context of screening out potential
Islamic fanatics. The use of wiretaps and security cameras are no longer debated as
weapons in the war on drugs; they are now touted as our only line of defense against
Arab militants. Retinal scans will someday be trumpeted as the only sure way to save us
from certain disaster. A film like *Enemy of the State* might be called naïve (or even anti-
American) in today's political climate, where security reigns supreme. However, we can
be confident that provisions are already being made to make sure that they keep an eye
on minorities, the poor, and political nonconformists. As illustrated earlier in this
chapter, the triad of culture, economics, and repression has been mobilized to facilitate
the rapid integration of the cutting edge into the everyday.

Notes

1 Urban household by income experiencing interruptions in service: $15,000 or less, 5.6
percent; $15–29,999, 2.4 percent; $30–44,999, 1.2 percent; $45,000 and up, 1.0 percent
(McGuckin 1999, table 1, p. 3). A comparison of inner-city blacks to inner-city whites for the
$10–14,999 income bracket reveals that 6.8 percent of African Americans compared to 3.1
percent of whites experienced interruptions in service (McGuckin 1999, table 6, p. 5).
2 "Sprint's decision to hire Vigilante marks the first time the telecommunications industry has hired
an agency to develop a full-scale campaign targeted at African-Americans" (Trollinger 1998).
3 "WindWire, the leading provider of wireless advertising and marketing solutions, today
announced that Afronet, a destination site for African-Americans, has joined WindWire's
wireless network" (WindWire 2000).
4 So much the better if they can be hidden anywhere. And it is really a two-fer if the enemy can
be said to draw on the words of civil libertarians and the freedoms protected by the Bill of
Rights for moral support and encouragement.

References

Songs

E-40. (1996). "Ring it." *The hall of fame.* New York: Jive.
Elliot, M. (1997). "Beep me 911." *Supa dupa fly.* New York: Elektra/Asylum.
Ice Cube. (1991). "Steady mobbin'." *Death certificate.* Los Angeles: Priority.
Kool Keith. (2001). "I'm a tell-u." *Spankmaster.* New York: TVT.
Lil' Romeo. (2001). "Don't want to." *Lil' Romeo.* Los Angeles: Priority.
Master P. (1992). "I'm going big time." *Mama's bad boy.* New York: No Limit.
Method Man. (1998). "Elements." *Tical 2000: Judgment day.* New York: Def Jam.
Mya. (2000). "Lie detector." *Fear of flying.* Santa Monica, CA: Interscope.
NWA. (1989). "Fuck tha police." *Straight outta Compton.* Los Angeles: Priority.
Smith, W. (1997). "Just cruisin'." *Big Willie style.* New York: Columbia.
3LW. (2000). "No more." *3LW.* New York: Sony.
A Tribe Called Quest. (1991). "Skypager." *Low end theory.* New York: Jive.

Films

Fuqua, A. (Director). (2000). *Bait.* Burbank, CA: Warner Bros.
Martin, L. C. (Director). (1997). *Def Jam's how to be a player.* Beverly Hills, CA: Polygram.
Martin, M. (Director). (1998). *I got the hook up.* New York: Dimension.
Pooh, D. (Director). (2000). *3 strikes.* Los Angeles: MGM.
Scott, T. (Director). (1998). *Enemy of the state.* Burbank, CA: Touchstone.

Books and Articles

Althusser, L. (1971). "Ideology and ideological state apparatuses." *Lenin and philosophy* (pp. 127–86). (B. Brewster, Trans.). New York: Monthly Review.
Baudrillard, J. (1996). *The system of objects.* (J. Benedict, Trans.). New York: Verso.
Bush, S. (1996). "African-Americans and technology: The community 'myths' are addressed by computer experts." *Sacramento Observer,* March 20, p. F3.
Conquergood, D. (1994). "Homeboys and hoods: Gang communication and cultural space. In L. R. Frey (Ed.), *Group communication in context: Studies of natural groups* (pp. 23–55). Hillsdale, NJ: Lawrence Erlbaum.
Crouch, C. (2001). "Will Big Brother track cell users." CNN.com, August 3. Retrieved May 26, 2005, from http://archives.cnn.com/2001/TECH/ptech/08/03/911.cell.tracing.idg/.
Gershenfeld, N. (1999). *When things start to think.* New York: Henry Holt.
Gramsci, A. (1971). *Selections from the prison notebooks.* (Q. Hoare and G. N. Smith, Trans. and Eds.). New York: International Publishers.
Jameson, F. (1991). *Postmodernism; or, The cultural logic of late capitalism.* Durham, NC: Duke University Press.
Krim, J., and R. O'Harrow, Jr. (2005). "Data under siege." *Washington Post,* March 10, p. E01. Retrieved May 26, 2005, from www.washingtonpost.com/wp-dyn/articles/A19982-2005Mar9.html.
McGuckin, N. (1999) "Analysis of households with interrupted telephone service using 1995 NPTS." *Nationwide Personal Transportation Survey.* Retrieved May 27, 2005, from www-cta.ornl.gov/npts/1995/Doc/publications.shtml.
McLean, A. (1998–99). "Erasing the boundaries: Drawing African-Americans onto the Internet." *Journal of Integrated Communications.* Retrieved May 27, 2005, from www.medill.northwestern.edu/imc/studentwork/pubs/jic/journal/1998-1999/mclean.htm.
McLuhan, M. (1966). *Understanding media: The extensions of man.* New York: Signet.
National Telecommunications and Information Administration. (1999). *Falling through the net: Defining the digital divide.* Retrieved April 19, 2002, from www.ntia.doc.gov/ntiahome/fttn99/contents.html.
Nelson, G. (1998). *Hip-hop America.* New York: Penguin.
Nonprofit Risk Management Center. (2000). "Perspectives on gangs and gang violence. *Community Risk Management and Insurance* (spring). Retrieved April 19, 2002, from www.nonprofitrisk.org/nwsltr/archive/n1100_3.htm.
Nua Internet Surveys. (2001). "African-Americans lead in U.S. Internet growth. February 1. Retrieved April 19, 2001, from www.nua.com/surveys/index.cgi?f=VS&art_id=905356501&rel=true.

Palast, G. (2000). "Florida's flawed 'voter cleansing' program." *Salon*, December 4. Retrieved May 26, 2005, from http://dir.salon.com/politics/feature/2000/12/04/voter_file/index.html.

Pintado-Vertner, R., and J. Chang. (2000). "The war on youth." *Color Lines* 2, no. 4 (January 31): 9.

Rose, T. (1994). *Black noise: Rap music and black culture in contemporary America.* Hanover, NH: Wesleyan University Press.

Trollinger, A. (1998). "Sprint to mount campaign aimed at African-Americans." *Business Journal*, September 14. Retrieved April 19, 2002, from http://kansascity.bcentral.com/kansascity/stories/1998/09/14/story8.html.

Walton, A. (1999). "Technology versus African-Americans." *The Atlantic Online*, January. Retrieved April 19, 2002, from www.theatlantic.com/issues/99jan/aftech.htm.

Wilson, W. J. (1987) *The truly disadvantaged: The inner city, the underclass, and public policy.* Chicago: University of Chicago Press.

WindWire. (2000). "WindWire adds Afronet to its wireless ad network." WindWire.com, December 12. Retrieved April 19, 2002, from www.windwire.com/news/pr_121200_1.html.

Zetter, K. (2005). "School RFID plan gets an F." *Wired News*, February 10. Retrieved May 26, 2005, from www.wired.com/news/privacy/0,1848,66554,00.html.

Zwerdling, D. (2005). "Electronic anklets track asylum seekers in U.S." [Radio broadcast]. NPR, March 2. Retrieved May 26, 2005, from www.npr.org/templates/story/story.php?storyId=4519090.

Section Three
International Perspectives

Mobile Sociality in Urban Morocco

Bahíyyih Maroon

In the Muslim nation of Morocco, mobile phone use has gone from zero subscribers to nearly 10 million users in less than a decade. In city centers, where mobile use is most dense, urbanity has come to be typified by the sight of roaming citizens utilizing global systems for mobile communication devices. The ether of contemporary Moroccan cities is layered with streaming digital signals flowing in a billion directions at once. On the ground, verbal communication between people whose bodies are not visible to one another now constitutes a normative feature of everyday life. The phenomenal popularization of mobile telephony in Morocco, as elsewhere, indicates the degree to which technological invention has embedded the mechanics of compressed space and time within the very substrata of contemporary human sociability.

The capacity to instantaneously collapse corporeal distance and engage in sociability beyond the restrictions of fixed place and time plays a critical role in the structural transformation of the contemporary Muslim public sphere. The nature of this role, however, is neither unitary nor predictable. As David Harvey (1990) writes, "The experience of time space compression is challenging, exciting, stressful and somehow deeply troubling, capable of sparking therefore a diversity of social, cultural and political responses" (p. 240). This chapter considers experiences of space-time compression enabled by mobile telephony in a Muslim city. Emphasizing the relationship between spatial practices and moral belief, what follows is an exploration of transitions in the public sphere produced by the dramatic rise of mobile communication.[1]

In urban Morocco, mobile telephony is used for establishing connections with potential "dates" and friends, privatizing the flow of personal information exchanges, "rewiring" the limits of gossip networks, and keeping up to date on the activities and movements of friends and peers. I argue that mobile telephone use reroutes moral codings dependent on the fixity of local place and produces an urbanscape of "mobile leisure." Utilizing mobile phones as pathways to anonymity, mobility, and individualism allows greater opportunity for transgressing moralized social roles. By providing an alternative modality for making and maintaining social connectivity, mobile telephony challenges the limits of moral citizenship. Drawing on ethnographic data, this chapter shows that the emergence of mobile phones in Morocco is transforming localized place-making practices and reconfiguring gendered divisions of public sociability.

The Emergence of Mobile Telephony

Mobile telephony was the first beneficiary of the Moroccan government's intensive campaign to liberalize the nation's telecommunication sector, which was previously state-run. In an effort to revitalize the structure of its economy, Morocco moved to expand its telecommunications industry in the 1990s. In 1997, after several years of debate, the landmark Post Office and Telecommunications Act—Law 24-96—was passed, creating a legal framework for the liberalization and market growth of the telecommunications industry (ITU 2001). The act clarified the procedures for privatization of the sector by carefully detailing the requirements for licensing telecom operators. Under the act, operators seeking to offer services in Morocco must participate in fair market practices and transparent operating procedures. Further, operators are obligated to maintain the technological standards in existence. Under this directive, the nation's impressively 100 percent digital network will continue to be improved. In addition to these provisions, the act mandated the creation of a regulatory agency. Accordingly, the Agence Nationale Regulataire des Telecommunications — ANRT — opened in March 1998. The Ministry of the Post and Telecommunications was also divided, creating the entity of the Secrétariat d'Etat des Postes et des Technologies des Télécommunications et de l'Information, SEPTI.

In midsummer 1999, hard work and fraught debate culminated in legislative change that brought Morocco its first successful licensing tender. Sent out to bid earlier that year, the license for the nation's second GSM operator was awarded to the Medi Telecom consortium (Meditel) for US$1.1 billion. The sale represented the most lucrative award for a GSM license ever in a developing nation. As a multinational group, the success of Meditel in gaining the license was another important signal to Moroccans regarding the the nation-state's intentions to participate in a global economic framework on the road to privatization. The success of the tender was indicated not only by the final bidding price received, but also by the transparent character of the selection process itself.

In 2000, the telecom industry in Morocco pushed further into the domain of privatization by selling 35 percent of the nationally held phone utility company. The sale of shares to Vivendi Universal netted the government over US$2.3 billion. Renamed Maroc Telecom, the operator has been iconized in national rhetoric as a potent symbol of successful market liberalization. In reality, the nation's greatest triumph in effecting a transparent liberalization of the sector is due to its oversight body—the ANRT. While stock sales, investment practices, and licensing revenues contribute to the actual and perceived success of the sector, the stability and growth of telecommunications in Morocco has necessitated constant transparent oversight and regulation of market practices.[2] In this regard ANRT has been persistently vigilant in attempting to ensure that fair market principles are legislated and enforced.

The growth of mobile telephony in Morocco has outpaced even the most optimistic forecasts. Currently, user rates are tripling on a yearly basis. Both Meditel and Maroc Telecom have adjusted their network structures to accommodate demand. Telephone users in Morocco have overwhelmingly opted to "cut the cord" or to simply bypass LAN lines altogether. Fixed line telephony rates are now decreasing yearly—as of 2004, there were fewer than 2 million subscribers nationwide. Mobile communication, in contrast, had a user rate of 9.4 million subscribers at the end of 2004 (ANRT 2004).[3] While efforts are being made to extend coverage areas into the nation's rural zones, mobile coverage is most reliable in cities. It is, accordingly, in the cities of Morocco that mobile communication is having a marked effect on the composition of the public sphere.

Follow the LEDs

To render visually mobile phones' proliferation in the cities, let us momentarily dim the city lights and map the Light-Emitting Diodes (LEDs) glowing from the faces of mobile devices.[4] To chart the LEDs, we must fade out the exact shapes of a city, flattening the specificity of streets, stairwells, and café terraces, darken conference arenas, theater foyers, shopping malls, outdoor souks, bus seats, and salon couches, turn into gray shadow beachfront promenades, lounge chairs at poolside, and milk carton stools on the sidewalk. We would see in all this blackened city space millions of randomly blipping and flickering lights. To grasp the appearance of "portables"[5] in this way would graphically mark the ubiquitous presence of mobile phones in the city sphere.[6]

To understand the role portable communication devices play in society, it is necessary, as is said in theater, to "turn the house lights up." With the physical features brought into focus, we see the bustling performances of social space where the precise character of actions happen in demarcated places. In social space, which is "a product and a making," the effects of mobile communication take shape in relation to the spatial parameters and moral beliefs informing the specificity of cultural practice (Lefebvre 1991).[7] In the next section, I describe an event advertising mobile telephones that took place in a public square in Casablanca, Morocco, in 2002. The staging of the event next to a gathering of Muslim men readying for midday prayer illustrates the religious character of the social space in which mobile telephony is proliferating. Following this ethnographic portrait, the chapter will turn to a more detailed explanation of the ways in which mobile telephony both displaces and is limited by practiced significations of morality in the Muslim public sphere.

Of Mosque and Mobile: An Ethnographic Event

Casablanca 2002

Located in the center of Casablanca, the quartier of Maarif boasts a thriving mix of neighborhood housing and commercial space. At the intersection of the quartier's main transportation arteries and vital side streets sits the district's only public square. The public square is a trapezoidal open space whose cement pathways are more pleasurable to behold than its parched grass, withered under the relentless North African sun. On the northern border of the open space, a one-way street provides prized parking spots in front of the *Marche des fleurs* (flower market). On the other side of the street a bland, cement-colored six-foot-tall wall hides a food market, which runs three quarters of the street's length. The food market offers fresh meats, vegetables, and assortments of cooking supplies all procured through the time-honored practice of price bargaining with independent merchants (Kapchan 1996). Where the wall of the market ends, the unassuming facade of the local mosque begins. Five times a day, there is an upsurge of pedestrian traffic toward the northeastern corner, where the mosque stands. Sundays through Thursdays, when prayer time nears, the usual stream of people on either side of the street becomes a river spilling into the autoroute. As the holiest day of the Islamic week, Friday mosque services—midday prayer in particular—draw the largest number of worshippers. To accommodate the crowds, officers come out each Friday and block off auto traffic, giving the mosque's adjacent streets over entirely to the movement of prayer goers. When the midday prayer is performed, an entire half of the public square, as we will see, is taken up by worshippers.

Early on a Friday morning in the spring of 2002, day workers descend on the paved area of the public square's southern corner and set up an event space. The show that follows is the "grand opening" of a red tubular kiosk at the southwestern tip. The kiosk has already been there for over a year, providing customers with three fixed phone lines. Now, though, the "teleboutique" function of the kiosk has given way to the sale of Meditel products and prepaid calling cards. To celebrate, event organizers choose to capitalize on the leisurely atmosphere of Friday. The timing of the event is intended to successfully capture the day's reliable upsurge in pedestrian traffic. In less than an hour, workers assemble a temporary stage while technicians connect and test an outdoor sound system. The stage backdrop boasts an enormous red plastic banner, with vibrant yellow lettering advertising the name and logo of Morocco's second largest mobile phone service provider, Meditel. Above the company's trademark banner, a twenty-foot wave of red, white, and yellow balloons sways as much due to the breeze as the intense vibrations of the sound system's heavy bass tones. By midmorning, the usually dreary south end of the district's only public square has been transformed into a bustling event space attracting a throng of eager spectators. Music blares from speakers, bouncing against the walls of the buildings that line the streets surrounding the square. Popular Rai tracks blend and reverberate with dance and hip-hop tunes, obliterating usual standards of public decency. The likes of Snoop Dogg and black America's answer to Madonna, Lil' Kim, rhyme provocatively on the benefits of liquor-laden sex acts in a sonic remix alongside Moroccan Rai celebrities Cheb Mami and Cheb Khalid, though the subversive content rendered in hyper-paced street English is effectively lost in translation to the Arabic-speaking crowd. By late morning, the south end of the square has assumed a rhythmic thumping that ingeniously serves as no more than another gloss of style intended to heighten the event's aura of "spectacular cool."

The master of ceremonies entices the audience with a streaming commentary advertising Meditel's mobile service packages and the wide choice in mobile phone models. On the sides of the stage there are enormous posters showing recent phone models and giant images of individuals talking on mobile phones. Still, the event's staging has been carefully constructed with obvious attention to the fact that for spectators the tiny technical bodies of mobile phones do not have anything approaching the captivating visuality of a shiny new car. Though the master of ceremonies teases the crowd with a series of giveaways, including portable radios, prepaid phone cards, and a variety of cell phones, the big draw is in fact a car. Situated in front of the stage, a generous length of rope partitions the spectator space from a dazzlingly red Volkswagen Beetle. The car's role as a central prop in the spectacle is reinforced by the fact that the entire interior of the vehicle is filled with neon green tennis balls. Everyone is given a chance to win the car. To do so they only have to guess the precise number of tennis balls inside and write their guess down on a form along with their contact information.

According to one spectator, it is "good" that Meditel is "giving something away," because "Maroc Telecom doesn't give things away." I point out to the spectator that

Maroc Telecom has just that past week given away a car, but the spectator is unmoved. "No no they [Meditel] do this all the time. So what if Maroc Telecom gives away something once—it isn't like this where they have it a lot for all the people," he says and flourishes his hands toward the spectacle. Meditel may be more successful at marketing itself to the masses as a company willing to supply limitless opportunities to win free merchandise, but both companies have aggressively marketed their products to the public by linking mobile phones to other products that form a totalizing picture of "consumer lifestyle" (Bourdieu 1984; Ferguson 1999). The mobile phone user is adver-tised as the owner of the latest cars, the most stylish clothing, the newest collection of technological devices.

Leaving the immediacy of the spectator zone, I walk through the center of the public square toward the *Marche des fleurs*, where I often go to take mint tea and talk with Adil, a part owner in one of the flower stalls. Shortly after I settle into my wooden stool in the flower stall, the speaker on the Meditel stage tells the audience that the event will be going on all day, though it is shutting down at the moment. He invites people to return *after* the lunch hour has passed to find out who has won the car. As the Meditel organizers go about temporarily closing their event, the stream of people in the square grows thicker in the opposite direction. People, specifically men, walk toward the north end of the square and begin forming orderly lines that extend back more than fourteen rows deep. The men are gathering for the Friday prayer, whose call is certain to erupt at any moment.

Seeing some of my friends walking toward public worship, I turn to Adil and ask him why he too does not participate in prayer. A slightly rotund man in his early thirties, Adil is generally very jovial and an endless supplier of interesting conversation. He says that he does not pray on Friday because he doesn't pray the rest of the week. I point out that many of the men prostrating themselves in the square on Friday do not do so on any other day of the week. Adil laughs at this and with his usual good humor says that this is the way of "too many Moroccan men" who try to wash off the "sins of the week, with one good prayer on the last day." He goes on to explain that he does not pray on Fridays or any other day of the week, because he engages in activities that are *haram*— forbidden. The act of smoking, along with "other things" that he does not name, prevents him from perceiving his lifestyle as one of purity. And purity, according to Adil, is what one needs in order to offer prayers to Allah. As he sees it, if one prays then one must also live one's life according the "good" or "right" path of those prayers. As Adil puts it, "If you cannot make the commitment to live your life according to this path then you contaminate your prayers." This is a common sentiment in Muslim cultures derived both from the *Hadith* (sayings of the prophet) and the Quran (Wadud 1999). What is significant about the exchange is the insistence that the body, its comportment and behavior, are the means of expressing belief and the notion that *the paths that bodies travel* are at once part of the body and outside the body as potentialities directed toward or away from the presence of Allah (Bourdieu 1999; Combs-Schilling 1989; Tami and Eposito 2000).

As we talk, the call to prayer rises up and the lines of men move in the ritual performance of worship. In unison, the male bodies filling the north face of the square fall to the ground, rise, and fall again in an act of submission and recognition of Allah's will. When the full formal prayer call ends, the multitude of worshippers go through a reassembling. Some of the men leave while others stay to hear the imam's Friday sermon. Only after the sermon concludes does the square's crowd disperse entirely, leaving the public space in a decidedly unspectacular state of quiet.

Postmodern Muslim Space: A Movement in Sociality

The Friday public square—beckoning on the south end with the enticing spectacle of chances to own free technology and filled on the north side with worshippers participating in the call to prayer—reveals the aura of modernity and the call of tradition performing their magic in one space. It is tempting to see these two features—the mobile advertising event and public prayer—within one local square as situated in a figurative face-off with one another. The nuances of the event space's performance cycle suggest something else, however. The Meditel mobile phone show was effectively closed down in deference to the timing of the call to prayer. The organizers, while inviting their audience to return later, suspended all activities in anticipation of the muezzin's impending call. The invitation to celebrate technologies of communication operated within the looming call of religious time and the honoring of Muslim practice. In this performance of public space, the embrace of new technologies and the face of tradition are not in opposition. The meaning of the postmodern, its insinuated techniques of mobility perfected to bytes via handheld semiconductors, and the experience of religious belief are mediated in social space by social bodies every day in Morocco. The issue is not one of "clashes" or, as some have argued, "cultural schizophrenia" (Majid 2000; Shayegan 1992). Rather, what the event space reveals is the lived domain of social transitions in a modern Muslim public (Zartman and Habeeb 1993). The significance of these transitions is a matter of ongoing negotiations in the daily production of social space in Morocco (Burke 1993; Entelis 1989).

The gender dynamic of the crowds within the public square indicates the practical form this negotiation takes on in the morally charged organization of the public. The audience before the Meditel stage advertising mobile telephones was mixed—men and women. Within the audience, men and women stood next to one another freely commenting and sharing the same public space. When the spectacle wound down, many of the men in the audience departed toward the other end of the square to join the growing congregation of worshippers preparing for prayer. The women, however, left the square altogether. Their absence turned the space into a sphere of gender segregation appropriate to the traditional practice of separating men and women during the time of prayer (Mahmood 2002; Rahman 1986). While women are not prohibited from praying in segregated spaces within mosques, it is an unacceptable breach of propriety for them to participate in the outdoor congregation of believers that sprawls across public squares on Friday and feast days. We can see, in this sense, how individuals move in social space that is at once modernized and traditional.

As a tool of everyday communication in urban Morocco, mobiles are active catalysts in reordering the conditions of possibility for sociability. Beginning with an encounter showing the use of mobile telephony as "social calendar organizer," the remainder of this chapter demonstrates mobile communication's position in realigning the limitations on morally gendered sociality in the public sphere.

Mobilized Sociality

I met Rita during fieldwork in the spring of 2002 in a cybercafé in the Parc quartier, named so for its grand "Parc de la Ligue Arabe."[8] The cybercafé was an underground garage in a former life that had undergone remodeling and in its cybercafé incarnation evokes the utilitarian spirit of a hospital cafeteria. The "cyber" offers connections to the Internet at computer terminals outfitted with Windows software. In the far right corner of the cyber, six high rectangular tables have been fitted to make a square with ten computers on the tabletops that have been designated for interactive gaming. It is at this table that I was introduced to Rita through my friend Hisham—a manager at the cyber. There are three other cybercafés within short walking distance of this one, but Rita comes here, because it is the only cyber where she can access Internet phone service. For ten dirham (US$1.10)[9] an hour she uses the café's computer to check her e-mail, surf the web, and talk on a headset with peers in the Middle East. She describes her Internet phone buddies as "friends in the Gulf." The connection is often faulty, and she usually has the other "talker" on her computer screen also in an instant messaging window. She sits at the gaming table, because it is set back from the rest of the cyber's terminals and offers some privacy. The gaming station is usually full in the late evenings, but generally empty in the afternoon hours, which is when Rita is there.

Rita lives far away from quartier Parc. She comes here on her "free days"—days when she does not have paid work or family obligations to fulfill. Her time on the computer is only one part of her social agenda when she visits the cybercafé. "I like to see all my friends when I come out [outside of her quartier]. I make plans with them, but then really it depends. Sometimes I think I am coming here and then I can't make it or my friend doesn't get here." During the course of one afternoon I spent with Rita, she facilitated meetings with three different people (including myself) in less than four hours. We started our visit together in the cyber, both because it was a mutually familiar meeting place and because it is the first place she goes on her excursions. The cyber functions as a sociability multitasking lounge in which she engages with people in the virtual world while notifying local friends of her arrival and organizing what she will do next. After leaving the cyber, we went to a Spanish-themed café that offered a light food menu in addition to its coffees and teas. We talked together for a little more than an hour and then left to meet her friend Yussef in a café two blocks away. After Yuseff left, Rita and I talked for a while longer until she had to go to meet another friend in yet another café.

Throughout the course of the afternoon, she facilitated her social encounters with the aid of a prepaid calling card and a Nokia mobile phone purchased through Maroc Telecom. Receiving and placing calls on her mobile, she confirmed and revised anticipated meeting times. The mobile phone as scheduling tool opens up the field of sociability for citizens by enabling them to traverse the city and roam leisurely from one location to the next within zones of coverage. With relatively basic digital competence, mobile users have the capacity to move through the city while remaining connected to personal social networks.

To explore the ramifications of the social competence provided by digital telephony in Morocco, it is helpful to turn to a comparative field observation recorded in 1988, just over a decade prior to mobile communication's meteoric rise in the Moroccan public. In *Picturing Casablanca*, anthropologist Susan Ossman (1994) describes sitting at a café with a young woman who is waiting for her boyfriend. As the intended meeting time comes and goes without his arrival, the woman becomes notably anxious as to his whereabouts. Ossman writes:

> She wonders aloud whether he is late because of negligence or lack of buses. Has he had to stop to have a coffee with a friend he met by

chance? "I just have to wait," she says, unsure what to think. She hasn't seen Khalid for three days and neither of them has a phone or a car. They plan to meet in advance, but other obligations sometimes prevent them from making their rendezvous. Often Khalid doesn't show up, and Fatima returns to work unsure whether to be angry with Khalid or the bus company. Should she express frustration with the contradiction between lunch hour schedules and social norms, or should she blame her lack of technical means to negotiate the distances of a large city like Casablanca. (p. 100)

This brief description is laden with rich allusions to the texture of social life in the Moroccan metropolis. Contextualizing Ossman's ethnographic slice highlights the conditions of sociability prior to mobile communication and by comparison delineates how social space is being transformed in the wireless city.

The young woman's suggestion that her beau is late due to an unscheduled encounter with another friend speaks to a pervasive manner of socializing by chance. I learned this pattern of socializing during my first stay in Morocco in 1998. After experiencing many frustrating missed connections with people, I came to realize that meeting times in Morocco possessed a decisively abstract quality. Setting a specific hour for business meetings or formal interviews was only a mildly reliable indicator of when the encounter would actually occur. For these types of meetings a window of between fifteen minutes to several hours was in general to be expected. Social appointments operated on an even more fluid abstraction of time. You were just as likely to encounter a friend by scheduling a time as by simply saying, "See you soon."

In all instances the last phrase spoken in regard to setting future meetings, is "Insh'allah," which literally means "Allah willing." For example, the statement "I will meet you tomorrow at two P.M." is followed by both parties stating, "Insh'allah." The use of this term is a cultural signifier the utterance of which acts as an acknowledgment of Allah as the ultimate force determining the outcomes of one's experiences. Moroccan Muslims believe that one's destiny is written invisibly on the forehead of every Muslim body. Individuals may assert their interests and desires for specific plans to be fulfilled, but it is Allah who determines how the order of things comes to manifest itself in one's life. The pervasive reliance on the phrase "Allah willing" to finalize intentions for connecting with people suggests one of the many ways in which religious belief operates in the collective consciousness of citizens moving through the everyday. The deference given to the authority of Allah in the design of one's life course is performatively declared with the utterance "Insh'Allah." It is meant to indicate at once one's acceptance of Allah's authority and one's recognition that fate and destiny may or may not line up with the plans people make between each other.

In a public in which meeting times are set at the hour of God's will, making consistent social connections require strategies of spatiality.[10] Without reliable time schedules or the ability to instantaneously contact people with phones, stable patterns of occupying specific places helped weight the odds for "chance" social encounters. Making a habit of frequenting a particular café, for example, ensured that friends knew where to look if they wanted to find you. Limiting the places in which one leisured meant that there was an easily negotiated parameter bounding the probable locations in which one could be found when not at home. Within the borders of a neighborhood community, people connected without appointments by simply going to the sites where they were most likely to find friends. Even if it you didn't immediately locate a friend you hoped to see, lingering in commonly frequented places offered a good chance of an encounter happening. Incorporating place into one's habits by repetitively selecting specific locations was an important means of maintaining social networks—among men.

The placement of the social body in specific sites within spatial borders that define a given neighborhood affected the chances of successfully connecting in two ways. One could simply occasion to see someone by limiting movement to an immediately localized series of places. Second, by being visible within known borders, social bodies rendered themselves accessible to neighborhood information streams. Without using phones and running on a timetable outfitted for spontaneity and happenstance, neighborhood chatter streams made it possible to locate people's whereabouts often in very little ticking time.[11]

This community information network is an institutionalized feature of everyday life in the Muslim public sphere. In Morocco the web of localized chatter runs through the public from the informal gossip of residents to written reports entered by authorities on the activities of specific precincts. It is understood by the public that this stream of information renders all members of the community potential participants in ongoing reportage of the happenings in localized place. The observational activities of street workers, for example, are a formalized feature of their work—parking attendants, corner cigarette vendors sitting on milk crates, street sweepers, and building concierges report their observations to authorities as a matter of course. If one senses that there are "always eyes watching," this is because indeed there are. In cities, local neighborhoods function much like small towns wherein the persistent awareness of people's public activities can be startlingly precise.[12]

Connecting through Community: Gendered Morality in Place

While community information flows serve a utilitarian purpose, enabling members of social networks to effectively locate and track one another, it is not a benign system of innocuous gossip. At its core, the function of local community chatter networks is to monitor and enforce moralized standards of public behavior. Ideals of moral conduct in the Muslim city are laden with notions of honor, shame, and dignity that are embedded in differential perceptions of permissible behaviors for men and women. When a woman makes herself visible within the public spaces of her local neighborhood, it can have dire consequences for her reputation that will affect her as an individual and impact the status of her family. To be seen frequently meeting in cafés within one's neighborhood, and particularly with members of the opposite sex, is to risk becoming a maligned figure of discussion in the chatter network and subsequently becoming stigmatized as a woman of "loose morals" (Afsaruddin 1999; Bouhdiba 1998; Smith 1980). Moreover, while women are free to utilize the chatter network for pure gossip, they cannot plug into the network to locate nonfamily members without exposing themselves to local judgments on their moral character.

As a single woman conducting research in a Muslim country, I came to personally understand the intricacies of how moral standards are imposed upon women's public behavior. After observing my male acquaintances and friends tracking each other through informal queries that tapped into the neighborhood chatter network, I took up this mode of locating people myself. I thought little of asking after people I wanted to socialize with just as the men I knew did. Further, I took the practice of identifying a finite number of local places in which to socialize as an expedient way of engaging in the local scene and often conducted interviews in the same small number of neighborhood cafés. Several months of this course of public socializing went by before I was made aware of its effect on my personal reputation as a woman in a Muslim public sphere. With great mortification, I listened keenly to a woman friend in my neighborhood patiently recounting some of the numerous stories about my supposed "illicit" behavior circulating in the local community. As a foreign-born researcher with a fieldwork agenda, I chose to ignore the circulation of erroneous information about my person and to continue pursuing public sociability with both sexes in order to collect data. Had I been a local woman, however, with not only my personal reputation but the reputation of my family to consider, such an option would have posed much more challenging consequences.

Neighborhood information flows serve different purposes in producing and foreclosing the public sociability of men and women. It allows men to easily track one another and thus to take part freely in the immediate public realm of their communities. For women, on the other hand, this information flow serves to circumscribe their activities. It acts as a policing agent, enforcing standards of honor and integrity based on chastity that are particular to women's bodies in the Muslim public sphere. The strategic use of local place in maintaining social connectivity—while a meaningful habitus for Moroccan men—is not an option for Moroccan women precisely because of local information flows. Socializing within the borders of their residential neighborhoods places women directly in the eye of community gossip and renders them subject to its consequences.

Mobilizing Urban Social Space

The social impact of mobile telephony's prolific growth in the Muslim public sphere is most powerfully understood at the level of place making and localized information flows. With ubiquitous mobile telephony, users can bypass the visibility of neighborhood socializing to make connections with others. Mobile use dismisses the need for strategies of maintaining social connectivity reliant on place-making practices in the limited domain of local neighborhoods. By providing individuals with direct, private, and expedient means of contacting others, mobile telephony disperses the usual structures for making sociality happen. It undermines the authoritative role of local place in manipulating the possibilities for public interaction with one's social network. Where clocks failed in establishing reliable time not bound to the movement of celestial entities and the call of religion's reminders, mobilized communication has triumphed. Mobile telephony displaces the former conditions of chance and revises the rules of opportunity. The ring of mobiles has, in short, effectively punctured the unreliability of social time.

The proliferation of mobile phones in Morocco provides people with the ability to effectively and privately organize meetings with members of their social network. People can be immediately located with the help of mobiles, which perform as communication tools and tracking devices at once. For the mobile user, finding members of a social network is a closed circuit between seeker and search object. This closed circuitry is a pivotal part of mobile communication's contribution to giving individuals a previously unattainable privacy. One does not have to worry about being overheard in a busy household making an appointment on the phone. Nor does one have to worry over the implications of tapping into other people's chatter, being able to now simply dial into sociality.

In addition to allowing individuals to privately organize their social time, mobile phones let people connect fluidly across the cityscape. As a kind of connectivity compass, mobile telephony gives social bodies a tool with which to "navigate the city." It acts as a practical aid with which to travel the city toward flexibly designated social encounters. Mobile users can move throughout the urban landscape while remaining locatable and connected to friends, family, and peers. This gives urban citizens the ability to explore beyond the borders of familiar community boundaries. Traversing urban space in search of sociability with mobile phones in hand and pocket, the distant spaces of the city are opened to individual users at once physically mobile and communicatively linked to social networks. For women in particular, mobile telephony offers possibilities for publicly socializing without suffering the consequences of judgment from their local community.

Moralism and Mobile Sociability

The freedom to move through the city while remaining communicatively connected does not displace the materiality of social conditions. Getting from one point to another in the city, for example, is as challenging for today's urban residents as it was ten years ago. The travel routes in cities remain overcrowded with cars driving in a maniacal clog along the boulevards and streets. Sidewalks are as often as not in states of disrepair, frustrating the pedestrian's effort not to stumble over broken stone and cracked pavement. Buses as well are as unreliable as ever—in fact more so as city government demolishes bus stops without prior notification and persistently haphazardly closes bus routes. Furthermore, mobile connectivity does not displace the moral conditions of sociability. Boundaries are challenged, stretched, reexamined, but not entirely overstepped or broken. To draw out the experiential quality of this point, I turn to a final ethnographic description of a mobile phone user in urban Morocco.

At twenty-four, Nadira is in the minority of women eligible to work who actually has employment. Still, she is within Morocco's vast legion of underemployed workers (Tessler 2000). Her work as informal secretary for a bookkeeper in the neighborhood where she lives is unreliable and low paying. Some weeks she works two days, other weeks not at all. When she does spend a day in the bookkeeper's office, she comes home with no more than 150 dirham—roughly US$18. The money that she makes is, as she puts it, "just enough to have spending change. It's not something I can take to pay for rent or buy food." The fact that Nadira is not married means she is expected to live at home.[13] There is no pressure for her at twenty-four to move out and support herself independently. Living at home means that Nadira, like most young Moroccans, has relatively little privacy. "There is always someone home," she says, "and when my father goes out I can't make a phone call at the house anyway, because he takes it with him." Nadira's father, like heads of households in many of the homes I visited, takes the dialing face of the home phone with him when he leaves the house. By doing this he makes it impossible for the other members of the household to use the phone and run up the phone bill. And until his adult children purchased mobiles, his "no dial" policy also prevented his wife and grown children from making social calls without his knowledge, thereby providing him a level of control over the social interactions of his family.

Nadira's possession of a mobile phone does allow her to circumvent her father's monitoring of the house phone. However, it does not mean that she is now able to spend lengthy time on the phone conversing with friends. Her lack of money prohibits this and makes use of the mobile one of utmost brevity. For her, as I would argue is true for most mobile phone users in Morocco, the mobile phone does not in any manner replace face-to-face encounters as the pivotal form of socializing. Just as people keep calls from fixed lines down to the fewest number of minutes possible, so too are mobile phone calls intensely brief exchanges. The concern with cost is evident in the fact that, contrary to the wishes of mobile operators who profit most from contractual service plans, over 95 percent of mobile users make calls with prepaid phone cards. This enables users to know precisely how much they are spending and to avoid overages that they cannot afford to receive as bills in the mail.

Owning a mobile phone allows Nadira to make appointments with friends. With it, she is able to maximize the little time that she has for public socializing. As a woman, Nadira experiences consuming demands on her available time. Unlike her two brothers, she is expected to share the task of household chores with her mother, including laundry, dishes, cooking, and cleaning the home.[14] On days that she does not have paid work—and there are many of them—these chores constitute the bulk of her waking time. She has free time between completing these tasks, but often it is not enough time to travel outside of her immediate neighborhood. It is because she only shares in the cooking a few days a week that she is able to sporadically leave for a long afternoon to socialize with friends. The gendered division of household labor impacts the amount of free time that Nadira has. The moral framework of Moroccan society affects the parameters of how she spends her available time.

As a Casablancan woman, she does have slightly wider latitude to acceptably navigate the public domain for leisure purposes than her female peers in other Moroccan cities. The degree to which women are segregated in the Moroccan public sphere varies among regions. However, while the morality police that exist in Saudi Arabia or Shiite Iran are nowhere to be found in Morocco, the presence of women in public remains inhibited by moral sentiment. In most urban centers, women have a high visibility in the educational system, the workforce, and spaces of consumption such as outdoor markets and shopping malls. But Moroccan women's visibility in leisure spaces is contested and subject to ongoing revision.[15] To clarify this, one can compare Casablanca's public sphere to the equally metropolitan Beirut, where women freely congregate, playing cards and smoking, or casually bare their midriffs as they stroll downtown holding the hand of a boyfriend. Casablancan women, in contrast, may push the limits of dress codes, but there are no bared bellies to be seen, certainly no careless card playing on sidewalks, and most definitively no casual displays of affection between men and women walking along the city streets.

Nadira is conscious of the fact that her conduct in public is subject to much more intensive social monitoring than that of her male peers. For Nadira, as for other Moroccan women, socializing outside of the gaze of her community is an important means of participating in the public without imminently risking her social status. Characterizing her neighborhood as a place where everyone knows her, she says, "When I have free time, I prefer to leave my neighborhood." By going outside of her community, Nadira, like the women described above, grants herself a pretense of autonomy. Leaving her neighborhood, she is engaging in a phenomenon of social practice that predates mobile phones. Mobile communication is not the inspirational spark for transforma-tions in public sociability. Rather, mobile telephony *extends* and *amplifies* the conditions of possibility for engaging in social conduct that presses the perimeters of what is morally sanctioned within traditional Moroccan interpretations of Islam. When Nadira leaves the familiarity and the watchful eyes of her local community, she charts a known but nonetheless mildly dangerous territory. Her ability to instantly connect over the phone with the person she is going to meet or, for that matter, to utilize the phone in case of an emergency, allows her "a sense of security" in branching out into the city (Da Costa Meyer 1996). Unlike the woman in Ossman's ethnographic description, today's mobile women are no longer left to the anxious waiting and frustration of missed connections and lost time. Instead they are able to capitalize on their scarce leisure time to pursue encounters with friends and love interests and to do so with the ability to be at once outside of their community and connected to their social network.

Moving beyond her own quartier into one of the city's stylish "hot spots," such as Gauthier, Maarif, or Anfa, Nadira understands acutely that she still runs a chance of being seen by relatives and judgmental peers also wandering the city's enticing leisure zones. Therefore, when she arrives at a café in another neighborhood she, as is customary of most urban Moroccan women, does not place her body in a chair on the terrace. Nor does she sit on the first floor of the café. Instead, Nadira makes her way to the second floor of the cafés in which she meets her friends for tea. She is elevating her ability to be anonymous, but she recognizes that it is only a partial anonymity. No matter where she goes in the city, she remains a Muslim woman.

Conclusion

Mobile telephony, perhaps more so than any other tool of advanced communications technologies, demands an emphasis on the specificity of bodies in place. It is as culturally situated bodies that people utilize inventions with the power to reorganize normative modes of sociality (Hard, Losch, and Verdicchio 2003; Soja 2000). The specificity of mobile communication's effects on social bodies is ascertainable through what Henri Lefebvre (1991) terms "textural" analysis. I have employed this method to portray the character of social space in which mobiles are accessed, the purposes of use, and resultant effects on social practice.

In Morocco, the phone call in an era of ubiquitous digital connectivity has not become a substitution or replacement for face-to-face conversation in the maintenance of social networks. Nor have convergent technologies like digital image capture, mobile Internet connections, or text messaging become as common as the simple, direct, and prolific use of mobile phones for rapid-fire verbal exchanges. Mobile telephony is most profoundly accessed to facilitate, locate, and create conditions of reliability for "face en face" social encounters. The emergence and continued spread of communicative mobility generates alternative strategies for connectivity that produce important slippages and openings in the spatial fixity and temporal uncertainty of sociality in the public sphere. In Moroccan cities, mobile phones are everyday devices held in hand that perform as a twenty-first-century improvement on the compass. Through the soft glow of light-emitting diodes and the sound of personalized ring tones, mobile devices act as communicative compasses guiding residents across new boulevards of sociality. With mobiles in hand, Moroccans subtly navigate the transitioning terrain of Muslim urbanity at once pressing apart and adhering to moralized social boundaries.

Notes

* The research upon which this chapter is based was carried out with generous support from the National Science Foundation and the American Institute for Maghribi Studies. The analysis benefited from participation in a round table with Michael Fischer at the Beirut Conference on the Public Sphere in 2004. I am grateful to Hugh Raffles, Megan Colleen Moodie, Jay Dautcher, and Patrik Lundh for their insightful comments.

1 To contextualize the phrase "Muslim public sphere," see in particular: Abedi and Fischer 1993; Anderson and Eickelman 1999; Farha 2002.
2 While ANRT officials are prohibited from owning interest in the telecom corporations, members of Morocco's SEPTI are active shareholders in the industry. The apparent conflict of interest among SEPTI officials has resulted in an ongoing controversy and a great deal of animosity between the two oversight bodies. International and national opinions on the matter generally recognize the greater contribution of ANRT in Morocco's success.
3 For a contextualization of the rate of growth see also ANRT 2002.
4 Additional conceptualizations of rendering "digital bodies" can be found in Mitchell, Inouye, and Blumenthal 2001. A particularly intriguing manner of thinking through the body-machine relationship introduced by handheld mobile devices is the Deleuzian notion of "fini-illimite," which Paul Rabinow (1992) elucidates as the state "in which finitidue, as empiricity, gives way to a play of forces and forms. . . . In this new constellation, beings have neither a perfected form nor an essential opacity" (p. 235; cf. Deleuze and Guattari 1987).
5 In Morocco, mobile phones are interchangeably referred to using the French terms *mobiles* or *portables*.
6 A similar exercise could be conducted in audio terms if one were able to hear only in particular the voluminous beeps, alarms, rings, music bytes, and speech generated by several hundred thousand mobile phones throughout the city.
7 Henri Lefebvre (1991) writes of social space as "at once work and product—a materialization of social being" (p. 102).
8 The system of dividing the city into quartiers (quarters) was introduced in Morocco during the administration of the French Protectorate, from 1912 to 1956. Within each quartier there are further localized domains that constitute neighborhoods. The distinctions among neighborhoods are often as much a matter of government administrative maps as the sentiments of community residents (Rabinow 1989).
9 This is figure reflects the price of cybercafé access per hour in 2001–2.
10 The relationship between spatial practices and religious belief is elucidated in, among others, Bourdieu 1999; Eliade 1987; and Ellul 1964.
11 Plugging into the local information stream meant asking another member of one's social network if they had seen the person in question. If they had not seen the person they would in turn ask someone else and so on until the last most reliable location of the person was ascertained. If the person being sought was anywhere in the neighborhood, one would know within an hour.
12 Elizabeth Fernea (1989) describes the phenomenon in her ethnography of an Iraqi town. On her way to visit women in a family on the other side of the town, she feels, but cannot see, eyes watching her. Upon arrival, her hosts indicate clearly that they were told she was walking to their home well before she herself got there.
13 Both men and women customarily remain in their family home until marriage. Although it is socially acceptable for men to move out on their own, particularly if they have arrived in their thirties still unmarried or if they are anticipating being married soon, this is not the case for women. To live alone is to inhabit an unchaperoned space, which brings connotations of impropriety and social aberration.

14 In Moroccan households without maids, it is typical for men rather than women to do the food shopping.

15 In 1999, for example, the newly anointed monarch Mohammed VI attempted to pass a reformed Family Code in the nation. In the nation's capital of Rabat, a small and amicable public march was held in favor of the proposed reforms, which would have amended divorce and property law so as to provide women with greater legal equity. In Casablanca, however, thousands of men and women took to the streets to protest the reforms, calling them "un-Islamic."tion and the American Institute for Maghribi Studies. The analysis benefited from participation in a round table with Michael Fischer at the Beirut Conference on the Public Sphere in 2004. I am grateful to Hugh Raffles, Megan Colleen Moodie, Jay Dautcher, and Patrik Lundh for their insightful comments.

References

Abedi, M., and M. Fischer. (1993). "Etymologies: Thinking a public sphere in Arabic and Persian." *Public Culture 6*, no. 1: 219–30.

Afsaruddin, A. (Ed.). (1999). *Hermeneutics and honor: Negotiating female public space in Islamic/ate societies.* Boston: Harvard University Press.

Anderson, J., and D. Eickelman (Eds.). (1999). *New media in the Muslim world: The emerging public sphere.* Bloomington: Indiana University Press.

ANRT. (2002). *Internet providers in Morocco: A country wide survey.* Retrieved August 4, 2002, from www.anrt.ma.

ANRT (2004). *The Moroccan telecommunications sector: Key indicators.* Retrieved May 5, 2005, from www.anrt.ma.

Bouhdiba, A. (1998). *Sexuality in Islam.* London: Saqi Books.

Bourdieu, P. (1984). *Distinction: A social critique of the judgment of taste.* (R. Nice, Trans.). Cambridge, MA: Harvard University Press.

Bourdieu, P. (1999). *Outline of a theory of practice.* Cambridge, UK: Cambridge University Press.

Burke, E. (1993). *Struggle and survival in the modern Middle East.* East Berkley and Los Angeles: University of California Press.

Combs-Schilling, M. E. (1989). *Sacred performances: Islam sexuality and sacrifice.* New York: Columbia University Press.

Da Costa Meyer, E. (1996). "La Donna e Mobile: Agrophobia, women, and urban space." In D. Agrest, P. Conway, and L. Weisman (Eds.), *The sex of architecture.* New York: Harry N. Abrams.

Deleuze, G., and F. Guattari. (1987). *A thousand plateaus: Capitalism and schizophrenia.* (B. Massumi, Trans.). Minneapolis: University of Minnesota Press.

Eliade, M. (1987). *The sacred and the profane: The nature of religion,* 6th ed. (W. Trask, Trans.). New York: Harcourt Brace.

Ellul, J. (1964). *The technological society.* New York: Vintage.

Entelis, J. (1989). *Culture and counter culture in Moroccan politics.* Boulder, CO, San Francisco, and London: Westview Press.

Farha, G. (2002). *Remaking the modern: Space, relocation, and the politics of identity in a global Cairo.* Berkeley: University of California Press.

Ferguson, J. (1999). *Expectations of modernity: Myths and meaning of urban life on the Zambian copperbelt.* Berkeley and London: University of California Press.

Fernea, E. (1989). *Guests of the sheik: An ethnography of an Iraqi village,* 3rd ed. New York: Anchor Books.

Goffman, E. (1963). *Behavior in public places: Notes on the social organization of gatherings*. New York: Free Press.

Habermas, J. (1999). *The structural transformation of the public sphere: An inquiry into a category of bourgeois society*, 10th ed. (T. Burger, Trans.). Cambridge, MA: MIT Press.

Hard, M., A. Losch, and A. Verdicchio (Eds.). (2003). *Transforming spaces: The topological turn in technology studies*. Retrieved January 8, 2005, from www.ifs.tudarmstadt.de/gradkoll;Publikationen/tranformingspaces.html.

Harvey, D. (1990). *The condition of postmodernity*. Oxford: Blackwell.

Harvey, D. (2001). *Spaces of capital: Towards a critical geography*. New York: Routledge.

International Telecommunications Union (ITU), Sector Reform Unit. (2001). *Effective regulation case study: Morocco, 2001*. Retrieved December 9, 2002, from www.itu.int/itudoc/itu-d/publicat/ma_ca_st.html.

Kapchan, D. (1996). *Gender on the market: Moroccan women and the revoicing of tradition*. Philadelphia: University of Pennsylvania Press.

Lefebvre, H. (1991). *The production of space*. (D. Nicholson Smith, Trans.). Oxford: Blackwell.

Mahmood, S. (2002). *Politics of piety: The Islamic revival and the feminist subject*. Princeton, NJ: Princeton University Press.

Majid, A. (2000). *Unveiling traditions: Postcolonial Islam in a polycentric world*. Raleigh, NC: Duke University Press.

Mattelart, A. (2000). *Networking the world: 1794–2000*. (J. Cohen and C. Libbrecht, Trans.) Minneapolis: University of Minnesota Press.

Mitchel, W. J., A. Inouye, and M. Blumenthal (Eds.). (2001). *Beyond productivity: Information technology, innovation, and creativity*. Washington, DC: National Academies Press.

Ossman, S. (1994). *Picturing Casablanca: Portraits of power in a modern city*. Berkeley: University of California Press.

Rabinow, P. (1989). *French modern: Norms and forms of social environment*. Cambridge, MA: MIT Press.

Rabinow, P. (1992). "Artificiality and enlightenment: From sociobiology and biosociality." In J. Crary and S. Kwinter (Eds.), *Zone 6*. New York: Urzone.

Rahman, A. (1986). *Role of Muslim women in society*. London: Sierra Foundation.

Shayegan, D. (1992). *Cultural schizophrenia: Islamic societies confronting the West*. Syracuse, NY: Syracuse University Press.

Smith, J. (1980). *Women in contemporary Muslim societies*. London: London Associated University Presses.

Soja, E. (2000). *Postmetropolis: Critical studies of cities and regions*. Oxford: Blackwell.

Tami, A., and J. Eposito (Eds.). (2000). *Islam and secularism in the Middle East*. London: Hearst.

Tessler, M. (2000). "Morocco's next political generation." *Journal of North African Studies* 5, no. 1: 1–26.

Wadud, A. (1999). *Qu'ran and woman: Rereading the sacred text from a woman's perspective*. Oxford: Oxford University Press.

Zartman, W., and W. Habeeb (Eds.). (1993). *Polity and society in contemporary North Africa*. Boulder, CO: Westview.

Zelinsky, W. (2001). "The world and its identity crisis." In P. Adams, S. Hoelscher, and K. Till (Eds.), *Textures of place: Exploring humanist geographies*. Minneapolis: Minnesota University Press.

Culture, Organization, and Contradiction in the Social Construction of Technology: Adoption and Use of the Cell Phone across Three Cultures

Paul Leonardi, Marianne E. Leonardi, and Elizabeth Hudson

Over the past several years, researchers have become increasingly interested in the effects of the cell phone on diverse cultures. Numerous studies examining the impact of this low-cost, highly customizable information and communication technology (ICT) have explored how the cell phone is changing the ways individuals communicate with one another and how they orient toward new technological innovations (Katz and Aakhus 2002; Leung and Wei 2000; Ling 2004). Although such studies have highlighted the important role that existing cultural practices play in mediating the acceptance of the cell phone, they have taken a relatively deterministic stance on the cell phone's ability to change cultures. That is, the cell phone is often viewed as an artifact whose effects can be prefigured by examining the particularities of the culture into which it will be introduced.

By contrast, scholars who study the use (Boczkowski 2004; Boudreau and Robey 2005; Orlikowski 2000) of ICTs from a social construction of technology (SCOT) perspective have shown that the consequences of a new technology are not determined strictly by social or technological forces. Instead, such research has shown that the shapes and effects of new technologies are instead negotiated through the interplay of social and technical elements (Jackson, Poole, and Kuhn 2002). Despite the ontological appeal of the perspective, few studies within the SCOT rubric have considered the important role culture plays in the social construction of an ICT. As a consequence, the majority of research on the interplay between ICTs and culture either depict the cell phone as a decisive agent of change that is causing unique cultures to become more homogeneous in their modes of communication (a deterministic perspective) or as an artifact whose meanings and effects are socially situated and thus inherently malleable (a social constructivist perspective).

In this chapter we attempt to reconcile these two perspectives by exploring the cultural implications of the social construction of the cell phone. Specifically, we solicited the participation of individuals from three distinct cultural contexts—the United States, Latin America, and the Ukraine—to begin to understand the similarities and differences in the way the cell phone is translated from a material into a cultural artifact. Whereas most studies of the cell phone suggest that the ways individuals use ICTs within a given social context are highly similar to the ways they perceive their utility (Campbell and Russo 2003; Leung and Wei 2000), our findings reveal that when culture is considered as an integral variable in the social construction of the cell phone, contradictions surface between the processes of perception and use. The findings of this study show that the presence of contradictions between perception and use persisted across the three cultures included in this study, while the social organization of the contradictions differed across cultures.

Existing research has documented that individuals in the Western industrialized world commonly adopt cell phones because they believe they will enhance safety (Murray 2001; Palen, Salzman, and Youngs 2000). Our findings indicate that individuals across the three cultures included in the study all acknowledged that safety was a primary reason they adopted the cell phone. Moreover, the primary perception of the cell phone across these three cultures was that this ICT was a device ideally suited to, as one participant put it, "save someone from big problems." Although participants across all three cultures gave nearly identical accounts of why they adopted the cell phone, further analysis of our findings reveals contradictions between the perceived usefulness of this technology and the actual uses of it across the three cultures.

While members of all three cultures indicated that they adopted cell phones for similar reasons, the findings reveal that members of diverse cultures actually used cell phones in ways that correspond with existing cultural values. In the following sections, we outline the methods used to collect the data analyzed in this chapter and present a detailed exposition of the findings. We conclude by considering four important areas: First, we explore why reasons for cell phone adoption are ubiquitous, and cultural uses disparate. Second, we expose several shortcomings in looking at "perceptions" and "uses" of ICTs as different abstractions of the same phenomenon. Third, we examine the role that contradiction plays in the instantiation of the cell phone as a cultural artifact. Finally, we discuss how the SCOT perspective can be enhanced by considering how culture serves to construct the uses of a new technology.

Methods

Most studies that have examined the impacts of cell phones on culture have focused on individuals' use of this ICT in one cultural context. Because we were interested in culture as a primary variable in the social construction of the cell phone, we designed a research study that would allow us to compare similarities and differences across cultures. At the outset, we identified three different cultural contexts in which research has documented that the impacts of the cell phone on social practice should be dramatically different—in Western industrialized nations, in highly collectivistic economically disadvantaged nations, and post-communist Eastern Bloc nations. From a deterministic perspective, the material properties of the cell phone should drive these cultures with distinct communication and social interaction patterns to become more similar. From a social constructivist perspective, the dramatic differences in communication and social interaction patterns that characterize these unique cultural contexts should construct radically different interpretations of the same cell phone technology. With this data collection strategy in mind, we next outline the characteristics of those who participated in this study and the procedures through which the data were collected.

Participants

To implement the plan set forth in this research design, we recruited participants who self-identified as members of three distinct cultural groups: North Americans, Latin Americans, and Ukrainians. Participants who self-identified as North Americans were recruited by a broad call to students who lived in university housing at two universities in the western United States. These individuals were pursuing a variety of undergraduate degrees and ranged in age from nineteen to twenty-five years old. In total, nineteen individuals who indicated that they were members of a broad "American" culture agreed to participate in this study. All of these participants were fluent English speakers and they all owned a cell phone.

Participants who self-identified as members of "Latin American" culture were selected from the among the local college community. The responses of seventeen individuals who were participants of a larger study were selected for inclusion in the present analysis because they were of roughly the same age group as the participants from the other two cultural contexts (for details of this study, see Leonardi 2003). Specifically, these participants ranged in age from twenty-two to twenty-seven years; all were fluent in Spanish and none speaks English at even a basic conversational level. These participants had resided in the United States for an average of 2.5 years and indicated that they had immigrated to the United States to find well-paying jobs and that they eventually planned to return to their countries of origin. All but two of the participants in this group owned a cell phone. The two who did not indicated that they hoped to purchase one soon but did not have sufficient funds to do so at the current time.

The final group of participants was comprised of twenty-two individuals who were students at a small Ukrainian university in the autonomous republic of Crimea. These participants ranged in age from nineteen to twenty-four and were pursuing a variety of majors. All participants self-identified with "Ukrainian" culture and all were fluent in Russian and had low levels of conversational skill in English. Further, all but three participants in this group owned a cell phone.

Procedure

The primary procedure for data collection utilized in this study was the focus group. As Krueger (1994) observes, focused group discussions among individuals of similar demographic backgrounds normally provides a comfortable environment for participants to share their stories and experiences, and thus tends to elicit in-depth comments and responses. Morgan (1997) suggests that a group that feels "comfortable" for individuals ideally requires six to ten participants, and to achieve robust, replicable, and generalizable results, three to five groups per project are needed. Additionally, focus groups have been shown to be a type of environment in which individuals from cultures that are typically considered to be characterized by high power will have high levels of personal disclosure and will speak freely without fear of reproach (Bradford, Meyers, and Kane 1999).

In order to procure ideas and statements deriving from the cultural identities of participants, focus groups were conducted only with members of similar cultures. Thus each of the authors was responsible for conducting focus group discussions with participants from only one specific cultural background. Following this design, three focus groups were conducted with "American" participants with an average of six individuals per group, three focus groups were conducted with "Latino" participants with an average of six individuals per group, and two focus groups were conducted with "Ukrainian" participants, averaging eleven individuals. Across the three cultural contexts, we conducted eight focus groups with a total of fifty-eight individuals.

Each focus group session lasted approximately an hour and a half and was held in on-campus locations that were easily accessible to all so that participants would feel comfortable in a familiar setting. Participants were first asked to discuss their general impressions of cell phones, including both positive and negative consequences that could arise from owning and operating a call phone. They were then asked more specific questions about why they chose to purchase a cell phone or why someone else decided to purchase one for them. Finally, participants were asked to describe their normal patterns of cell phone use and to share stories about incidents that characterized both regular and irregular interactions with them. All participants were encouraged to share both personal experiences and stories they had heard about cell phones, and to comment whenever they felt it appropriate. The focus group sessions were conducted in the native language of the participants (English for participants from the United States, Spanish for participants from Latin America, and Russian for participants from Ukraine) and were recorded via audiotape with the informed consent of all participants. All audio recordings were later transcribed by the researchers and translated into English for comparison.

The data were analyzed separately for each cultural context by a researcher who was not familiar with the data collected from members of the other two cultures represented in the study. To coincide with our conceptual interest in understanding similarities and differences between adoption and use across cultural contexts, each of the data sets were first coded into these two broad etic categories (Lindlof 1995). Within each of these broad etic codes, the researchers coded the data based on emic categories represented that surfaced inductively within each specific cultural context (Strauss and Corbin 1998). Once the data had been coded in both etic and emic ways *within* each culture, they were then compared *across* the three cultural contexts. By comparing these various data sources and highlighting their similarities and differences, we were able to triangulate the ways in which cell phone use affected and was uniformly affected by the culture while still uncovering the specific practices that constituted these broader effects.

In the sections that follow, we detail the findings uncovered through this process of data collection and analysis. The data are presented in terms of the themes characteristic of adoption and use of cell phones in each of the three cultures included in this study.

North Americans and Cell Phones

Adoption

Individuals who participated in the North American focus groups discussed a number of prominent reasons they chose to adopt cell phones. Of these various accounts, two themes surfaced consistently in the data. First, individuals adopted cell phones explicitly for peace of mind. Second, many adopted cell phones because, as one participant put it, "everyone else has one, so I should too."

Peace of Mind. A common story recounted by American participants was that they first purchased a cell phone, or one was purchased for them, when they began to drive. For most participants, parents were the motivating factor in persuading them to adopt the cell phones in this situation, as they wanted to ensure their child's safety. Two respondents reported similar stories of buying their first cell phones. "I got my cell phone when I was, I think, at the beginning of my senior year in high school and umm, my parents got it for me just for like driving purposes, like there's an emergency and stupid stuff like that and we had to drive through like a bad part of Chicago on the way to school. So just for like safety purposes." After hearing this story, another participant replied, "That's exactly how it was for me too. When I started driving they [parents] wanted me to have a cell." American participants frequently noted that cell phones provided a "safety net" for new drivers while at the same time establishing a sense of security and peace of mind for parents. The adoption in this instance was beneficial to all parties involved. Thus, safety was not only an important adoption criterion for young individuals themselves, but also for those who might potentially buy them a phone. As another participant explained, "I wasn't even sure if I wanted a phone or not. I mean, I think it's good to have one to be safe and all—that's the best reason to get one—but my parents were convinced. I guess it's just a time when parents need to let go, and they think they can let you go easier and you'll be safer if you can be in constant contact if you need to."

Many participants also felt a tension between knowing that they *needed* a cell phone for safety reasons and *wanting* a cell phone for more personal reasons. In these cases individuals frequently couched their reasons for adoption in terms of safety and security and then noted that they quickly discovered that the cell phone could be used in many other ways. As one participant noted, "In the beginning, it [the cell phone] was only for the car, but then senior year of high school I started realizing I could talk on it to my friends, so I talked a lot." Other participants recounted similar experiences of adopting cell phones for safety reasons and then discovering that they could also be used for other communication tasks. Some participants even admitted that they used the trope of "safety" as a reason to convince themselves or others that they actually needed a cell phone: "I got my first cell phone after 9/11. I always wanted one and it seemed like a good excuse to get one and my mom said all the phones didn't work, and I'm like I think I really need an emergency kinda phone." Or in the words of another participant, "I got my first cell phone after my, like right at the end of my freshman year of college because I was moving to D.C. for the summer . . . it's like a security thing too because I was working really late at night and coming home late at night." Participants also gave numerous examples of how cell phones could not only be used to react in a situation in which an emergency occurred, but that they could also be used proactively to thwart emergencies or avoid dangerous situations: "When I am walking somewhere that I think is kinda sketchy or I'm alone and like at night I get on my phone and talk until I get to where I'm going." Another participant provided an example of a similar scenario: "Whenever I go running my dad's like, 'Take your phone like so I know you're not somewhere in a ditch.'" In these examples, the cell phone is seen not only as a savior in a dangerous situation, but also as a means of self-defense.

Clearly, participants chose to adopt cell phones for a variety of safety-related reasons. The ability to call someone instantaneously in times of distress was comforting to participants and provided peace of mind. However, participants in this cultural context often displayed an overly optimistic view that the mere possession of a cell phone could prevent or discourage dangerous situations.

Imitation. Participants who identified with a broad "American" culture also frequently noted that at a certain age most individuals are expected to adopt a cell phone. In other words, that idea that one should have a cell phone for the sheer sake of having one was quite common among participants in our study. As one individual described, "When you're in high school you can get away with not owning a phone. I mean, I guess nobody really expects you to even have one. But by the time you get to college you just have to have one. I mean, you know, everybody has one and it's just like you say, 'Hey, what's your cell number?' and if they don't have one its just weird." The comments provided by this participant demonstrate an important point uncovered in the data: that the adoption of cell phones within American culture is often taken for granted. That is, individuals often read the adoption of cell phones by others as a sufficient reason to adopt one themselves. On this score, another participant commented, "I wasn't sure if I needed a cell phone till I kept seeing that everyone else had them. I mean I don't really even like them, but in some sense if everyone else has one and you don't, then you're kind of out of the loop. I guess you just have to follow the crowd." In such cases, participants gave no principled reason for deciding to adopt the cell phone other than for reasons of mimetic isomorphism.

In fact, many participants discussed how their desires to "follow the crowd" in terms of cell phone adoption were so strong that they often trumped more principled reasons for not adopting. On participant provided this interesting example: "I hate when people are on the phone all the damn time talking here and there. Like I want to hear their conversations about who did what to whom while I'm in the grocery store. I swore that I wouldn't get a cell phone because they are such a distraction. I guess I just caved in or something because suddenly I was like the only person I knew who didn't have one and everyone would be like, 'Uh, you don't have cell phone, that's weird.'" Other participants suggested that cell phone users were often characterized as certain types of people to whom they had negative reactions. However, despite an initial attempt to refuse cell phone adoption on moral grounds, many participants admitted that they soon became cell phone adopters themselves: "I always thought that those kind of people who always had to be talking to someone were annoying. It's like get some self-esteem. And also, I always thought if something is that important the person will find me, so I don't have to worry about having a cell phone. Now I own a cell phone so I guess I'm a bit of a hypocrite. I just got tired of being the only person who didn't have one."

These data demonstrate that American participants were either often unclear why they adopted a cell phone other than to imitate the practices of others or that they decided to adopt because the cost of not following the crowd became too high. It is possible that these findings could be interpreted in light of critical mass theories of media adoption (for example, Markus 1990), which argue that once a new technology is widely diffused within a population laggards will be forced to adopt if they are to "keep up." However, while critical mass theories provide a "utility" explanation for cell phone adoption, our findings uncovered a "normative" or "symbolic" explanation: that the stigma of not having a cell phone was great enough to encourage adoption independent of whether or not the cell phone provided increased utility for communication within a given social context. Clearly, both utility and normative explanations are needed to explain technology adoption (Kraut et al. 1998), but the data collected with American participants showed strongly that normative reasons were much more salient for participants.

Use

Although participants boldly expressed safety concerns and imitation as reasons they adopted the cell phones, further analysis of the examples participants provided describing how and when they used cell phones told a different story. In fact, not one of the American individuals who participated in this study ever provided an example of a time when they actually *used* their cell phones for safety or self-esteem reasons. Instead, we found that participants often used cell phones to be able to talk whenever and wherever they wanted and to avoid the discomfort and stigma of being alone.

Ego-Centric Communication. Given that all of the American participants in this study were college students, it is not surprising that they spent much time discussing the difficulties of maintaining contact with family and friends who lived at a distance. As participants often discussed, the fear of losing contact with loved ones when they moved away to college was great: "Yeah, I was always worried that it would be tough to stay in contact with people when I moved to college. You know, you just get busy and at home you can use the phone whenever you want or you can just drive over to someone's place, but if people are far away that's a lot harder." For most participants, this initial preoccupation with losing contact with others was important because it marked a more fundamental issue: that one would not be able to talk to someone whenever they pleased as they had done in the past. This is what we term ego-centric communication—the desire to have the ability to make contact at the focal actor's convenience. Many studies have shown that within American culture the idea that "I want to communicate therefore I should be able to communicate" is quite strong, as it represents and supports cultural values of individualism impatience (Cameron 2000).

Participants in this study regularly described how they used their cell phones to enable ego-centric communication. Moving away to college was seen as a major impediment to ego-centric communication, and the cell phone was used as a means to overcome this problem. As one participant commented, "I have a big family and I wanted to stay in contact with everyone. . . . It's like the only way to stay in contact with everyone, not the only way, but it lets me do it when I want to." Other participants expressed similar patterns of use: "I need to make sure I can talk to people when I want to and I use my cell phone to make that happen. It is ridiculous to think that you would have to wait around till someone else gets off the phone these days. Just get your own!"

In addition to keeping in contact while in college, participants reported using cell phones for keeping in contact while abroad. Many discussed that they had heard stories of study abroad experiences in which individuals did not talk to loved ones for weeks on end because telephone communications were poor in other countries. This situation proved unacceptable to many participants who felt that they should be able to stay in contact with others at their own convenience. Thus, while writing letters, e-mails, and postcards were some ways that participants could control communication relationships with those back in the United States while they were in other countries, the cell phone was used as the primary communication tool for ego-centric communication. One respondent related his time abroad with his first purchase of a cell phone. "The first one [cell phone] I ever got I was while I was stationed in the Peace Corps in Guatemala, and that was the first time, if I actually had something happen at home, my parents could contact me like now. My grandpa died while I was there, and they [my parents] picked up the phone and called me, and otherwise I don't know how, it could have been weeks before I had any direct interaction and found out." As the findings indicate, the actual physical distance of the participants from those they were communicating with was not important, but rather it was more important to speak and remain in contact with those who were not directly in front of them as if they were.

Other participants also noted that when living with others they had trouble divvying phone time among themselves and their roommates, both in the dorms and in apartments off campus. This situation proved troublesome because it impeded ego-centric communication. To overcome this difficulty, many participants advised that one could use one's cell phone: "I live with two people, and we have one phone cause it's in the dorms and it's hard. Sometimes there's like peak hours when everyone wants to use the phone so I'll just use my cell phone." Other participants suggested that a cell phone provided an important "always on" connection not only for outgoing calls, but for incoming calls as well: "If I am at my apartment and my roommate has been on the phone for like hours, I don't have to worry about like no one's gonna be able to get through." Students use the cell phone as a second phone line to better coordinate their lives with roommates or dorm life on their own schedules.

Not Being Alone. The findings also indicate that American participants used their cell phones to avoid the stigma of being alone. Although individualism is a well-documented hallmark of American culture (see, for example, Shkodriani and Gibbons 1995), researchers have observed that there is also a stigma associated with acting alone in this broader cultural context (Zimbardo 1969). This means that while there is a cultural value placed on individual *accomplishment*, there is paradoxically a cultural stigma placed on *being alone*. Participants in this study were quite aware that the idea of being alone was uncomfortable in public situations in which they could be seen acting in isolation from others.

For these reasons, many participants discussed using their cell phones as tools to overcome the stigma of being alone. For example, numerous participants admitted to making phone calls while walking across campus to and from class. As one participant noted, "Yeah, I totally use my cell phone when I'm walking around. I mean, if you don't have anyone to talk to you just don't want to be alone all the time." Another participant was a bit brasher in her account of the way she used her cell phone to avoid the stigma that is so often placed on being alone.

> I really find myself talking on the phone a lot in public places when I'm alone. I never really thought about it before, but then one of my friends told me, "Hey, I always see you walking on campus on your phone." So I thought about it some and I guess it makes sense, I mean you don't want to look like a loser walking around by yourself. That sounds really bad. I don't mean that people who do are losers, but it's just that you don't always want people to think that you have no one to talk to.

Thus, participants who were reflective on this practice often recounted using their cell phone not only to avoid the *reality* of being alone, but also to avoid others' *perceptions* that they had no one to talk to.

Latinos and Cell Phones

Adoption

The individuals who participated in this study and self-identified as members of a broad Latino culture were also quite explicit about the reasons they chose to adopt cell phones. All but two of the participants owned a cell phone at the time of this study, and the two who did not indicated that they hoped to purchase one within the next several months. Two themes surfaced through data analysis that indicated why Latinos made the explicit decision to adopt cell phones. First, they indicated that cell phones provided security in times of trouble and that they could be used to save individuals from dangerous situations. Second, participants were quite conscious of the digital divide and frequently acknowledged that if they did not adopt cell phones as a communication technology they would fall behind many of their peers.

Security. Latino participants in this study told numerous stories of times in which cell phones had saved people from dangerous situations. Although none of the participants indicated that they had used a cell phone to escape a dire situation, most participants described stories that they had "heard" about the advantages of having cell phones for security reasons. One participant recounted a story that she had heard from a friend about how cell phones had helped to save individuals in the World Trade Center buildings after the 9-11 attacks: "I heard that some of those people who were in the buildings in New York were saved by using their cell phones. They were able to call loved ones and to tell them where they were and people could come get them. This is why cell phones can be so good. They provide one with security and help people to be safer. They even said on the news that some people were able to say goodbye to loved ones for the last time." Other participants shared stories about traumatic events whose perils were mitigated by the use of cell phones.

Not all stories, however, involved specific events of this sort. Instead, most participants projected scenarios in which cell phones could be used to reduce the risk of harm or injury. As one participant who did not own a cell phone commented, "I don't own a cell phone yet, but what if something happened to me? Like what if I was driving and something happened like I crashed and I needed help? I could call my husband or tell someone and they could save me. It is safe to have a cell phone and I'd feel more secure with one. I don't know how I can be without one now." Another participant responded similarly, projecting a scenario in which the use of a cell phone would make her feel more secure:

> I don't have one in my car yet, you know how it is, but as a woman sometimes I really think I need one. I could talk with someone if there was a problem or use it if there was some kind of emergency. But it doesn't have to just be for the car. I told my husband we should get one for my daughter so she can be safe when she's away, or if she gets sick or if something happens to her. All of these are good reasons to have a cell phone. They're very positive.

These stories position the cell phone as a type of security agent that can aid individuals in times of emergency or tragedy.

Many male participants also commented on the potential for cell phones to provide security, but in a more protective way. In many of these types of discussions, males described how they did not need cell phones themselves, but that they often bought them for their wives or daughters. "I think if anything happens to me I'll be OK. I can get myself out of lots of problems. But I think it's good that my wife has one and we are thinking about getting one for our daughters so they can use them if they need to and if they are in some sort of trouble. I think I'd feel much safer with this because you never know what can happen." Clearly, both men and women participants in the Latino focus groups agreed that one of the primary reasons for adopting a cell phone was that it provided a sense of security that could not be easily achieved with any other type of technology.

Not Falling Behind. Another strong theme that emerged from the data was that participants saw the cell phone as a sign of progress. As one participant noted, "Cell phones are a new technology, and I think Latinos have a stereotype of not liking new technologies, but we want to be involved in progress just like anyone else." Most partic- ipants were quite concerned that, in general, Latinos were losing many opportunities because of a digital divide between those who had access to new technologies and those who did not: "They say that many Latinos are falling behind in the digital divide and that they are not learning the new technologies like other people. This is sad because nobody wants to fall behind or not be seen as good at using technology as others." In most cases, participants professed a desire to be savvy technology users and consumers and cited the lack of sufficient funds as the primary impediment to this goal.

Despite the issue of cost, many participants acknowledged that adopting cell phones was one of the more affordable ways that individuals could keep up on current technology. One participant described how he chose to buy a cell phone rather than a computer because it was less expensive and it gave him the sense that he was "keeping up" with his peers: "I can't really afford a computer so I bought a cell phone. At least that way I feel like I'm keeping up with the latest technology, and they say you can do many of the same things on a cell phone than you can on the computer." Another participant commented similarly about the effects of the digital divide on her decision to adopt a cell phone. "It is a terrible feeling to think that you're falling behind everyone else. But at least for many Latinos like me you can actually get a cell phone and be part of the world that uses new technologies." Yet another response in a different focus group session illustrates the prevalent concerns of the digital divide and the feeling of falling behind. "They talk about this something divide, digital divide. I don't want to be left behind, and I don't think anyone wants to be left behind. So my cousin told me to get a cell phone and I'd have the latest technology. It's just that I don't want to be another Latina that isn't up to date on what's going on."

Most individuals who participated in this study acknowledged that the cell phone marked a certain fluency with new technologies and that they felt happy not only to maintain contact with friends and loved ones, but to participate in the use of a "revolu- tionary" new technology. Thus, cell phones became a symbol of technological sophisti- cation at an affordable price.

Use

By looking carefully at the way Latino participants talked about their cell phone usage patterns, we identified two important practices. First, participants rarely used the cell phone for everyday conveniences, such as calling the store; instead, they used their phones primarily to keep in touch with friends and family who lived back home in the Latin American countries from which they emigrated. Second, participants made extensive use of the three-way calling and speakerphone features of their phones to create situations for group communication.

Keeping in Touch. As much of the existing research on cell phones in the United States indicates, individuals use their phones primarily as a convenience tool. That is, they use it to call to ask questions, find out information, and be "in contact" when they need to be. Accordingly, our research with American participants presented earlier demonstrates how individuals' enactment of ego-centric communication supported this practice. For Latino participants, however, the idea of the cell phone as a "convenience" tool was not present. Rather, this interchange between facilitator (F) and participants (P) demonstrates how Latino participants regularly used their cell phones:

F:	When do you normally use your cell phone?
P1:	To call my family back home.
P2:	For family.
P3:	Me too.
P4:	I call my family and friends.
P5:	I talk to the family back in Salvador.
P2:	If you don't use it to talk to your family, what else are you going to use it for?

As is clear from this excerpt, the idea of using cell phones to maintain contact with loved ones in another country was very strong for Latino participants. Many participants commented that they had left spouses, siblings, parents, or best friends in their native countries when they immigrated to the United States in search of work. Therefore, finding a means of communication that would keep them in constant contact with home life was important.

Interestingly, participants reserved cell phone use for familial contact and used regular land line phones for most everyday activities. As one participant commented, "Let's see. I use my cell phone to call back home to Mexico, and to talk with my friends here. It's really good for that because you have these plans that are not so expensive and then you can always have your phone with you in case someone calls and you don't have to worry about missing them. But I don't use it to do errands or to see what time the movie is. Those things aren't so important so I just use the phone in my house." A participant in another focus group session discussed a similar pattern of alternation between cell phones and land lines: "Oh, yes. I use my cell phone to talk to my loved ones. That's very important because they can call you anytime. But when you're doing something not so important, like calling to check at your bank, then you might as well use a normal phone for that or just go there yourself." These comments illustrate an interesting distinction between when and when not to use cell phones. For most participants, cell phones were used as a personal communication device rather than as an instrument for inquiry. In such a way, the cell phone took on a special status and gained a unique "importance" in the eyes of participants. Unlike their land line phones, the cell phone could afford them the possibility to ensure that they would never miss a call because they are not at home. Therefore, the cell phone became a primary way of keeping in touch with friends and loved ones.

This use of the cell phone as a tool for maintaining contact coincides with the important value placed on family communication within Latino culture (Flores Niemann et al. 1999; Marin, Gamba, and Marin 1992; Stavans 1995). In practice, then, the cell phone became an important device for supporting a cultural value. That participants began to view the cell phone as a tool almost elusively meant to be used to maintain contact with loved ones shows how the existing cultural practice of a group can transform a technology with many applications into one with one dominant use.

Group Communication Device. Latino participants in this study were highly proficient users of their cell phones. In fact, comparative analysis of the data across the three cultural contexts suggests that they were more familiar with the various technical features of their cell phones than were any of the other groups represented in this study. Two of the features that Latinos frequently used on their cell phones were those of three-way calling and speakerphone.

First, numerous participants discussed the advantages of three-way calling for enabling multiple-party talks. As one participant described, "Oh, I use the three-way feature all the time so I can talk with my two sisters at once. It's much better that way because you're all there and you don't have to worry about leaving someone out. It's more ideal that way." Another participant also expressed her happiness with the three-way calling feature on her phone in order to talk with friends as a group: "I like that my group of friends can talk at the same time. Since I live here and one of my friends lives in Texas and the other lives in Guadalajara, we can all talk together and gossip with each other." Together these examples illustrate participants' interest in holding conversations with multiple individuals simultaneously. The three-way calling feature afforded by most cell phones was seen as an easy way to maintain group communication.

A second way in which participants used their cell phones to talk in groups was by taking advantage of the speakerphone function. Many participants admitted that they were conscious during the purchase of their cell phone that they wanted to buy one equipped with a speakerphone. As one participant commented, "I wanted to buy one with the speakerphone so the whole family could talk to the grandparents back in Michoacan at the same time." Many participants discussed the fact that speakerphones allowed multiple individuals to interact simultaneously, thus enabling effective group communication: "When we use the speakerphone we can all talk, you know, like a group together. You can't do this if you're just talking one to one on the phone. It is much better that way because then you have everyone involved in the conversation. Sometimes it's a little hard to hear, but it is still better than not being able to talk."

As these experts demonstrate, using the cell phone's technical features to encourage and maintain group communication practices was common practice for most Latino participants. Moreover, many purchased cell phones precisely with such goals in mind, looking for devices and providers that supported these functions.

As a predominantly collectivist culture, researchers have documented Latinos' affinity for group communication (that is, communication with multiple alters) over one-to-one communication contexts (Coon and Kemmelmeier 2001; Zsembik and Beeghley 1996). This cultural practice served to condition particular uses of the cell phone, thus establishing it as a tool for group communication. In such a way, participants noted that they often used the cell phone as much for multiple-party conversations as they did for individual ones.

Ukrainians and Cell Phones

Adoption

Ukrainian participants cited a variety of reasons for adopting the cell phone. Many were open about why they wanted it or, in some cases, why they did not want it. Their responses and discussion reflecting uses and adoption align well with cultural distinctions regarding alliance with the West and its attention to image. The analysis of our data suggests two pervasive themes characterizing the reasons Ukrainians chose to adopt the cell phone. First, the cell phone represented a security blanket in its ability to allow individuals the opportunity to get help in difficult situations. Despite this advantage, participants also displayed an overt fear of negative consequences that the cell phone could bring to their users. Second, cell phones were adopted to aid in the process of social acceptance among ones' peers.

Security Blanket. Throughout the focus group sessions, participants regularly commented that one primary reason to adopt cell phones was that they served as security blankets for young students. In other words, when an individual found him or herself in a difficult situation he or she could use the phone as a lifeline to call for help. Although most participants clearly viewed the cell phone in this capacity, they expressed that their parents were more often concerned with adopting the cell phone for this reason. As one participant described, adopting a cell phone allows its owner the possibility of providing real-time communication to worried parents and friends, thereby allaying their fears: "The thing that I like the most is that I can communicate from many places. For example, if I am at the disco, I can send a message to my parents where I am and what time I will be home. I think that ah, uh, I may make calls in the institute and at home."

Although most participants discussed the fact that they chose to adopt the cell phone because it could serve as a security blanket, Ukrainian participants were distinguished in their identification of an adoption paradox: while people adopted the cell phone to stay safe, the mere act of adopting could lead to even more dangerous situations. For example, many participants mentioned that because Ukraine was a somewhat impoverished area with sharp class distinctions, the threat of robbery was greater if one carried a phone. Many participants provided stories about the dangers of phones being stolen and about people being killed for their mobile phone. As one participant commented, "I saw a young girl with a mobile phone and it is a very expensive one. And I think it is very dangerous for children, for a child, to carry such an expensive toy because everyone can just take it, and what can she do? I heard a story about when three young men killed a man for a phone." Although these dangers and fears associated with cell phone use in Ukraine surfaced during discussion, they were not strong reasons for deterring all students from owning one. In the case of most participants, there were many other factors keeping them for adoption. In the case of the man getting killed for the phone, many students seemed surprised by this story, but several showed familiarity with it.

In addition to the risks of assault and theft perceived, many students perceive health risks from using a cell phone. During the discussion, students often mentioned the importance of carrying the phone away from the body. As one participant suggested, "It is very bad for us for our health. Not only for— Mobile phones we have to carry them in bags . . . My boyfriend carries his mobile phone in his front pocket. I tell him that is dangerous, but he said, 'We have Chernobyl. [The phone] is so small.'" So while her boyfriend was joking about the magnitude of the danger in comparison to the radiation from the Chernobyl disaster, this participant perceived a danger that was worth warning her boyfriend about. Another participant showed a similar understanding of the dangers of owning a mobile phone in her discussion with the facilitator:

> **F:**   Would you like to buy another telephone?
> **P:**   Yes. I would like to very much . . . [but] it is not very good
>   for our health.

Again there are concerns about the perceived radiation associated with the mobile phone. At the same time, however, this is not a risk that outweighs the desire to own the phone for the potential security blanket that it can provide for other, more common situations.

Social Acceptance. Participants in this segment of the study frequently cited "keeping connections" and "keeping up" with their peers as reasons for adopt or wishing to adopt a cell phone. Although it was often the parents who gave participants their cell phones, participants mostly used the phone to keep in touch with friends via phone calls, or more often SMS. As the following interchange between the facilitator and a participant who did not own a cell phone at the time of this study shows, participants often wanted cell phones for what they represent socially:

> **F:**   Do you feel discomfort for not having a mobile phone?
> **P:**   I have a phone at home. I use phone cards in the street to
>   call my sister and my relatives. I am not disturbed about it.
>   I do not regret not having it yet.
> **F:**   But you still want to have it. Why?
> **P:**   Because it is a modern thing. It is a modern item and I am
>   a young girl and I want to be modern, to have an
>   opportunity to speak with my friends.

Another participant shows that even more than having a desire to keep in touch with friends, she noticed that she was in an awkward position as the last of those in her social circle to purchase a mobile phone: "I have had my mobile phone for nearly one year. I got it when my mom gave me some money for my birthday and I bought my mobile phone . . . all of my friends had it already. And I didn't. This way I can find them anytime." On a basic level, this participant's espoused ability to keep in touch with her friends who already owned phones encouraged her desire to purchase it. On a more fundamental level, being the last of "all my friends" served as a more symbolic and deeply penetrating social reason for adopting the cell phone.

Similarly, many participants in the Ukraine often admitted to adopting a mobile phone because "everyone else has one." From this statement alone, it is not clear whether students wanted to maintain communication with "everyone else" or if they simply wanted to keep up with their peers, though this ambiguity was clarified in some participants' speech. As one participant commented, "Frankly speaking, I always wanted a mobile phone. My friends all had a mobile phone. For example, if I go to the disco. I can send a message to my friends." Another participant discussed the idea that most people have no objectively technical needs for a cell phone, but that they choose to adopt them for symbolic reasons: "I think that most people don't need them. They do not really need them because, like me for example, I am not a business lady, and I have a regular phone and my mother has a regular phone and it is just fashionable to have a mobile phone."

Use

In considering the ways that Ukrainian participants actually used the cell phone, one dominant theme emerged from the data. We found that, overwhelmingly, individuals used their phones as a status symbol. In fact, many participants admitted that they did not regularly use their cell phones for conversation, but that the act of carrying a certain type of phone with them and displaying that phone for all to see gave others a clue as to their social standing in a context in which differences in social status were quite prominent.

Status Symbol. Ukrainian participants are quite brand-conscious of their phones and realize that the recent models are the most fashionable. Participants carrying older phones may try to hide them, but students with newer phones will mention the quality of their phones early in the discussion. As one participant commented in the opening of the discussion in which students were asked to introduce themselves and talk a little about how they got their phone, "I have had my phone for ten months and it is a Nokia model, one of the best." This participant, similar to many others, wasted little time before mentioning her phone as "one of the best." Similarly, another participant, a second-year student, was concerned with the social image the cell phone provides an owner: "First of all, I would like to look fashionable. Because me and my mom are two women who are very fond of looking smart and fashionable. Using a mobile phone in our country is considered very fashionable and stylish in our country. I don't know why." Here, this participant chooses not to go into an in-depth examination of the reasons for the mobile phone's fashion status in Ukraine, but rather she highlights it, and her desire to achieve the image offered by carrying a mobile phone. Phones seem symbolic of a certain amount of disposable income, but they also serve as a status symbol; having a nice modern phone will keep the users fashionable.

In fact, the idea of using a cell phone as a fashion accessory to mark one's status in informal social relations was so prevalent that many participants purposefully decided not to use their phones for communication purposes. For instance, in this interchange, one participant admits to the facilitator and the rest of the group that she rarely carries her mobile phone because of its older design.

P:	I have had a mobile phone for about three months. My father gave it to me when he bought a new model. I do not use it often—only when I phone to my friends.
F:	Do you call your parents?
P:	No, never. I only use it two to three days a week. Of course I want to buy a new phone.
F:	Why?
P:	Because my phone is old.
F:	Old fashioned?
P:	It is an old model.
F:	You would like it to be a more modern design.
P:	Yes, for example Nokia.

F: Where do you use it the most?
P: At home . . .
F: Do you always receive your calls at home?
P: I do not always take it with me.
F: Why?
P: I do not like it. I do not like my mobile phone.

This participant's reluctance to carry her phone with her in public, as an accessory as many other participants mentioned, reinforces the idea of status implied by carrying a nice mobile phone, or in the case of this particular participant, the lack of status conferred by carrying an older, less popular model.

To this end, participants often decided that despite the communication advantages that cell phones could provide, these advantages were not worth the risk of being perceived as someone who was "low status" as evidenced by their possession of an "old" or "ugly" phone. That status and cell phones would be linked comes as no surprise within the context of Ukraine culture. Because Ukrainians are highly cognizant of various socioeconomic subcultures (see, for example, Dalton 2001), the cell phone marks a way of transcending or reaffirming social class. Thus participants regularly used the phones not as technical objects, but as social objects that signaled some sort of status to their peers.

Discussion

Examining the reasons participants gave for adopting cell phones across the three cultures reveals startling homogeneity of practice. As table 1 indicates, by comparing the themes uncovered for adoption in each of the cultural contexts, we can see that they fall into two broad categories of practice. The first practice of adoption is one of *safety*. American participants acknowledged that they adopted cell phones for "peace of mind," while Latino participants discussed how cell phones were adopted because they provided the opportunity for "salvation" from difficult situations. Similarly, Ukrainian participants discussed their practice of adopting cell phones so as to have a "security blanket" in times of trouble. Together, these three themes support the idea that participants across cultures adopted cell phones for safety reasons. This corresponds with the findings of other studies that suggest that Americans adopt cell phones for safety reasons (Murray 2001; Palen et al. 2000). Our findings demonstrate that safety concerns dominated across cultural contexts, and individuals outwardly admitted to adopting cell phones for this reason.

Table 1
Practice of Adoption across Three Cultures

Practice	Safety			Signaling		
Theme	Peace of mind	Salvation	Security blanket	Imitation	Not left behind	Social acceptance
Origin	American	Latino	Ukrainian	American	Latino	Ukrainian

A second broad practice of adoption that was supported across the three cultural contexts was that of *signaling*. In addition to adopting cell phones because they provided a tangible means of maintaining safety in troublesome situations, adopting cell phones also served a symbolic purpose. American participants, for example, discussed how they often adopted cell phones to "follow the crowd." Latino participants enacted a similar practice by adopting cell phones so that they would not be "left behind," while Ukrainian participants acknowledged that cell phone adoption could increase "social acceptance." Thus it appears that across the three cultural contexts the adoption of cell phones was a clear signal to others that the user conformed to some socially desirable position.

What is interesting in these findings is that reasons for adoption appear ubiquitous and somewhat impervious to changes in cultural context. That is, we found both safety and signaling practices to be the primary reasons participants gave for adopting cell phones in each of the cultural contexts we studied. Thus, from the outset it does appear that, at least for adoption purposes, the logic of cell phones is culturally catholic. Notwithstanding changes in cultural contexts, safety and signaling are legitimate reasons for adopting cell phones. This finding bolsters the argument that the material (safety features) and social (symbolic features) properties of this new technology exert a relatively uniform pressure on individuals in a variety of cultures (Katz and Aakhus 2002; Leung and Wei 2000; Ling 2004; Schlosser 2002).

When comparing the actual ways in which individuals in various cultural contexts discussed their uses of cell phones, however, we uncovered tremendous variance in usage practices. As table 2 indicates, cell phone use was unique to contours of the cultural context in which it was embedded. Moreover, participants used the cell phones in ways that were influenced by and supported existing cultural values.

Table 2
Practice of Use across Three Cultures

Cultural Context	American		Latino		Ukrainian
Practice of use	Ego-centric communication	Not being alone	Keeping in touch	Group communication device	Status symbol
Cultural value	Individualism	Need for attention	Importance of family	Collectivism	Socioeconomic awaremness

Usage patterns among American participants showed that cell phones were most often utilized to support extant cultural values. For example, participants used cell phones to enable "ego-centric communication," which supports the cultural value placed on individualism. Similarly, individuals used cell phones so that they could avoid the stigma of "being alone," which supports a cultural value of need for attention—especially prevalent among American youth.

Latino participants used the exact same cell phone technology in dramatically different, and at times conflicting ways than Americans did. For example, while American participants used the cell phone to promote individual communication practices, Latinos used it as a "group communication device." By using features of the cell phone that allowed them to talk with a number of individuals simultaneously, Latino participants upheld the cultural value placed on collectivism and the belief that individuals are in better communion with others in group contexts. Participants also used the cell phone as a tool to "keep in touch" with family members who lived both close and abroad. While purposefully deciding not to use the cell phone for information-seeking purposes, Latino participants upheld the high value placed on strong familial relationships in their culture.

Finally, usage of the cell phone by Ukrainian participants showed markedly different patterns than did use by Americans and Latinos. Participants talked at length about using the cell phone as a "status symbol" among their peer group. In fact, many participants admitted to not talking on their cell phones often, but instead were satisfied if the phones conveyed a certain image to those who saw them in possession of one. This practice of use is strongly influenced by the heightened awareness of socioeconomic status and the importance of identifying subgroup membership within the culture.

Together, these findings show an interesting pattern: that the actual ways individuals use the cell phone are highly dependent upon cultural values. Participants frequently discussed using cell phones in ways that were in line with the practices of their particular culture, and this continued use supported and encouraged the culture. This finding supports the arguments of those who suggest that technology use is culturally malleable and that the same technology can take on different meanings across changes in cultural contexts, and thus be used in radically different ways (DeSanctis and Poole 1994; Leonardi 2003; Woolgar 1996).

By looking simultaneously at the reasons participants in the three cultural contexts gave for adoption of the cell phone and the actual ways that they used this communication device, we can see that contradictions are present across changes in culture. In other words, in all three contexts, individuals professed one reason for adopting cell phones, and then proceeded to use them in radically different ways, and sometimes in ways that actually conflicted with their avowed reasons for adoption. Moreover, while reasons for cell phone adoption appear ubiquitous, the actual practices of cell phone use are culturally variable. What this insight suggests is that the culture of which an individual is a member, along with the way that those experiences are organized into a coherent interpretive framework, allows for the presence of contradictions between adoption and use.

Contradictions imply that there are certain "acceptable" reasons for adoption that are taken for granted. Surely as analysts of media discourse suggest, the discursive construction of the usability and value of electronic devices influences individuals' perceptions of the value of a new technology (Boczkowski 1999; Lemke 1999). For cell phones in particular, this means that certain reasons for adoption are standardized and inhere precisely because they meet universal criteria for effectiveness (Campbell and Russo 2003). What our findings show, however, is that these discursive constructions are not strong enough to carry over into practices of use. In other words, while discourse about the new technology may drive individuals in distinct cultural contexts to adopt the cell phone for similar reasons, culture then influences usage patterns. The contradiction between popular and cultural practices of cell phone use can prove (as revealed in the study of the three cultures presented herein) contradictory. These findings indicate that deterministic perspectives that view the cell phone as an agent of change that influences disparate cultures to become more similar help to explain patterns of adoption, but they do not predict actual cell phone usage. To understand this latter practice, social constructivist perspectives are needed in order to capture the nuance of cultural practices in influencing technology-using behaviors. Thus, our findings show the utility of both deterministic and social constructivist perspectives in that they explain differences in adoption and use and point to the rise of contradictions between them.

Importantly, we have shown that in contrast to authors who claim that perception and use of a technology are but different abstractions of the same phenomenon (Fulk, Schmitz, and Steinfield 1990; Prasad 1995), perception and use are actually two fundamentally different processes. Participants in our study perceived the utility of cell phones in such a way that adoption seemed natural and acceptable. However, they began to use those technologies in ways that often contradicted the reasons for which they adopted them. Thus researchers must draw a finer distinction between the practices of perception and use if they are to understand the processes whereby technologies are socially constructed.

Finally, our findings indicate the importance of considering culture as an integral part of the social construction process. While many authors have argued that the features of social context do lead to certain interpretations of a technology (for example, Orlikowski 1992), further attention should be paid to important differences among cultural practices. Few studies of technology implementation have examined culture's role in mediating the impact on new technologies (Leonardi 2003; Rice, D'Ambra, and More 1998; Robey and Rodriguez-Diaz 1989). Our study shows that it is essential for researchers to show what types of practices (that is, adoption) are impervious to cultural influence and which (that is, use) are susceptible to it.

In sum, we have shown that individuals in different cultures adopt cell phones for similar reasons, but use them in radically different ways. We believe that understanding how culture binds or cleaves adoption and use is essential to ensuring productive use of this new medium by individuals around the world.

References

Boczkowski, P. J. (1999). "Mutual shaping of users and technologies in a national virtual community." *Journal of Communication* 49, no. 2: 86–108.

Boczkowski, P. J. (2004). "The processes of adopting multimedia and interactivity in three online newsrooms." *Journal of Communication* 54, no. 2: 197–213.

Boudreau, M.-C., and D. Robey. (2005). "Enacting integrated information technology: A human agency perspective." *Organization Science* 16, no. 1: 3–18.

Bradford, L., R. A. Meyers, and K. A. Kane. (1999). "Latino expectations of communicative competence: A focus group interview study." *Communication Quarterly* 47, no. 1: 98–117.

Brown, B. (2002). "Studying the use of mobile technology." In B. Brown, N. Green, and R. Harper (Eds.), *Wireless world: Social and interactional aspects of the mobile age* (pp. 3-13). London: Springer.

Cameron, D. (2000). *Good to talk? Living and working in a communication culture.* London: Sage.

Campbell, S. W., and T. C. Russo. (2003). "The social construction of mobile telephony: An application of the social influence model to perceptions and uses of mobile phones within personal communication networks." *Communication Monographs* 70, no. 4: 317–34.

Coon, H. M., and M. Kemmelmeier. (2001). "Cultural orientations in the United States: (Re)examining differences among ethnic groups." *Journal of Cross-Cultural Psychology* 32, no. 3: 348–64.

Dalton, M. (2001). *Culture shock! Ukraine.* New York: GAC.

DeSanctis, G., and M. S. Poole. (1994). "Capturing the complexity in advanced technology use: Adaptive structuration theory." *Organization Science* 5, no. 2: 121–47.

Flores Niemann, Y., et al. (1999). "What does it mean to be 'Mexican'? Social construction of an ethnic identity." *Hispanic Journal of Behavioral Sciences* 21, no. 1: 47–60.

Fulk, J., J. Schmitz, and C. Steinfield. (1990). "A social influence model of technology use." In J. Fulk and C. Steinfield (Eds.), *Organizations and communication technology* (pp. 117–40). Newbury Park, CA: Sage.

Jackson, M. H., M. S. Poole, and T. Kuhn. (2002). "The social construction of technology in studies of the workplace." In L. A. Lievrouw and S. Livingstone (Eds.), *Handbook of new media: Social shaping and consequences of ICTs* (pp. 236–53). London: Sage.

Katz, J. E., and Aakhus, M. (Eds.). (2002). *Perpetual contact: Mobile communication, private talk, public performance.* Cambridge, UK: Cambridge University Press.

Kraut, R. E., et al. (1998). "Varieties of social influence: The role of utility and norms in the success of a new communication medium." *Organization Science* 9, no. 4: 437–53.

Krueger, R. A. (1994). *Focus groups: A practical guide for applied research.* Newbury Park, CA: Sage.

Lemke, J. L. (1999). "Discourse and organizational dynamics: Website communication and institutional change." *Discourse and Society* 10, no. 1: 21–47.

Leonardi, P. M. (2003). "Problematizing 'new media': Culturally based perceptions of cell phones, computers, and the Internet among United States Latinos." *Critical Studies in Media Communication* 20, no. 2: 160–79.

Leung, L., and R. Wei. (2000). "More than just talk on the move: Uses and gratifications of the cellular phone." *Journalism and Mass Communication Quarterly* 77, no. 2: 308–20.

Lindlof, T. R. (1995). *Qualitative communication research methods.* Thousand Oaks, CA: Sage.

Ling, R. (2004). *The mobile connection: The cell phone's impact on society.* San Francisco: Morgan Kaufmann.

Marin, G., R. J. Gamba, and B. V. Marin. (1992). "Extreme response style and acquiescence among Hispanics: The role of acculturation and education." *Journal of Cross-Cultural Psychology* 23, no. 4: 498–509.

Markus, M. L. (1990). "Toward a 'critical mass' theory of interactive media." In J. Fulk and C. Steinfield (Eds.), *Organizations and communication technology* (pp. 194–218). Newbury Park, CA: Sage.

Morgan, D. L. (1997). *Focus groups as qualitative research,* 2nd ed. Thousand Oaks, CA: Sage.

Murray, J. (2001). *Wireless nation: The frenzied launch of the cellular phone revolution in America.* Cambridge, MA: Perseus.

Orlikowski, W. J. (1992). "The duality of technology: Rethinking the concept of technology in organizations." *Organization Science* 3, no. 3: 398–427.

Orlikowski, W. J. (2000). "Using technology and constituting structures: A practice lens for studying technology in organizations." *Organization Science* 11, no. 4: 404–28.

Palen, L., M. Salzman, and E. Youngs. (2000). "Going wireless: Behavior and practice of new mobile phone users." In *Proceedings of the ACM conference on computer supported cooperative work* (pp. 201–10). Philadelphia.

Prasad, P. (1995). "Working with the 'smart' machine: Computerization and the discourse of anthropomorphism in organizations." *Studies in Cultures, Organizations, and Societies* 1: 253–65.

Rice, R. E., J. D'Ambra, and E. More. (1998). "Cross-cultural comparison of organizational media evaluation and choice." *Journal of Communication* 48, no. 3: 3–26.

Robey, D., and A. Rodriguez-Diaz. (1989). "The organizational and cultural context of systems implementation: Case experience from Latin America." *Information and Management* 17: 229–39.

Schlosser, F. K. (2002). "So, how do people really use their handheld devices? An interactive study of wireless technology use." *Journal of Organizational Behavior* 23: 401–23.

Shkodriani, G. M., and J. L. Gibbons. (1995). "Individualism and collectivism among university students in Mexico and the United States." *Journal of Social Psychology* 135, no. 6: 765–72.

Stavans, I. (1995). *The Hispanic condition: Reflections on culture and identity in America.* New York: HarperCollins.

Strauss, A., and J. Corbin. (1998). *Basics of qualitative research: Techniques and procedures for developing grounded theory,* 2nd ed. Thousand Oaks, CA: Sage.

Woolgar, S. (1996). "Technologies as cultural artifacts." In W. H. Dutton and M. Peltu (Eds.), *Information and communication technologies: Visions and realities.* Oxford: Oxford University Press.

Zimbardo, P. G. (1969). "The human choice: Individuation, reason, and order versus deindividuation, impulse, and chaos." In W. T. Arnold and D. Levine (Eds.), *Nebraska symposium on motivation,* vol. 17 (pp. 237–307). Lincoln: University of Nebraska Press.

Zsembik, B. A., and L. Beeghley. (1996). "Determinants of ethnic group solidarity among Mexican Americans: A research note." *Hispanic Journal of Behavioral Sciences* 18, no. 1: 51–62.

The Cell Phone as a Cultural Technology: Lessons from the Indian Case

Anandam Kavoori and Kalyani Chadha

> *The spanking new Tata Sumo careened crazily through the New Delhi traffic. On each side of the Sumo, smoke billowed from other cars, buses, and rickshaws. Through the smoke, one could see emblazoned on the sides of many vehicles bold claims of a new connectedness: cell phones. Similar advertisements hung everywhere: on crooked telephone poles, adorning the sides of slums, schools, railway stations, homes, and offices. The car driver clasped a cell phone to his ear as he narrowly missed a line of pigs heading straight for a garbage heap piled outside a tiny cell phone shop. The cultural vertigo was complete.*

Introduction

Media technologies in the developing world are usually mediated through global relations of unequal access and disjunctive growth (McChesney 1999; Schiller 1999; Reeves 1993; Hardt 1992).[1] Technologies, theories, and inventors rarely originate in the developing world; rather they are part of a matrix of global relations that has historically placed the developing world in a derivative relationship. This relationship has been reiterated in earlier histories of television, radio, the newspaper, and the Internet (Kavoori and Chadha 2001). The cell phone, we shall suggest, is no different.

One way to theorize the role of the cell phone in the developing world is to examine it narrowly as a set of technological developments coordinated through policy prescriptions by politicians and institutional regulators. Much like the Internet in the last decade, the cell phone is being framed in this decade as the new vehicle for the developing world's information revolution. Focusing only on policy issues, we could review current and past institutional and legal developments and then develop a prescriptive logic for yet to emerge technological, social, and political developments. Rather than attempt such an exercise, what we have tried to do is to ask the more difficult—and perhaps more interesting—question, How is the cell phone shaping issues of identity in the developing world? How is the cell phone a site for the articulation of a specific cultural consciousness that will both underpin and legitimize the future of economic and institutional development?

Recognizing that technologies are always understood in cultural contexts (Leonardi 2003) and that each technology is fundamentally different in the way it is socially constructed by its users, we would argue that thinking about technology in this sense provides a way to place communication in a position of importance rather than regarding it as ancillary to and shaped by technology (Leonardi 2003, p. 161). Decentering technology at the interactional site allows it to be reconstructed as a social practice and communication as an "object of interest itself, rather than keying only to characteristics of communication that seem derivable from technology" (Leonardi 2003, pp. 161–62).

By taking this path to analysis, we are not saying that the cell phone cannot be understood by examining issues of technological innovation, state governance, or infrastructural development. We are saying, however, that an exclusive focus on the institutional and individual basis of assessing a media technology globally ignores how such technologies are mediated in cultural terms. The role of a technology can be better understood when you place it in a vision of a *cultural* future rather than an exclusively *technological* future. In other words, we propose that the cell phone is a cultural technology that is appropriated and internalized by the culture within the matrix of global and cultural relations framed by processes of global capitalism. In an ongoing project called the Cultural Technology Project[2] at the University of Georgia, we have argued that this process of appropriation of cultural technologies in the developing world takes place not so much through new media such as the Internet but rather through its framing in traditional mass media, such as magazines, newspapers, and television. It is through messages in these media that the cultural frame for understanding cell phones is sold.

The selling is done through a well-known form of persuasive communication—advertising. Our paper examines the terms in which the cell phone is being sold in the developing world, with a focus on India. Based on a qualitative reading of a sample of advertisements,[3] we make an argument about the cultural role of the cell phone framed in cultural terms. We focus on the cultural values and discourses that advertising emboldens and hence the discursive blueprint for society and the nation-state that it presents.

Why Advertising?

Simply put, it's everywhere. As the personal narrative that opens this chapter conveys, traveling in any of India's cities, the presence of cell phone advertising is overwhelming. The research question as to the function of advertising shouts at you from every intersection in India's urban landscape. As Stuart Ewen (1989) puts it,

> Urban imagery—advertising—bears the imprint of the lives of the people that they address. To approach an understanding of urban commercial imagery, images must be seen as engaged in a social-historical process, responsible to the changing terms of social life, of social institutions. Thus, advertising images, though they lay claim to an enormous sweep of vision, must be placed upon the social and political battleground they often intend to mask. (p. 83)

What kind of social and political battleground exists in the developing world? As theorists of globalization remind us, we are seeing a sea change in political ideology, as market liberalization and cultural homogenization sweep across the developing world (Price 1999; Thussu 2000). In other words, the cell phone needs to be assessed as an agent in the developing world's negotiation with issues of modernity, capitalism, and economic development.

That negotiation is unproblematic for advocates of the new communication technologies, who see it as a force for economic development. As Alok Mittal, a software engineer puts it, "we are part of a second freedom movement" (*India Today*, July 10, 2000, p. 65). Such euphoria shows us that the cell phone is not just about information, as is often argued, but has a specific cultural placement. As Vicente Rafael puts it in the context of the Philippines, the cell phone is a "technological thing that has been idealized as an agent of social change, invested with the power to bring in new forms of sociality" (2003, p. 402).

In sum, as one important space of communication—advertising—engages with the cell phone it "becomes a site for the reception and formation of everyday life and therefore a site of ideological formation" (Schwoch, White, and Reilly 1992, p. 22).

Cell Phone Advertising and the Cultural Ecumene of Globalization

The universe of advertising by cell phone companies (and others) needs to be first contextualized within a larger universe of advertisements articulating a fundamental shift in (the marketing of) new cultural sensibilities in the developing world as it grapples with the paradoxes of global capitalism. It can be seen as part of what Ulf Hannerz has called the "cultural ecumene" of globalization.

Every issue of the *Times of India*, for example, has at least two pages of full advertisements, where advertisements for cell phones appear alongside others. These include those for call center jobs, Internet service/companies, English language schools, computer schools, exam preparation centers (computers, law, MBA, SAT), and for admissions to schools in Europe and the United states.

Reading across such advertisements, two contextual themes emerged, which we termed "technology acquisition" and "consumer culture." These themes refer to both learning a new language (English) and a technological language (computers, Internet, call centers, and so on) and gaining entry into a system of cultural commodification and consumer culture that ties cell phone use into the technological/education/employment options offered by computer centers, cell phone centers, careers in medical transcription, and modes of employment that are focused on technology and closely tied to a valorized global/European/modern marketplace. In sum, these careers/lifestyle prescriptions are interpellated and create a new subject: the consumer.

In addition to linguistic acquisition and consumer culture, other advertisements reflected a third contextual theme, which we termed "technological national development." Elements of these themes were articulated by different advertisements. The first ad (in the magazine *India Today*) by the Indian government's Ministry of Information Technology, advertises "Community Information Centers," "Where a new dawn of freedom—freedom from distance" is promised. It invokes the nationalist poet Rabindranath Tagore and suggests that new technology will lead India "into that heaven of freedom" where "the mind is without fear and the head is held high, where knowledge is free."

The second ad comes from the Reliance Infocomm (one of India's leading industrial houses), entitled "Reliance India Mobile." It frames the reader as a national subject: "Get Ready India." The text of the three-page advertisement is centered on the chairman and managing director, Mukesh Ambani, who writes, "A digital revolution is being unleashed in India today with the launch of Reliance Infocomm. I invite you to take part in this revolution." The third ad is from the global media company Samsung, and has a cell phone being held by a number of young, attractive, and exuberant Indians who ask, "The future is calling. Are you there?"

Taken together, each of these advertisements signals an important element in "technological national development." They represent the collective valorization of technology by three separate agents (the government, transnational capital, and indigenous capital). The valorization of this technology is tied to issues of reimagining the nation as a cell phone nation and the role of information technologies as the *economic* arm of nation building. Historically, media in much of the developing world was seen as the *cultural* arm of national building, and media content was seen as fulfilling both entertainment and information functions. This frame for constructing cell phones mirrors and extends a process of cultural commodification and national reimagination already established by the Internet in India (Kavoori and Chadha 2001).

The Discourse of Motorola Cell Phone Advertisements

We now turn to a detailed textual reading of one set of advertisements that occurred across sites—billboards, newspapers, magazines, and television. These were the Motorola advertisements.

Our analysis draws substantially on an excellent analysis of cell phone advertising in Slovenia by Mojca Pajnik and Petra Lesjak Tusek (2002), in which they examine issues relevant to our analysis: culture and technology using an Althusserian and structural-semiotic analysis. Our reading of these advertisements also drew on a research report by Motorola researcher Sadie Plant (2002), who conducted extensive field research for Motorola across the world in order to identify the sociological and ritual contexts for cell phone use. While we don't cite from the report extensively, it helped us to frame and contextualize the advertising/marketing logic behind these advertisements.

Pajnik and Tusek's (2002) analysis focuses on cell phone advertising by Mobitel in Slovenia. They argue that cell phone advertising functions like most

> [a]dvertising discourse, where ideology functions through the "inter-pellation of viewers" (Althusser 1994). Interpellation is a process by which we organize ourselves into the position offered by advertising discourse in the presentation of a particular product. There is a discourse of the inner voice used in advertisements that address the reader as "you" continuously telling you what it is you want and need. (p. 279)

To counter pose, the Motorola report, in its introduction (written by the Motorola Company and not Dr. Plant), draws on a very different institutional and pedagogical discourses to make its case: "We live in an age of intelligent machines that are in perpetual communication, creating new networks of knowledge, information and empowerment across the globe. At the heart of any technological change is the human experience. And it's in understanding how the digital world is being experienced by all of us, as friends, colleagues and families, that we gain the most insight into the shape of things to come" (Plant 2002, p. 1).

The Advertisements

The six advertisements from Motorola that we will focus on are part of a single advertising campaign using Indian models to frame the use of cell phones and the cultural discourse it interpellates viewers with. The six advertisements had the following titles: GlobalMoto, JetsetMoto, MastermindMoto, HeadsturnMoto, ColormeMoto, and TranceMoto. We saw these advertisements on posters, walls, newspapers, and magazines—in other words on both the media and urban landscape. The advertisements discussed here were all taken from the bestselling news magazine *India Today*.

Like the Mobitel advertisements in Slovenia, the Motorola advertisements "were presented through the images of people, although they do not speak at all" (Pajnik and Tusek 2002, p. 285) and created "the illusion of people connected, gaining friendship, love and social approval, while the phone as a technology stood as a substitute for personal communication" (p. 297). But there was more than just interpersonal communicative messages being framed here. We now turn to these.

Technology and Masculinity: Analysis of GlobalMoto, JetsetMoto, MastermindMoto, and HeadsturnMoto

Each of these advertisements are focused around different Indian male models that center the act of mobility and of the machine-body combine that has come to characterize so much of our use of mobile technologies. The models hold up, flash, and "display" the phone as part of their body and the performance they enact. In this centering of both display and use, the cell phone advertisements replicate our general intimacy with machines. As Donna Haraway (1990) put it in a seminal article, "Late twentieth century machines have made thoroughly ambiguous the differences between the natural and the artificial, mind and body, self-developing and externally designed. Our machines are disturbingly lively, and we ourselves frighteningly inert" (p. 194).

In this sense, the cell phone is very clearly located within a wider matrix of technology relations seen, for example, in earlier narratives of beepers, cameras, watches, transistors, portable CD players, and even cars. Cell phones thus keep open the "technological determinism and ideological space opened up by the reconceptions of machines and organism as coded text through which we engage in the play of reading and writing the world" (Haraway 1990, p. 194).

Beyond this overall reiteration of a cultural positionality toward technology and body-machine relations, the Motorola advertisements do a lot more: they frame a specific cultural relationship to this technology and predicate a gendered mode of accounting, to which we now turn.

The GlobalMoto has the following elements: a slim Indian male, dressed in a business suit holding a silver briefcase. He is on the go, he looks at the viewer in midstride, his expression a mixture of satisfaction and aloofness. His eyebrows are marginally quizzical; he conveys both assurance and a self-consciousness of the effect of his presence. This presence is framed with the accoutrements of being global—a blue jacket, unbuttoned and open; a cell phone receiver in his ear; and the silver briefcase, with labels for five cities: Taipei, Tokyo, Mexico City, Sydney, and Montreal. It is an image in which the idea of "mobility"—central to both the technological and discursive constitution of the cell phone—is emphasized. As the Motorola report puts it, "All around the world, the mobile has become associated with a handful of phrases which recur like samples in a global dance track. These include 'on my way,' 'on the bus,' 'on the train.' If 'where are you' is the perfect mobile question, the perfect mobile answer is 'on the mobile' (Plant 2002, p. 5).

Being on the mobile in the context of the GlobalMoto advertisements signals not just mobility but economic mobility—the ready inclusion of the Indian male presence within the work and cultural space of global capitalism. The man on the move in the advertisement is no ordinary man—his mobility is *fashioned* by global capital and he is *made manifest* through its rearticulation in the context of a local masculinized presence. We can assume that similar national models and narrative strategies would be used to sell Motorola's global vision to different national markets and cultural sensibilities.

The MastermindMoto ad extends the logic of mobility and corporate masculinized Indian identity and presents it with a narrative vehicle that is less tangential, less inflected with ambiguity. It is focused on an Indian model that takes the value of globality and mobility and presents it in a direct mode of address. It shows a twentysomething business executive wearing a shiny leather-look business suit with a pinstripe yellow tie. The model faces the camera, his head tilted up so that he is looking down at the reader. His expression is aloof, the disdain barely concealed. In his left hand, he holds an open cell phone, its screen lit up with colorful content (which is not decipherable). Behind him in small letters are the words "Pocket Internet Explorer" and "Windows Media Player." The model's legs are spread open, he leans forward, lightly balanced on a bright red sofa. His gaze (and by implication that of the cell phone) are emblematic of a wider logic offered by global capitalism: get in the game or get left behind. Its sheer inexorability appears to inform the personification of these models. As Pajnik and Tusek (2002) put it, "the Individuals in the advertisements are personified even if they are represented as members of a particular social group and the *individuality* is represented to be a *crucial new value*" (p. 297; emphasis added).

The last two advertisements, JetsetMoto and HeadsturnMoto, take the logic of corporate Indian masculinity and extend it into the realm of popular culture and youth identity politics and center the cell phone within the frame of cultural performance and play. JetsetMoto shows an Indian male model wearing a leather jacket and informal business shirt balanced on a skateboard. The picture is taken from the ground up, so that the businessman/skateboarder is flying over the viewer, who looks up at him. The model balances himself with two barely outstretched hands, one of which holds a cell phone. He wears dark glasses; the graffiti under his skateboard says "switch." His gaze is away from the viewer, positioned at his destination (the point of landing or perhaps somewhere more abstract). What stands out from this corporate/popular culture performance is the effortless control and balance of the model. Unlike many other skateboarding-themed advertisements, the emphasis is not on contorted moves but rather on the almost unconscious pleasure that such control gives to the businessman/skateboarder. JetsetMoto is an extension of the logic of both GlobalMoto and MastermindMoto (in its reliance on the centering of corporate male masculinity), but it also articulates a more assured, comfortable, and pleasurable set of uses of this technology. It personalizes the technology and links the critical new values of globalization with the promise of popular culture and personal enactment.

HeadsturnMoto takes the logic of Jetsetmoto and firmly places it within the realm of popular culture and an aggressive youth identity politics. It shows a young Indian male in his late teens, early twenties, poised in stride. His legs are spread confidently apart as he looks intently and texts on his cell phone. His clothes serve as diacritical signs for a new Indian masculinity. He wears tight black pants with shiny red markings running down each leg. His striped black jacket swings open like a cape (Batman style), and his shirt is made of a thin black mesh through which his skin can be seen. His hair is carefully rumpled and his eyes invisible behind large, wraparound dark glasses. His expression is hostile, his gaze zeroed in on the cell phone that he cradles carefully as he texts. His shoes are shiny black leather and placed apart in a free-swinging but balanced style. HeadsturnMoto provides the viewer with a set of messages that draw on and take sustenance from the other Motorolo advertisements. They are firmly placed within the idea that the neo-liberal global marketplace has arrived and is made possible by the discursive strengths of a corporate male masculinity, but there is more to HeadsturnMoto—it is the idea common to popular culture representations: the moment also calls for a counter-culture that uses technology to represent its identity politics—which like most corporate-sponsored youth cultures is defiant, aggressive, flamboyant, and deliberative in its self-reflexivity and self-centeredness. HeadsturnMoto is strikingly eye-catching and strikingly commonplace. It is easily placed within the MTV-generated world of youth culture images that have now come to be synonymous with the youth face of global capitalism.

Cultural Technology and Femininity:
Analysis of ColormeMoto and TranceMoto

A beginning point for examining the two cell phone advertisements that used women models is the history of the use of women in advertising. There is an extensive body of feminist and postmodern analysis that has focused on issues of patriarchy, marginality, and representation. While we do not reference this literature in this chapter, we reiterate with Anna Reading (1997) some of the key issues and concerns:

> Research work has focused on the ways in which women in different regions and countries are represented through "cultural stereotypes," for example the mother, the virgin, the whore or the good daughter or wife. The media, from this perspective, is seen as playing a detrimental role by providing women with a limited number of role models which ignore the diverse character of women's lives. What is needed, it is argued, are more positive role models for women. (p. 2)

Connecting these issues with those of globalization and gender is important as we examine the representational import of using women in cell phone advertising. Following Krishna Sen and Maila Stivens (1998), we suggest that scholars see consumption as a pivotal concept to use in thinking about the place of gender in the "newly affluent" cultures and the middle class–centered neo-liberal marketplace. As they put it, "Consumption is central to the constant search for and the construction of new identities. Linking market and identity is important to think about gender and globalization in affluent Asia" (p. 5).

In the context of the Motorola advertisements ColormeMoto and TranceMoto, such consumption needs to be examined in the context of historical representations and the very politicized space of India's public sphere. As Sen and Stivens (1998, p. 5) put it in the context of developing countries in Asia, "Consumption patterns provide a way of tying gender directly into theorizing the connections between macro-level global processes and local complexities and specificities. In particular, the development of elaborate new femininities based on the consumer/wife/mother and the consumer/beautiful young woman can be seen as central to the very development of these burgeoning economies" (p. 5).

The first ad, ColormeMoto, has the following elements: an "oriental" model, her hair styled in a twist over her head, her neck adorned by a white lace collar, holds up a cell phone to her left eye so that it becomes an instrument of viewing rather than use. Around her right eye is a tight arrangement of peacock feathers. The image on the cell phone is also that of a peacock. The peacock, a bird seen in the Indian context as a bird of beauty, color, and vanity, is thus centered as a defining characteristic of this gendered use of technology. The model evokes both Asian cosmopolitanism (as seen in the historically constituted "made in Japan"), but also Asian anxieties, where the economic history of the "Asian tigers"—Japan, Korea, and Singapore—are seen as the emulative model for other Asian countries. It is an unusual placement of discourses: the traditional geisha-centered narrative focused around sophisticated grace with the promise of swift, assured sexuality are transferred into the Indian context with its own national and regional ambitions in the realm of economic growth. Perhaps the key lies in the framing of the picture, "Color*me* Moto" (emphasis added), where the agency is presumed to lie elsewhere, not in the woman herself but perhaps with one of the other male models for control of this technology or even more abstractly in the idea of local subjects opening themselves willingly to the use and pleasures of corporate-sponsored performance in both personal adornment and body-machine relations (hairstyle, telephone as eye) and so on.

The second advertisement, TranceMoto, parallels the discourses around popular culture and identity politics as seen in HeadsturnMoto. Here an Indian female model dressed in the skimpiest of clothes—a mesh, almost see-through sleeveless top, and shorts—cradles a cell phone to her throat. Her legs are arched, her eyes look directly at the viewer, and her hair is in careful disarray. Her expression is hostile but sexually available, her lips and eyes immobile in the fixity of their expression. It is a familiar trope in corporate pop culture products—the young, hypersexual woman, available but hard to get. In the Indian context, it is a departure from the traditional symbols of sexuality—which are often coded with a repressed domestic sexuality (the submissive beautiful wife) or a voluptuous siren. What is also new here is the adoption of a kind of poverty chic (emaciated, thin women models) that mirror less the real poverty in India but the fashion-based constructs of femininity that underwrites the beauty industry. Finally, the ad is also a departure from the sexualized "Western" construct in Bollywood histories of the vamp and the slut. TranceMoto, as the name suggests, is a different animal—the trance is as much in its making—through the deliberate assumption of such a role by Indian women and in being entranced—through the possibilities presented and offered by globalization.

Assessing the Motorola Cell Phone as a Cultural Technology

The Motorola cell phone, we have argued in the preceding section, frames and constructs Indian consumers along a semantic/narrative story line that centers individuality, references corporate-sponsored identity formations, and is reiterative of very specific modalities of identity formation in the Indian context in the wake of market liberalization. We now turn to some theoretical speculations that such an analysis calls attention to.

Our findings mirror Pajnik and Tusek's (2002) analysis of Mobitel's advertising in the context of Slovenia. They see advertising as part and parcel of the formation and maintenance of class-based ideological formations. In their words,

> Ideology functions in such a way that it recruits subjects amongst individuals or transforms the individuals into subjects—by interpellating or hailing. This is how the inner voice of advertising works. The rhetoric of Mobitel's advertising, both verbal and pictorial, is based on the inner voice. With shaping promises, assurances and illusions, the voice promotes the good things about buying the product and also implicitly or explicitly warns the consumer what might happen if he or she does not buy the product. (p. 279)

The idea of consumption is centered in the case of both India's Motorola advertisements and Slovenia's.

> Mobitel's advertisements speak to consumers about identity and appear to offer solutions—they open the path toward new and better identities. A new look can be synonymous with a new me (Jenkins 1996, 7–8). People in advertisements are not a realistic representation but an imaginary one. As Williamson (1978) suggested that if we buy the product we actually buy the image and at the same time contribute to the construction of identity—through consumption. (Pajnik and Tusek 2002, p. 281)

But as we have suggested, the cell phone in the Indian context does not merely reproduce the same problematic reification of consumption; it also structures gendered identity formations that are symptomatic of wider structural and social divides that globalization generates. There are a number of implications that we will now describe in a thumbnail fashion.

First, the Motorola advertisements perpetuate a ghettoization of women within the realms of sexuality, ritual, enactment of tradition, and submissive performance while taking on the kind of technological accoutrements that corporate modernity signals as its leitmotif.

The Motorola advertisements systematically restrict the mobility of women as players in the economic and political arena, even as they are centered unproblematically in the commodity world. There is considerable precedence for this in the developing world-historical engagement with media and advertising. To use one example, an analysis of women's representations in Ugandan media examined the press images of women in national newspapers over several months and discovered that women were rarely portrayed in relation to economic or political issues. They were rarely included as experts in subjects outside the home (Reading 1997, p. 2).

Second, the Motorola advertisements perpetuate an equation between masculinity and technology so that the relationship becomes durable (Faulkner 2000, pp. 87–119). The use of cell phones by the Indian male subjects in the Motorola advertisements accentuate an assumption about male agency in processes of globalization, but to this is added a very clear rearticulation of "the design cultures" of modern engineering and science (Oudshooron, Romes, and Stienstra, 2004), and it is in this overall sense that the cell phone becomes both an agent and a creator of a regressive, powerfully gendered cultural technology.

In sum, the discourse of the cell phone in India—that is, its framing as a cultural technology in the Indian case (for both men and women)—reiterates the problematics around gender. Ulf Mellstrom's (2004, pp. 368–82) work in Malaysia suggests that (much like in India) masculine bonds are mediated and communicated through interactions with machines and where technologies become a means of embodied communication for male bonds. "These masculine practices continuously exclude women and perpetuate highly genderized social spheres where men form communities based on a passion for machines. Such passion transforms technologies into subjects in what might be termed a heterosexual, masculine, technical sociability and subjectivity" (p. 368).

Assessing the Cell Phone as a Cultural Technology in the Developing World

We now return to some thoughts about the questions we began this analysis with: How do we assess the cell phone as a cultural technology rather than just as an easy, accessible technology? In addition, what do the discourses used by advertising tell us about the future blueprint for society in the developing world? And perhaps, most crucially, what kind of ideological formation for a developing country is the cell phone?

Grappling with these questions is difficult, especially given the fact that India is often seen as an example of a third-world country successfully encountering and dealing with new technologies such as the Internet, call centers, and cell phones. So, we offer some initial thoughts to begin formulating an understanding of cell phone advertising in the developing world.

We would argue that cell phone advertising such as we describe creates and masks the role of new technologies in three linked ways: by creating/masking the future of publicity and image making; by creating/masking the future of cultural dislocation; by creating/masking the future of capitalist expansion.

To understand these ways of creating and masking the cell phone's future we must first understand the role of the omnipotence of such advertisements in the urban-media landscape. With the evanescent nature of cell phone and call center companies (replacing the dot-coms of just a few years ago), what is important, as John Berger (1977) says, is to understand that

> [p]ublicity image belongs to the moment. We see it as we turn a page, a corner, on a vehicle as it passes by, on a television screen. Publicity images also belong to the moment in the sense that they must be continually renewed and made up to date. Yet they never speak of the present. Often they refer to the past and always they speak of the future. . . . Publicity is not merely an assembly of competing messages: it is a language in itself, which is always being used to make the same general proposal. It proposes to each of us that we transform ourselves, or our lives, by buying. (pp. 129–30)

The process of buying is simultaneously one of image making and of being absorbed into the image of advertising. This willing absorption by people and institutions of all economic and political backgrounds in India is indicative of the power of the cultural value of the new technologies such as the cell phone and the Internet. Advertising simultaneously creates and masks the future of the centering of this commodity world. As Sut Jhally (1989) puts it,

> In advertising the commodity world interacts with the human world at the most fundamental levels: it performs magical feats of transformation and bewitchment, brings instant happiness and gratification, captures the forces of nature, and holds within itself the essence of important social relations (in fact, it substitutes for those relations). What is noteworthy about such scenes is not that they are concerned with daily life; it is the extent to which goods enter into the arrangements of daily life. (p. 218)

As the cultural value of the cell phone becomes part of the arrangement of daily life, what results is not prosperity but cultural dislocation and alienation, words rarely used in the euphoria over the easy access promised by the cell phone. Cell phone advertising becomes by its constant reification of an other space simultaneously a creator of urban futures and a mask of its hidden contradictions (of class, gender, and consumption). As Stuart Ewen (1989) puts it, "Cultural dislocation is the central experience of urbanization and modernity. Within the shadows of progress stands the culturally eviscerated individual . . . consumption it might be argued is the most widely available mode of psychotherapy. Advertising speaks to emotional hungers, presents its commodities as emotional nourishment" (p. 84).

In the end, however, cell phone advertising is what advertising is always about: a form of persuasive communication that masks its true function in late capitalism: to sell commodities. It speaks to the interests of buyers rather than nations, to consumers rather than citizens. Historically, in the developing world, media technologies were seen as the cultural arm of nation building. They worked with the notion of informing and creating a citizenry rather than consumers. New technologies such as cell phones, on the other hand, create a culture of consumption and mask the cultural contradictions they creates. Advertising is centrally implicated in this relationship, especially "those centered on the production and consumption of telecommunications, information, and computer services—they present to viewers through their visual and verbal discourses the faith and beliefs that underlie what might be called `corporate soul' . . . (they work) through their dual epistles of technological utopianism and consumer culture" (Schwoch, White, and Reilly 1992, p. 22).

Cell phone advertising in India (and perhaps in the rest of the developing world), then, reflects the emergence of a fundamental change in market relations from a mixed economy to a capitalist one. Under current conditions of globalization, cell phone advertising (like other advertising in the developing world's urban-mediascape) fills the discursive space created by the structural transformation of society. Jhally's and Ewen's comments about other forms of advertising appear to be even truer about cell phone advertising: "Capitalist production methods mean more than merely a new way to produce goods—it entailed a revolution in the cultural arrangements of traditional society . . . the world of goods in industrial society offers no meaning. The function of advertising is to refill the emptied commodity with meaning" (Jhally 1989, pp. 220–21). "While reinforcing the priorities of corporate production and marketing, advertising offers a symbolic empathy to its audience, criticizing alienation and offering transcendent alternatives. Needless to say, these 'alternatives' are contained religiously, within the cosmology of the marketplace" (Ewen 1989, p. 86).

We close with the idea that the cell phone and its discursive construction as a cultural technology need to be properly framed and contextualized before we embrace them euphorically as either indicative of a new popular consciousness (as evidenced in the Philippines) or as a restructuration of traditional communication patterns. Haraway (1990) provides us with a final reminder: "We are living through a movement from an organic, industrial society to a polymorphous information society—from all work to all play, a deadly game. Simultaneously material and ideological, the dichotomies move from old hierarchical dominations (white capitalist patriarchy) to the informatics of domination" (pp. 203–4).

Notes

1 This chapter draws extensively on our earlier analysis of Internet advertising in India (Kavoori and Chadha 2001). This includes reference material and some of the contextual analysis. On both a personal and theoretical level, our experience of cell phone advertisements was structurally similar to our experience of Internet advertising and, in fact, pushed us in our analysis.

2 The Cultural Technologies Project is housed in the Department of Telecommunications at the Grady College of Journalism and Mass Communication, University of Georgia, is aimed at a critical assessment of the various cultures of the cell phone, new media (the Internet, including the media of virtual cultures—for example, MUDS), and is generally focused on issues of technology and popular culture. As part of its international focus, the authors have been involved in data collection of the current state and future of the new media in Asia. Other papers from this project look at the evolution of Internet and telecommunications policy and the nation-state; the development of international regulatory regimes in the developing world; a comparative analysis of Internet advertising on first-world and third-world websites; and, finally, data collection on popular culture and the Internet focused on Bollywood websites.

3 This chapter is based on data collection that consisted of field work in India during May 2004, when the first author visited the cities of Bombay, New Delhi, Jaipur, and Mussouri in India and made a visual record of cell phone advertising in the urban landscape of New Delhi (a photo essay will be available in the near future on the Web). Insights from this field experience were gleaned from all cell phone–related advertising in the newspaper the *Times of India* for the month of May 2004, and all cell phone–related advertisements in the news magazine *India Today* for March, April, and May 2004. Textual analysis of these advertisements was conducted with a focus on identifying emergent themes and recurrent motifs. These readings were related to the personal field experience in India. The specific examples of advertisements discussed in this chapter were chosen from this inductive process. Their function, thus, is both representative and illustrative within a textual and literary analysis tradition rather than a social-scientific/content analysis tradition. No quantitative tabulation of these themes was made and none is offered here. This analysis remains, in the end, a "reading" of advertising texts. While no claims of objectivity can be made, there is no reason to suspect any systematic bias in interpretation.

References

Berger, J. (1977). *Ways of seeing*. London: BBC Penguin.

Ewen, S. (1989). Advertising and the development of consumer society. In I. Angus and S. Jhally (Eds.), *Cultural politics in contemporary America* (82–95). London: Routledge.

Faulkner, W. (2000). The power and the pleasure? A research agenda for making gender stick to engineers. *Science, Technology and Human Values*, 25, 1, 87–119.

Haraway, D. (1990). A manifesto for cyborgs. In Nicholson (Ed.). *Feminism/Postmodernism* (190–233). New York: Routledge.

Hardt, H. (1992). *Communication, history and theory in America*. New York: Routledge.

Jhally, S. (1989). Advertising as religion: The dialectic of technology and magic. In I. Angus and S. Jhally (Eds.) *Cultural politics in contemporary America*. (217–229). London: Routledge.

Kavoori, A., & Chadha, K. (2001). Net tarot in New Delhi: Reading the future of the internet in advertising. *Convergence: The Journal of Research into New Media Technologies*, 6, 7, 82–95.

Leonardi, P. (2003). Problematizing new media: Culturally based perceptions of cell phones, computers and the internet amongst United States Latinos. *Critical Studies in Media Communication*, 20, 2, 160–179.

McChesney, R. (1999). *Rich media, poor democracy: Communication politics in dubious times*. Champaign, IL: University of Illinois Press.

Mellstrom, U. (2004). Machines and masculine subjectivity. *Men and Masculinities*, 6, 4, 368–382.

Oudshoorn, N., Romes, E., and Stienstra, M. (2004). Configuring the user as everybody: Gender and design cultures in information and communication technologies. *Science, Technology and Human Values*, 29, 1, 30–63.

Pajnik, M., and Tusek, P. (2002). Observing discourses of advertising: Mobitel's interpellation of potential consumers. *Journal of Communication Inquiry*, 26, 3, 277–299.

Plant, S. (2002). On the mobile: The effects of mobile telephones on social and individual life. *Motorola Company Report*.

Price, M. (1999). Satellite broadcasting as trade routes in the sky. *Public Culture*, 11, 2, 69–85.

Rafael, V. (2003). The cell phone and the crowd: Messianic politics in the contemporary Philippines. *Public Culture*, 15, 3, 399–425.

Reading, A. (1997). Women, men and the mass media. *Common Concern*, September, 1997. Available online at www.worldywca.org/common_concern/sept1997. Accessed 5/23/2005.

Reeves, G. (1993). *Communications and the third world*. New York: Routledge.

Schiller, D. (1999). *Digital capitalism: Networking the global market system*. New York: Routledge.

Schwoch, J., White, M., and Reilly, S. (1992). Television advertising, telecommunications discourse and contemporary American culture. In J. Schwoch, M. White, and S. Reilly (Eds.). *Media knowledge: Readings in popular culture, pedagogy and critical citizenship* (21–37). Albany: State University of New York Press.

Sen, K. and Stivens, M. (Eds). (1998). *Gender and power in affluent Asia*. New York: Routledge.

Thussu, D. (2000). *International communication: Continuity and change*. London: Arnold.

Contributors

Paul Levinson

Paul Levinson, Ph.D., is currently a professor and department chair in the Department of Communication and Media Studies at Fordham University. Strongly influenced by the works of Marshall McLuhan, Levinson has authored more than a hundred scholarly articles and eight books on the history and philosophy of communication and technology, including *The Soft Edge* (1997), *Digital McLuhan* (1999), *Realspace* (2003), and *Cellphone: The Story of the World's Most Mobile Medium and How It Has Transformed Everything!* (2004).

Adriana de Souza e Silva

Adriana de Souza e Silva is an assistant professor at the Department of Communication at North Carolina State University (NCSU). Adriana holds a Ph.D. in communications and culture from the Federal University of Rio de Janeiro, Brazil. From 2001 to 2004, Adriana was a visiting scholar at the UCLA Department of Design and Media Arts. Her research focuses on how new media interfaces change our relationship to space and create new social environments via media art and pervasive games. She holds a master's degree in communication and image technology from the Federal University of Rio de Janeiro, Brazil.

Janey Gordon

Janey Gordon is a senior teaching fellow in radio at the University of Luton, U.K. She has written and published extensively on the role of radio, specifically local radio networks and their link with social activism, and she started a broadcasting station for the University of Luton, now LutonFM. She is the author of a monograph on ultra-local radio.

Rich Ling

Rich Ling is a sociologist at Telenor's research institute in Norway and also the Pohs visiting professor of communication studies at the University of Michigan in Ann Arbor. Ling has published numerous articles for academic and nonacademic publications, and has held posts at and lectured at universities in Europe and the United States. He is the author of *The Mobile Connection: The Cell Phone's Impact on Society* (2004) and, along with Per E. Pederson, he edited *Mobile Communications: Renegotiation of the Social Sphere* (2005).

Wendy Robinson and David Robison

Wendy Robinson, Ph.D., is a visiting assistant professor in the Department of Communication Studies at the University of Michigan at Ann Arbor, where she teaches courses in multicultural and mobile communication. She previously taught at Duke University and the University of North Carolina at Chapel Hill. She is currently writing a book about recent intersections of mobile media and mass communication.

David Robison earned his master's degree in media and English literature at Leeds University. He researches and implements mobile design and application courses in the School of Informatics at Bradford University in the U.K., where he is currently a teacher in the Department of Electronic Imaging and Media Communications. Robison is also director of a popular Web and WAP lifestyle community site, 4clubbers.net.

Collette Snowden

Collette Snowden has worked as a journalist, public relations practitioner, and in the mobile communications and information technology sector as a consultant and researcher. She was the inaugural Donald Dyer Research Scholar in the School of Communication, Information, and New Media at the University of South Australia, where she undertook doctoral studies on the impact of mobile communications on the practices of media professionals. She has a particular interest in the social uses of telephony.

Allison Whitney

Allison Whitney holds a Ph.D. in cinema and media studies from the University of Chicago. She is currently the Social Sciences and Humanities Research Council of Canada Postdoctoral Fellow in The Institute for Comparative Studies in Literature, Art and Culture at Carleton University, Ottawa, Canada.

Heidi Campbell

Heidi Campbell is an assistant professor of communication at Texas A&M University. She has done extensive research on the religious use and perceptions of digital and mobile technologies. Many of her publications deal with issues related to the role of religion in a global information society, including her recent book *Exploring Religious Community Online*, in Peter Lang's Digital Formation series.

Gerard Goggin and Christopher Newell

Gerard Goggin, Ph.D., is an Australian research fellow in the Centre for Critical and Cultural Studies, University of Queensland. He has published extensively on telecommunications, the Internet, new media, and disability. He is the editor of *Virtual Nation: The Internet in Australia* (2004), and is working on a cultural history of the Internet. He is in the midst of a five-year international study of mobile phone culture and regulation, and is writing a book entitled *Cell Phone Culture: Mobile Technologies in Everyday Life*.

Christopher Newell, Ph.D., is associate professor in the School of Medicine, University of Tasmania. A person with disability, he has long researched disability and technological systems. His many government and industry roles include being chair of the Australian Communications Industry Forum Disability Advisory Body and a member of the council of the Australian Telecommunications Industry Ombudsman.

Gerard and Christopher are the authors of *Digital Disability: The Social Construction of Disability in New Media* (Rowman and Littlefield, 2003).

Davin Heckman

Davin Heckman is an assistant professor of English and communications at Siena Heights University. He recently earned his Ph.D. in American culture studies from Bowling Green State University, and is working on a forthcoming text on smart houses and everyday life. Davin is co-editor and cofounder of the journal *Reconstruction*.

Bahíyyih Maroon

Bahíyyih Maroon is an architectural anthropologist completing her Ph.D. at the University of California, Santa Cruz. Her research examines the relationship between advanced communication and information technologies situated in the built environment and transformations in social practices. In addition to scholarly work, she is an active practitioner in the architectural community. Currently, she is coordinating the construction of a Herzog de Meuron building in San Francisco, California.

Paul Leonardi, Marianne E. Leonardi, and Elizabeth Hudson

Paul Leonardi is a doctoral student at the Center for Work, Technology, and Organization (WTO) in the Department of Management Science and Engineering, Stanford University. His research interests include the impact of new technologies on work practices, the relationship between ICTs and culture, and the management of technical work. He has published research on technology implementation in organizations and on the ways in which technological artifacts are enrolled discursively in organizational change initiatives.

Marianne E. Leonardi is a graduate student in the Department of International and Intercultural Communication at the University of Denver. Her primary focus is on intercultural training, and she has conducted research on the connection between culture and communication and the influence of power and privilege on this relationship.

Elizabeth Hudson earned a master's degree in communication from the University of Colorado in Boulder, focusing on organizational communication. She currently teaches research methods in the Communication Department at Salem State College in Salem, Massachusetts. Most recently, she served in the Peace Corps as a TESL volunteer in Ukraine.

Kalyani Chadha

Kalyani Chadha is associate director of the Media, Self, and Society Program at the University of Maryland, College Park. Her research interests are in media globalization, telecommunications policy, and Hindi cinema.

The Editors

Anandam Kavoori

Anandam "Andy" Kavoori is associate professor of telecommunications and director of the Cultural Technologies Project at the Grady College of Journalism and Mass Communication, University of Georgia. He is the coeditor of *The Global Dynamics of News* (Ablex, 2000) and *Media, Terrorism, Theory* (Rowman and Littlefield, 2006), *Bollywood Culture and Cinema* (New York University Press, forthcoming) and has published scholarly articles in most major international communications journals.

Noah Arceneaux

Noah Arceneaux is a doctoral candidate in the Grady College of Journalism and Mass Communication, University of Georgia. Prior to returning to academia, Arceneaux developed websites for the ABC, CBS, and Fox television networks. His research interests include the origins of American broadcasting as well as contemporary forms of electronic media.

Index

Digital Formations

General Editor: Steve Jones

Digital Formations is an essential source for critical, high-quality books on digital technologies and modern life. Volumes in the series break new ground by emphasizing multiple methodological and theoretical approaches to deeply probe the formation and reformation of lived experience as it is refracted through digital interaction. **Digital Formations** pushes forward our understanding of the intersections—and corresponding implications—between the digital technologies and everyday life. The series emphasizes critical studies in the context of emergent and existing digital technologies.

Other recent titles include:

Leslie Shade
Gender and Community in the Social Construction of the Internet

John T. Waisanen
Thinking Geometrically

Mia Consalvo & Susanna Paasonen
Women and Everyday Uses of the Internet

Dennis Waskul
Self-Games and Body-Play

David Myers
The Nature of Computer Games

Robert Hassan
The Chronoscopic Society

M. Johns, S. Chen, & G. Hall
Online Social Research

C. Kaha Waite
Mediation and the Communication Matrix

Jenny Sunden
Material Virtualities

Helen Nissenbaum & Monroe Price
Academy and the Internet

To order other books in this series please contact our Customer Service Department:
(800) 770-LANG (within the US)
(212) 647-7706 (outside the US)
(212) 647-7707 FAX

To find out more about the series or browse a full list of titles, please visit our website:
WWW.PETERLANGUSA.COM